ERNEST HOLMES AT ASILOMAR

Lectures and Classes from the 1950s

TITLES BY ERNEST HOLMES

The Basic Ideas of Science of Mind

The Beverly Hills Lectures

Can We Talk to God?

Change Your Thinking, Change Your Life

Creative Mind: A Metaphysical Classic

Creative Mind and Success

The Ernest Holmes Papers: A Collection of Three Ernest Holmes Classics

Ernest Holmes Seminar Lectures

The Essential Ernest Holmes: Collected Writings

Extension Study Course in the Science of Mind:
A Complete Commentary on the Science of Mind Textbook

How to Use the Science of Mind: Principle in Practice

Living the Science of Mind

The Science of Mind

This Thing Called Life

This Thing Called You

The Voice Celestial, with Fenwicke Holmes

What Religious Science Teaches

ERNEST HOLMES AT ASILOMAR

Lectures and Classes from the 1950s

COMPILED BY REV. MARK GILBERT FOR

SCIENCE OF MIND®
ARCHIVES & LIBRARY FOUNDATION
Where the Past Illuminates the Future

Science of Mind Publishing is an imprint of Centers for Spiritual Living
573 Park Point Drive | Golden CO 80401

Ernest Holmes at Asilomar: Lectures and Classes from the 1950s
Copyright © 2023, Science of Mind Archives and Library Foundation

All rights reserved.

No part of this book may be reproduced in any form without permission in writing from the publisher, except for brief quotations embodied in critical articles or reviews.

Science of Mind Publishing
573 Park Point Drive
Golden, CO 80401-7402
720-496-1370
Shop.CSL.org./Books

Printed in the United States of America
Published August 2023

Made possible by funding from Rev. Dr. Kristina Collins
Editor: Julie Mierau, JM Wordsmith
Design/Layout: Maria Robinson, Designs On You, LLC

ISBN paperback: 978-1-956198-27-0
ISBN ebook: 978-1-956198-28-7

Contents

Letter from the Executive Director vii

In Gratitude x

Acknowledgments xi

Introduction by Rev. Mark Gilbert xiii

    Asilomar xv
    Ernest Holmes xvi
    Summer Conferences xviii
    Ernest Holmes at Asilomar xx
    The Talks xxv

Chapter 1: 1954 — Discovering God 1

Chapter 2: 1956 — The Nature and Development of Consciousness . . . 17

    Wonder, Love, and Praise 19
    Spiritual Mind Treatment 29
    Resistance 43
    The Purpose of Evolution 57
    What Does It Mean to Us? 66
    Our Religious Science 77

Chapter 3: 1957 — Practice of the Presence 89

    Abiding Place of Presence 91
    Contemplating the Presence 107
    Grace 124
    Exaltation of the Presence 141

    Religious Science 157
    Classes on Mysticism 171
    Mysticism Class One 172
    Mysticism Class Two 184
    Mysticism Class Three 197
    Mysticism Class Four 208
    Mysticism Class Five 222

Asilomar Photo Album 234

Chapter 4: 1958 — Oneness 255
    Fear Is Faith 257
    Bondage Is Freedom 270
    Time Is the Timeless 284
    The Relative and the Absolute 297
    The Finite Is the Infinite 312

Chapter 5: 1959 — The Basis of Religious Science 327
    Personal Responsibility 329
    Self-Existent Cause 342
    Nonresistance 354
    Evolution 365
    Spiritual Maturity 376
    Sermon by the Sea 387

Index A: People 396

Index B: Subjects 399

About the Author: Ernest Holmes 403

Letter from the Executive Director

What would you give to step back in time, to be at Asilomar when Dr. Holmes was there during the height of his talks and spiritual revelations? What if it were possible to relive this sacred time now?

Asilomar. Just the way the word rolls off your tongue, you can practically feel the mystical magic of this sacred place for our Religious Science movement. Imagine feeling and smelling the salt winds coming off the sea, hearing the waves crashing along the shoreline. Envision Dr. Ernest Holmes standing at the front of Merrill Hall or in the Chapel, speaking with Spirit flowing through him. Hear his unique and powerful voice, proclaiming in his famous "Sermon by the Sea":

> *Find me one person who is for something and against nothing, who is redeemed enough not to condemn others out of the burden of his soul, and I will find another savior, another Jesus, and an exalted human being.*
>
> *You find me one thousand people in the world who know what Religious Science is and use it and live it as it is, and I'll myself live to see a new world, a new heaven, and a new Earth here.*

The people Dr. Holmes proclaims are for something and against nothing, who live the teaching of Religious Science to create a new world, a new heaven, and a new Earth are you and me. Right now.

With the publication of this book, we get to be at Asilomar with Dr. Holmes. We get to be encouraged and inspired by his deep wisdom to transform our own lives and the world today. That is what this book does for each one of us.

The Science of Mind Archives and Library Foundation is honored to be the curators and guardians of our Religious Science history. As the executive director of our Archives, I constantly am amazed by the treasures tucked away in our archival boxes—wisdom that needs to be brought to the Light. Mysteries to be solved. But none of these items does anyone any good if it remains there—boxed up, old, dusty, crumbling, never to be revealed.

Until now…the Light has come!

Enter Rev. Mark Gilbert. He joined the Science of Mind Archives' Board of Directors in January 2022. He is a natural researcher, writer, and seeker of knowledge, specifically the wisdom of Dr. Holmes. As a member of our Archiving /Digitizing Team, he quickly discovered the wealth of untapped resources that needed to be brought to the light. He began organizing all of Dr. Holmes's works into inventories and spreadsheets. He takes items not yet released on the Archives website and polishes them up, adding fresh cover pages, and uploading them to the website, truly making the invisible visible. He is dusting off these treasures and breathing new life into them so anyone can easily access them online.

In this process, he discovered the transcripts of Dr. Holmes's Asilomar lectures from the summer "Spiritual Advances" in the mid to late 1950s. You could feel Gilbert's enthusiasm as a Divine Idea was formed: to create a book on Asilomar during the Holmes years, filled with the wisdom of this true mystic, presenting readers with timeless wisdom as pertinent today as it was then.

In his introduction to this book, Gilbert expertly leads readers through the history of Asilomar, Ernest Holmes's background, the Summer Conferences, the history of our Religious Science movement, Ernest Holmes at Asilomar from 1954-1959 (including wonderful background stories), leading readers into the lectures and classes. At the beginning of each talk, Gilbert shares a concise summary of the topic, and then Dr. Holmes takes it from there, sharing the Wisdom of Spirit that supports each one of us through what Holmes called "This Thing Called Life."

This is your invitation to step back in time, go to Asilomar, and experience the direct revelations of Truth flowing through our founder of Religious Science,

Dr. Ernest Holmes. You will experience the wonder and wisdom of Dr. Holmes at the magical Asilomar all through the pages of this book.

Who knows? Maybe you can help us solve the mysteries of where the transcriptions and recordings are from 1954 and 1955. Maybe the wisdom of Dr. Holmes within these pages will ignite your Inner Light and cause your own personal revelations of Truth, further transforming your life for the better. Maybe it will deepen your passion and pique your curiosity to explore more of the hidden wisdom and teachings available on the Archives' website.

Come, experience the recently uncovered treasures, dusted off and now available to you, thanks to the Archives and Rev. Gilbert. There is only the Now. Come with me. Let's go!

Peace and Blessings,

Rev. Kathy Mastroianni
Executive Director
The Science of Mind Archives and Library Foundation

Access the many treasures of Dr. Ernest Holmes and the Science of Mind history on our website at www.scienceofmindarchives.com. Please also prayerfully consider becoming a Friend of the Archives so you can be a part of making the invisible visible for us all—and for generations.

SCIENCE OF MIND®
ARCHIVES & LIBRARY FOUNDATION
Where the Past Illuminates the Future

In Gratitude

The Science of Mind Archives and Library Foundation is deeply indebted to Rev. Dr. Kristina Collins for her generous donation in support of this book. She is Senior Minister at Sanctuary Center for Spiritual Living in Covina, California, and a member of the Foundation's Board of Directors. Her generosity helps bring the philosophy of Dr. Ernest Holmes to life for the Religious Science movement and beyond.

Dr. Collins has a deep connection to Asilomar, this sacred place for Dr. Ernest Holmes and the Religious Science movement, where she and her husband, Jim Montgomery, RScP, met and were married. She is the first recipient of the Hazel Holmes Award for the Love of Our Asilomar Conference.

Thank you, Dr. Collins, for enabling us to bring this volume to reality.

Acknowledgments

The Science of Mind Archives and Library Foundation would like to thank the Infinite Presence for the divine idea to create this book of Dr. Ernest Holmes's lectures and classes from Asilomar in the 1950s. We are grateful for answered prayer to manifest this work in the world.

Our gratitude goes to Dr. Ernest Holmes for his clarity of thought and sharing his wisdom that continues to impact and awaken countless lives worldwide.

We are grateful to Rev. Mark Gilbert for his divine idea and willingness to create this book, including his countless hours of research, writing, compiling, and editing the information contained within these pages. His passion for Holmes's teachings and his determination brought this book to reality.

Long-time Archives volunteer Nan Agriesti, RScP, diligently transcribed all of Holmes's works, for which we express our gratitude. Her attention to detail and understanding of this teaching are reflected in each page of this book. We also are grateful to whoever originally recorded and transcribed these talks.

We are indebted to Park Peters of Audio Park Recording for donating his time to digitize the audio recordings of Dr. Holmes, including the only audio recording from Asilomar located thus far, available through the website of the Science of Mind Archives.

Thank you to Centers for Spiritual Living's publishing experts for their kindness, professional services, and deep dedication to continuing to bring Science of Mind teachings to the world. We are especially grateful to Publishing Manager Holli Sharp for overseeing the production, to Editor Julie Mierau for smoothing the transition between audio transcripts and the printed page, and to Graphic

Designer Maria Robinson for her dedication to making the book readable and visually appealing.

The Science of Mind Archives and Library Foundation, as the keepers of our Science of Mind teachings, ensured these lectures were preserved and made available to readers. We are grateful to Rev. Dr. Marilyn Leo, founder of the Archives, for her continued vision and dedication to ensuring the preservation of our history. Thank you also to the members of the Archives' Board of Directors, each of whom is a beacon of light for this project, for propelling forward the high purpose of the Archives: *To Preserve, Protect, and Present Science of Mind Philosophy and History.*

Thank you to the Archives staff: Executive Director Rev. Kathy Mastroianni; Certified Archivist Kim Larmee; Administrative Support Melinda Eskridge, RScP; and Prosperity Manager Rev. Valerie Torphy. We appreciate their assistance with finding the materials needed to make this book a reality and their behind-the-scenes encouragement, enthusiasm, and support.

Finally, the Archives is grateful to all our visionary donors, Friends of the Archives, volunteers, and everyone who supports this vital work, keeping alive the vision Dr. Holmes decreed in his 1959 "Sermon by the Sea."

Introduction

ASILOMAR AND ERNEST HOLMES

Asilomar and Ernest Holmes. Asilomar and Religious Science. Asilomar and Science of Mind.

For many of you, the connection between a retreat center on the shores of the California coast and the New Thought philosophy, the Science of Mind, and its founder, Dr. Ernest Holmes, needs no explanation. They are most likely already indelibly linked in your awareness.

Somewhere along your journey, you may have attended a conference at Asilomar, where you listened to wonderful music and inspiring speakers in Merrill Hall, searched the grounds to find the location of a workshop that interested you, and shared food and wisdom at Crocker Hall with fellow attendees. You may have journeyed down the meadow and along the boardwalk to find the beach so you could feel the sand beneath your feet and dip your toes in the ocean. You may have felt a deep sense of history—the history of Asilomar itself—and with it, the history of a spiritual philosophy that has given meaning to your life.

If the connection between this sacred place and this spiritual leader's teachings is not yet formed in your mind, you will forge that link by exploring the pages of this book. And the following pages contain so much more.

At the heart of this volume are the words spoken by Holmes to those who attended the Religious Science conferences at Asilomar in the 1950s, the final decade of his life. These summer gatherings were a special time, not only for Religious Scientists but for Holmes himself.

Throughout his time as a public teacher, Holmes gave weekly Sunday messages in public halls, taught many classes, wrote numerous books and magazine articles, broadcast his message on radio and TV programs, founded *Science of Mind* magazine (in continuous publication even today), and spread the message of Science of Mind to as many people as he could. He was driven to help people see that there was a "Power for good in the universe" and that they could tap into it to create the lives they desired.

Although Holmes certainly touched on deep spiritual topics during many of his presentations, he always attempted to meet people where they were, presenting his philosophy in a way both understandable and applicable to people's daily lives. There were, however, some occasions when Holmes gave his listeners a deeper metaphysical presentation on what he was thinking. These included the coveted "Tuesday Invitational Classes" he taught in the last decade or so of his life, as well as the week-long series of talks he gave during summer gatherings at Asilomar in the 1950s.

The transcripts gathered here offer a glimpse into what Holmes believed was important to share with those people who were already deeply involved in the movement. As such, they are, to a degree, advanced metaphysics presentations and most assume some familiarity with basic concepts of Science of Mind and New Thought. For those who may be approaching Holmes for the first time, you might not find this the easiest on-ramp to the philosophy. Although you will no doubt obtain some helpful nuggets for your spiritual search, there are other books by Holmes and others that would serve as more logical introductions to Science of Mind.

However, for the long-time spiritual seeker and one familiar with the basics of Science of Mind, these lectures will help reinforce your understanding and take you deeper into the philosophy. Be prepared to be challenged.

Most of these transcripts appear here for the first time. Of those that have been published previously, probably only one item included in this collection is well known to most students of Science of Mind: Holmes's famous "Sermon by the Sea," his final talk given at the close of the 1959 Asilomar conference.

This was also his final presentation at Asilomar, as he made his transition in early 1960. Fittingly, this lecture outlines Holmes's vision for the future of the philosophy.

Before we delve into the words of Holmes, let's take a few moments to consider how this spiritual teacher and his philosophy came to intersect with what is now a California state park a short drive south of Monterey.

ASILOMAR

Asilomar opened on August 7, 1913, as a leadership camp for the YWCA. Its dedication drew more than 2,000 attendees, which the local paper reported as being "a vivid and true and living symbol" of the work "the young ladies are attempting to accomplish toward a betterment of the world." What a fitting intention for the location that became so coupled to Science of Mind and Centers for Spiritual Living's global vision to "create a world that works for everyone."

A veritable who's who of influential women supported the YWCA in the early 20th century, lending their influence and money to the growth of Asilomar. These included, among others, Phoebe Apperson Hearst, mother of famous newspaperman William Randolph Hearst; Ellen Browning Scripps, cofounder of the Scripps newspaper chain; and Mary Sroufe Merrill, author of a book on the history of Asilomar. Noted architect Julia Morgan designed many of the original buildings, most bearing the names of these famous founders.

The facility expanded by twenty additional acres a few years later, and as the YWCA received more donations, additional buildings and structures were added. The center grew such that by the year 1921, the facility was open year round and could accommodate up to 500 people. By then, it hosted meetings held by various religious groups, colleges, and women's training programs.

The Great Depression brought about a steep decline in the use of Asilomar, and the YWCA closed it in early 1934. Unable to find a buyer, the organization at times leased portions of the facility for various other uses, such as a motel and a youth training camp. During World War II, many of the buildings were used as living quarters for military families. It was not until a couple of years after the war that the YWCA returned Asilomar to its original purpose as a conference center.

In the early 1950s, the YWCA sought to sell the facility. Eventually an arrangement was worked out that led to Asilomar becoming part of the California State Park system in July 1956. This agreement led to the nearby City of Pacific Grove leasing and operating the center, followed by a two-decade period of construction of new, contemporary structures.

In later years, operations at Asilomar would return to the control of the California State Parks system. The state would turn to private contractors to handle rentals and run the day-to-day operations, a practice that continues today. In 1987, many of the original Julia Morgan-designed buildings were designated as National Historic Landmarks.

Today, Asilomar is still an active and vital conference facility, hosting guests and groups from all around the United States who come to experience its unique and tranquil environment. Its peaceful nature and its feeling of harmony certainly contribute to its intention toward a "betterment of the world."

ERNEST HOLMES

Just as the history of Asilomar could take up a full volume, so could the story of Ernest Holmes. Here we offer the briefest description of the man to set the context for this book. Those who wish to know more can certainly seek out one of several biographies.

Holmes was born in a small town in Maine in 1887 to a family whose spiritual beliefs were as pure Congregationalists. His parents encouraged reading the Bible but did not want their children to take in any fear, calling them to ignore lectures on hell and damnation. Ernest, though, had a curious mind and sought out local sources such as the library to pursue other religious teachings, philosophy, and more. Ernest grew up with an open and inquisitive mind, curious about the world and his place in it. Early major influences on him included Ralph Waldo Emerson, Mary Baker Eddy (Christian Science) and various metaphysical writers of the day, such as Christian D. Larson and Ralph Waldo Trine.

In 1912, Holmes moved to the Los Angeles area, following his brother, Fenwicke, who was leading a local church there. Ernest found work in a desk job for the City of Venice that afforded him free time to pursue his main interest, reading various metaphysical books. Discussing metaphysical ideas with a coworker in 1916 led to his speaking to a local group—to rave reviews. This began a period when Holmes continued his studies, combined with an increasing number of public talks. During this time, Holmes discovered the writings of English judge Thomas Troward, who became another major influence on his developing philosophical outlook.

By 1919, Ernest published his first book, *Creative Mind,* outlining the key elements of his spiritual philosophy. More books followed, along with his continued lectures, now being held at local theaters to accommodate his growing audiences. Holmes also spent time studying with well-known New Thought teacher, Emma Curtis Hopkins, the so-called "teacher of teachers." By 1922, Holmes began work on his summary of what he was now calling "Science of Mind." His book by that name was published in 1926 and later was revised into the current 1938 edition, popularly called "the textbook."

The following year, 1927, saw the incorporation of the Institute of Religious Science and School of Philosophy (later renamed the Institute of Religious Science and Philosophy), the formal educational organization focused on bringing Science of Mind to the world. Also at that time, he began the monthly *Science of Mind* magazine, briefly titled *Religious Science Monthly.*

The key components of Science of Mind fall into what is generally termed New Thought philosophy, along with similar teachings, such as Unity and Divine Science. Holmes never claimed that what he created was any kind of divine revelation. Instead, he saw it as a synthesis of the best of science, religion, and philosophy. What perhaps contributed to its initial and continuing success is its practical nature. Adherents could learn practices they could employ in their lives to change their thoughts, so as to correspondingly change their experiences.

As Holmes and Science of Mind grew in popularity, there arose a number of followers who wanted to move beyond teaching educational classes and begin creating churches. Although Holmes was initially reluctant, he eventually approved this approach. This led to the growth of what were called Churches of Religious Science and an eventual separate organization, the International Association of Religious Science Churches (IARSC), to coordinate their efforts.

Throughout the 1940s, the Institute continued to explore ways to best support their educational endeavors, which had expanded into radio programs and other activities, and ensuring the consistency of the growing number of Religious Science churches, ministers, and practitioners (individuals who provided spiritual prayer support). Eventually, the Institute moved further toward becoming a religious organization by changing its name to the Church of Religious Science (CRS) in late 1953.

SUMMER CONFERENCES

At this point in the growth of the Religious Science movement in the early 1950s, which coincided with Asilomar becoming a state park, Ernest Holmes and his blossoming number of followers began seeking out a beautiful natural setting as the backdrop for an annual spiritual retreat. Their first such conference in the summer of 1953, however, was not at Asilomar but rather at Camp Sierra near the village of Big Creek in the Sierra Nevada Mountains of California.

Coordinated by the IARSC, more than 300 people convened on the afternoon of Saturday, August 15, 1953, for the event that ran through the morning of the following Saturday. Each day there were parallel agendas, one for the adults and one for the children. Daily activities began with a sunrise meditation in the Hillside Chapel at 7:15 a.m. and concluded with a nightly campfire for everyone.

The theme for this first retreat was "The Christ in Action," and each evening various Religious Science ministers spoke on topics such as "The Christ in Action in the Individual" and "The Christ in Action in the Group" and so on. However, the place to be each day was the Assembly Hall at 11 a.m. when Holmes gave his hour-long daily talk. This pattern repeated each day until Friday, when Dr. William Hornaday spoke at the morning session and Holmes gave his final talk for the week right after the evening meal.

In his first remarks for the week, Holmes began by reframing their time together. Their gathering was not to be considered a retreat in his eyes. He challenged all by saying, "Generally speaking, we think of such a gathering as this as a 'retreat.' But in Religious Science, a spiritual retreat really is a 'spiritual advance.' We should acquire a greater consciousness in uniting our thought with each other in a common cause and purpose for which we work, and upon which our whole practice is based: a consciousness of the Presence of God within everything and everyone. Our spiritual advance, then, is devoted to a deeper awareness, a higher perception, and a greater realization of spiritual Truth: the reality of a Divine Presence, whose impulsion is love, and a Universal Principle, which acts as law."

In other words, even though the setting is one where participants might have been retreating from the outside world, the purpose was to advance the evolution of each person's own consciousness.

Overall, this week long "advance" was considered a great success and plans moved forward for future summer conferences. The October 1953 newsletter of the IARSC gave a glowing review of the entire week, capping it off with these words:

> *And we could not close without a word about the magnificence of that climactic lecture by Ernest Holmes following a picnic on a huge rock (which is a solid granite helicopter landing). There Ernest Holmes truly fed the souls of the multitude with his modern "Sermon on the Mount." This was on Friday evening at sundown and a truly awed audience trekked back down the mountain to Camp Sierra where the last service—a beautiful candlelight service, Lora Holman in charge—was preceded by the "Little Theater," cleverly prepared entirely by the children.*

Ernest's talks that summer were considered so special and so inspiring that with the help of Georgia C. Maxwell as editor, they were compiled and printed in book form in 1955 under the title *Seminar Lectures*. This volume was later revised and reprinted by Science of Mind Publications in 1987 (available on the Science of Mind Archives website).

Unfortunately before the next summer rolled around, organizational differences would impact future summer conferences. Rising concerns about having two separate organizations and differences of opinions between Holmes and some leaders of the IARSC on administrative issues led to a break (in what became known as "the split") between the CRS and the IARSC in early 1954.

From that point there were two organizations teaching the Science of Mind and bringing to the world the philosophy that Ernest Holmes birthed. This continued up until the early part of the twenty-first century when, in 2012, the two groups came together to form what is now called Centers for Spiritual Living.

Until then, though, the year 1954 began a half-century period of separate summer conferences for the two groups. That summer, Holmes and his organization began a long relationship of annual summer meetings at Asilomar. Meanwhile, the IARSC met again at Camp Sierra in 1954 and 1955 and then at the Hotel del Coronado in Coronado, California, in 1956. During those early years, programs show that the highlighted speaker each day was Dr. Raymond Charles Barker.

Starting in 1957, both groups were each hosting their own summer meetings at Asilomar, although on different weeks. This tradition continued up into the early part of the twenty-first century, setting the stage for the members of both organizations to forge in their minds and hearts that deep connection between this spiritual setting and their beloved Science of Mind philosophy. That connection continues.

ERNEST HOLMES AT ASILOMAR

Beginning in 1954 and continuing through 1959, Holmes came to Asilomar each summer to meet and interact with Religious Scientists. Although he was there as a speaker, and his presence no doubt attracted a fair number of attendees, he also came to interact with people and learn from them what was on their minds.

Most valuable was the time he spent roaming the grounds, weaving his way among the trees and finding his way down to the white sands of the Pacific Ocean. It was in these locations that people approached him, asking for a photograph and wanting to speak with the famous Dr. Holmes. What they found was a humble, approachable man who dressed casually and relished his interactions with everyone he met.

If someone wanted a longer conversation, Holmes was not opposed to grabbing one of the chairs outside Hearst Social Hall, facing the large meadow ringed with walkways heading toward the beach, and sitting and visiting with that person for an extended time.

Holmes's preferred place to retreat for discussion was the suite of rooms he lodged in, located in a building formally called The Tide Inn. That original name gave way through the years to the name by which the building is more popularly known today, the Pirates' Den.

The large cottage was originally build to house young men who came to Asilomar in the early days to work in such jobs as grounds maintenance, mechanics, kitchen help, bus boys, dishwashers, bellboys, and similar jobs. These young men, known for their propensity for raiding pies from the dining hall, became known as pie rats. Relishing the name, they took great honor in being "pirates" and organized themselves into The Membership of Pirates, with leaders and an established hierarchy.

By the 1950s, The Tide Inn served as quarters for select visitors. Although many Asilomar guests at that time slept in dormitories, The Tide Inn and a few other lodges had rooms with baths and a main living area, a characteristic Holmes appreciated due to its homey qualities. Close associate Reginald Armor and his wife, Elsie, also usually stayed in one of the rooms in the building.

Holmes appreciated his inns's proximity to Merrill Hall where larger gatherings occurred. Merrill Hall was where he usually gave his well-attended lectures, giving him the convenience of having his lodging just a few feet away. An extra bonus was that The Tide Inn was also fairly close to Asilomar's dining facility, Crocker Hall.

As Dr. William Hornaday recalled in his book *The Inner Light*, coauthored with Harlan Ware, "Ernest's favorite cottage was near the lecture hall, put down amid dwarf cypress not far from the long rocky beach. The living room, looking out on dunes which funneled to the sea, boasted a big fireplace and comfortable armchairs.

"After the lectures, Ernest often invited a few potential critics in for coffee." recalled Hornaday. There Holmes would ask his guests if they understood what he had just lectured on. When one group stated that they had, he replied to them, "Good. Explain it to me then. There was a lot of it I didn't understand myself."

Hornaday's chronicle details one memorable Asilomar where he and Holmes, while on their way to the conference, stopped to pick up a hitchhiker, a young college man from Chicago named Bernard. On discovering he was in a car with a couple of ministers, the young man confessed that he considered himself to be an atheist. Holmes took an interest in learning more from Bernard about his beliefs, as well as, perhaps, supporting him in his grappling with such questions about God. He offered to have him stay at Asilomar as a guest and attend the talks and classes.

When Bernard tentatively accepted Holmes's offer, Hornaday was charged with getting him some food and taking him up to one of the hilltop dormitories where other college-aged men were housed. At this point, Hornaday describes the following interaction he had with Bernard:

What does Dr. Holmes really want of me?, he demanded. Is he saving souls or what?

He's after material, I imagine.

Sir?

He'll deliver five lectures before the week is out. He wants to know if the thinking of young people has changed lately.

Holmes was well known for giving his talks without notes, leaving the impression that he had not prepared anything. Nothing could be further from the truth. It has been described that he was always preparing. He was always listening, thinking, reading, and mentally considering the subject of his talks. But then when the time came for him to give the talk, not only had he prepared, he allowed himself to be open for the Divine to speak spontaneously through him.

As Hornaday described his talks, "He always insisted he'd never had a revelation, yet when the creative obsession was upon him, there were times when his lecture could best be described with the embarrassing word 'illumined.'"

Although Holmes loved these interactions with the people gathered at Asilomar, reports indicate that after the passing of his wife, Hazel, in May 1957, Holmes also sought solitude at Asilomar. He found the place gave him a good opportunity to be alone with his thoughts and to contemplate certain questions that were central to him as he moved toward the closing of his ministry.

One area of focus during this time, as his brother, Fenwicke, states in his biography *Ernest Holmes: His Life and Times*, was "an increased urgency to clarify, unify, and protect the message, to lift his flock to his highest understanding of Truth before he left them." To that end, Fenwicke stated that in the later years, Ernest wanted to address three subjects with his followers at Asilomar: mysticism, the religion of the future, and the new literature. As we will discover in the words of Holmes in this book, he did just that.

But there was one other topic clearly on Ernest's mind in those final years at Asilomar and that was the question of mortality and immortality. Fenwicke writes of the two of them sitting in the living room of Ernest's suite in The Tide Inn, working on their epic poem later published as *The Voice Celestial*. Ernest had just recently finished his part of the chapter, "Life and Death," and Fenwicke found this topic very much on his brother's mind.

Describing Ernest's final two years at Asilomar, Fenwicke wrote:

During those two summers, there was a wistfulness about Ernest as he came and went on the campgrounds, a man who walked alone in this temple-like grove with its soft carpet of pine needles, its pillars of pine, and its lofty canopy of green. He sought solitude on the shore beyond the wall of sand dunes, dressed informally in the oversized lounging jacket that was his favorite attire at the retreat. Sometimes admirers would search him out to snap a picture or secure an autograph.

He welcomed them kindly, complied with their requests, and turned his face again toward the sea. Was he thinking the long, long thoughts of youth or the longer thoughts of age and eternity? I do not know. Sometimes his mind went back to Hazel, and then he would respond with unconscious warmth to the slightest affection bestowed on him by those he met on the paths. "I lean on love," he said. By leaning on love, he was made strong. His words at Asilomar were of unusual power.

Hornaday concurs on this point. He described this exchange late one evening in 1959, as they concluded their discussion at The Tide Inn:

That was the evening that Ernest Holmes, a lifetime student of all religions, said with such conviction that no one could doubt his sincerity, that he and his beloved wife Hazel and his old dog Prince would meet again.

"Prince has a discrete bark, just for me," he said, "and I'll hear it. And Hazel will be waiting in some dimension I can't envision now, but there they'll be."

The fire crackled in the room's warm silence, and I thought of what he had said in the lecture that morning: "What the average man means when he says he doesn't believe in God is that he doesn't believe in immortality."

His own belief was a reassurance, a glimpse down an endless corridor where, far away and in the mists, all his true loves were ready to welcome him. And that he did truly believe. This I know because I was with him on that last day when it was tested.

He walked out with me that evening when everyone else had gone. He loved the view at any hour but especially when the evening silence came. From where we were standing, dwarf cypress trees made a soft, green, low-growing accent against the white sand. He enjoyed walking to the top of the highest dune to watch the cresting waves in the moonlight. At certain daylight hours, there was a color, an aquamarine, to be seen in the rays of the sun; it was caught in the underside of the wave and was almost unbearably beautiful.

That evening, leaving him at The Tide Inn, I knew that his thoughts went with us after we had said good night. He is gone now and the months and the years are passing, but the warmth of the man is with us still.

THE TALKS

We are blessed to have a written record of most of what Ernest Holmes lectured on during this final decade of his life. In some regards, those around him did a wonderful job of ensuring that they captured almost all of his public output. The methods used differed, depending on the circumstances.

In some instances, handwritten notes by Holmes (or someone's typed version) were retained. Additionally, many of Holmes's lectures were recorded on early reel-to-reel tape recorders and later transcribed. This was true for his Sunday talks, his radio shows, his classes, and, fortunately for us here, some of his presentations at the summer conference. Although we currently have only one recording of Holmes speaking at Asilomar (more on that later), some of the transcripts have notes on them, suggesting they were taken from a recording.

Another popular practice was to have his talks transcribed by a stenographer. These would later be typed up on thin onion-skin paper with sheets of carbon paper between each page, allowing multiple copies to be prepared. We can thank these original carbon copies for most of the talks in this book.

However, even though we are blessed that so many of these talks were captured, given the luxury of distance and time, we also can see that frequently this wonderful material was not always filed and maintained in the most organized and protective manner. Recent research resulted an inventory of what we know is available and what currently is not. This research included reviewing available transcripts and notes, as mentioned, but also reading the various board notes of the Religious Science organizations and physically going through all relevant materials contained in the Science of Mind Archives.

These efforts uncovered some rich material, such as many program guides for the summer conferences, reports in various newsletters about the Asilomar gatherings, and more. We also located many photographs of Ernest Holmes at Asilomar, a sampling of which are included in this book.

Yet there are some things we have not located. Even though we would love it if this book contained all of Holmes's presentations at Asilomar, sadly, it does not.

We hope that the publication of what is available here will somehow lead to the discovery of certain missing items.

What we have discovered is that similar to his week at Camp Sierra in 1953, Ernest generally prepared a lecture for each day of the week. Records clearly show that the CRS first met at Asilomar in 1954. Although we do not have the full program, we do have one previously unpublished transcript of Ernest's talk "Discovering God," which was given that summer and is included in this volume. Hence, we believe that there were other talks in 1954 for which we have neither the title nor the transcript.

The program for 1955s Asilomar shows the dates for that meeting were July 23-30, with Holmes giving six lectures. The titles of the first six are as follows: "New Foundations for Faith," "The Science of Mind and Inspiration of Spirit," "Unfoldment of Spiritual Mind Treatment," "The Transcendent and the Immanent," "Synthesis of the Philosophy of Troward," and "Spiritual Awareness and Psychic Hallucination." Unfortunately, we have unearthed no copies of these talks.

Additionally, the program from 1955 shows that Holmes gave a concluding talk on the final Saturday morning before attendees left the conference. This is listed simply as "Sermon by the Sea." Research shows that Holmes consistently gave a final concluding morning talk every year, which was always entitled "Sermon by the Sea." The only one for which we have a copy is from 1959, included in this book.

Even though we do not have the transcripts or notes of any of these talks, that doesn't mean that somewhere in the vast amount of material produced by Holmes we don't have this content under some other title or format. We know Holmes frequently updated and used similar content with the same name in the various modalities in which he released content (magazine articles, radio shows, phonograph records, etc.).

Even after 1960, Science of Mind Publishing continued for many years editing together Holmes's content from different sources to produce "new" Holmes magazine articles and books (such as the annuals published into the 1970s).

Frequently, this new material was given a new name, making our identification of the origin of its source material difficult or impossible.

There is a possibility that any documents or recordings of the missing talks from 1954 or 1955 may have been used to produce other material. Of course, there is also a chance, although doubtful, that no one captured the words of Holmes in those missing years. At this point, we simply don't know.

All of that being acknowledged, let's celebrate the wonderful treasure trove of what we have.

In the summer conference from August 13 through August 18, 1956, Holmes gave six talks, for which we have all the transcripts, although the transcript from August 15, "Resistance" may be incomplete. Our research indicates that only two of these talks have been published previously, although with the content edited. Holmes's talk on August 13, "Wonder, Love and Praise" was edited and published as an article in the December 1957 issue of *Science of Mind* magazine. Similarly, the talk from August 14, "Spiritual Mind Healing" was highly edited for a two-part article in the February and March 1958 issues.

In 1957, Holmes gave five talks (July 8-12). Included here are the transcripts of all the talks, none of which are we aware have appeared previously in print. That year, he also taught a five part class on Mysticism for which we have the notes for all sessions. Previously, one session's notes were published online by the Science of Mind Archives, but the others are previously unpublished.

In 1958, Holmes gave a series of five lectures on August 11-15, all of which are available here. The first two, "Fear Is Faith" and "Bondage Is Freedom," previously appeared online through the Science of Mind Archives. The others are published here for the first time.

Finally, we have a complete set of the transcripts of all six of Holmes's talks from his final year at Asilomar, August 10-15, 1959. Most of these talks have not been published previously. His final talk, given on the last day, is well known among students of Science of Mind and was previously released by Science of Mind Publishing as a small volume entitled "Sermon by the Sea," which is the last lecture included in this book.

The Science of Mind Archives and Library Foundation continues to research and inventory the tremendous volume of Ernest Holmes's works. Although our intention with this book is to bring you these valuable presentations, which we know can benefit your study and understanding of the Science of Mind, we also hope the release of this book will help us in furthering our exploration of Holmes. Specifically, we would love to find the transcripts from Asilomar not included here and to track down any audio recordings we currently do not have in our historical collection.

Already in the preparation of this book, we have identified a previously unidentified audio, recently digitized in the Archives' collection, as being from Holmes's Friday night presentation at Asilomar in 1957, on the topic of "Religious Science." I hope at some point we will be able to report that we have found more recordings.

Listening to that recording offered us the opportunity to answer the question of how accurate these transcripts are. After all, there is a degree of trust that the work done to capture Holmes's words adequately and accurately did so.

From my review of the transcript compared with the recording, I have to say that we have nothing to worry about. Although there was an occasional word difference here and there, which we corrected, there was never anything that led to Holmes's meaning not being accurately recorded. I would add that a handful of the transcripts contain missing words. We did not attempt to guess at what Holmes said and left that gap for you and your imagination. In some instances, the lectures were slightly edited for clarity, never changing or reinterpreting the meaning.

There is something, however, that we need to keep in mind: Reading transcripts of talks is much different from reading an edited book or article. Holmes frequently moves from idea to idea with the stream of his consciousness. Sometimes there are stories and asides in the middle of a point he is making. This can sometimes make for difficult reading, as we attempt to keep up with where his thoughts were going.

Yet once we become comfortable and familiar with the pace and direction of reading his verbal presentations, we find ourselves enthralled and excited by the new places he takes us in our metaphysical exploration. We also get great insights into both the humbleness and the humor of Holmes.

With all of this background now outlined for you, let's turn our focus to what I know you truly want to explore—the words that Dr. Ernest Holmes shared all those many years ago with the individuals who came to be with him at Asilomar. May these words reach across our experience of time and space to both inspire you and support you as you grow along your own spiritual journey.

Rev. Mark Gilbert
Summer 2023

ERNEST HOLMES AT ASILOMAR

Lectures and Classes from the 1950s

CHAPTER 1

1954

Discovering God

Discovering God

AUGUST 1954

In this talk, Ernest Holmes discusses the natural tendency, the urge within all humans, to seek meaning of this mystery we call life. Each of us must be left alone to use our free will to discover answers to life's questions on our own. This quest calls us to discover ourselves, and as we do so, we recognize that we also discover the Divine.

Records indicate that the first Asilomar conference in 1954 was held on August 11 through August 14, although the date of this lecture by Dr. Holmes is not clear. We can presume he spoke each day. Within this talk, Holmes references his talk from the preceding day, so this was not his opening lecture. Unfortunately, this is the only transcript we have been able to identify as coming from that summer.

Plotinus said that nature is the great "no thing" but it isn't exactly nothing because it has an office to perform: to receive the images of the contemplation of the Spirit. There is no more doubt that there is such a neutral field of creative action in the universe in the realm of mind than that there are different kinds of trees growing out of the same soil. There isn't the slightest doubt that mental action and reaction takes place and that it is analyzable, but the theoretical supposition that it takes place in an individual or separate mind is entirely fallacious. It is not an entity but an apparently "entitized" field of reaction in that it has no volition of its own. As Plotinus said, this mind principle is a blind force — not knowing, only doing.

I remember when [Thomas] Troward's book [*The Edinburgh Lectures on Mental Science*] first came out; it was a long time ago. I had chosen a certain broad-minded Ph.D., and I used to go and spend about a half a day each week and pay her a five dollar gold piece—that was the kind of money we had then; it would be worth about fifteen dollars now—just to ask questions to satisfy my own curiosity. So after about a week or two she said, "Now there is no sense in you coming anymore. You can get all the teachers together and teach them!"

That, of course, was an extravagant statement. I couldn't have. They wouldn't have listened and would have hanged me if I had tried, like Meister Eckhart. You know he was excommunicated 200 years after he died because it took them that long to find out what he was talking about. It was like the anathema they pronounced on Spinoza. One of our greatest troubles is that we do not know that sugar is sweet unless we take it out of the sugar bowl. Shakespeare understood this when he said, "A rose by any other name would smell as sweet." The Bible said, "God made man upright but they have sought out many inventions."

Troward tells us the story of the Garden of Eden. It is the story of every man's soul. Eve represents the feminine principle in us and Adam the masculine: Adam, the intellect, and Eve, we would say, the inward psychic receptivity, which may or may not be right. It has got more error than truth in it. It is Eve or the feminine who is seduced by the serpent, who represents the life principle arguing on behalf of isolation, separation, and duality. "And the Lord God said, 'Behold, the man is become as one of us, to know good and evil and now, lest he put forth his hand and take also of the tree of life, and eat and live forever.'" And it said that God didn't like that because He didn't want them to gain the knowledge of good and evil if they were going to live forever.

Now this has a meaning. All of these allegories have a teaching, a spiritual meaning, a cosmic meaning. It is merely the way they have to tell it. It means that even God cannot make a self-choosing individual who will have the possibility of self-choice without letting this instrument alone to discover itself. It is the meaning of life, it is the meaning of what is going on right now. Man must be let alone to discover himself. He must be a creature of choice. Ignorance excuses no one from the result of his choice.

Emerson said that there is no sin but ignorance and no salvation but enlightenment. We say there is no sin but a mistake and no punishment but the consequence and that apparent punishment is the eternal action of a changeless equilibrium that itself never gets out of balance. It always acts as justice without judgment. You see there is no final judge in the universe as theology teaches, else you would have a God who is just a gigantic human being. There is balance, there is equilibrium so complete that if you shift the weight of a grain of sand across your thumbnail it changes the physical weight of the whole sidereal universe to compensate for the movement, because the universe itself is self-existent, self-energizing, self-perpetuating, and self-expressing. That is the deepest thought we have.

God didn't make God! I wrote something once, and I can only think of one verse:

For Cause has neither why nor what.
Original, It stands alone.
Of Its own self-sowing,
Itself was never sown.

That is just another way I took to say God was not created. God didn't make God. God didn't make law. God and law are coexistent, coeternal, and self-existent, and therefore, self-perpetuating, self-energizing, self-acting, self-realizing, and self-fulfilling. That is the basis of our whole philosophy.

And so man was left in the Garden of Eden (that is, the garden of the soul) to discover himself. In the process, he ate of the fruit of the tree of the knowledge of good and evil, which is duality. Now remember, it is the serpent that tempts Eve; she is the feminine. Then she goes out and seduces Adam. This is just a story you know, though it is rather realistic. Why did Adam get knocked over first? We know today in the operation of the human mind there is action and reaction, that wherever there is an emotional bias, there is always an intellectual blind spot. Where that bias exists, in that place the intellect cannot think straight. It is impossible. When Troward's book came out, I saw for the first time something I never understood: that the human mind alone gets sick and suffers, that the

Divine Mind alone heals. He said this is true, but it isn't explained. I sat up all night and read his book.

I went to my friend, and I said, "I have found something." She said, "I never was so disappointed in my life. I thought you knew so much; you don't know anything." Well, I still knew I was smart, and I had never heard that an emotional bias will create an intellectual blind spot. So I said to her to wait another week while I thought it all over, because I knew I was using a terminology she was not familiar with. The next week I went back and explained it all over again, and she said, "Where did you get this? This is taught only in the schools of advanced teaching." I said, "It was exactly what I said last week," but I failed to put it in terms she was used to. That is the thing we must avoid in our field. We are not a group of people running around saying there isn't any ocean, that the man scratches because he doesn't itch, and that this man is a moron because he is so intelligent. We do not do that. We are very realistic. We believe completely that there is only One Mind, which is God, and I can only tell you what I believe.

I believe we are pretty much hypnotized from the cradle to the grave. Emerson said that it seemed as though when we entered this life, somebody gave us something too strong for us. He said we are gods on a debauch. But once in a while, somebody wakes up and looks about him, but he goes to sleep again. He is describing the flashes of illumination of cosmic consciousness where we see no longer as through a glass darkly.

We have what is called a spirit, soul, and body but we are not thinking of them like a three-layer cake. The Platonists were the greatest line of intellectual thinkers the world has ever known. It is reflected in their art. How perfect the Greek art is, but how cold. While the Italian art is not nearly so perfect—their figures are grotesque, the babies don't look like babies, they look like old men and women—but it has color and feeling. Right balance is the balance between the feeling and the intellect, the thought, and the emotion. The Greeks had an absolute, a spirit, a soul principle, then a mind principle and a body.

Part of our philosophy is taken from the intellectual concept of the Greeks, except I put the absolute and the spirit together, called the body completely the effect, and the soul or the mind I divided into its two aspects of action and reaction. (If you want to call it conscious and subconscious, it doesn't matter. Or call it the seed and the soil.) So, I grafted these two together and these two and left this one out here to do the best it could do for itself because it is more than nothing and less than something. It is entirely an effect. Of course, out of the body, the body in a split second starts to disintegrate. A factor has gone, at any rate.

Plotinus said that it was almost impossible to differentiate between what he called the Spirit and the Absolute. The effort of the Greeks was to postulate what they called an Absolute, which was behind existence, and then to have that which is behind existence step down from the Absolute to the Spirit, which begins to differentiate the nonexistence. The next principle, below [the level of Spirit] was the Soul and the business of the Soul was to receive the images of the Spirit. It was a sort of proxy for the Spirit. Then they had the id principle as a blind force, not knowing, only doing. And the body. We just call it Spirit, soul and body.

We were discussing yesterday something that every person in our field should understand. We are not psychologists anymore than we are physiologists, but we know there has to be circulation, assimilation, and elimination if we are going to get well. Let this represent the Absolute, the Unconditioned, out to the point of differentiation. What stops it? The subjective state of our thought, the sum total of human thought. Mrs. [Mary Baker] Eddy called this "animal magnetism" or the "mortal mind." The Bible calls it the "carnal mind, enemy to God." Troward called it the "human mind in the subjective state." Jung called it the "collective unconsciousness." I just call it "what everybody has believed that may or may not be so." Who cares what you call it, so long as you know what you mean by it. For instance, Mrs. Eddy said consciousness constructs a better body when instructed by light, truth, and love. Well, that doesn't mean anything until you realize what it does mean and then it means something. The Bible said, "Make all things according to the pattern showed to thee in the mount." It says again, "Beloved, now we are the sons of God and it doth not yet appear what we shall be, but we know that when he shall appear, we shall be like him, for we shall see him as he is." We are never going to be sons any more than we are. We are already where we are going, or as the Bhagavad Gita says, "The unreal has no existence and the real never ceases to be." It also says, "The self must raise the self by the self." That would have to be true because no man can know himself without knowing God. No man can know God without discovering himself. Rabindranath Tagore said, "Nirvana is not absorption but immersion." We are not lost but found in God.

This is our whole business, to discover God, but something is in the way. Whether we call it the mortal, the human, the carnal, the race thought, the race suggestion, the race hypnotism. "Beloved, now are we the sons of God and it doth not yet appear what we shall be." We don't see what we are going to be because we see as through a glass darkly, but we know that "when he doth appear, we shall be like him." Whenever we see him, we shall be like him, and he shall appear when we see him as he is. It is one of the most remarkable statements in the Bible. Our whole philosophy is based upon the eternal, changeless, reality of a divine pattern in the universe, which not only includes us but which would be incomplete without us because we are the beloved of It, existing for Its delight. Robert Browning said, "Whence the imprisoned splendor may escape / From the developed brute, a god, though in the germ."

We find that during this process, we have to get from here to here, from the wilderness to Jerusalem, to the center, the whole of the soul. When Jesus started to cast the devils out, they said, "What have we to do with thee, Jesus, thou Son of God? Art thou come hither to torment us before the time?" Joseph Jastrow, psychologist, said that one of the greatest troubles in getting the clearance is what he called "the inertia of thought patterns." The thought patterns argue as though they were entities. This is what argued to Jesus.

When Mrs. Eddy spoke of the argument of error, they thought she was screwy, of course. Jesus forgave people their sins. At the center of the human mistake, the human isolation, the thing that thinks it is separate, there is always a sense of guilt, of insecurity, of anxiety, of not being wanted, needed, and loved. This is why Jesus forgave people. At the core of the human error or mistake (which is mistakenly called your subjective mind; there is no such thing; it is merely a reaction in a field of Universal Law now acting as though it were you), it will argue. Quimby, perhaps without knowing it, devised what is called the argumentative error. That is why Edward Kimball said this argument logically presented to mind produced this principle. What academic psychology mistakenly calls my subjective subconscious or unconscious is merely where a universal law of cause and effect is operating through me, taking on the color of my thought and therefore, reacting to me as though it were an entity.

It is interesting to me that now they no longer talk of a neurotic but a neurosis. In treating, you must separate the neurosis from the neurotic. And in our field, we have always said you must separate the belief from the believer. What is at the center of the strange animal that is called my subconscious mind? Because there is no such thing. There is no individual anything in the universe. There is an individualization of all things. If there were an individual thing in the universe, that which is individual would be isolated from the universal and no man could discover God because God is here. Remember, when we say there is no individual anything, we are not denying that all things are individualized, but for the first time we are coming to understand the uniqueness of the individualization. All of God is back of every poem that was ever written. There is only one poet. Emerson said, "There is one mind common to all individual men. Every man is an inlet to the same and to all of the same," and he may become an outlet. He said that human history is the record of the doing of that mind on this planet, and the mind that wrote is the mind that reads or it couldn't understand it. One of the great things in our philosophy is the doing away with duality. Einstein has done away with it in energy and mass. Some day psychologists will get enlightened enough to do away with the human and the Divine, and then they will become metaphysicians.

They have discovered at the University of Redlands two very interesting things in prayer therapy. First of all, they have discovered that affirmative prayer takes precedence over the negative. "I am the Lord and there is none else, there is no God beside me." The name of God is the statement of the verb "to be" and the affirmation of Its action without opposition. And they have discovered that the one who believes in hell cannot pray as affirmatively as the one who doesn't.

There are two things in the Bible that interest me very much. When God came down to the Garden of Eden to have a little talk with Adam, and Adam isn't around. "Where are you Adam? Where art thou?" Now Adam sticks his head from behind a cactus bush or a redwood tree or something and said, "I am over here." And God said, "Why don't you come out? Let's talk things over." Adam said, "I am naked." Now, there is the payoff. God said, "Adam, who told you that you are naked? How did you discover it?" When John the Baptist was baptizing people, a man came and threw himself in the dirt and said, "What shall I do to avoid the wrath to come?" John looked at him and said, "Son, that is a dirty proposition you are in, very unsanitary. Why don't you get up and shake the dirt off yourself? Let me explain something to you. I didn't come to tell you how to avoid the wrath to come. I came to tell you that the kingdom of God is at hand."

This is the thing we find. This is what interferes with the seeing. Now whether you want to call it the psyche, the subjective, the subconscious, the unconscious, let us call it the accumulation of human beliefs that seem to operate through all of us and argue to all of us saying, "You can't heal; he can't heal; she can't heal," and so forth.

I was talking to one of our ministers, Ethel Barnhart, and she said we must create a subjective entity of right action for the whole field of Religious Science. We must create a subjective entity for our own beliefs and the beliefs of the whole race, and then they either control us for good or ill. We all have a subjective state of thought in the universal field. Every group and every nation has one. They all become hypnotized by their own beliefs, lighted by false beliefs. You will find this in Robert Browning's poem *Paracelsus*, when David wakes up Saul and sings to him first of the glory of the physical universe: hunted the lion in his den, the wonderful silver shock of a plunge in cold water, and then the theme comes up and finally reaches the climax where he is revealing Saul to himself. And he said, "Saul, a hand like this hand shall throw open the gates of new life to thee! See the Christ!" And he is revealing the universal man. This wakes Saul up. He has been mesmerized. He slowly resumes his old motions and "he is Saul, ye remember in glory, ere error had bent the broad brow from the daily communion." When David, the little shepherd boy, sees this awakening of the human to the Divine, this whole theme is awakening the imprisoned splendor, he steals out into the night. Here Browning uses the most significant and I think the most beautiful thought of looking about him, feeling the pulsation of the invisible, and he calls it "the Elan," where everything is alive.

We are individualized centers in the consciousness of the Universal, whose center is everywhere and whose circumference is nowhere. There is no individual anything in the universe, but man has sought out many inventions. They have been mental ones, and at the center of everything, that keeps us from getting back to "that imperial palace whence he came." It was what William Wordsworth was talking about when he said that the youth is nature's priest. He said of man's experience: "Shades of the prison-house begin to close upon the growing boy and he forgets the glories he hath known and that imperial palace when he came." But he says at times "in moments of calm weather (he means meditation)/Though inland far we be (encased in materiality)/Our souls have sight of that immortal thither—/And sea which brought us hither/Can in a moment travel thither—/And see the children sport upon the shore and hear the mighty waters rolling evermore." It was always there. Like him when he lost the littleness, he merged with the other. It was immersion but not absorption.

As we discussed yesterday, we must get from here, which is the subjective, to the Universal or Spirit, which ought to flow without interruption. If it did, we would know intuitively, we would work without effort. As Emerson tells us, everything falls but everything falls in a circle because a circle is the only movement that describes infinity, without beginning and without end. That is why the ancients used the serpent as a life principle, with the tail in its mouth, a hoop. Now we encounter what everybody has believed, what we have believed. It doesn't matter what you call it, we have got to get through it. The argument is not about God, other than to affirm that God is all there is, but it is to get rid of that which says God is not all there is. Clear the passage. Mrs. Eddy said, "Destroy the enemy and leave the field to God." In modern academic terminology they call it coming to the light of day or self-awareness. Now here is an interesting thing. I like the saying of Jesus, "Where the blind lead the blind they both shall fall into the ditch."

I believe in a synthesis of all the different forms of analysis. There is a danger that we do not get caught in any one form so that we are unable to make the synthesis. To borrow from everything, such light as it has, that is the genius of our movement. In doing this, if we were to start out here and try to find out what is in here (and they do this professionally), they have what they call transference.

Now to me this has a great spiritual meaning. In other words, a person being treated has a sense of inferiority perhaps, or isolation, or insecurity, or anxiety, or guilt. The one treating, be he a preacher or a teacher, is in a sense a savior to him, for he transfers all his original emotions to this person. This is both good and bad. Sometimes it is positive, and sometimes it is negative. It depends on his own relations in his early life. He will go from this quickly; it is just a phase. Sometimes there is a counter transference. The thing I am interested in is this: if the time comes in the operation where the doctor strikes a place in the mind of the patient where the same condition has not been healed or still exists in his own mind, even though it is unconscious, the whole performance stops. That is the end of it, it can't get any further. Now Jesus said it in a different way, "If the blind lead the blind, both shall fall into the ditch." In this method they are supposed to get through this and then they are supposed to do what they call "break the transference." The Bible says, "Thou shalt have no other gods before me." I interpreted it that way, because as long as we depend on anything external to the self, we are depending upon a reed broken by the wind. And that is why the Bhagavad Gita says, "The self must raise the self by the self."

All I wish to point out in this operation is merely this: We start up here, although we do not recognize that. There is some confusion in here that keeps this from reflecting or manifesting down here, and if it is true then that four things exist at the center of this whole morbidity and isolation, which are rejection, guilt, insecurity, and anxiety, and there is no question about that, what is our divine medicine for this human ill? Jesus started right out with what is now called the neurosis. He said, "Your sins are forgiven you." That is why he did it. He knew what was in man. It is scientific when you begin to treat a person to forgive his sins. But Jesus also said, "Go and sin no more." How wondrously kind his words of love to the woman who "stood at his feet behind him weeping, and began to wash his feet with tears, and did wipe them with the hairs of her head, and kissed his feet, and anointed them with the ointment."

Jesus taught justice without judgment. He was no softy, no sentimentalist. "This ought ye to have done and not left the other undone." Jesus taught a rule of ethics and what we perhaps today would call morality or right living, so absolutely complete that he placed the possibility of our being forgiven in our own ability to forgive. Not because God needs anything but because he knew that the eternal flow of Divine givingness is inhibited by our unforgivingness.

Don't make God a great big man. It is awfully hard to get away from superstition, bigotry, and fear. God doesn't need to forgive, and the real man doesn't need to be forgiven, but the man you and I seem to be has got a lot of troubles, a lot of misery. And while he refuses to forgive, the Divine givingness, which ever presses against his unforgivingness, cannot get through. Thus Jesus said, "Forgive us our debts as we forgive our debtors," because it is done unto us as we believe. He said if you take your gift to the altar and find you have something against your brother, take it home. Here is cause and effect again, which Emerson called the High Chancellor of God.

So if we need to be forgiven, let us forgive. That is the first step to get a clearance from this that appears to be so isolated and so separated and is looking and looking. As St. Augustine said, "Thou hast made us for thyself, and our heart is restless until it find rest in thee." Every man's search is for God, but not the God of theology. We are looking for the God of joy, the God of laughter, the God of love. As James Whitcomb Riley said, "As it's given me to perceive/I most certin'y believe/When a man's jest glad plum through/God's pleased with him, same as you." God is laughter, of course. It is only through our own forgiving that the Divine givingness resumes Its natural currents. There isn't anything that is mad at us, trying to blast us or withholding anything from us. That is all twaddle. It doesn't belong in as great a concept as we have. We have something grand, something great, something majestic, something cosmic. It is titanic. From the human standpoint, as Emerson said, "The finite has wrought and suffered. The infinite lies stretched in smiling repose."

We have to forgive, then we have to have a sense of no guilt. "Who told you thou art naked?" Whatever it is that is too painful to bear all by itself it projects.

Sometimes it is called aggression. I have said the ego must have self-esteem. We must think well of ourselves, but rightly. But we project this unconscious sense of guilt, have a need for a sense of punishment, create a devil, hell, and all the rest. I believe that everything that the human mind believes in, no matter what it is called, that denies the supremacy and the immediacy of the unborn moment, of that which has no history and breaks forth free, clear and complete and boundless, and now is alive from the standpoint of the truth, has drugged the mind of man until we finally forget that "imperial palace from whence we came."

That is all that psychology has taught me—the blocks! Because all they do is deal with the abnormal people, and if they believe that 10 percent of all people are abnormal, for every ten persons they analyze whom they say are abnormal, they have got to pick out ninety of the most normal, happiest, glorified souls ever discovered. That is why this psychologist knows only about the diseased mind. That is good, but don't tell me that this puts up a standard for the Divine! How can a person who deals only with unhappiness know what a happy person feels like? Jesus said, "Behold, the kingdom of God is at hand."

We have to be forgiven. We have to get over the sense of guilt. I have healed many a person with the thought that God within this person approves of him. You know, often if they have stomach trouble, it will heal it. We have to get the sense of security. We have to get over anxiety. If we will take these four morbidities, we will heal 75 percent of all the people who are sick. Therefore, you and I start up here and let it down here. We know what goes on in here, but we don't want to stop there. We start with the unborn moment of the eternal here and the everlasting now. If we are to work back this way, we do it by argument. If we work down this way, we do it by the inspiration of some divine interior knowingness, which Plotinus said all men have, but few people use.

This, I think, is a lesson. It is a thought that helps you to understand that which has been eternally established. We are that thing now which we seek. After all, all that stands between heaven and Earth is an idea, and I am a great believer in this, that we must treat every man's problem—poverty, sickness, unhappiness, no matter what it is—as something that is operating through him because it is identified with him. But it does not belong to him or to anybody else. I am a great believer that if we can get that clearance, the pattern to which we have been eternally attached will assert itself. And I would add one other thing, since we are individualized centers of the consciousness of God, we have the privilege to initiate a new pattern. I believe fervently and enthusiastically with Meister Eckhart that the Eternal has never had but one son. God is begetting the only begotten and He is begetting him in me now. I believe with Emerson that the ancient of days is in the latest invention. Right here and right now as I speak, something new is born out of the unborn.

CHAPTER 2

1956

The Nature and Development of Consciousness

Wonder, Love, and Praise

AUGUST 13, 1956

In this first lecture from Asilomar in 1956, Ernest Holmes sets the stage for this summer's series to focus on "the nature and development of consciousness." First up are the concepts of wonder, love, and praise. Holmes reminds us that we are here to seek meaning and that the awe and wonder with which we approach life serves our search. A lack of wonder means that on some level we are no longer living. A life of wonder serves our evolution as we discover the Christ consciousness within ourselves and everyone we encounter. This recognition brings us to a sense of universal love and calls us to adore and praise this thing called life.

Welcome to Asilomar and this meeting.

Let us not forget this: Every man is a center in the consciousness of God (that includes women because we are speaking of generic man), and one is not more important than another in the kingdom of God. One is not smarter than another. One is not more intelligent than another. And if there are those in this world more dedicated and more spiritual than others, I have failed to meet them in seventy years, but I have heard about them, and I no longer believe they exist. Every man is on the pathway of an eternal evolution, and so far as you and I are concerned, he is hell-bent for heaven. I believe only in the hell we are getting out of, not in any one we are going into. It is self-created, and therefore we will have to become self-annihilated. We are all going to the same place because we all came from the same place.

Religious Science is no place for stupid dopes. It is no place for souls who have not become aware that they are now part of the universe in which they live. What we need is an increasing group of people who will prove what they believe before they try to believe anything else. We believe too much already, 75 percent of which is probably not true, even though people think I made it up, which I didn't.

We are not a system of thought forever staid and fast, and once written and delivered to the saints and forevermore static. Everyone will contribute something but it will never deviate from the two fundamental propositions of the ages: The universe is impelled by love and propelled by law. These are the two great realities and the polarization between the two, of action and reaction, constitutes the mystery of the universe in which we live, declares its self-existence, fills the mind with wonder and contemplation and awe. I am so convinced of that that I look forward with wonder, with awe, with reverence, with adoration, with love to the possibility of every person in this room, because I believe we are destined. We are the most consecrated persons to accept universal conception free from the superstition of secularism and dogmatism the world has ever known. All we need is more consciousness of what we now have.

We are going to conduct a series, not of lessons but of discussions, on the nature and development of consciousness, with nothing to win, not to heal somebody or get an extra nickel—all of that is good—but to develop the system, the capacity to be aware of the invisible in which we are rooted. This is the very essence of our teaching.

Our subject is wonder, love, and praise. When Jesus was talking with the disciples, asking them what is the reaction of the multitudes to his speech, what do people and whom do people think that I am, some of them said, "You are a prophet come back, you are the Messiah that was to come. Some of them say this and some say that." He turns to the impetuous Peter, the most human of the lot, and he said, "Whom do you say that I am?" And Peter, with one of those quick flashes of intuition, the only avenue through which revelation can come to the mind, said, "Thou are the Christ, the son of the living God." Jesus replied that flesh and blood had not revealed this unto you but your God inside you by some flash of consciousness has lifted the veil of sleep that hangs so heavy over the eyes of all of us from birth to death, and you have seen that which I came to proclaim, this is my mission: to reveal to you that which is the truth about myself. Or as the poet James Russell Lowell said, "I behold in thee, an image of him who died on the tree."

We are here to more deeply penetrate into the nature, the meaning, and the wonder and the reverence, and the awe and the adoration of the living Christ, not as an historic Jesus but as that which lives and moves and breathes today. "A hand like this hand, shall throw open the gates of new life to thee! See the Christ stand" (from *Saul* by Robert Browning). If God is omnipresent, God is both over-dwelling and indwelling, and the highest God and the innermost God are the same God. No man hath seen God, only the son hath revealed Him, which son we are. Not by virtue of any good thing that we have ever done—we are not that good, we are not that intelligent—nor by virtue of any evil thing that we could ever do shall we lose one iota of it until God has made the pile complete. The dismal story of sin and salvation does not belong to the new order of thought, which has come to enlighten the world. "Behold the kingdom of God is at hand."

I have never met and know that I never can or shall meet one single individual who, having gotten a clearance for himself, has ever denied it to anyone else. I know in such degree as you and I condemn anyone, we are not sure of ourselves. Harmony knows nothing of discord. Love has never heard of hate. God is not acquainted with the devil. If God is the transcendent and the imminent and the omnipresent, it is only when we translate the commonplace into the terms of the transcendence that we shall recognize and realize the imminence. It is only when we elevate the commonplace to the mountaintops that we shall understand and enter into the transcendence, for they are one and the same, equal and identical, even as the Divine Spirit is equally and evenly distributed like the ethers of space in the vast cosmos, not moving but causing everything within it to move.

Let us start out with a concept of wonder, as a child. I wrote once something about children. I remember the last verse only, "They hailed the day with glad delight, their feet in naked gladness shod, their eyes with wonder gleaming bright, such is the kingdom of God." Peggy Lee has recorded it and made it into a beautiful song.

The wonder of life. You know when wonder goes out of living, we begin to die, psychologically and physiologically. It is now known that 75 to 90 percent of all physical weariness is occasioned by a lack of enthusiastic viewpoint on life—that is wonder. The wonder and the joy. And what is going to happen next. Every day is a fresh beginning; every day is the world made new. And if we could discover that split second that the Zen Buddhist looks for, that Jesus referred to, and all the great and good and the wise have told us about, that moment in the eternal presence when we are no longer conditioned in the present by the past and when the future anticipation does not condition the present. For these are the two millstones that grind the joy out of the day in which we live, sandwiched in between two impossible negations, such little happiness and joy, such little wonder and delight as we should experience.

All creation, in my estimation, exists for the delight of God, the self-expression of the Infinite, the articulation of that which needs instrumentality for its own identity. Therefore, only as you and I in wonder, with reverence but with an enthusiasm, identify ourselves with the living Spirit can we hope that the living Spirit, through this instrumentality, shall shape the course of our existence, sing the song of eternity, the wonder at the heart of love, the mother crooning over her babe, suddenly is a part of the Divine heart, surrendering its being to its own creation—human love. Thus identified with Divine givingness and grace, as it is called, the most wonderful, the most entrancing concept and the human intellect surrendering itself to Divine wisdom, that intuition shall speak in its own language of eternity to the human mind.

This is the only revelation we have, and I would not give anything for all the dogmas that ever existed. Find one man or woman or child who has become acquainted with the Divine Presence and you will learn more from him than from every book you have ever read. This was the secret of Jesus and of Gandhi. Gandhi called it nonviolence; Jesus called it nonresistance. They have reduced all the laws of the universe to liquidity. It is only when solid meets solid that there is an obstruction. But Jesus and Gandhi understood that there is a nonviolence, a nonresistance because it is as Emerson meant when he said, we see the universe as solid fact, God sees it as liquid law. And they practiced the nonviolence, nonresistance wonder of unification with life, until there was nothing left to resist it and they triumphed. You might say Jesus was crucified and Gandhi was shot. So what? We will all get dead physically someday fortunately. With some impatient gesture, the soul will grab us by the seat of the pants and the nape of the neck, and throw us into the next kingdom of our expression. All the art and planning and wit and science of man shall not deter it one second, anymore than we could command the wind and the waves to be still, or tell the sun to no longer revolve.

There is an integrity beyond ours. There is an imagination beyond ours. There is a feeling deeper than ours, and yet we are akin to it. Who listens closely to his own soul shall hear a song no other person can sing. Who listens to the harmony of his own being, though he be in the desert or on the mountaintop alone, shall compose a symphony that no human instrument had to be attuned to and can play it only in wonder and reverence and awe on the heartstrings of his own heart, his own mind, in his own soul, for we are that instrument.

So we come together to realize the value of the individual life and its relationship to the universe. "'Who say ye, Peter, that I am?' 'Thou art the Christ, the son of the living God.'" Christ means the one and only sonship. Jesus put off the old man and put on the new man, who was Christ, until the old man, crucified and dead in the graves of obscurity and isolation, gives birth to the new man, universal, divine, eternal, everlasting, and perfect. This is the meaning of the symbol. For Christ is the universal sonship, hid with Christ in God. If all of you who have brought your textbooks will read again the chapter on the perfect whole, hid in the heart of cosmic love, some of the meditations at the end of the book, which are found in "Contemplation of the Spirit," for we wish to elevate the consciousness of our whole movement to the perception of the meaning of this divine incarnation. Everything I shall talk about this week will be but the development of one theme: There is hid within the mind of man "a divinity that shapes our ends, rough hew them how he will."

By a slow process of compulsion and impulsion, apparently outside man, he is compelled to go through the process of evolution, "A fire mist and a planet/A crystal and a cell/A jellyfish and a saurian/And caves where the cave men dwell; Then a sense of law and beauty/And a face turned from the clod—/Some call it evolution/And others call it God" (William Herbert Carruth). That is our whole theme. There is incarnated in you and in me that which we call Christ, but it is the incarnation of God, and ye are Christs and Christ is God. That is the meaning of that. The Divine sonship is not a projection of that which is unlike our nature, it is not a projection of the Divine into the human. There is no such thing that knows such projection. God cannot project Himself outside Himself. God may only express Himself within Himself. That is why Jesus said, behold the sermons in stone and running brooks and God and good in everything. We are to discover the divine essence individualized. There is and can be no such thing as a distinct individual that would be separate from the universe, and if you will think this out—and we are here to think and study and consider together 'til we arrive at something we may take home that will, we hope, increase the possibility of our spiritual awareness and the destiny of the human race.

Consider that an individual means something separate from something else. Man is not an individual in God; he is not an individual one with God, because this presupposes isolation and separation and disunion. Man is an individualization of God. Our unity is neither in or with but of. "He that hath seen me hath seen the Father." Now this was the genius of Jesus, as it has been of the great and the good and the wise of all ages, every great soul and the poets and the philosophers who perceived their spiritual identity. Let us consider the nature of unity that they came to see and know. Unity permits no division. The altar of God cannot respond to the gift that is made in the sense of isolation or fear or appeasement. It is only the pure in heart, the simple in mind, and the meek who shall inherit the Earth. There is no arrogance in spirituality. Spiritual arrogance is intellectual stupidity. It is spiritual blindness. It is temporary death to the soul. "Judge not that ye be not judged, for with what judgment ye judge, ye shall be judged," and many a person would rather remain in hell that he may still entertain animosity then to give it up. Isn't that strange, how perverse we all are, humanly speaking?

The stupidity of the intellect, of the conceit, of the social order is so terrific that it staggers me at times. The stupidity and the ignorance and the futility of it and the nasty littleness of it—a crime against the soul, a denial of that sublime and divine thing within us that waits to take flight to greater things, that Jesus taught, differentiating him somewhat and a departure from ancient Judaism, although it was built on that, partly on ancient Hinduism and the philosophy of the Greeks, the greatest line of intellectual thinkers the world has ever known. He forgave people their sins. He announced the importance of the individual life, the root of spiritual democracy. These are the two greatest teachings of Jesus. The Jews had held that the sins of the fathers are visited on us from generation to generation; the Hindus held the theory of reincarnation. Jesus may or may not have believed in them, I do not know. If he did, he believed in them only as relativities, hampering the human mind, for he said that your sins are forgiven you. "Today shalt thou be with me in Paradise." And he said every hair of your head is counted—the value of the individual life. Jesus gave us back to ourselves. And he might have said with Emerson, "I tread on the pride of Greece and Rome…/For what are they all, in their high conceit/When man in the bush with God may meet?"

What is the thing that Jesus proclaimed, "Ye are of more value than many sparrows." I Am the son of the living God, "He that hath seen me hath seen the Father." "I Am the way and the truth and the life, no man cometh unto the Father but by me." He was not talking about Jesus, he was talking about *you*. How are you ever going to reach God other than through your own nature? There are no prophets other than the wise. There is no God beyond truth and no revelation higher than the realization of that divinity within us. There cannot be what the ages have failed to reveal; you and I must reveal each to himself in the secret chamber of his own heart, the secret place of the Most High, where only and alone does he abide under the shadow of the Almighty. But that aloneness, which the great have spoken about, was not a loneliness. It was the one all-inclusive, all-penetrating unity of everything that is. This shall generate within us a wonder, the spirit of adventure. What can we bring forth?

The life without wonder is dead. Life comes from the innermost resources of our own divine nature. This was the claim Jesus made upon the universe. We must make the same one and identify ourselves with the same presence and power in the same principle. This is why we are here; this is the meaning of our work. If we have anything to offer the world, it will be this. The new catholicity of the mind and the soul and the spirit cannot help but generate love. And we realized that since I am one with all life, I wish to express the most life that I can. Your life is my life; my life is your life. I cannot leave you out and understand myself. I am incomplete. I am lame and blind and halted without inclusion. Remember this: We are talking about the kind of inclusion that Buddha, Jesus, Gandhi, Walt Whitman, and Emerson understood. When Emerson said that who in his integrity worships God becomes God, and when Jesus said that God causes the sun and rain to fall alike on the just and the unjust, and when Walt Whitman said of the prostitute, "Not 'til the sun excludes you do I exclude you/Not 'til the waters refuse to glisten for you, and the leaves to rustle for you, do my words refuse to glisten and rustle for you." This is inclusion. Our littleness, the narrow vision of our spiritual perspective causes the horizon of God's boundless skies to press so close to us that we are suffocated by that which alone could give life, and we must reverse the process. It is impossible to be filled with spiritual wonder.

We are falling into a deep reverie of universal love. You know there is no person whom we could hate if we loved him. It is a terrible thing to feel disunited with life and the world and each other because this is to us a reflection of our own soul, this is to us this vast panoramic picture mirror. Whatever it may be, it is more than nothing and less than something. It has an office to perform, to give expression to that which animates what we see and what we animate, and we animate what we see, and this to us is the projection of our own soul. We cannot help but be filled with love. It is true that love is the lodestone of life and, as Ella Wheeler Wilcox said, "A love so limitless, deep and broad/That men have renamed it and called it God."

Now love is of the alone to the alone in everything we meet. It asks to return just the joy of the giving. The moment it asks for a return, it is fearful, it is doubtful, it is weak, it trembles, it becomes anemic and exhausts itself because it opens no channels to the enlargement. This is what Jesus meant when he said, "Who loses his life shall find it." Love.

And that brings us to adoration and worship and praise. I wish to write on the spirit of worship, and the title came to me: Do We Worship to Appease or to Adore? That is the way I shall handle the subject. Do we worship to appease or to adore? The altar of God receives no appeasement. The wine that is poured into the chalices of the Lord has no bitterness in it. The eternal, the everlasting, the Infinite knows nothing about our little ways, our petty thoughts, our little divisions and subdivisions until we have stifled the soul and the mind and the intellect and the imagination, the will, and I know people who by a repression shut themselves in from their friends and their comrades and their children because of some little petty damned thing. We have tried to contain the Infinite in a pint measure, and the pint measure will not hold it. We have tried to reduce the Eternal to the level of the temporal, and the temporal will not take it. And in our anguish, we have besought the living God to save us from the error of our ways.

Psychologically, emotionally, and religiously, it is good, but spiritually, from the standpoint of the revelation of the soul to the soul, it hasn't arrived very far. The chalice of the Lord contains no bitterness, no fear. The wine that runs over from the chalice of the eternal is not trampled from the grapes, nor does the divine forgivingness we seek come as an answer to our appeal that the Infinite shall enter into our mistakes, but rather shall it be as the prodigal son who would feed his belly upon the husks that the swine did not eat but no man gave unto him. No man shall ever give unto you or to me other than that which we take.

The universe shall continue its song. Someday, when we come to it in adoration, having surrendered our littleness, our hopes, our fears, our longings, our heavens, our hells, our saviors and our way-showers, naked and clean and unafraid, shall our horizon be extended and the night shall cease and the chariots of celestial fire shall spill their lights across the hilltops of our new vision. And our valleys shall be elevated to the mountaintops, and God Himself shall go forth anew into creation through you and through me. And may angels light your path to that indwelling city of God in your own soul. Amen.

Spiritual Mind Healing

※

AUGUST 14, 1956

In this second lecture in 1956, Holmes continues discussing the nature and development of consciousness by describing the practice within Science of Mind of spiritual mind treatments. Here he defines this type of affirmative prayer, including how it works and how you do it effectively.

The subject today is spiritual mind treatment. Note that we use the word spiritual mind treatment rather than Christian mind treatment, or Jewish, or Hindu, or some other kind of mind treatment. We use it as we would use the word beauty. Beauty is the essence of the beautiful. That is why we speak of a work of art as an object of art. Art itself, beauty, is subjective. It projects itself into a form, and that is what we call an objective. But it is an objectivity of a subjective essence, felt but not seen. So we use the word "spiritual" in the same sense. It applies to every race, every color, every creed; it would be just as effective for a pagan as a Christian. Now we happen to be Christians, if such there be. We happen to belong to that faith by background and culture. It has nothing to do with spiritual mind healing, either as a spiritual essence or active law or science.

We believe there is a science of spiritual mind healing that can be taught, definitely used, and consciously applied with certainty of a definite result. That is what we mean when we speak of the Science of Mind. We do not speak of "healers" in our movement. In our movement, there is no such thing as a healer, any more than there is someone who makes a garden or makes a cabbage. Nature creates the cabbage; we plant the seed. In our movement, there is no such thing as a healer or a natural healer or some person who has more healing power than others. There is no such thing. We are always fighting against superstition in our field. It is so easy for the little truth we have to be clothed by so much superstition that finally we lose sight of that which makes it work and begin to do a lot of things that make it not work. We are not superstitious.

You do not have to be superstitious to be spiritually minded. Remember this: A spiritually minded person is not one who puts on an asinine look or vacant stare and walks around proclaiming that nobody is at home and not likely to get there soon. That is not spiritual mindedness. Spiritual mindedness is a persistent and consistent person who understands all and will accept all. The person who builds too high a wall around his very small mental estate will shut out more spiritual scenery than he can let in.

Spiritual mindedness is the capacity to not only believe in, to perceive, to feel, and to react to a unitary wholeness, a divine presence, an essence, an infinite personalness, a beauty, a love, and, I believe, a laughter that exists in the universe because I do not believe the universe is serious. We get all weighed down by our little virtues, which instantly become vicious. For such people, there is nothing to do anything with. Spirituality is normal, natural, spontaneous, effervescent, or never studied. Emerson said that we have confused Jesus with virtue and the possibility of all men, and that virtue, self-conscious, becomes vicious.

Spiritual mind healing then means exactly what it says: The healing, the spiritual healing of the mind with the idea that the mind reacting on, in, through, and as the body and environment will change the environment because the mind is changed. "Be ye transformed by the renewing of your mind, cutting off the old and putting on the new, which is Christ, Christ in you." Now the Greeks said that man is numa, psyche, and soma. That means spirit, soul, and body. Psyche means the feminine. We speak of psychology, the science of mind. Psychosomatic medicine deals with relationships between body and mind or between body-mind relationships. We believe in it. It is one of the approaches, in fact, to spiritual mind healing.

We also believe in the relationship of the spirit or the numa to the psyche, which is mind. Therefore, without contradicting what we get from other fields, we add to and say we believe in spiritual psychosomatics. We really practice spiritual psychosomatics in spiritual mind healing because the mind automatically establishes a relationship to the body without our having to even try to make it. The mind should have a relationship to the spirit that is automatic and spontaneous. There are emphases on spiritual psychosomatics, because if we change the mind, the mind will change the body.

Now why is this? This is something you and I understand, and but a few people in the world do understand it, and only people in the metaphysical fields understand it. Science doesn't. Philosophy doesn't, as I have only encountered in rare instances, like Baruch Spinoza saying, "I do not deny mind is one thing and matter is another, but there ceases to be a distinction between mind and matter so the greatest metaphysical problem also dissolves." Theology, as such, except in the new metaphysical movement, does not appear to understand it because we deal with concepts that [Phineas] Quimby announced when he said, "Mind is matter in solution and matter is mind in form."

It is very important to understand this. In other words, Quimby says mind and matter are the same thing, but there is a phase of mind that is liquid and a phase that is in form. But he said, "There is a superior wisdom to which this principle of mind is as the matter of the Spirit." That was no different than Einstein saying that energy and mass are equal, identical, and interchangeable. He doesn't say energy energizes mass; he says it is mass. Spinoza understood that when he said mind and matter are the same thing. Therefore, in spiritual mind healing, we deal with a concept that there is no difference between the essence in form and the essence of form, because the essence of form in form is form.

We deal with it in the same way that we deal with the mysticism of the Divine Presence: God as man in man is man. I coined that after the saying of the mystic who said that the highest God and the innermost God is one God, or the overdwelling and indwelling are one.

So just as Einstein established the principle of energy and mass, all that means is the visible and invisible, what you see and what you don't see, as being the same thing but automatically announced a wisdom superior to them because he could analyze both of them. This is the thing we must not overlook. When Einstein said energy and mass are equal, identical, and interchangeable, he did not disappear into the picture he had drawn. His identity remained that of a conscious intelligence, analyzing that which as energy and as mass has intelligence but not self-awareness. Therefore, it has no consciousness. It is inconsistent, as [Sri] Aurobindo would have said, or it has such a low degree of intelligence that it has no self-awareness. It is necessary for us to understand that because we have an identical belief in the field of body-mind relationships. We do not deny either the body or the mind but we do affirm Spirit. We add to but do not take from.

Jesus understood this. Jesus understood the system of the Jews and of the Hindus. From the ancient Jews and Hindus and Greeks come most of the best philosophy we have. Christianity says it is a combination of the Palestinian impositionalism and Grecian Eminentism. All that means is the God that is up there and the God that is in here is the same God. But we must understand that our belief is that mind in solution and mind in form are the same thing. In other words, we are not trying to reach a known fact with an unknown or unknowable principle. We are not spiritualizing matter to heal disease or materializing spirit to perceive matter and control it. There is no such thing as spiritual control of the material universe. The very theory is a suppositional opposite, which annihilates its fundamental premise and you start out with chaos.

This isn't very clear to me but I am sure it is true. What I am trying to say is there is no God who is supervising a human kingdom. There is no law in nature above another law of nature that is translating a law, opposite and different from it, into a likeness of it. There can't be. Nature is one system. God is one. Existence is one. Therefore, spiritual mind healing deals with the concept of disease, not as an unreality in experience but as a form of intelligence in a wrong arrangement, and thought rightly arranged will automatically rearrange it on the basis that mind and matter are equal, identical, and interchangeable. This is what Quimby taught and nothing has changed. Mrs. Eddy said, "All is infinite mind and its infinite manifestation, for God is All-in-All."

Now I want to talk about physical disease and our approach to it because it is a part of our practice. It is not the most important thing we do, but it is a very important thing. If a man has a pain or is suffering from disease, I don't know of anything that will make a man happier than to get him well. And I don't think it is egotistical to want to do it. I don't have to believe in lost souls because if they are, neither you nor I nor God nor anybody else would know where to look for them because they would be lost, and that is that. But I don't believe any of us has completely found ourselves, discovered that thing which makes him tick, that mystery that Omar Freed said, "which without asking wither hurried hence and without asking wither hurried whence, like water, willy-nilly flowing."

Now we believe in spiritual mind healing and our approach to it is very simple. First of all, we believe that the universe in which we live is a spiritual system governed by laws of intelligence or the law of mind in action. Spiritual mind healing is not a gift that somebody possesses. There is a technique: Its thought is form and doth the body make (or soul is form because thought and soul are interchangeable here). Then Quimby said, "I represent the man of wisdom and the man of wisdom enters the man of opinions and he explained that his opinions are opinions and you ask me, what is the cure and my answer is, my explanation is the cure." This is psychosomatic medicine carried to rather a high degree. Jesus said there is a truth that sets man free, or as we would say, which known, demonstrates itself.

In psychiatry they say if the thing can be brought to self-awareness it probably will be dissipated because it is the nature of every neurosis to heal itself and every physical disease to heal itself. I was reading recently a testimony of some psychiatrists and very excellent medical men and they stated that 75 percent of all physical diseases would heal themselves if we would forget them, and 75 percent of all emotional disturbances would adjust themselves if we would let them alone.

Why? Because life is self-existent. It is the nature of everything that is wrong to make itself right, and everything that is wrong has within itself the ability and power and capacity, should have the intelligence to adjust itself to that fundamental harmony to which, in which, and with which nothing can be wrong.

Now the one who practices spiritual mind healing, if he wishes to really heal, he must explain these things and demonstrate them because in our field, as in medicine there is a cure without there being a healing. People who, every time they get a headache or their foot itches, have to have a practitioner aren't in much better shape than a neurotic person who has to go to a doctor every few weeks to get examined to see how he feels. It is a very bad practitioner who hopes that his patient will have to come back, even the second time. It is just as bad as a practitioner who won't work with him until he doesn't have to come back. We are not making bypasses or meaningless inane statements in our work. We are not saying peace when there isn't any peace. We are not saying people are not ill or why would we try to work on them if they weren't? We are admitting there is something wrong but it could be made right.

Therefore, we start with an explanation. I believe in our work, treating is subordinate to teaching, even when you are practicing and with just an individual, that is if you really want to get somebody somewhere. However, in the necessity of our practice, it often happens that about half the time you don't have a chance to do that. Somebody calls you up and says give me a treatment, and you know you have a science, a way to give a treatment, and you help him. And that is good, but it will be better if he will come to you and you explain body-mind relations.

Now spiritual mind healing will not be complete until it tunes the individual to the Infinite. It can't be. It will not be complete until you get a clearance from the sense of rejection and guilt. Therefore, you will have to forgive him. Someone will say, how can I forgive him? Well, you just forgave him. Jesus said, "Your sins are forgiven you." He also said, if you go and do the same thing again, you will create the same cause. Troward said that you can initiate a new chain of causation, but if you go right back to the old, you merely repeat it.

Spiritual mind healing must assure the consciousness that there is nothing in the universe to be afraid of. There is no fundamental evil. There is no duality. This is the essence of spiritual mind healing because as the consciousness perceives this transcendence, it almost automatically sloughs off the other thing. There is a rhythm in the universe. Rightly understood, there would be no conflict.

There is a peace in the universe, a freedom from confusion, that rightly understood would heal all troubles. There is an all encompassing love in the universe that, rightly understood, would heal emotional trouble. It will do it because when we do this individually, it does it. All you have to do is to apply the rule and multiply the thing and you arrive at certain conclusions that have not been arrived at in other fields. Somebody said to me the other day, we shouldn't give degrees, etc. You will never get anywhere if you stop and ask people what you should do—sit astride the ass or carry him on your own back.

The intelligence of God has presupposed that man should no longer remain witless. Interesting concept and worth playing around with whimsically. Someone will say, we want to know how to practice specially; this is the way to do it. There is one thing that psychiatrists taught metaphysics, but metaphysics hasn't learned it yet, and that is a psychiatrist or analyst who judges his patient or condemns him is unethical in his science. He is absolutely wrong and won't get very far. Now this means that when we say love is a great healing power, we are right. Love is the great healing power. The fire of love is the essence of reality that burns the eros from the heart and the soul and the mind that has seared the body. The body is the effect. A corpse doesn't know whether it has a cancer or not.

Everything below the threshold of consciousness that is aware is insentient to the level of awareness at which consciousness has evolved. It is what Troward meant when he said, "The higher mode of intelligence controls the lower." Everything less than conscious intelligence is unconscious intelligence, which can function only on the pattern either inherent with it by the cosmos or injected in it by us being subject. Somebody will say, how can we do what God didn't do? We can't. When we do it, God is doing it. That is where we make our mistake. One of our greatest errors is that we think the universe was created, wound up, and is now running down and that the Mechanic deserted it when He wound it up. This is why Emerson said that the Ancient of Days is in the latest invention. And he said, the mind that wrote history is the mind that reads it, can interpret it only from this viewpoint because history is a record of the doings of that mind on this planet. You have to forgive people their sins. The Catholic Church does it, and there are fewer neurotics among those who go to confession than the others, although Fritz Kunkel said the deepest confession is what he called meditative or confessional meditation.

Now then the practitioner has the tool of thought, and this is based on the assumption that, thought or substance, there is no difference between the thought and what it is going to do. But what it is going to do is announced by the definiteness of the thought, but its ability to do it is not injected by the thinker. This is very important. This is why I started out by saying we have no natural healers, no spiritual healers, we do not use the word "healers." It is a mistake in our science. And in our philosophy, we use the word "practitioner." We do not say that a physicist is a natural energizer, do we, because he deals with energy. Of course not.

Here is where Quimby arrived at the concept that there is a superior wisdom independent of mind, as fluid and mind as form to which the word, the treatment, and the form it takes—which are themselves equal, identical, and interchangeable—are but as the matter or the substance to be molded by the consciousness that uses it. And so Quimby said that the use of this he calls the Science of Christ. This is where the term originated and this is what Jesus understood.

This means that the practitioner doesn't do the healing, but if he didn't do his work of meditation and prayer, it might not be done. He doesn't inject himself in as a healer, but what he does is to consciously use a natural energy, intelligence, and creativity at the level of his consciousness, his recognition, and his feeling of it. In this sense the practitioner uses the Law of Mind.

When that divine moment comes, as Emerson said [in *Self-Reliance*], "Leave your theory, as Joseph his coat in the hand of the harlot, and flee." Who shall tell you how to pray when you feel like praying? Only you know your relationship to that which is greater than you but which is you. This is a sacred precinct; it is the Holy of Holies; this is the secret place of the Most High and in you is that Light, that being, the candle of the Lord that can never be extinguished. Shakespeare caught a vision of this when he said, "How far that little candle throws its beam, so shines a good deed in a naughty world."

A practitioner is a practitioner. He is a user. Troward said the original meaning of the word "husbandman" is a dispenser of the Divine Gift. I think that is good. I have come to believe that all our interpretations of the Bible are what we make up.

What would be a technique of spiritual mind healing? It is merely the formation of words to conform with an idea—an idea, of course, that harms no one and with the insistence that they are true until nothing in your own mind, your own consciousness rejects what you said and have what you said identified with the person, place, or thing you want changed. That is all there is to it. It is simplicity itself, but it is so elusive that we look for a greater profoundness, not knowing how profound simple things are. I have studied Plato all my life. Jesus knew everything Plato knew, but you would never know that Jesus knew what Plato knew by reading of Jesus, and you would never know that Plato was talking about what Jesus knew by reading Plato. Because where one has the intellectual evolvement, the other speaks direct from the fire of the heart with the simplicity of a man who looked about and found in nature the object lesson of the spiritual reality of the universe in which he lived. Look at the sun, the lilies of the field, etc.

We of necessity believe that there is an Intelligent Principle in the universe that receives the impress of our thought as we think it and acts upon it deductively without question, without argument, without rationality, so far as acceptance or rejection, and with complete accuracy and mathematic and rationality so far as operation is concerned. In other words, I think a man by the name of Edward Kimball said, "Argument logically presented to the mind produces the result." I use that frequently because everything happens and that is the logic of your treatment. God is all there is, and God is perfect. There is One Life, that Life is God, that Life is my life, therefore that Life is now pulsating through me. There is One Divine pattern of harmony—it beats in perfect rhythm, it is in accord with the universe, the undulation of the universe is this. There is nothing separate from it. Now as a result of this, the logic of the argument produces the essence of the conclusion, which becomes what we call the realization in which lies the power of this movement. That is the starting-off place of the thing that can fly faster than sound.

Therefore the argument, since there is only one mind principle, convinces no one but the one who gives it. No one else. It doesn't convince the practitioner. It doesn't go out anywhere. There is no such thing as your subjective mind and my subjective mind and somebody else's subjective mind. There is a law of subjectivity equally distributed, just as the Spirit is, and reacting to the individual and individualizing in and through him. And in this sense, the thing you change is where you are and the person is where you are because it is where you are and everything is in it and it is all being its own law through each person.

And so what you correct in your own thought, whether you call it an argument, this is where affirmation and denial come in. Charles Fillmore thought the denial was equal and necessary as the affirmation. Emilie Cady did. I think the Christian Scientists do. Quimby in a certain sense did. But all have realized that the affirmation and denial are for the purpose of building up a subjective acceptance that the mind itself can no longer reject, which now becomes part of the universal law and order of that individual, and because it is identified with him, it will operate through him.

Now the technique is very simple. This treatment is for John Smith. He lives at such and such a place, and this is the truth about him because it is that which appears is opposite to this that is eliminated from his experience. This is all that is left—the Divine Pattern, and nothing is attached to it. Somebody might say, "Every plant my heavenly Father hath not planted is rooted up and cast out." "Behold ye, I make all things new." These are statements to convince the mind of the one giving the treatment, but any statement that will *convince* you is good. Make up one. No two treatments can ever be alike, lest we should listen to ourselves speak, and we must not listen to what we say but what we think that now says what we don't have to listen to. But that is true of all art, all public declaration. It is the one and only rule I tell our students. They say, "How do you become a good speaker?" and I say, "I, beyond all the usual things that are needed and necessary, never listen to what you are saying, always say what you are listening to, and you will impart yourself to your audience if you love them."

Who then is a good practitioner? Everybody who believes what we are talking about. There aren't any good and better and more spiritual than another. It has nothing to do with God being God. These are the little ratholes we fall into. If you and I could divorce ourselves from our littleness, we would never have to become great. We would be great. Because greatness inheres by virtue of the divine incarnation, which you and I didn't have a thing to do with. I never have a funeral without saying we believe in immortality; therefore, we believe it is a principle in nature. All people are immortal or no people are immortal. No one is bad enough to destroy it or good enough to create it. We all got to the same place here, we will all get to the same place there. Sam Walter Foss said in *"The Song That Silas Sung,"* "Let the howlers howl/And the scowlers scowl/And the growlers growl/And the gruff gang go it/But behind the night/There's plenty of light/And everything is all right/And I know it."

Forget all about being spiritual, and that peculiar look will disappear. It is a mild form of insanity. Do the thing spontaneously, joyfully, gladly. Out of the mouths of babes and sucklings. And he sent a little child unto them and said, "Suffer the little children to come unto me and forbid them not, for of such is the kingdom of heaven. And a little child shall lead them."

Let the child in you counsel the man of experience that the man of experience, out of what he has learned, shall have found out what is good, better, or worst and seek to follow that which is good, but always by this wise counselor—the infinite child—and it will always tell you what to say. We have no formula because every time you give a treatment you expect it is the only time you are going to give that one. And it is a new formation and must be spontaneous. The moment it becomes mechanical, it seems to lose power. The technique may be correct, but the fire and feeling and temperament isn't there, and it is out of the fire of the heart that the mouth must speak.

Therefore, don't wonder what words you are going to use. You may know this: A treatment, I believe, follows a law of intelligence, and I believe the objective manifestation of it corresponds with the subjective use. The treatment is involution; the other is evolution. The treatment is spontaneous; the rest is mechanical. Someone may ask, "How will we apply this to the treatment of affairs?"

In just the same way. There is no difference between treating somebody to remove a disease or treating somebody to remove an impoverished state. It is all mental. We reduce everything to a mental concept and then clear up the mental concept, spiritualizing not things but our own consciousness of a greater perception of substance and supply. There is one person in the universe, only one. That person is what I am; I am the only personality there is but it is differentiated and individualized in me in a unique way. I do not compete with anybody and nobody can with me. There is neither competition nor monopoly in God.

Then we know that thoughts have the action of creating new experiences out of the primordial substance in the original mind. I spoke about the wonder of it yesterday. It is an adventure. For instance, take a person who is alone and lonely, and you point out to him there is but one person and you must expect this and that. Then you say, new experiences are coming to this man, he is going to meet new people, new experiences, new conditions. Wonderful, and as you do that, out of what you have done through the law that operates upon it because I think everything is operated upon. We know it is physically. It is mentally and spiritually, too, in my estimation. You will find whole new sets of circumstances. We must remember that out of the impulsion of our thought there is a creativity set in motion that has a prerogative and initiative, as well as a reciprocal action toward us, and something new will come, something new will come. I write that way when I want to write inspirationally. I take a thought and say, now do your stuff and see what happens. Sometimes it is silly and sometimes it is good enough to keep, but who knows. There is but one Creator in the universe, and we individualize It. It individualizes us, I guess.

There is only One Mind; we use It. One Spirit; we live by It. One Law, which governs everything, One Presence responds to everything, but we are individualizations of It and we do initiate. The Universe is not an endless and monotonous repetition of the same old thing. Charles Kettering said that every invention is an intuition and the development of it and technique is but a series of intuitions. I believe that.

There is nothing ridiculous to the Infinite. The only thing the Infinite cannot do would be that which denies the Infinite. We must never forget that. Aurobindo says, "How do we know but what the tigers fighting in the jungle are but expressing the fierce delight of the Infinite."

Something new is being done every time you think. God is not a static God. There is no time when creation begins. It is beginning now. In the eternal Now, the Spirit moved upon the face of the waters. In the eternal Now, my thought moved upon the subjectivity of the universe, and out of it arose that creation from the void, and it never existed before. We are not, as some of the Hindus think, endlessly repeating incarnation after incarnation.

Therefore, so complete is what Troward calls the reciprocal action of this thing, that you and I can initiate a new chain of causation without knowing what it is going to look like. Now, let me make an illustration, because to me this is terrifically important. (Somebody said to me, "I heard you have retired." Well, I have retired like you put four new tires on a good car so you can travel faster and farther. This is the only kind of retiring there is.) I am treating every day to know new and better things are going to happen to me than have ever happened before. And they will.

We can initiate a new chain of causation just by saying that something new is going to happen. If I send to the Department of the Interior, they send me a packet of seeds I don't know anything about and have never seen. I would never have seen the kind of a flower or plant this seed would make. I have no mental equivalent of it in my own mind. This we should be careful about. But the Mind that created the seed invoked in it and involved in it its own idea, kind after kind, and when I subject it to the Law of Creativity, it will provide me with that which I did not give an equivalent for. My equivalent was only in the ability to expect to receive something I knew nothing about. We make a mistake if we think we have to have an exact mental equivalent of every experience. If we did, we would be caught in a trap right now. We should have painted the picture and stepped into it, and we would really and truly be framed. That is not the nature of the universe in which we live.

And so remember this: No matter what you are treating, people or conditions, find out what is wrong, know that the opposite thought will erase it. Start as simple as that, and you can do it. Because nobody can think any better than you can think. No one has any more authority about it. Nobody is any better than you are. Take somebody who is willing to abandon himself to the genius of the universe, the realization of his intimate relationship to it, who is willing to put his foot forth into an apparent void, and he certainly will find it on a solid rock. Take someone who can worship the God in the tree and see no difference between a saint kneeling in high ecstasy before the altar of his faith and the man who is drunk in the gutter, and let him apply his thought and feeling and all that he is to his conviction, and you will have discovered a spiritual genius.

Resistance

AUGUST 15, 1956

In this third lecture from 1956 on the nature and development of consciousness, Holmes describes the resistance that arises in us as we seek to grow and evolve. Part of this resistance comes from our individual desire to protect our egos, and part comes from the collective consciousness of humanity. On an individual level, we question our worthiness to accept the goodness of life. On a collective level, we believe in duality, which pushes against the internal urge to know unity. Holmes asks how we can overcome these patterns of resistance and suggests, ironically, that the answer lies in nonresistance (a topic he returns to in 1959).

This is a meditation about the ego. People seem to labor under what to me would be a mistaken concept that our endeavor is to get rid of the ego. As I suggested, that would be like throwing the baby out with the bathwater. Our object is not to destroy that which the universe has created and projected in us in discovering what we call the "Christ," which means the universal pattern and prototype of God as His own son. It doesn't mean something else. This is God, the Son. But you are that son. We are not seeking to destroy but as [Rabindranath] Tagore suggested, nirvana is not absorption but immersion, not lost but found in its truest sense. The ego, rightly understood, is the only thing that we have or are or can be or ever hope to evolve into more of the same, which is which. Whatever that means. We are not here to annihilate what God has created but to accentuate the relationship of Creator to created, of Father to son, so intimate that the Father becomes the son and the son the Father, without confusion. That is the meaning or interpretation. Tomorrow's title is "The Purpose of Evolution" and Friday's title, "What Does It Mean to Us?—from the Father of Light to the Son of Love."

Please don't anyone ever think that Religious Science teaches the absorption of what we miscall the finite in what we misinterpreted as the Infinite, the loss of the identity of individualization of that instrumentality of the Infinite, the whole purpose of evolution of which is to produce, accentuate, and increase. You are the most important thing you will ever meet, the only divine being you will ever know, merely because you can never know anything outside of yourself. This shocks people at first. This is not blasphemy; it is the correct interpretation.

This morning I want to speak on a subject that is partly theoretical and partly, I believe, demonstrated in our field and in a field of psychic and psychological sciences insofar as they are scientific, which isn't far enough but which is gradually extending its horizon of scientific investigation, of something that is true because science is the knowledge of laws and causes in nature and how they operate. So I chose the subject called resistance. This means a psychological resistance, individual and collective. The word "resistance" is borrowed from psychology. In analytical psychology, they speak of the resistance. Joseph Jastrow said one of the main difficulties of the analyst that the psychiatrist has is to deal with what he calls the "inertia of habit thought patterns." This comes to us out of the field of science. He said the thought patterns in there laid down do not like to give themselves up, and they argue as though they were entities. Now seventy-five years ago when Mrs. Eddy and the early Presbyterians spoke of the argument of error, I suppose everybody said, "Well, they are a little bit screwy, but unless they become violent, let's not make them a charge of the state."

It is an interesting thing that many psychic revelations and intuitions of the ages that reflected our theology, philosophy, and science came in the back door of intuition—like the modern concept of the nature of the physical universe, that it is a flow. They do not appear to know whether it is regular, intermittent, or steady. It is no different from the ancient concept of Pythagoras that everything is motion and number. Not a bit different. The modern equations of Einstein, that everything bends back upon itself, is the law of karma of the East, which Annie Besant said, "binds the ignorant but frees the wise." One of the prophets said, "He led captivity captive." It was Isaiah.

He, Christ, in me shall take the law that bound me and rightly understood, it will free me, because karma, which is the law of cause and effect, is the law that binds the ignorant but frees the wise.

Einstein's first concept that everything bends back upon itself is the basis of the law of compensation, of Jesus and Emerson saying that as a man sows, so shall he also reap, that everything in the universe moves in circles. Einstein's next concept—that energy and mass are equal, identical, and interchangeable—is the very basis of all of our practice, as I discussed yesterday. The theory of our practice must be based on the liquidity of the universe and that there is no such thing as a solid fact, not yesterday or tomorrow or ever was, can be, or will be. Facts only appear to be solid, and form only appears to be solid.

One of the last findings in modern physics is that we must now think of the physical universe more as a shadow cast by an invisible substance than as a thing in itself. Plotinus, in trying to explain the mystery of the physical universe, said it is no thing but it is not nothing. It is more than nothing and less than something. It is more than nothing in that it is; it is less than something in that it is not an entity. But, he said, its business is to project the form, the contemplation of the Spirit.

Einstein's last equation, which he didn't elaborate very much on but said a couple of years before he passed on, that he was convinced that at last he had found one consistent law that synthesized all physical laws. That is every law in physics, every known law in science, and I believe it will include the psychological laws: The universe is one system. What is true on one plane is true on all. As above, so beneath. As below, so above. As within, so without. That is why Jesus in all of his parables used the examples of nature. Jesus was not a theologian or a religionist, as you and I understand the term. He was one who perceived and proclaimed, "Behold, the kingdom of heaven is at hand." They probably said, "We don't see anything but rocks and falling stars and sand and grime and dirt and horror and birth and tragic experiences and death, that which was not invited and goes uninvited as water, willy-nilly flowing."

So when Einstein said there is one law common to all other laws, he was synthesizing or putting together, joining together in a unitary wholeness every law that science knows anything about, and he said there is one law that finally governs them all. This is no different than the ancient Jews saying, "Behold, O Israel, the Lord thy God is One." Just existence. The name of God is existence. And in the Greek Catholic Church they now use the word "existence" in their services, so I am told. I learned a long time ago to accept the saying of [Lucius Annaeus] Seneca, "Keep faith with reason for she will convert thy soul." And someone else will say there are no prophets other than the wise.

I've also learned that everybody made everything up, and you just have to listen to the story that sounds the best. Aaron Burr said of law, it is that which is "boldly asserted and plausibly maintained." We get in the habit of accepting the authority of the ones who scream the loudest. There still are no prophets other than the wise. Seneca was still right in his admonition: "Keep faith with reason for she will convert thy soul."

One of the first things I learned was that the interpretations of the Bible were so confusing they could not be either sensible or scientific because both science and sense deal with principle and will have to deal with principles that are alike. They will have to interpret them the way they are. And out of the knowledge of the laws of nature, the way they are, will grow the philosophy of life that is correct and the religion, which is our relationship to the Invisible, which is right. But with it will be combined the mystical intuition and synthesized. We will discover in them what James Russell Lowell called "that thread of the all-sustaining Beauty which runs through all and doth all unite."

Our talk this morning on resistance, individual and collective, is based partially on the scientific knowledge and partially on what I think and many others think must happen if we carry the known into the unknown and multiply the collective group by the individual members and arrive at what must be, so far as to say, almost but to most at least control of the human race, blindly, merely by what the human race has always believed, blighted by false beliefs. First this sounds strange. We know this is what happens in individual life. We know that mental and emotional unbalance is the usurpation of the prerogative of the intellect, of the objective faculties or the conscious faculties by this subjective, until there is no longer any point of discrimination or decision or action. It is like a blind force.

Plotinus spoke of this mind principle as a blind force, not knowing only doing. In order to understand this, we must suppose (and we do) that there is a neutral principle of mind reaction described by Troward, by Hudson fifty years ago, individual and collective, and described by Carl Jung, no doubt the greatest living psychologist or psychiatrist and, I think, the greatest whoever did live. He deals with the mystical, the spiritual, and the religious, in which I believe, because from them and through them has come and still comes the greatest hope and the most nearly right action we have. When I say anything critical about men's spiritual beliefs, it is not a criticism about religion. Religion is the intuition that strikes the intellect through the emotions and interprets itself to any individual at any age it can, through the culture and background of that individual, at that age and, once in a while, somebody rises beyond his own background, creates a new horizon, shoves the possibility of experience farther out. That is what all great reformers have done.

But so often they get so confused in the psychic that the vision which of itself is fair and cosmic does not get through to the surface but brings with it the fringes of that which is not true. The psalmist wrote in Psalm 91, "He that dwells in the secret place of the Most High shall abide under the shadow of the Almighty." And what can be more exalted than what David wrote in Psalm 23, "The Lord is my shepherd; I shall not want."

But the same man, David, wrote in Psalm 18, in a different mood, "Thou hast also given me the necks of mine enemies, that I might destroy them that hate me." One day Mohammed got a vision that there were 600 Jews in Mecca who were in his way, and whatever it was that told him, told him to go over and slit their throats, which he did. God is life; life does not ordain life.

Jesus saw more than that. They said to him, "What is God's relationship to the dead?" And he said, "For he is not a God of the dead but of the living, for all live unto him." We have to separate the intuitive perception, which is the only way revelation comes from the psychic reaction of the ages, which appears to be revelational but is psychic hallucination. That is part of the genius of Richard Bucke, who wrote *Cosmic Consciousness*. He knew how to do that because on top of knowing Cosmic Consciousness, he had charge of an insane asylum.

Now, the resistance: We must suppose while it is psychological, it is both individual and collective. Freud said that a neurotic thought pattern will repeat itself with monotonous regularity throughout life until it is changed. He said a psychological repression is a group of highly emotionally charged thoughts, feelings, and ideas so deeply buried in the unconsciousness that they cannot be brought to the surface either by an act of will or through the imagination. We would think the will or the imagination would do it, if anything, but he said no. Why? Because the ego must not be rejected, and therefore they are so deeply buried that they cannot be brought to the surface by any conscious or volitional act. And he further said that there they remain in a dynamic state. They are not corpses; they are buried alive. And they are in there kicking, sputtering, and spitting, and that is the nature of the inner conflict between the out-push of the cosmic urge and the back-push of that which would hurt our ego or reject our libido. This is known to every psychologist and every psychiatrist.

We must suppose then that this takes place in a field of mind that is neutral, impersonal, plastic, creative and reactive, reflective and reciprocal, just as Troward has said. No student of Religious Science has completed his study unless he has studied Emerson, Troward, and Meister Eckhart and all the great and good and wise because our attempt is to analyze only that we may synthesize. We must maintain the integrity of our movement because we have the best techniques and the most teachable, presentable system the world has ever known. But having that as a background, we must add to it continuously. And you and I and everybody must write new stuff for us. I often think the reason Jesus never wrote except in the sand was to confuse the people who were condemning somebody, the sand in which the next puff of wind was to erase, but he wrote in the records of the intuition, in the plastic material of the psychic, those deathless words of life, because Jesus, like Emerson and Whitman, was not psychically confused. The world is.

We must suppose that, just as there is an individual resistance—which says I can't be happy, I am guilty, I will probably go to hell anyway, and all this irrationality that disturbs the equilibrium of life and its balance produces all the insanity that there is, or at least 90 percent of it—we in our field must take a step further. Now Carl Jung is the only one who has really taken it a step further (or the Jungians in the field of psychology) and suppose that there is what he called a "collective unconscious," which is what the Bible meant by the carnal mind and Mrs. Eddy meant by mortal mind, the repository for the thoughts and feelings of the ages now operating through every individual collectively as a unit, the sum total of human thought governing human action. This is what produces mass hysteria. Individually, it could produce what the Hindus call "darshan." A relationship between the speaker and those listening forms a third thing that operates back again through them all. Every speaker has this, but it will be on different levels because it will be on the level on which his consciousness is functioning.

Now then if it is true, as Lady Pearl Moore said last night—and it is scientifically certain that we are born with a birth, life, and death urge—that when the life urge is exhausted, as far as it appears, the liability of human experience weighs down to the expectation of more pain than pleasure, according to the pain-pleasure principle that exists, disintegration starts in because mind begins to destroy the body because we cannot keep a body very long after we lose the will to live. But beyond that, there is something else. The death urge of Freud we will accept up to a point of its operation, but we will reserve the right to interpret its meaning. It isn't a death urge at all; it is an urge to more life. There is that in all of us that is getting tired of the monotony of this part, that is caught in the trap of its own unconscious setting, wishes to extricate itself from it, and therefore even the death urge of Freud is to us interpreted as the voice of life saying, "There are no dead people, but this part of me has already died, so let it shuffle off, it is no longer useful," and with an impatient gesture, the soul throws it aside. As the Bhagavad Gita says, "But as when one layeth his worn-out robes away and taking new ones, sayeth, 'These I will wear today,' so putteth by the spirit lightly its garb of flesh, and passeth to inherit a residence afresh." That is from Edward Arnold's translation of the Gita, the most beautiful I think of all.

Now then this is what I mean by the resistance, individual and collective, the argument of error. If we will accept what science now knows to be true about the individual psyche as being true about the collective unconscious, the sum total of all human thinking, then we shall discover this. I believe it is true, and I started out by saying part of this is a theory, part of it we know to be true. I believe this to be true because if the theory is correct, all you have to do is increase it. If it is true that the extreme escape mechanism is suicide, then it is accepted. Now according to Dunbar's experiments of ten years in the Presbyterian Hospital, know that 85 percent of all of our accidents are unconsciously invited. And Arnold Hutschnecker, who wrote *The Will to Live*, said all of our diseases are also unconsciously invited. These people are not in the metaphysical field; they are in the field of science, but this is metaphysics.

It doesn't say to go out in front of a car to be killed or do anything like that. You just unconsciously put yourself in a position that you have an accident so you won't have to meet the liability of the incident that you do not know how to handle. It is called an escape mechanism. I believe all you have to do is multiply that by 2.5 billion people, which is approximately the population of the world, and you will have what produces war, pestilence, and famine. Psychologically, a secret that is not shared with somebody else is the worst possible emotional liability. But shared with other people, it is the best. That is why we have fraternal organization.

We have a secret, which is that we don't care how crazy we are so long as we find out something we want to know. We are not concerned whether it pleases philosophy, theology, religion, science, or anybody else. If it is true, we must dehypnotize the self first of all. This is where you start. Psychology says the first adjustment is to the self, the next to the family, the third to society, and the fourth with the universe. And we are not whole until we have made these adjustments. We are all like what the Apostle Paul said, "For that which I do I allow not, for what I would, that do I not, but what I hate, that do I." And also in Romans, "O wretched man that I am! Who shall deliver me from the body of this death?"

He was giving himself a good analysis, but he didn't know what made it happen, he thought strange, malign forces, denominated spirits, unliberated souls, etc.

All these things are another part of the resistance of the human mind to the knowledge that will set it free. The theory of sin and salvation, fall and redemption, that we are caught between the devil and the deep-blue sea. Let's admit it because there is no correct psychological analysis until the cause of the neurosis is brought to the light of day to be self-seen. It becomes dissipated because there is no longer any psychic energy to energize it, to give it the life borrowed from us. We create our own persecutors and nothing else could, and that is true. In my own little way I just say, limitation and bondage are evidence of freedom. It is not an evidence of duality. It is an evidence that freedom is so great it can produce what we call bondage. But it isn't bondage in itself, you know, it is freedom expressed that way; I believe even pain is.

Now the resistance or inertia of the thought patterns of the ages, this is what was said to Jesus when he stopped to cast the devils out. (There are no devils to cast out, there are no spirit obsessions; I have been through all that and know what I am talking about). What I announce shall be the truth to me until, with Emerson, I can say that consistency is not something we have to completely carry through life because when we get a greater good, we will let the old go, like a new truth makes ancient good uncouth. Emerson said, over the doorway of consistency, "I would write on the lintels of the door-post, Whim! I hope it is somewhat better than whim at last, but we cannot spend the day in explanation."

We can have a perfect logic based on an imperfect premise and arrive at false conclusions without ever departing from the mathematics of logic or induction or deduction, and we will be farther away from the truth than we ever were before just because our logic is so good. If you start with the assumption of sin and salvation, you can build up. You are the only prophet you will ever know. If you are wrong, be wrong until you know why you are wrong and get right when you know why you are getting right, and you won't be hypnotized.

I don't want to get to heaven by being hypnotized any more than I want to get to hell by being hypnotized, because I know hell isn't a place that is hot. It is the state of consciousness that has neither a sense of humor nor a sense of rhythm. And I know heaven is not place where the streets are paved with gold because we will have no use for gold. It is merely a place where we are in harmony and happy and no longer afraid.

Alfred Lord Tennyson said, "But what am I?/An infant crying in the night./An infant crying for the light./And with no language but a cry." And from [Henry Wadsworth] Longfellow, "That the feeble hands and helpless/Groping blindly in the darkness/Touch God's right hand in that darkness/And are lifted up and strengthened." And it won't even be the outstretched hand of the greatest savior that ever lived that will place your hand in the hand of the Eternal or press you to its bosom. The discovery has to be made by each one of us, and that is why Jesus, at the height of his power, when they sought to deify him, said, "It is good that I go away that the Spirit shall bear witness to you." For YOU, you and you, this is what I have been talking about, to reveal the self to the self. That is why the Gita said the self must raise the self by the self.

There is a resistance, individually and collectively, to every good thing and every change that takes place in the world, the inertia of the thought patterns established throughout the ages, individually and collectively, and I believe it operates through this impersonal field of subjectivity, hypnotizes the race from the cradle to grave.

You and I might as well accept these things. Enough is known scientifically for us to follow this and go out into a broader field and discover that the inertia and resistance of the thought patterns of the ages, everything that decrees by alleged revelation of the prophetic visioning. Now remember, it doesn't matter how much people scream or how loud or how many people clap their hands and say amen. It ain't necessarily so. There is nothing in the universe that can destroy life. There is no energy known to science that will destroy itself. The universe is not operating against itself. This was one of the great revelations of Jesus. "They said, 'This fellow doth not cast out devils but by Beelzebub the prince of the devils.' And Jesus knew their thoughts, and said unto them, 'Every kingdom divided against itself is brought to desolation and every city or house divided against itself shall not stand. But if I cast out devils by the Spirit of God, then the kingdom of God is come unto you.'"

He taught the transcendence of the individual mind over what today we will call the individual and collective unconscious of the resistance, because, remember this, the belief in limitation can only limit the belief in limitation. From accepting a less limited viewpoint, it can never create limitation. There is no such thing as limitation. There is no such thing as getting lost. There is no such thing in the universe as evil, of itself. There is no such thing as disease, in itself. Now I am not denying the experience of these things at all. I don't believe we have to deny the experience to affirm the reason why it doesn't have to be in the larger synthesis.

I believe we are hypnotized from the cradle to the grave. Jean de La Bruyere said, "Life is a tragedy for those who feel and a comedy for those who think." This is what the Bible calls "antichrist." It is not an entity of evil; there is no entity of evil. Antichrist is the sum total of the denial of good. But it resists the advent of good. When two solids come together, they will clash. We have to discover a non-resistance that by its fluidity resists, not by resisting but by annihilation, that which can oppose only when it descends to the level of the opposition. (Trim the guy down to where you can knock him out.)

Here is the resistance, and now how are we going to overcome the resistance? Jesus said, "Resist the devil and he will flee from you." We are not dealing in a field where we are pitting good against bad. You are not bringing a terrifically good power and a spiritual consciousness that makes you so sweet, you are not bringing that to overcome the devil. There is no devil. There is no evil. There is no opposite other than suppositional. Every apparent opposite is a suppositional opposite of truth. Mrs. Eddy said, "The greatest wrong is but a supposititious opposite to the highest right," which is completely right. Therefore, people like Jesus and Gandhi, they had worked this thing out, this was the greatest problem they solved. Jesus didn't come to save people. He never preached any salvation. He preached, "Behold! Behold! Look again; look at it differently. Behold!" He said, "These people said this and that but I say, you have to transcend by nonresistance until that which resists on its own level no longer exists because the universe is not divided against itself."

How do we do it? I know everybody has a different idea, but I like a virile and robust idea, even in spiritual things. Right now, I don't believe the altar of faith must receive the gifts of morbidity in order to elevate us to that place where the eye views the world as one vast plane and one boundless reach of sky. I believe we shall come singing a song or a funeral dirge. We shall wade through the waters of morbidity and become submerged in them like every one of the saints who spoke of the long night of the soul. There is no dark night of the soul. They were suffering the experience of the resistance of the human mind or else the universe is not a unity and a totality at any and every point of its infinity, equally and evenly distributed, and the truth declares it has to be. And this we may be certain that it is: This is the truth.

This is what Jesus was talking about: A truth, made known, liberates. While we have adversaries, we shall fight them on the level of their own contention. I do not believe in spirit possession because I have seen them myself. How do you think you or I or anyone else in the psychiatric field could knock out ten devils if they actually existed at the point of contact with the individual? You could not throw them out and that is that. If you know they are not there, but it looks as though they were there, then things are not what they seem to be. Then you correct the mistake in thought and the manifestation that looks like ten devils will disappear. These are the only devils there are.

We have to have a conviction. This is the meaning of our spiritual culture—that we shall have a conviction. Jesus said, "Heaven and Earth will pass away, but my words will never pass away." The presence and power and activity of whatever you want to call it, God or truth, it doesn't matter in your word in such degree as this word gives your consciousness a transcendence over the belief of the necessity of the apparent opposite. Only a fool has seen through the ridiculousness of the wise; only a child can enter heaven. Why did Jesus, among the lords and gods of their day, when they had to feed the multitude, whether it was symbolic or literal, why did he have to choose a child? Jesus, the man of wisdom, knew how it could be done. The child of unwisdom had not yet learned that it could not be done. And putting the wisdom of spiritual adulthood with the spontaneous proclamation of the child, the multitude were fed—and that is the only way they will ever be fed. It is the only way you and I will ever be fed by that transcendence, this thing which is nature and nature's God and the law of our own being. If they were an entity in this resistance, there would be nothing you and I could do. It is only in psychiatry, when they reduce it to liquidity of self-awareness, that it is dissipated by the knowledge that it is not an entity. People are not obsessed by anything but ideas. And if we will multiply that in human consciousness of the collective unconscious, we will arrive at a simple something, like all great simplicities, the profoundness of which will shiver your timbers.

Suppose we are blighted by a false belief—and I believe one other thing: None of us is smart enough to think up all the hell we have been through, nor are we intelligent enough to think up all the good we have ever experienced. This is a terrific truth. Evil is neither person, place, nor thing, law, cause, medium nor effect. It only acts as though it were, but it acts like a law while we believe in it. You and I are not good enough to have earned immortality, and we are not evil enough to destroy it. "For he is not a God of the dead but of the living, for all live unto him." "Today shalt thou be with me in paradise."

We are not healers. We are, as Emerson said, beneficiaries of the divine fact. Robert Browning said, "Tis thou, God, that givest, tis I who receive." This is the nature of reality. What will happen to us when we know evil doesn't belong to anybody? The psychiatrist is discovering this, and he says it is not the neurotic but the neurosis talking. We shall no longer have these nasty little spiritual sidelights of uncovering people's error. But how do we know? I don't know, and I don't believe you know. I am not an agnostic until it comes to opinions, and then I am the worst agnostic who ever lived.

What will happen when we no longer judge others? Jesus said, "Judge not, that ye be not judged. For with what judgment ye judge, ye shall be judged and with what measure ye mete, it shall be measured to you again." I used to know an old guy who was a retired minister who had nothing evil to say about anybody and didn't think anybody was too wrong and found something good in everything. It was at least thirty years after that before I knew why. He had gotten a clearance of the unconscious sense of guilt in his own mind; therefore, there was nothing there to project.

"What thou seest, that thou be'est." And from St. Augustine, "But if thou love not the brother whom thou seest, how canst thou love God whom thou seest not?" All our condemnations in the name of God and righteousness and truth and analysis that are real dirty and downright hellish are projections of our own inferiority complex. And the whole human mind conspires to immerse us in the sea of despondency of negation, of disbelief or isolation, and it is the only hell there is. Emerson said, let us then arise and taking the torch, the light of truth, "obeying the Almighty effort and advancing on Chaos and the Dark."

The Purpose of Evolution

AUGUST 16, 1956

In his fourth lecture from 1956 on the nature and development of consciousness, Holmes brings us to the idea of our spiritual evolution. He points out that the deepest thinkers of the ages have come to the same conclusion—that the Creative Force embedded Itself into Its creation through the process of involution and then left it alone to discover its source, its power, and its freedom through the process of evolution. Now we are at the point where we are called to consciously cooperate with the Creative Force as we move toward the next steps of our evolution.

It is what we think in mind and not what we say that registers. In the ethers of the universe or in what we call the mind of the person for whom we are working, that intention is its own direction. You cannot have any intention without having direction, and it is the intention that will register. In analysis, if you think something different from what you say, what you think is what you will register. Shakespeare said [in *Hamlet*], "My words fly up, my thoughts remain below. Words without thoughts never to heaven go."

Our talk is based on the concept of the ages, upon whose highest concepts I think we must place reliance if we are going to place it upon anything. The only reason Emerson knew more about some things than somebody else was he set up what he called "a lowly listening." And the reason Einstein knew more about mathematics than someone else was he spent more time thinking about mathematics and opening his consciousness. The only reason we have great creative geniuses is that they are listening.

We all have access to that which projects everything. How does it do it and why does it do it and what is it and the process by which it does it is our discussion this morning. If you were to read the ancient Upanishads or Gitas you would find it there. It is the sum in the substance of the whole story of creation in the Jewish religion. It was taught by the Greeks. It is fundamental to every great concept and philosophy the world has ever had. Therefore, it is not a revelation to me.

Our comments on these realities may or may not add something to their explanation. They should, if the comments are intelligent. Gandhi said in the first part of his life, God is truth, but in the last part of his life, he said Truth is God. There is a vast difference. When he said God is truth, this was dogmatic. He might be talking about the God of the Jews; he might have been reared as an Episcopalian, as I was reared as a Congregationalist. We have two different kinds of Gods. But Gandhi said with adult reflection and greater experience, he realized by saying God is truth that would be dogmatic because then we would say, "Whose God is Truth?" He then said truth is God, which is correct.

We interpret the nature of the universe by discovering the nature of what it does and how it acts. There is no other way to know what it is other than through the mystical revelations of the intuition, of which William Wordsworth said, be what they may, they are still the guiding light of all our days.

But when these mystical feelings—which impact the intellect with some message from the unknown—cross the border of the unknown and the invisible, strike our emotions and intellect and create our religion, because that is where every religion comes from—I mean religion, not the philosophy of the dogma of religion, which may or may not be correct—they are largely projections of our own guilt or we would never have created hell out of them. So Gandhi was right. He realized these things and he said, Truth is God.

A young man who bought the textbook, when asked what he did, said he was a physicist and works on government stuff. When I asked him why he was buying *The Science of Mind* textbook he said, "Someone loaned me one, and I read enough to know I want to study it. I thought it was terrific." I said, "Do you think it is true? Does it contradict anything you know?" He answered, "No, there was nothing in it that a scientist could not believe." I said, "If you believe this, I want you to write another textbook that I want to put along with this and it will explain from your viewpoint and the science of physics everything that is in this work."

The reason is that the universe is one system, just one. Emerson said, "Nature is an endless combination and repetition of a very few laws," and they repeat themselves over and over again on every plane. This is what Gandhi meant by saying Truth is God. Muhammad's son-in-law, husband of Fatima, was a poet, and he said if you split the atom, you will discover the sun. Jesus split the human atom and discovered the son of God, cryptic in it as it is in everything, because the universe is an indivisible system.

Today, I want to consider what the deepest thinkers of the ages have believed. It is the meaning of evolution, incarnation, and emancipation. I am not discussing this from the problem of good and evil, which I know nothing about, or sin and salvation, which I care nothing about. I am discussing it not from the viewpoint of my opinion, which I have no regard for whatsoever because it is either right or wrong, but I am able to give you a presentation today and tomorrow of what the greatest spiritual thinkers who have ever lived believed. I am not even going to say they were right, although I think they were. As Evelyn Underhill said, "Man is free and holds the keys of hell as well as the keys of heaven." The only knowledge we have of heaven and hell has come through the consciousness of man. The Bible says in John 1, "No man hath seen God at any time; the only begotten Son, which is in the bosom of the Father, he hath declared him."

The universe is defined as that whose center is everywhere and whose circumference is nowhere. The infinite, which without being concentrated or concentrating itself is automatically centered everywhere and equally distributed, that is what we mean by Omnipresent, and being the Divine Intelligence, Omniscience and all-knowing, and Omnipotent. We suppose a preexistence, a self-existence cause, God or whatever you want to call it. Let's just call it God because we know what that means, which means the cause of everything.

Now it makes sense that it is the nature of the eternal to forever beget its own son. Meister Eckhart said, "God never begot but one son, but the Eternal is forever begetting the only begotten," and, "All that God ever gave His only-begotten Son, He has given me as perfectly as him, no less." It is the conviction; it is the teaching. All the great thinkers and philosophers believe what I am talking about. It is the nature of reality to forever pass from being, we will call it, into what they call becoming. They believe it is the nature of reality to forever incarnate itself in everything and through everything. The theosophist speaks of the mind that sleeps in the mineral, waves in the grass, wakes to simple consciousness in the animal, to subconsciousness in the human, to cosmic consciousness in some humans, and to super consciousness in, let's say the archangels.

We have here in the known, an atomic intelligence in the mineral. We have the animal kingdom and several kingdoms. Here are four or five levels of intelligence that we know about. What reason do we have to suppose that this does not go on ad infinitum and that there are people beyond us as far as we are beyond the tadpole? The logic of all these is part of the teachings of all the great thinkers and of Jesus who said, "In my Father's house are many mansions. If it were not so, I would have told you so." It is the teaching that the process is the nature of the Infinite to forever incarnate or the divine spark to ignite and impregnate the mundane clod. That is the meaning of the ancient symbol of Lucifer being thrown out—the fight they had among the angels, like we have among the different spiritual groups of religiously activated people. They are trying to say that it is the nature of the Infinite to incarnate.

Now remember when we speak of the nature of something, we are not talking about a divine plan or a divine purpose but a divine pattern; not a divine need or desire as we understand it, but an impulsive part of the nature that is the Creator and must create or it won't be a creator.

We are also referring unknowingly to the case back of the psychological ego, the true unconscious id, and the psychological libido. It is all one thing. That system has been at least. And this is Lucifer being thrown out, striking the clod. From Robert Browning's *Rabbi Ben Ezra*, "Finished and finite clods, untroubled by a spark…A man, for aye removed/From the developed brute; a god though in the germ." This is what James Russell Lowell meant when he said, "Every clod feels a stir of might/An instinct within it that reaches and towers/And groping blindly above it for light/Climbs to a soul in grass and flowers." That is an intuitive perception of this ancient teaching. The spirit comes to what they call the lowest arc or level, the outermost rim or fringe. This is the way they describe it. It is symbolic but it is literally true now that divinity is hid in everything by an automatic principle of involution. Read Troward and you will find this.

This is what the ancients called, what we would call perhaps, the true unconscious or intelligence in nature, the insentient. It means that which has intelligence operating, but it has no conscious volition up unto this point. There is an arbitrary part of our evolution because it appears to be the nature of reality to incarnate and then let the thing alone to discover itself. "Before Abraham was, I am." "But Jesus answered them, 'My Father worketh hitherto, and I work.'" Now remember, this is an up-push of the incarnate, the involution that always creates an evolution. And evolution follows involution with mathematical precision and mechanical certainty and irresistible purpose—but not a desire. Robert Browning said, "There is an inmost centre in us all/Where truth abides in fullness; and around/... This perfect, clear perception—which is truth.../Whence the imprisoned splendour may escape."

I don't think God planned it, I think God is it—and there is a difference. It is like Gandhi saying, Truth is God and this isn't the way Truth works, it is the way God works, toward a purpose that separates Him or It from Him or Itself, but rather not from the need but from the nature of being what It is, this is what It does. This is the generation of the time when the plant was in the seed before the seed was in the ground. The idea comes prior to the evolution. They are talking about the principle of involution, which precedes evolution. "In the beginning was the Word and the Word was with God and the Word was God. He was in the beginning with God. All things were made by him."

This is the unconscious—the unconscious but not unintelligent. It is the nature of reality that in the individualization of itself and the multiplication of its expression of that individualization has *[word missing from transcript]*. There shall still be, let us say, this period that no one knows anything about. It has been called the Fall or the Great Ignorance; it hasn't woken up yet. Now naturally when the unconscious is pushed by an evolutionary principle to the point of reflecting consciousness or self-awareness, the arbitrary and mechanical processes of evolution must cease, although they are functioning back of us like the automatic functioning in the human organism that neither our will nor lack of it has anything to do it with.

Let's say this thing, which was the impulsion by involution, becomes now a propulsion by evolution, and the moment we have arrived at, which is referred to as consciousness: "Then a sense of law and beauty/And a face turned from the clod/Some call it evolution/And others call it God"—William Herbert Carruth. When that moment arrives, the arbitrary and compulsory processes of evolution are held in abeyance until there comes a conscious cooperation with the evolving instrumentality and its principle and the presence back of it. The Father works and now the son works. That is the meaning of that place in the New Testament where it says if there had been anything more under grace whereby they could say, verily by grace, that law would have been given.

Nature does not want us to be serious too long and never did. If the tree did not bend in the wind, the pressure in the atmosphere would break it off. That flexibility, which we do not dare ignore against the liability of tension, causes most of our diseases. If there had been any more grace whereby men must have been saved, verily by grace it would have been given. If the All-Seeing Wisdom, which you and I call God, desires to project Itself into Its own son and take back Its own son into Its own bosom, It could have made a mechanical spontaneity. Grace, which means the divine givingness and the infinite love, would have done it. But even a divine wisdom cannot create a spontaneous mechanism or a mechanical spontaneity. Therefore, by grace, that could not be given which through law must be learned in experience. And that is the meaning of evolution. It has nothing to do with salvation, nothing to do with a reward in heaven. It has to do with karma, which is not kismet, cause and effect, which is a plaything of the gods, a tribute to the wise and an overlordship to the unwise. The Christians call this the teaching of grace. We discover we are the beneficiaries; we believe in grace. That which the law could not have done, Christ or the divine incarnation now will do. This is also the meaning of the mystical saying of Jesus,

"And no man hath ascended up to heaven, but he that came down from heaven, even the Son of man, which is in heaven," because there is no line of demarcation.

Jesus also said, "Beloved, now are we the sons of God; and it doth not yet appear what we shall be: but we know that when he shall appear, we shall be like him, for we shall see him as he is." "Beloved, now are we the sons of God." The incarnation is already made; we haven't anything to do with it. "Which of you by taking thought can add one cubit unto his stature?" Then he turns around and says, "Why do you believe it will be done?" This means that you don't concentrate, you don't wish, you don't beseech, you don't hold thoughts—that doesn't do anything. We now are the sons of God, and there is nothing we can do about it. Even in a treatment, my firm conviction is that the treatment is absolutely independent of the one who gives it but will operate at the level of his consciousness when he gives it and for the purpose with or for or whom he identifies it, consciously or unconsciously.

Now are we the sons of God. We are already where we are going, but we don't know it or we don't see it. Now are we the sons of God, but it doth not yet appear what we shall be. It is certain that out of this we shall become something, because we are on the pathway of evolution. It makes no difference who believes what, except what we believe. We are here to evolve ourselves; but in the process, we discover there is only One Self and we are part of every self and the biggest concept is the one that includes the most, not for salvation but for the expression of that which will not be stilled. We don't know what we will be like or look like, by and by, but we know that when he shall appear—he is already here—what is going to appear is already here. When he shall appear, we will be like him (but we already are like him), when we shall see him as he is.

It is only then when we see him, "What thou seest, that thou be'est," but action and reaction is what goes along with it—action spontaneous, reaction mechanical, and an infinite field. Emerson said, "We animate what we can, and we see only what we animate." Out of the God that is, every man creates the God that is believed in. And I believe in the God who is believed in because it is that which is awake in us and we now have it. But as we progress in evolution,

"When he shall appear, we shall be like him, for we shall see him as he is," no different from the Lord's Prayer, and we shall see him as he is. He already is as we are going to see him, but only when we see him and identify ourselves with him shall he appear to us. Looking steadfastly at his face, we behold him.

Therefore, you and I have nothing to do with involution. The first stages of our evolution were the stages of the out-push of the involuting principle by a mechanics or mathematics of its own projecting, that which we may now recognize and consciously become a co-partner with: the Infinite. I suppose that was the first dawn of human history and from then 'til now, nothing has said "you must" any more than the father said to the son, "Son, don't do it." And when the guy came back, he didn't say, "What did you do?" God never argues, he contemplates.

There must be conscious cooperation. Therefore, the ancients said, nature unaided fails. And that is true. Every new invention is a new impartation of the out-push of evolution to the consciousness of man. One thing we fail to remember that the Ancient of Days is the newest invention. Therefore, the universe is not cut and dried, and once wound up to run down, the creative act continues in and through our own minds, as original and primordial as it ever was, because it never was any more original or any more primordial than it is now. I am the same yesterday, today, and tomorrow; I change not. That will answer whether when you treat, you treat for what is or what you want, you treat out of what is for what you are going to do, and out of what is, something will form that never was before. This is the wonder of the universe in which we live. But there are those who have skipped certain periods of evolution and have taken a step farther because they know. And the next thing we have to remember is that just as the evolutionary impulsion contains in that seed of our individualization that which was to arbitrarily carry it to the point of conscious differentiation, as Troward points out, it still has that thing which we are not aware of; it is bigger than we are. The intellect doesn't perceive, the eye does not perceive the wonders, as Plotinus said. Its beauty is terrific, and even in our slight experience there is that impingement upon us and the intellect and the will and the thought and the feeling of time, which is so transcendent, we see Him just a little more as He is. But from that moment when the incident part is a conscious reflection, all arbitrary processes of evolution must have ceased. "Verily, verily, I say unto you, the Son can do nothing of himself, but what he seeth the Father do, for what things soever he doeth, these also doeth the Son likewise. For the Father loveth the Son, and showeth him all things that himself doeth, and he will show him greater works than these, that ye may marvel." As the Father has inherent life within Himself, real life, it is existence and not subsistence. For as the Father hath life in himself, so hath he given to the son to have life in himself.

This concept I want to complete tomorrow is the most glorious concept, the deepest spiritual philosophy, the most impersonal and impartial philosophy, the most true philosophy. It comes from the Jews, the gentiles, the Greeks, the Hindus, medieval mystics, and modern scientists. It has come out of the united intelligence of the race, and there is no law of nature that contradicts it. There isn't a law in psychology that contradicts it. There is no argument against the universe in which we live.

What Does It Mean to Us?

AUGUST 17, 1956

In his fifth lecture from 1956 on the nature and development of consciousness, Holmes builds on his previous talk on evolution. Here he describes how evolution has moved us through various transitions in the physical world and now with humanity into the mental world. He says that another transition from the mental to the spiritual is upon us and that the teachings of Religious Science can assist us in moving forward as "eternal beings on the pathway of an endless progression."

I have been trying to give more or less of an academic lecture this week. I am a teacher, and I have been trying to teach what to me seems to make sense in this metaphysical field. There is so much nonsense attached to it. The metaphysical field in America is made up of wonderful people with the greatest idea, and I believe the concept they have is destined to reshape the evolution of the human race, ultimately. Yet, in the process there are a lot of people, naturally, who project rather strange ideas upon the stream of the experience of the evolution of this movement. But we don't have to be worried by that. If we watch the performance and the pageantry in any of the more picturesque churches, such as Catholic or Episcopalian, we realize that it is accepted because it has been going on for so long. If we did the same thing tonight that the Catholics do, and I am not saying there is anything wrong with it, everyone would think we were a bunch of nuts because everyone does not have the wit to know that there is a universal nut tree and it bears more than one kind of fruit.

A man who knows only one religion is a theologian and a dogmatist because there are more candles that burn on the altar of the Lord. Now our altar, which is in the heart, permits the placing of each and every one of these candles, dedicated to the universality of God and of truth and a beauty, of the divine nature of man. Jesus was a Jew, we believe the greatest of the Jewish prophets, who was crucified by the Romans because they thought he was a rebel. Jesus's philosophy was confusing to the Greeks because he spoke from the Jewish heart of sentiment and emotion and feeling, the greatest line of such prophets the world has ever known. It doesn't seem strange to me that his own people misunderstood him because of the dogma of that time, just as Gandhi, by a system of nonviolence, was really the cause of the disarming, so far as his nation was concerned, of the most militaristic power the world has ever known.

Of course, these things are not understood, and Jesus has been just as misunderstood by the Christians. He confounded the philosophy of the Greeks, who spoke from the intellect, the greatest intellectual line of philosophers the world has ever known and with the least feeling, although they spoke of the Divine Imminence. It is the warmth and the color of the Latin art, the Roman art, that appeals to us, not the form. The form is grotesque, but it is the warmth, the color, and the feeling that makes an everlasting appeal, and they will never die unless they fade from the canvas. In the Greek art, you will notice how perfect it is. There never was such architecture, and their sculpture is the most perfect the world has ever known. But you do not wish emotionally to embrace it; you admire it intellectually.

The warmth and the color are a part of the human need. Therefore, they are a part of the Divine answer. There is no human need that has not already been Divinely answered, even though the answer hasn't been caught up with yet because the human need seems to draw a veil between it and the human rejection to even receive the possibility of its discovery.

It is no wonder then that the Jews repudiated their greatest prophet. The Greeks repudiated Socrates, and on his dying bed, when Plato burst into tears because Socrates's feet were already getting cold, Socrates laughed because, he said, Plato thinks this body is Socrates. And his last act was to say he owed a rooster to somebody and to please pay the debt. He then drew the blanket over his head and expired. He had already said, "They think they are going to kill Socrates but they will have to catch him first." They never caught up with him.

It is no wonder the Greeks repudiated Socrates. It is not strange that somebody seeking revenge for the South assassinated Lincoln. It is not strange that the Greeks did not understand the philosophy of Jesus, a philosophy of the heart, which with the nicety of their hearts, they were not able to analyze intellectually to discover that it would finally emerge in the heart as well as in the head, because they are a part of one organism, one unity. They hadn't made that synthesis. It isn't it strange to me that Rome might have been afraid of a rebel who excited and incited the vast crowds of people. They were jealous of his power. I can see why the Roman legions crucified Jesus. They said it was not the Jews who did it. I don't think it is even strange that Christianity has looked on Jesus too much as the great martyr and there have been too many thoughts of morbidity.

And I was wondering this morning when I woke up, before the bells tolled, I thought to myself, I wonder what would have happened to the Christian world if instead of every cross of agony (not the cross itself; it is a symbol; it is beautiful; and I'll tell you in a moment what it means because the Christian world hasn't the slightest concept of what it means) if there had been a beautiful, artistic colorful picture of the tomb or if it had been made into a sculpture and the glow of a beautiful light showing that it was empty, I wonder. "That thou seest, man, become too thou must; God, if thou seest God, dust, if thou seest dust" — St. Angelus.

The cross really stands for the great Trinity of being and the transition of this Trinity or the interchange between the human and the Divine. The ancient Jews had three Adams: the Adam of the earth, the Adam of the air, the Adam of the sky. As in Adam or the first Adam means we all die. Even so in Christ or the last Adam, all are made alive. The first man is of this Earth. The second man is the Lord from heaven, and as we have all born the image of this Earth, so shall we also bear the image of heaven. This is what that means. So they had the three-headed serpent because the serpent stood for the life principle, crawling flat upon the ground, viewed materialistically. It is that which tempted Eve because she stood for the subjective. Then she tempted Adam because where there is an emotional bias, there is an intellectual blind spot. Perfect with modern psychology, this allegory of Eden, you all know that.

We must differentiate between the dramatic picturing or in the attempt to portray a cosmic order and never mistake the symbol for the substance. We can mumble all the prayers in the world but unless they come from the heart, they will not ascend beyond the intellect.

But a child, not even knowing he has an intellect, might far surpass the wisest philosopher who ever lived in the enthusiastic acquiescence of that which he has not yet rejected, because we have to learn to be afraid. This in no way will take away from the majesty and the might, the purity, the adoration that the Christian has for Jesus or the Jew might have for the great lines of prophets proceeding him, or the Greek might have for the father of philosophy, as Socrates is called, or that the Hindu might have for the light of Asia. And until you and I see what Mark Carpenter and Elmer Gifford have told us, the meaning of the warmth and color of the indwelling Lord of Life, I think all evolution culminates. Its purpose is to culminate transition from the kingdom of the human to the kingdom of the Divine, from the kingdom of the mathematics of the law, of cause and effect which has caught everyone, not to the place where the human as individualization is annihilated or the law destroyed.

Is the law then of no avail? God forbid. The universe is a combination of law and order and person, the principle and the law of action and reaction, and there is nothing else fundamental to all creation.

This ought not to seem strange. What I am saying is no different from Einstein saying there is one law that governs all physical laws. Or Emerson saying, "There is one mind common to all individual men," and in Deuteronomy 6:4, "Hear, O Israel, the Lord our God is one Lord." Mathematically certain, whatever it is, it is One, and it includes what you and I are. But it is not inclusive of what you and I might think we are. According to the great teaching of the ages, and I accept it because I cannot help but believe the united intelligence of the greatest thinkers who ever lived, particularly those who were free from the superstition of idolatry and the subtle hypnotic insinuation of psychism, these are the only people who ever lived who brought us prophetic news from the Kingdom of God. There are no others.

Over the doorway of alleged revelation of the individual or the group, I would write, "Stop, look, and listen." We may hear many voices psychically that are not of God. The Divine incarnation, which is the nature of the Divine Creative Spirit, is to forever give. And this is grace, which imparts itself. This is love. The need to give is grace. The only way in which the giving can be by the impartation of the self is love. But the universe is not a chaos; it is a cosmos. Therefore, the law also remains as the servant of the eternal Spirit throughout the ages. Coexistent, coeternal with God, and being a part of the natural order of the truth, which means that it (no matter who thinks what is what or which or how hypnotized we can get to be) will always be exactly what it is. As I said yesterday, Gandhi's precept that Truth is God will lead us further than the concept that God is truth, if we try to follow every revelation in the world, even the modern one.

If we do not have a religion, we are sick. An irreligious person is not normal. A person who must be superstitiously religious needs some kind of help, too. It is difficult to discover the nicety between these things, but people like Jesus did that.

In the process of evolution, all creation is caught in the operation of the law. The law is a taskmaster. The law is a cold, unfeeling, relentless, impersonal thing. Therefore, from what we call the insentient—that is the divine incarnation—it is as though God had said, "I will bury myself in the possibility of man and see what happens, but someday he will remember where he came from. He must be subject to the law of his own action and reaction. The suffering is of no consequence in the evolution of the soul."

What is the moment of pain compared to the hour of deliverance? What is the truth in comparison with eternal life because of some instinctive morbidity born of the universal sense of rejection? We have felt that God has imposed and ordained, and we say God has brought this to the world to teach us a lesson, which is nonsense—which means it makes no sense. There is no God whomsoever imposed suffering; ignorance has done it. And if it had been enlightenment that did it, we could not extricate ourselves from it. Impossible. Therefore, it is said there is no law against those who are in Christ, that is those who have found the Divine pattern.

Yesterday we discussed remembering that this is the thought of the ages. I didn't make it up because these are all made up by somebody, remember. And you and I have to judge, not who tells the sweetest story or who magnifies the coloration of the most dramatic story, but what is the truth. That is what we want to discover. It will not hurt us to know there is a mechanics and a mathematics to the truth, if we do not get caught in the mechanics. It does not harm us to believe in evolution because evolution is true. But we shall put the cart before the horse unless we always remember that evolution itself is an effect and not a cause. It is a secondary cause, as Troward points out, but itself is a result of a Divine involution imposed upon and incarnated in the nature and the constitution of everything from an atom to an archangel, merely by the fact that the involuting principle is the evoluting principle. It is all what we call God: Omnipresent, everywhere, manifesting in and through by Its nature, giving of Itself by Its nature, demanding of Itself the results of Its own self-knowingness, that It may behold the Father in the son and the son in the Father.

And out of the great matrix of nature and the creative principle that is also a part, symbolized perhaps by the mother of all creation, the universal womb—which indeed the Catholic church has masculinized for several hundred years—now we call the universal psyche, the mother principle in nature because it exists, impregnated by the Divine ideas, gives birth to the cosmic patterns generically, which must then become individualized by the group and the person. In other words, the Divine pattern is universal; what we do with it is individual. There can be no conscious cooperation with the Divine pattern individually to specialize it personally until we have first realized that it is a part of the universe and it is generic.

This is where the arbitrary processes of evolution (by a slow millions of years, no doubt, on this planet) gradually push up that instrumentality that may look about reflectively, may cogitate upon its own conclusions and choose its own pathway, and from thence all arbitrary processes cease. That is why I said yesterday, if there had been any law under Grace, Divine givingness, and love whereby man must have been free, why by compulsion they did what is only best, verily by love or Grace, such would be given. But even God could not make a mechanical spontaneity. It is impossible.

You know there are some things that God cannot do. Strangely enough, God cannot do anything that contradicts the nature of the thing that is doing it. It couldn't without being self-destructive. And this is what Jesus pointed out when they said, "You are in league with evil and you cast out devils by the devil." He said, "No, that won't work. Any kingdom divided is doomed." This is why science has found no law that would destroy its own energy. It will transmute it, transmit it, change it into another form, and all of this, but it will never destroy it. There is just so much energy in the universe, but it can be used for infinitesimal purposes. There is just so much substance in the universe, and it can be formed and reformed and eternally formed.

Now Jesus came singing a song proclaiming a freedom, rejoicing in a knowledge of the law and the perception of a presence. That is why they said he was crazy. It repudiated much of the Jewish system; it confused the Greeks; to the Romans it was rebellion; and later to the Christians it became a morbid crucifixion. Too much. This was not what he came to proclaim. In as nearly as it is possible for a human being, as Troward said, Jesus's understanding the nature of the Divine, embodied by reciprocal action that which he understood and no doubt did. As far as possible for God to walk in man and with man and be man, he was. "The works that I do shall ye do also and greater works than these shall ye do."

Now Jesus did another thing that has a psychological connotation. He broke the transference of their ignorance. And when he saw that they would not let go of him, he said, "I will let go of you." In other words, he knew that the image of freedom exists in the cosmos, not in mother or father or leader or preacher or anyone. This is what Jesus did. Why do you think he did it? He never did anything without knowing what he did. He knew what he was about. He said, "It is expedient that I go that the Spirit of truth shall bring to you the knowledge of what I have said and all truth may be yours, that they may be one."

Now this, psychologically, we would say was breaking the transference. We know as practitioners the sooner we can get a client on his own feet so he knows we don't have anything to do about healing, the sooner the guy who is sick will heal himself. Why? Because the thing that is in him isn't sick, and as he discovers this he gets well. We may help him see the Truth. That is why I say there are no healers in our field; there are only practitioners. There are no teachers, as such.

Someone came to Jesus and called him good and he said, "Get up. Why do you call me good? There is none good, save one, who is God." Someone came to John the Baptist and said, "What shall I do to avoid the wrath to come?" John said, "Get up out of the dirt. I did not come to tell you how to avoid the wrath to come. I came to tell you that the kingdom of God is at hand." It is a long way between the city of the wrath to come and the city of God, so far that 1 million journeys around the world will not reach it, nor eons of searching find it, because it has no existence. There is no dualism in the universe. The self looks for the self because the self knows the self.

And so by a process of physical evolution, a physical identity and personality is thrown out. Now having some greater control over its own destiny because of its understanding of objective laws of being but not the subjective yet, nor the spiritual, and so the next step in evolution must be and that is the transition through which the world is going. But now the processes of evolution must be slowly pushing everything to another transition. The first was the physical to the mental, and now it is from the mental to the spiritual. It must be doing it. I don't believe it is doing it because of any revelations. I suspect all revelations, and I am going to continue to until I receive a revelation that has no negation in it.

Did I tell you I went through the Psalms and marked every paragraph that had no negation in it whatsoever and compiled them and wrote them out. And there were just seven pages of double-spaced ordinary typed manuscript. That is the part of the context of the Psalms that I call the "Psalms of Psalms," the praise of praises, because it epitomizes what the rest are trying to say, synthesizes what they mean. It is beautiful:

If I make my bed in hell, thou art there.
If I take the wings of the morning and dwell in the uttermost parts of the sea,
even there shall thy hand lead me, and thy right hand shall hold me.
If I say, surely the darkness shall cover me, even the night shall be light about me.
Yea, though I walk through the valley of the shadow of death, I will fear no
evil for thou art with me.

Just seven pages. Isn't it terrific how hard it is to speak in affirmative language? We are always like Peter, denying our Lord.

Now the next transition must be what Troward called from the fourth to the fifth kingdom. It is the meaning of the crucifixion and death and resurrection of Jesus. Everything he did was to reveal the pattern behind everything; it was to reveal the nature of that whole thing to which the whole creation moves. As Alfred Lord Tennyson said, "One God, One law, One element and One far-off Divine event, to which the whole creation moves."

"Blessed are the meek, for they shall inherit the earth." No one else can. "Blessed are the pure in heart, for they shall see God." It is the same as saying, love only understandeth and comprehendeth love, Jesus saying if you understand this and know it and do it, if you see it, you will understand it. You cannot tell a person something that the meaning of which has not evolved in the comprehension of its possibility in his own mind. It doesn't mean he is unintelligent. He just does not know what you are talking about.

There are no people today outside the metaphysical fields who have the slightest concept of what spiritual mind healing is or means, or how it operates, or the law operating through it. No one. I hear them explain it and explain it, and it has nothing to do with it at all. It isn't a lack of intelligence; it is a lack of the knowledge of the subject. I would go to some physicist to have him explain physics. I wouldn't go to him and try to explain physics to him because I couldn't do it. You have to ask the man who knows. Strange that it has to be done here. Strange that the repository for this Divine knowledge is in the hands of such ignorant people as we are. Isn't it funny? Isn't it funny that the chalice of the cup of heaven has been given to the unwise because the wise repudiated it? Only the pure in heart shall see God. And they shall not see Him gazing steadfastly at an archangel but deep in the longing eyes of the most destitute person on Earth.

This is what the great have understood—and only the great—and the great are so few that these pearls of great price that we gather from them should become a new rosary. And we shall count each bead until the end, and there shall be no cross. In my estimation if we need a symbol, let it be an empty tomb. That is all that Jesus left behind. Jesus knew the transmutation of flesh into some higher etheric form that cast no shadow on the pathway of human existence, where the sun stood always at high noon and no shadow could be cast. Destroy this body, and I will raise up another. Now this is Christ, the perfected man, and when Jesus found they thought it was him, he said no. "I came to tell you how wonderful you are, I came to tell every one of you that you are eternal beings on the pathway of an endless progression, forever and evermore and never less than himself, because I am the son of the heart and the delight of the eternal God, and I know my Father and He knows me."

I want you to know before you leave here that, whether you understand it or not, Religious Science has the most exalted concept of Christ and the most exalted concept of the personalness of the Living Spirit of any system of thought —modern, medieval, or ancient—that has ever been given to the world. But our movement hasn't caught up with it. We, too, might be caught in the law. That thing that Elmer read from last night was written in five minutes of time, and I didn't know it until after fifteen years of studying.

Much comes through the mystical revelations of the heart that lifts itself, possibly, perhaps unknowingly, to whatever this thing is. A chalice is filled. It is necessary then, in the transition from the next kingdom, not that we repudiate the other but remember that people who have received cosmic consciousness in this world still have molecules in their body and eat food. On that plane, they followed its laws. On the mental plane, they followed its laws.

We have provided the first synthesis of science, philosophy, and religion and laid a plank down across what would have otherwise been a gulf throughout the ages that the world has ever known. One place I stand firm and sure and certain—

and I am willing to battle it out with every intellect on Earth—is that Religious Science reveals the only God that can be eternal and human at the same time. And it is true. For unless the Father is his own Son, if there be a unity of life, how shall the Son evolve into his own Father? Absolutely impossible. And unless the mother heart that broods over creation shall give birth to that cosmic dual unity, there is no way in which it could transpire, and the universe is intelligent. But what will happen to the perfected man?

It is in Aurobindo and Troward's denouement. It is in the resurrection of Jesus, for students of the New Testament. To that perfect embodiment toward which all evolution moves, ring on ring and sheath on sheath and circle around circle, until at last to eternal life it brings the fruits of incarnation, less ascending into greater, that perfect eternal pattern, forever one with its Creator.

What does gnostic man or the resurrected man or the Christ mean? That is the next kingdom into which we are going. Some have entered it while they were in this world. There is no law against entering it, because while we are caught in the law, it represses itself in a second to what would we expect, the ability to function on any plane. There will always be an embodiment, an absolute dominion over everything we understand now as physical, obliterating complete supremacy over the past and fear of the future. This is the meaning of all evolution. This is the preface of the endless ages. This is the meaning of every religion, for every one of them has brought some candle lit from the central flame of the eternal fire, whose ashes and flame and light are one and the same thing. They have all brought some offering to the universe, some in reconciliation but generally in fear, generally with a feeling of guilt and repudiation. It won't be that way, as Alfred Lord Tennyson said, "When God hath made the pile complete." And my brother and I wrote [in *The Voice Celestial*], "Thou within all things, around them, Brahma, Light of Life Divine, change our being into Thine. Rob the mind of its illusion, strip the ego, naked, bare. 'Til the waiting heart within us finds Thy Presence hidden there."

Our Religious Science

AUGUST 18, 1956

These final words from Holmes as Asilomar of 1956 comes to a close center on his hopes and intentions for the movement of Religious Science, the uniqueness and usefulness of its message, and his charge for the attendees to take the message of love from the conference back into the world as "four-dimensional beings living in a three-dimensional world."

Rev Irma Glen: It's just about over, this 1956 annual summer conference of the Church of Religious Science, and I believe that it is only in retrospect that we shall become fully aware of all the good and high consciousness we have experienced here. I don't believe some of us shall ever again be as we were before because this Christ light we have found together here this week will surely live and grow and expand on and on in our hearts and our minds. Our love and gratitude to our beloved leader and founder of Religious Science, Ernest Holmes, is unbounded, for all he has given us of himself in what he has shared with us. Our joy is unbounded and our gratitude unlimited. God has been very good to Ernest and very good to us through him. And now, after he delivers his traditional Sermon by the Sea, we are going to observe a five-minute silence, which we know will be very deep and profound, and then our beloved soloist, Dick Froeber, is going to sing a new composition of his and of Ernest's, entitled "May the Lord Still Walk with Thee." This is the first time it has been sung. After Dick sings, we will silently leave the chapel, and I don't have to tell you with what feeling. And now, here is the man without whom none of this would have been possible, none of this sweet fellowship could take place, the star of our conference, Dr. Holmes.

Ernest Holmes: Rudyard Kipling said, "Far-called, our navies melt away/On dune and headland sinks the fire: Lo, all our pomp of yesterday/Is one with Nineveh and Tyre!/Judge of the Nations, spare us yet/Lest we forget—lest we forget!"

And so as we prepare to leave the beauty of this Asilomar and the golden shores washed by the ageless ocean, as Henry Wadsworth Longfellow stated, "The ocean old/Centuries old/Strong as youth and as uncontrolled/Paces restless to and fro/Up and down the sands of gold." I am sure we shall carry with us from the beauty of this scene and contemplation of our own soul something that shall more nearly approximate an unconscious but spiritual memory of that which we really are.

The whole process of evolution is one of discovering something that existed before you and I discovered it. The evolution is to us, the advancement is to us, but not to the Eternal. The only thing that marks the difference between Religious Science and the modern metaphysical movement and other spiritual movements, all of which are good and sincere, all of which earnestly seek the same thing that everyone is looking for, the only thing that marks the difference is that we believe we have found it. And we believe that no man can find the cause of that destiny, as Shakespeare said, "that shapes his ends, rough hew them how he will," until he discovers in some degree the nature and reality of the spiritual universe in which we now live.

This discovery is, of course, only in part. Now we see as through a glass darkly, but we are all aware at times, sometimes it seems to me almost intensely aware, that the tree speaks to us. One of the first things I learned when very young, going out into the woods with a very great artist who happened to be a woman, and she wanted to paint trees. And when she would paint a tree, she would go up and hug it and kiss it and talk to it. And I didn't think she was crazy, I was only about ten. I knew she knew something I did not know, but I didn't think she was crazy. I knew she was communing through what I later discovered is an interior awareness with that which otherwise seems so static, so inanimate, so uncommunicative—and there is such a reality to everything.

Everything in this physical universe gives forth a light. All things give forth an inner light, emanations thin as air. Light clouds draped around the luminous form are in all things, everywhere. That is as much as I can remember of this (I wrote it a long time ago): "This light is real, it is not a fantasy, it is not a psychic hallucination, there is a light that lighteth every man's path."

We have sought to discover the avenues through which we approach this light and loose this imprisoned splendor. Now I would like to say to you that what at least is one of the characteristics of what I hope Religious Science started in and will remain, is a sort of flexibility with human life that at times seems strange. They said of Jesus, "Can any good thing come out of Nazareth?" As Mark Carpenter told us the other day, they said it could not be that a man who eats with publicans and sinners and permits a prostitute to anoint his feet could be a good man. And I thought of that one day, and I said to myself, without trying to put any words together, how wondrously kind his words of love to the penitent kneeling there who bathed his feet in tears of joy and dried them with her golden hair.

One of our great troubles is exclusiveness. What God has made, God has anointed. What God has created, God has provided with a light. The Infinite makes no mistakes and never errs, and our whole trouble is our inability to interpret the symbolism of the objective, to understand the difference between psychic hallucination and spiritual illumination and to find sermons in stone and good in everything. I trust that out of this thing which we call Religious Science and the Science of Mind will come the greatest spiritual tolerance the world has ever known.

The only thing Jesus ever condemned was a liar and a hypocrite. He never condemned people because of their sins, strangely enough. He said, "Sin no more, lest a worse thing come unto thee." Jesus understood the law of cause and effect and how to become emancipated from any particular sequence in it. He was a very rational man, and therefore he understood that if we remain in water, we will still be wet.

He didn't particularly condemn: "Judge not that ye be not judged. For with what judgment ye judge, ye shall be judged, and with what measure ye mete, it shall be measured to you again." Jesus did not say God will condemn you. He said you condemn yourself. With the judgment you judge, you will be judged. There is no other judgment, but this is a terrific judgment. This is a judgment so intimate that we can no more jump away from it than we can our own shadows. We have no pomp, no glory, no special revelations, no great prophets whom the Almighty has tapped on the shoulder and said, "I will tell you how to make split pea soup but no one else." We have nothing like this, thank God.

We have yet to prove—and I say it soberly; of course, I am always sober but I am not always serious, and if I ever get to be, I shall know this is the end of my trail, it has run out and stopped—we have yet to prove that Religious Science because of its liberality can survive. We have yet to prove that because of its totality and humanity and all inclusiveness, it cannot be destroyed by little people whose vision has not got beyond the psychic condemnation and projection of a false ego. I said last Sunday night that I believe Religious Science, if it evolves and develops, will become the next great world religion. I believe it. There has been no great religion given to the world, except Mormonism and Christian Science, since the rise of Islam 1,200 years ago, many Christian sects, but no great, new, terrific spiritual impulsion. And as much as I admire Mormonism and the Christian Science movement (I praise it and bless it and know it is terrific), it will never do it. The tenets are too set, the precepts are too hard, the corners are too square. It is efficiency-plus but it is not spirituality-superlative because there are no corners in the mind of God.

Now whether we can get around that corner to where there are no corners but not to where everything moves in circles will depend on US. With what measure you mete, it shall be measured to you again. Unless we become a living embodiment of love, we have no way to say to somebody else, "God is love." Unless there is something that lights our path and people know, we have no rational justification in saying, "Man is a candle of the Lord," because somebody will say, "What man? Where did he go? How do you know?" And then we resort to the shibboleths of Jacob and Moses and Jesus and Buddha, all of whom were terrific, but there isn't a one of them here. Did you ever stop to think of that? I have never seen them, and the only pictures I have ever seen of Jesus make him look like a Swede, and I know he was a Middle Eastern Jew. You see, the artist has painted the traditional and not the historic Jesus. He has put on the canvas a symbol of what the sum total of people with anemic religious conceptions conceive its leader and founder must have been. Strange, but I didn't make it up.

You see, you and I have not got the authority of authoritative religion. I never said you will have to do this or that. No one ever heard me say Religious Science will always have to study what I wrote. Ten moments after I shuffle off this mortal coil, they may take everything I wrote and tear it up and put it in the trash can. And I shan't care because I am not even going to look sideways, much less backwards. Our eyes are put in the front of our head to see the expansive panorama of an ever-broadening horizon. As Oliver Wendell Holmes said, "Build thee more stately mansions, O my soul, as the swift seasons roll!/Leave thy low-vaulted past!/Let each new temple, nobler than the last/Shut thee from heaven with a dome more vast/'Till thou at length art free/Leaving thine outgrown shell by life's unresting sea!"

We have yet to prove that there is enough integrity in the present evolution of spiritual mindedness to bind people together on principles and embodiments, where there is no other kind of authority—and I have consistently refused and shall, while I live, persistently refuse any other kind of authority. We only have organization enough to keep the walls from falling out.

Now this is the greatest hope of the world and, at the same time, the greatest danger of our movement. People like to have you say, "Thus saith the Lord," and, "I got a revelation." I have been all through that, and I would no more be an instrumentality of perpetuating a new kind of spiritual ignorance than I would cut my throat, physically. I wouldn't wish to leave this world with a burden, if there is such thing as a memory, that I tied anyone and bound him even to the Lord God Almighty, because it is wrong.

So Rudyard Kipling wrote:

When Earth's last picture is painted and the tubes are twisted and dried,
When the oldest colours have faded, and the youngest critic has died,
We shall rest, and faith, we shall need it—lie down for an aeon or two,
Till the Master of All Good Workmen Shall put us to work anew. ...

And only the Master shall praise us, and only the Master shall blame;
And no one will work for the money, and no one will work for the fame,
But each for the joy of the working, and each, in his separate star,
Shall draw the Thing as he sees It for the God of Things as They are!

Those stars were there before we arrived on scene. They will be there when our little boat puts out across the trackless ocean of the unknown, in the last culminating adventure of human experience that Plotinus called "the flight of the alone to the Alone." The alone to the Alone, a journey everybody makes confidently, looking forward to it with complete composure. We have yet to prove that there are a group of people—and I believe there are a group of leaders, which we yet have to prove—who can see the bigness and the depth and the breadth of what we are doing and treasure it enough to hand out to the generations yet unborn, maintaining the integrity of its simplicity and the profoundness of its childlikeness.

These things confuse the intellect. They disturb the thought patterns of overly authoritative beliefs, and they do the one thing to the individual that makes it the most difficult thing in the world for him. Freedom is dearly bought. It is won at great cost, and half the world mistakes liberty for license and unity for uniformity.

There will have to be an integrity in those who point the way. We have such an integrity, and as this movement expands and spreads and deepens and broadens and heightens, it will not be the consecration and the dedication of medieval beliefs or ancient cultures or modern contentions that will hold such a movement together. It can come only from the fire of the heart and the intellect, directed by Spirit and a soul impregnated by the divine pattern.

We have set before us what may to the world look like the greatest simplicity. A doctor of divinity said to me one day, "Ernest, I know why you always have such big audiences." We were speaking then at The Wiltern and turning about 1,000 people away every Sunday morning. And I said, "Why?" And he said, "You get all these people to fold their hands over their stomachs, and they say everything is all right." I said, "Let me tell you something, brother. Our philosophy is so tough that we don't even dare to criticize anybody." Of course we do but we are reminded that Jesus said to look after a woman and lust after her is to commit adultery with her in his own heart. He was not even condemning adultery, he just said this is the way it is. Can't you see it? Jesus said there is nothing concealed from the universe in which you live. The Chinese say, it is impossible for a man to conceal himself, and they also said, "Oh man, having the power to live, why will ye die?"

You know, Emerson said truth is like a candle. You and I have to prove, as best we may, that there is at least on Earth a group of people with whom freedom and liberty are safe. And if there is no such group of persons on Earth, I would pray to God our institution would fall apart before I do. And I still feel quite well put together, everywhere except mentally. I have never known what it is to have much pain, guess I never did. I know I never had fear like I have seen people have in their religious culture. I don't know what it is that they are afraid of. When I see people who are afraid of hell and the devil and what is going to happen to them, I haven't (what we call in our field) the mental equivalent. I am glad I haven't. I think it must be terrible. It must be the most horrible thing in the world to be afraid of the universe in which we live. I can't and I don't want to conceive it. I know it is a disease of the mind. We have yet to prove that there is a group of people organized for the fraternal benefit of mutual cooperation and communion, but philosophic in spiritual essence and human things. We are evolved enough to accept the freedom and destroy it, mistaking it for license.

That is going to be the testing point: whether or not individuals can do that and teach thousands a new freedom, without saying we teach you can have what you want, do what you want, go where you want, be what you want and it doesn't make any difference what happens. We *don't* teach that. We do teach that, to a certain degree, man has a freedom. As Tolstoy said in *War and Peace*, within the laws of inevitabilities, we have a freedom to love because God is love. Love never hurt anybody. We have a freedom to hate within the law of inevitability of the dominating power and principle, love, for when we have hated too much, it will destroy our physical embodiment. It is just that we will have to start over again. It is an impatient gesture of nature. Nothing has happened to the soul or to the spirit; the mind is confused, the body is destroyed—that is all that happens. We have the freedom to enjoy all the peace we want, but the law of inevitabilities determines that when our confusion has reached a certain point, we shall have to dissolve its instrumentality in order to return to peace.

Why?

Because the nature of the eternal is self-existent, and the nature of self-existence, of a necessity, is self-preservation for self-perpetuation. Not that God thinks these things out. That is the way it has to be. That is what is back of the thought when they say that self-preservation is the first law of nature. It is. But it isn't a law as people think it. It is a law of flowing out of the inevitability of the nature of the Divine Creative Being. God is eternal and cannot destroy Himself.

You and I have, I believe, the greatest challenge that has ever come to any religious group of people. We are very small in number, a few thousand members. I don't know how many, and I couldn't tell you. Many hundreds of thousands of people are interested in Religious Science and the Science of Mind as introduced by our organization. There is no way of counting them. In the middle of the ceremony last night, I looked up and saw all those people and said to myself, how did I get here? I am not the ministerial type. What are we here for? And I got to thinking about it, right there in the middle of the ceremony, and I missed my cue. I said to myself, what is it? Wouldn't it be terrible if we were to start another monstrosity? Wouldn't it be awful if we were again to besmirch the pages of the desire of humanity in its search for evolution and sidetrack it into another mistake?

This is a confession. Fritz Kunkel said that a secret held by only one person is the worst psychological liability he can have, but if he has friends to join it, it is the greatest psychological asset he can have. So I ask you to join with me in my sins. And I thought, wouldn't it be terrible, won't it be awful unless and while I live I will see to it that it is at least the hope of spiritual freedom. Do you know what I am talking about? I do. And I know it is the most difficult thing on Earth for an individual to be on his own pathway in the evolution of his own soul, in the light of the eternal. And I know it is a very difficult thing for a group of people who have not again been hypnotized into the mesmeric spell of another revelation, because many people will do anything if you can sell them that bill of goods.

I have nothing to sell, and I do not wish to buy anything. I have all the worldly goods I need. I am not afraid of the future, and I do not think the destiny of the world depends on what I have written or what I am doing or our being here. God would certainly be very finite if that were the case.

But I do believe somebody is going to project on the screen of human experience, out of the accumulated intelligence of the human race, something that has never happened before, a real spiritual democracy of this country, as this country attempts to project an economic and political democracy. It is a very difficult thing. It is difficult not because of the idea, but because of the embodiment. So I hope, as we all think of what we have done and been and said here, we shall remember, you and I and all of us, you are just as much a part of this experiment as I am, because I couldn't do it alone. Our leaders are just as much as I am—more than I am—because it has to have many places where it is accentuated and spread and multiplied. But we couldn't do it as leaders, planners, or thinkers unless people come to it. There would be no object in it. We don't want to get together, a hundred or so of us, and tell ourselves how terrific we are when we know we aren't.

There is nothing so wonderful as what I am, strange as it looks, crazy as it seems. Where else shall that thing that appears to be me discover what that which appears to be me really is? And what other starting point is there for you other than where you are? I know this: We are going to take a physical journey in a few moments, to eat more of this good food. We are all going to get into some kind of a conveyance, and we are going to start toward a destination, but we will get in and start from where we are. I am leaving from Asilomar. I don't know any other way to get to Los Angeles. You and I have to start from where we are spiritually. We have to put up with ourselves as what we are, psychologically and physiologically right now, until we can do better. And no one can live for us. That is why Shakespeare said, "To thine own self be true. And it must follow, as the night the day, thou canst not then be false to any man."

We have yet to prove what Jesus taught about forgiveness. He said if you take your gift and lay it on the altar and find you have something against your brother, take it home. He said it isn't acceptable to God; it isn't going to do you any good. Now Jesus, the greatest intellect and mind that ever lived, knew God wasn't going to get mad at somebody; this is not what he was talking about. Jesus was a cosmic man, disclosing universal truths in a language of relativity, which is the only language we humans have. That is one of our difficulties. We are four-dimensional beings living in a three-dimensional world. And the world in which we live has very little in it to describe that other thing, that light we all see. I know I have seen it many times, and you must have. It must be a common denominator. That light that lighteth every man's path is real.

Jesus was merely saying that your heart is the altar of God. You wish to extend your experience in what we would call consciousness, farther out into the realms of the unknown, and by that through marriage, unite yourself with the eternal love of God. And, therefore, you bring an offering, which is good. He didn't condemn it or praise it. This was the objective symbol of an inward grace. Like the sacraments in the church, they are beautiful, but he said to search your own consciousness. Do you hate anyone? Do you even dislike anyone? Do you condemn anyone?

Love only knoweth and comprehendeth love. The gateway to love is not to be open to hate, so hate may not enter; it cannot get in. There is a secret and a sacred pathway of the soul that only you and I may trod, each for himself, and as Rudyard Kipling said, "Each in his separate star/Shall draw the Thing as he sees It, for the God of Things as they are!" But some light, some diffused light from that does certainly shine through the pores of the skin. I have seen it in people, and I can tell you, sometimes they are all white light and sometimes it is pretty murky. And I am sure I am the same way when they look at me. I am sure if anyone could see himself the way he really is, it wouldn't matter if anyone else ever saw him again anyway while he lived.

So Jesus is saying this: God is all love, givingness, joy, peace, happiness, beauty forevermore. How are we going to get the nature of reality to deny itself, that it shall satisfy the whimsical petty fancies of our little ambitions? The soul requires a complete surrender. The Spirit knows nothing about degrees of givingness, and even the intellect cannot be satisfied until something dominates it which is beyond logic and our process of reasoning. It falls like mercy, like Shakespeare says, gentle dew from heaven.

We have yet to prove that there is enough spiritual development in us, enough of the actual unification with love and joy and peace, enough intelligence to bind it together with what organization is needed to keep it from falling apart. And rejoice. We will never do it unless people sitting in the shadow of our consciousness automatically become healed without our will or wishing or knowing. Shakespeare said, "How far that little candle throws his beams! So shines a good deed in a naughty world."

Now somebody might say I am not ready for this great thing, I am not good enough for this great thing. Don't worry about that. I never met a man in my life who thought he was good enough that I would want to spend any more time with than it took to say goodbye. He wouldn't interest me at all. That isn't the way it works. It is something entirely different that, dress it up as we may, a child can penetrate the mask and will unmask us before we walk one block.

It is a submission. It is a recognition. It is a unification. It is a joy. It is a calm. It is a confidence and an inward peace, something that seems to so bind itself to the universe with the invisible cords of a new kind of love and adoration, that heaven and Earth objectively shall pass away, and it shall not change it one iota. This is what you and I have to prove, shouting, as Rudyard Kipling said:

The tumult and the shouting dies,
The captains and the kings depart,
Still stands Thine ancient sacrifice
A humble and a contrite heart.
Lord God of hosts, be with us yet,
Lest we forget, lest we forget!

CHAPTER 3

1957

Practice of the Presence

Abiding Place of Presence

MONDAY, JULY 8, 1957

For Asilomar 1957, Ernest Holmes spoke each evening in a series he entitled "Practice of the Presence." Here he offers thoughts on the "transcendence of the living Spirit" and its relationship to the "immanence of the divine incarnation"—that is, the relationship of God to Its creation. As we are that creation seeking God, Holmes offers guidance on where and how to look. As we discover that abiding place of Presence, we move from ignorance into enlightenment.

NOTE: We were not able to transcribe the first few opening sentences of this talk due to technical glitches.

. . . because there is more that he does not say than there is that he does say. If he shoots his wad, he has shot his wad and that's that. It is only that which is thought and felt and partially said that refers to that corresponding something in everyone that feels it. Whether he is outwardly aware of it or not, it is true. This is the only reason you or I will listen more than once to a speaker. We don't go twice to hear the same person tell bad jokes and that's why. When I say bad jokes, I mean jokes that aren't funny, but if very many of them were made up that weren't bad, I didn't hear them. Something funny about that, isn't there? I wonder why somebody who thinks them up couldn't think of decent ones and equally be funny, but they don't.

This is the only reason we ourselves sit down to try to think, meditate, practice the presence of God, practice the transcendence, and realize the immanence is because something is indelibly written in our own minds—and we didn't put it there—that causes us to listen to the silence, to listen to some rhythm of the wind in the tree, to listen to the waves, and to hear something that is just a little beyond the physical perception.

This is the transcendence in everything. It is why we look at great art, because there is a transcendence that suggests an immanence. There is a beauty overshadowing it. When the future shall translate the art of this age, it will be called interpretive and symbolic, but it will not be called great art. It will not be called beauty, if beauty is a synonym for art. It will be interpretive of an age that had not yet inwardly assimilated, in its consciousness, the impact of a mechanical evolution. It hadn't put it together, the nuts and the bolts. It has nothing to do with the artist; some are just a little too dominant. The mechanics and the spontaneity haven't quite come together.

We find the same thing in much of the sciences. You see, science is necessary to our evolution, but science as such is a thing without a soul. This is no criticism of it. We certainly need knowledge and more knowledge, but the knowledge we now have causes the world to totter on the brink of a possible abyss, from which it shrinks in horror as it contemplates the possibility of the annihilation of the whole human race. And I have often thought if there were the kind of God that most people believe in—thank God we are not as other men—it seems to me He would wet His thumb, place it on the brow of humanity, and wipe it out and say it was just a sad mistake.

Now, I am not a pessimist, I'm an extreme optimist. I have said if there were the kind of God that people believe in—but you and I say or I say and I hope you say, then I'll think it sounds better—that I thank the God that is that the God that's believed in isn't and couldn't be.

Now we have a right to analyze this situation. It looks as though these talks I am going to give on the transcendence, the immanence, and the presence should be entirely inspirational, and we should soar on clouds of heaven over Asilomar. I would like to soar all around Asilomar and out over the ocean, but I would like to be careful that I don't fall to Earth with a dull and sickening thud. The ideal and the real must be brought together, definitely. The transcendence of the living

Spirit and the immanence of the divine incarnation must unite or we shall not understand the meaning either of the immanence or the transcendence, for the immanence reaches up to the transcendence, even as the transcendence reaches down to the immanence, that the two may join by a natural affinity of like with like and produce the mystical marriage referred to in all spiritual literature, which means the conscious union of the soul with its source. I would like us to reason for a while before we try to ride the clouds. I like riding the clouds. It's the easiest thing you can do because even though you get all wet, you're not conscious of it. It's like someone taking a sleeping pill and going to sleep. But we must wake up; that's the only trouble with sleep.

Emerson said, you know, that it seemed as though when we came to Earth, something gave us a drink too strong for us. He said we are gods on a debauch, but every once in a while somebody wakes up and looks about him, but very soon sinks back. And he said, "Beware, lest thou sink back into that slime from which thou hast so recently emerged."

I like the idea of the slime because when I was a kid, I loved to squeeze mud between my toes. You probably never did such a thing, but I would like to do it today just as much. Where is the child? What killed him? Who slew the innocent? Who threw the baby out with the wash water when he cleaned the tub? Who destroyed happiness to find salvation or introduced the devil to be a companion with God? Only those of low vision, only those whose consciousness could not read in apparent duality and multiplicity the lesson of unity—a unity so great, a power so profound, an immanence so dynamic that out of the transcendent and boundless possibilities of limitless freedom, even bondage is made. For unless bondage is made out of the stuff that is freedom, and unless some inner perception transmutes and translates and converts and sublimates the one into the other, the universe is a dualism, and it wouldn't stand for one moment.

Where is God? Where is the transcendence? Where is the Divine Presence? That's the first thing we have to establish. We may establish it mathematically or logically or inspirationally, revelationally, intuitively, but not dogmatically. If it so happens that there is only one power in the universe, one ultimate, one final power—which I think science, philosophy, and religion have now determined, certainly according to the last thoughts of Einstein, when he said that there was in his estimation but one physical law which coordinates, synthesizes, and unifies all known physical laws. I do not find that any different from the Hebrew saying: "Hear, O Israel, the eternal, the Lord thy God is one." I don't think it is any different from Emerson saying there is one mind common to all individual men, and it is no different when you and I say that whatever the nature of the ultimate reality is, it is one and only, and therefore we are faced with a multiplicity.

There are many things in the universe and more things in reality than are dreamed of in our philosophy. For now we see as through a glass very darkly, very dimly perhaps, but shadows outlined on the wall of experience are merely suggestive of a reality, even of a copy that is indistinct. I recently read an interpretation of Einstein, and Eddington, the man who wrote it, said that modern science now thinks of the physical universe more in the terms of a shadow cast by an invisible substance. The Bible says the invisible things of God from the foundation of the world are made manifest or known by the visible. What Eddington is really saying is what you see comes out of what you don't see. What you see does not cause itself; it's an effect. What you see has a pattern, a likeness, in the invisible. It is the shadow of the invisible imperfectly cast on the screen of our experience. It is a copy of a reality that is true, but the copy may be false, may be pretty much as you and I interpret it. "As thou seest, that thou be'est."

Wouldn't it be funny, and I believe it's true, if there is as Walt Whitman said, "Enclosed and safe within its central heart/Nestles the seed Perfection." And I believe it. Wouldn't it be funny if that perfect thing were here, were now, were complete, were perfect, as indeed it must be, and that our whole process of evolution, as indeed I believe it to be individually, is merely the experience through which we go to the awakening of that which never slept. As the Apostle Paul said in his letter to the Ephesians, "Awake thou that sleepest, and arise from among the dead, and Christ shall give thee light."

Now where is God? If God is one, just one, you and I may not conceive of such infinite unity. We see strewn about here and there little variations of it, which is difficult enough for us to put together. It's hard for us to put together love and hate, peace and confusion, poverty and wealth, heaven and hell, sickness and health. But until we finally get them together, we shall understand neither the transcendence, the immanence, nor the unity because we shall have dualism. No person can live in a universe and remain sane, really, who believes that half of his experience is false and the other half is real. And all people who try to do that whom I have ever observed finally end up by denying everything they do not like and affirming everything they do.

A very good friend of mine and a good practitioner said to me one day, we were talking about some case and that somebody ought to reveal something to somebody. "Well," I said, "we cannot treat that anybody is going to do anything. I've treated people for forty-five years. I never once in my life even thought of treating anybody to do anything, never even entered my head to do so. I should have suspected myself had I done it." I said, "We don't treat people to do things." "Well," she said, "no, but if there's any good reason. . . ." I said, "Hold everything, sister. Grab your hair, because I think it's a little loose." I said, "You're telling me if there's any good reason why this man should reveal this. . . ." "Well," she said, "he certainly will." I said, "Do you think there's a good reason?" She said, "There certainly is."

She was telling God what to do. You see, you can't do it that way. If there is a transcendence at the center of anything and if it so happens that our evolution is not the evolution of it but the unfolding of it to our consciousness in our experience, what is there in us that recognizes it? How shall we know? How shall we know when we see Him?

How shall we know? John Greenleaf Whittier said "The riddle of the world is understood/Only by him who feels that God is good/As only he can feel who makes his love/The ladder of his faith and climbs above/On the rounds of his best instincts; draws no line/Between mere human goodness and divine/But judging God by what in man is best/With a child's trust leans on a Father's breast."

How shall we recognize Him when we see Him? The New Testament says, "Beloved now are we the sons of God and it doth not yet appear what we shall be; but we know that when he shall appear, we shall be like him for we shall see him as he is. And everyone that hath this hope in him purifieth himself even as he is pure." And Jesus said, "And no man has ascended up into heaven except he who came down from heaven, even the Son of Man, who is in heaven." These are mystical sayings, the equivalent of which would be for us to say, "No one shall go to heaven unless he came from heaven, and no one shall either go or come unless he is already where he thinks he's going."

Now this is what Jesus said. I didn't say it. I wouldn't be that intelligent, but I demand an intelligent explanation of it of myself and one that satisfies me, because I learned a long time ago that the great are great to us only because we are on our knees. Let us arise. So far as you and I are concerned, Emerson said when we walk down the aisle, we give them the only greatness we are going to get back. Emerson knew that the immanence meets the transcendence and only through the complete surrender of the human to the Divine. Now this isn't the loss of the human. It's a surrender of the lesser to the greater, the ignorance to the intelligence, the weakness to the strength, the fear to the faith, the hell to the heaven, and the hate to the love, but how shall we know Him when we see Him? "And no man ever ascended up into heaven except he who came down from heaven, even the Son of Man, who is in heaven." You won't go; you won't come; you are there. There is nowhere to go to and nowhere to come from but an eternal state of being. "I am that I am, beside which there is none other," is what Jesus taught.

It says further in the New Testament, as I have just said: "Beloved now are we sons of God. It does not yet appear what we shall be." We are that now, it doesn't appear, we don't see it, WE ARE. It doesn't appear but when He shall appear, we know that we shall be like Him. We're like that. We don't see Him, but when He appears we shall be like Him and we shall see Him and He will appear and we shall be like Him when we have seen Him as he is. Now this is one of the terrific mystical sayings of the ages. We shall appear when we shall see Him as He is. Onlook the deity and the deity will onlook thee.

Act as though I am, and I will be. Wouldn't it be strange if it so happened that He appears every moment but only in the way we look? This is what I happen to believe. Why? Because every great and glorified spiritually evolved soul that has ever lived has taught it. All the great masters, all the great saviors, all the great saints, all the great poets have written about it. All the great music is around this theme. All of our highest thoughts are there, if we but knew it, to that same thing until, as Wordsworth says, "The prison walls of experience close him round about/And he forgets that celestial palace whence he came." But, he says "in moments of calm" whether that's in meditation, prayer, thought, identification, "though inland for we be," in that which seems dualistic, materialistic, "Our souls still have sight of that immortal sea/That brought us hither, can in a moment transport us thither/And see the children sport upon the shore/And hear the mighty billows rolling ever more."

See, this is a testimony of the poet. You know, Emerson said, "Sometimes the muse too strong for the bard sits astride his neck and writes through his hand." All great music is done this way. All great writing is this way. Something takes over, which is not separate from the self. It does not produce a split personality or a multiple personality or a confusion. It is that which we are, now shining through enough to take over this particular situation and out of its transcendence, within its immanence—that is, out of its over-dwelling and indwellingness—something speaks, and when it does, a power is loosed in the universe. And it is only the loosing of such power on such occasions that has given the world its great literature, its great art, its great music, its great sermons, its great mysticism, because the whole search of man is after that which shall make him whole, nothing else, whether we shall call it God or whether we shall call it heaven or whether we shall choose to call it salvation, which I don't like, but it's all right as long as we don't have to sin too much to get there. Of course, I think salvation is so sweet, one would want to get lost along the way a number of times. It is like the boy who was pressing his nose very hard and his mother said, "Son, why do you do that?" He said, "It feels so good when I take it away." Now, he had something. There's logic in that, and it is true: In our littleness, how little we are.

I said to someone last night, "My ego is about the size now of a marble, and I hope it will roll away." "Well," she said, "do you really want to get rid of your ego?" I said, "No, I wish to find it."

This transcendence does not lose the immanence, you know. Who loses his life shall find it, the wisest Jew who ever lived said. Who loses his littleness shall find his greatness. Who loses fear shall find faith. Why? Something Mrs. Eddy said that I always liked: "All prophets are prophets to me and truth belongs to no one." She said the greatest wrong is but the supposition of opposites to the highest right. I think it's one of the great sayings in the spiritual culture of the ages, that the greatest wrong is merely a false interpretation of the natural equivalent to its need, which is the transcendence within the immanence, that is, the God within the man, that one, the same and identical, because all that the immanence is in the transcendence now individuated, not as a separate or distinct individualization, but as an articulation in a unique way of the totality of its own being. Does that mean anything? This is a lesson. This is not a dramatic display. I don't know how to do that stuff. This is important. This is what we're here for. This is what we're here for. This is a seminar. If it were entertainment, we'd charge admission and get better entertainers than we are. I know somebody that for a dollar you could get to hear and he's much better than I am, and if you only paid a dollar to hear me, I don't think I'd like you very well, because I'd think you didn't think I was good enough. Isn't that interesting how strangely we react to things.

Now I said that the immanence is God. Where is God? We're trying to locate God now. Somebody said you can't locate Him. I am going to say you can, but in locating God, you can't divide Him. I happen to think you can locate God as a moving something, and if you can't, what's the use in chasing Him? I couldn't see any sense to that. It's like a cat chasing its own tail; it never quite catches up with it. I think it would be better to cut the cat's tail off and do away with that illusion. It will be kinder in the end. And give it a false mouse to play with. They're mostly playing with mice anyway. The Divine immanence, God in me, is the transcendent God that's in all things. Therefore, we'll have to locate God, but not in any particular spot—in all, over all, and through all. I happened to write the things we read last night about our belief. I wrote them in about twenty minutes about thirty years ago, without any thought. That's why they're good. Now it said God is in everything but not absorbed by anything. He is in all things but not absorbed.

We have a certain sort of a panpsychism—God in nature. I think God's in the tree. I even think God is in myself, though when I look at myself sometimes, I say how funny can God be? But God must be that, too. How do we know but what

God laughs at Himself? I don't know that He does; I don't know that He doesn't. But if you and I laugh, at what do we laugh? I'm not willing to settle, in my philosophy and in my thoughts, for denying everything I don't like just because I don't like it. I don't think it makes any sense. Psychologically, I happen to know that it produces a split personality. That is not a desirable thing. It would be better at least to have a multiple personality, and there would be more people to talk with. I think that would probably be better, but just a split personality, it seems to be settling for too little, in my estimation only, and I speak as a man and not as a god.

But we're trying to locate Him. "Whither shall I go from thy spirit? Or whither shall I flee from thy presence? If I ascend up into heaven, thou art there: if I make my bed in hell, behold, thou art there. If I take the wings of the morning and dwell in the uttermost parts of the sea; even there shall thy hand lead me, and thy right hand shall hold me." If I say, "Surely the darkness shall cover me; even the night shall be light about me." "Yea though I walk through the valley of the shadow of death, I will fear no evil for thou art with me." There is a perception of the Presence. "If I take the wings of the morning and dwell in the uttermost parts of the sea," he will be there. This is a transcendence. But what recognizes the transcendence but the immanence? How shall that which is unlike God, know God? It shall not.

I wrote something about friendship in which I said, "Perhaps God has saluted Himself in us. Perhaps God was lonely until we met." It's just a play on words, but who knows what that thing is that happens in new situations and meeting new people. When an influx does take place, it takes place on all levels—physical, mental, and spiritual—not to fill a vacuum within itself, but to fill a vacuum within in our need, our own want, that will erase our own fear, extinguish our own loneliness by its aloneness. Plotinus said, "The one to the one."

Now, how are we going to find Him unless He is everywhere? You're not, not at all. But if He is everywhere, how are we going to find Him unless we discover Him anywhere? Every anywhere is in the total of the all-comprehensive everywhere. The greater includes the lesser. This I think we overlook.

We don't quite realize that the only love we shall ever know is what we experience, express for each other. God may be love, but we don't know it in any other way. The only happiness that we shall ever know is the happiness that we are. And suppose, for instance, that that transcendence, now this is the next great step to me. As I said this morning, these are the two greatest revelations of the ages, the transcendence and the immanence, the Divine Presence overshadowing and the same Presence indwelling. "Not I but the Father within me; yet the Father is greater than I. Yet whatsoever things the son seeth the Father do, that doeth the son also, so that the Father may be glorified in the son. Let your light so shine that men seeing your good works shall glorify your Father in your heaven, that kingdom which is within."

Now you and I are going to agree right now, at least I am going to agree with myself right now, I don't always agree with myself. When you don't, you've got some kind of a mental indigestion. You see, everything in the physical plane is but a copy and a poor imitation of its mental equivalent, and its mental equivalent is almost as poor an imitation of its spiritual prototype, because the spiritual prototype is the universality step down into our mental equivalent, which step down into their physical and outward correspondences. Is that clear? Does it make any sense? If it doesn't, forget it. It sounds kind of confusing to me. I'll think it over awhile, two or three weeks, and if it makes any sense, I'll let you know next year. I'm inclined to think it can, if I can come to understand it.

You know, there is much that the intellect can arrive at that doesn't even invite the soul. Whitman said he liked to loaf and invite his soul. Mathematics can arrive at the conclusion that a light-year is light traveling 186,000 miles plus a second, across an emptiness of space for a billion light years. It can do it only by a symbol. Let us call this distance, if such exists, or space, if such is. Nobody knows, but all that you and I know about distance, really, we got in an automobile and drove to San Francisco and Mexico and New York. Maybe some of you have driven around Europe. That's all we know. The rest is a theory.

And so Moses was taken up, theoretically, of course. I don't think God took Moses by the hand and said, "Come up yonder now. We're going to climb a mountain." I just don't happen to believe in this. I don't believe in any anthropomorphic

God or any Divine power that I'd use with anyone, because it doesn't make sense. There has to be a logic to reality and a mathematics to reality, which in no way dissolves the inspiration or the illumination but rather gives it validity, so that when we finally get on the right track, we can let the reins loose and we shall not become confused. There is a transcendence; there is an immanence. Only the immanence can know the transcendence. Love only knows and comprehends love.

Let's locate God then, right here. Now whether we locate God right here—we're not dividing Him, because all of here is there—but let's locate all of God right here and all of God right there, for all of God is wherever God is. We just happen to call it the omnipresence. It means the indivisible unit, which means that all things are everywhere present at all times, neither beyond the point nor approaching it. Now if this is true—and I do not doubt it—we can agree with it, but something else goes with it, as I just said. Put the two together and you have, I believe, at least an intellectual answer to the greatest inquiry the human mind has made. What is it all about? That which, without asking, whither hurried hence, and which without asking, whither hurried whence like water willy-nilly flowing. In other words: Why, why, why? Every intelligent person asks over and over in the continual adjustment to life and just living: Why?

I want us to know that our philosophy, at least that part of it that I believe in, is both transcendent and immanent. I do not know how we are going to find a Creator separate from Its creation. I do believe I know how finding one in His creation, we shall see the revelation of that which transcends His creation. But the other part that goes with the first says this: Very few people have found, the other sounds so grand, the God that is transcendent will have to appear to the God that is immanent in the form, in the way, in the manner in which the God that is immanent looks at the God that is transcendent. Does that make any sense?

Here is another way of saying it. There is something in the universe that looks right back at us the way we look at it. On-look the deity, and the deity will on-look you. But somebody will say, "You don't think God looks back at me, as mean as I am, the way I look at God?" The only God you and I will know reacts to our action. But there is a greater reaction from that to us, if our action holds itself up to it in a transcendent manner.

We are not limiting that God that is because the God that appears is only a half-God. "Naught is the squire when the king's at hand, withdraw the stars when dawns the sun's brave light." It is destined by that everlasting pressure against us. "The wind bloweth where it listeth but canst not tell when it cometh and whither it goeth. So is everyone that is born of the Spirit." I believe there is an incessant, ceaseless pressure, urge. I think that's what the psychologists mean by the libido. We call it the divine urge. God is a spirit and the spirit seeketh such. There has to be a pressure. It's what is back of evolution. Browning said:

A spark disturbs our clod; ...
And I shall thereupon
Take rest, ere I be gone
Once more on my adventure brave and new:
Fearless and unperplexed,
When I wage battle next,
What weapons to select, what armor to indue....
All that is, at all,
Lasts ever, past recall;
Earth changes, but thy soul and God stand sure:
What entered into thee,
That was, is, and shall be:
Time's wheel runs back or stops: Potter and clay endure.

What transcendence? He's talking about Divine Immanence, which endures because the immanence is the transcendence and nobody ever made God. God wasn't born; God does not cease to be. Beloved now are we, the sons of God. It doth not yet appear but he shall appear when we shall see him as he is, and he shall not appear until we shall see him as he is.

Then the immanence must see the transcendence and see itself in the immanence, that the immanence may reflect back to it that which it sees and what's going on in this great cosmic mystery to us, but probably a simplicity so simple, so very simple that a child could understand. As a teacher said, "Verily I say unto you . . . do always behold the face of my Father which is in heaven." Well, if we beheld the face of our Father which is in our heaven, our seeing reality as it is will cause it to appear. But it cannot appear, the passage says, until we see it as it is. We are between the devil and the deep sea. This is an enigma. This is a dilemma. This is a conundrum. This is a riddle. And it is said in the mythology of the Egyptians that when the pilgrim asked those questions of the sphinx, rather the sphinx asked these questions of the pilgrims, if they could not answer, the sphinx swallowed them up, or I guess it swallowed them down, because if it swallowed them up, they wouldn't have been down. We always should be careful of the direction we take. But if they did answer, the sphinx had to get out of the way, it just moved over to one side. That's the mythology that goes with this colossal figure, and it's a good one.

We either answer the problems of life or they are problems. Evil will be evil while we look at it. Hell will be hot while we believe in it. Heaven is that which we have harmonized in our own consciousness, and God is what we have accepted. But wouldn't it be strange if, without limiting the Infinite, we bound ourselves with the cords of freedom, phantom, illusionary but real, like the slaves in the cave of Plato, bound by shadows. But you know if we couldn't be bound by shadows, we wouldn't be free. Freedom is the stuff that bondage is made of or else there is dualism in the universe—and there isn't. This is hard for people to see. It's hard for me to see. I'm just as thick as everybody I meet. I hate to admit it, but it's true.

It's hard for you and for me to say "my God is my pain pleasure." It isn't for me. Is my bondage freedom? It must be or else there is dualism or else some part of my life is living an illusion. It does not satisfy my curiosity for somebody to say that's all unreal and this is real, because I know they're coercing their own mind, projecting their unconscious desires, and not sublimating the restrictions one bit. And the harder they fight, the bolder the devil gets, because he, too, is an illusion. The fork and flaming breath and tail and the whole works and hell, etc., limbo, purgatory, and all the other nonsense theology has strewn down the pathway of a long-suffering humanity, which took it because it was so ignorant it didn't know how to reject it. But believe me, it is rejected by this movement forever. There is no dualism.

The immanence views the transcendence only because without division, the immanence is the transcendence. This is what Jesus said, knew, and understood. "Not I but the Father who dwelleth in me, but yet the Father is greater than I." This is not idolatry. This is not setting ourselves on the throne of the Almighty God. It is honoring God at last. To say, well at long last we admit that there is such a thing as an incarnation—of what?—the transcendence, how we have located Him. He's not very far away. He isn't a distant scene. He isn't the day after tomorrow, a coming event that casts its shadow before it. He isn't even the grand perception. I mean, He's more than that. As Tennyson said, "One God, one law, one element, and one far-off Divine event, toward which the whole creation moves." He's that but more.

Now, it's only because, as Alfred Lord Tennyson said, "Our little systems have their day/They have their day and cease to be./They are but broken lights of thee, And thou O Lord, art more than they." Now we're going to have to come to the place, if we're going to discover the transcendence, that it's here. All of the immanence indwelling shall know the over-dwelling. I and the Father are one, and that's the first half of the greatest discovery the human mind has ever made. The next half is equally important: "That thou seest, man, become too thou must; God, if thou seest God, dust, if thou seest dust."

Mrs. Hopkins says in that transcendence, *High Mysticism*—which I feel is the best example for us because among all the mystics whom I have read and studied, she is the only one who ties mysticism to what you and I believe in, even for utilitarian purposes—she said there was a race of people who produced great prophets, perhaps the greatest spiritual prophets of feeling the world has ever known, but she said they kept their vision too much on a valley of dry bones and persecution and oppression and continuously fed the belief that it should manifest in their history. "As thou seest, that thou be'est." Now its very difficult because we don't like to believe that we are reflecting our limitations, and I don't like to believe it either, but I accept it. But I appease my pride, and I think rightly, by saying it's my ignorance, but the ignorance of laws excuses no one from their effects.

Aurobindo, that's one reason I like Aurobindo, he didn't speak of sin and salvation. He spoke of ignorance and enlightenment. Isn't that much better? It covers it all, and he speaks of those processes as coming up out of the ignorant into the intelligent by evolution. We are certainly in the process of evolution. Wouldn't it be wonderful if we could accept that that transcendence—that thing that we see in the morning light and the evening sunset, in the rose that glows the varied colors at early dawn, and in the face of the mother crooning over her baby, and the child at play, and the wisdom of the wise, and the dance of life, and the song, there's ever a song somewhere should we sing it—if we could see in all this transcendence, that you and I could not recognize it without the immanence, we should never know about an indwelling God, an over-dwelling God, unless the indwelling God reveal Him. When we see Him, we shall know Him when He appears, but since He's already there, He shall not appear until we see Him as He is and everyone that hath this hope in Him glorifieth and purifieth himself, even as He is pure.

Now this is very simple: God is all there is. God is everywhere that is and every what that it is. Don't think you're going to take some what out and leave where and have a creation without a creator or through dualism. There is no such a thing in our category. Our bondage is made of our freedom. Hell will cool off only when we open the gates of our consciousness to let in the wind of heaven. Lift up your gates, and the King of Glory shall come in. "Prove me now herewith, saith Jehovah of hosts [the indwelling presence], and see if I will not open unto you the windows of heaven and pour out such a blessing that ye shall not be able to receive it."

And you and I come alone to the alone, and there is no mediator. Fortunately, there are instructors. We all try to help. You try to help somebody. There are ones we help, we treat; we believe in it. But in the long run, that gift of yourself upon the altar to the Greater Self that is that self, you shall bring in your own hands, singing your own song, until the stars themselves shall sing together and a new day shall break across the horizon of your eastern sky.

And may the light of heaven guide you, and may the harmony of celestial music accompany you to that pathway which leads inward, even as it spans outward to the city of God and wholeness.

Contemplating the Presence

TUESDAY, JULY 9, 1957

In this second evening's talk on our Practice of the Presence, Holmes discusses our contemplating the Presence, where we enter into the essence of the Thing within us "from that which exists externally to that which subsists internally." Our contemplation of the Presence is not to make anything "happen" but rather to deepen our sense of personal relationship with this Presence and know It at the deepest level possible.

NOTE: The final lines of this talk were not captured on the recording.

No man has ever seen the Spirit within us, but what artist has ever seen beauty? Beauty is subjective; art is objective. Out of that inward awareness, that subjective sense, the artist creates the object of that subjectivity, and that's why we speak of an object of art. Who has ever seen truth or integrity? Who has ever seen energy? And yet science deals with energy mostly. Who has ever seen life? And yet the biologist spends his life studying the action and reaction of life. Psychology is a study of the human mind, but no psychologist has ever seen the human mind. Philosophy is supposed to be a study of reality, and no one has ever seen reality. Well, no, we haven't seen each other. We only feel each other. We haven't seen life. We live it; we feel it. We haven't seen beauty. We appreciate it, and I think cannot live without some form of beauty. We have not seen peace. No sane person doubts the reality of peace. You know, we may kill the nightingale and dissect him, but we shall never discover his song nor capture it. It's a very interesting thing.

All the things that are real are invisible. All the things that cause the visible are invisible. So the Bible says the invisible things of God, from the foundations of the world, are made manifest by the visible. What you see comes out of what you don't see. And it is only as we interpret what we don't see by what we do, which merely suggests it, that we arrive at the nature of reality in our own conclusions. And it is only as we do something about it that we go beyond the mathematical and the intellectual arrival and have a sense of something more, of something beyond the border of our objective lives. Rufus M. Jones wrote a little book called the *The Testimony of the Soul.* He was the great American mystic of his day, as Evelyn Underhill was of her day in England, and they were both of our day. And he says that the testimony of the soul is just as real as the testimony of the sense.

In other words, if you were to take away from us that which enables us to know, there wouldn't be anything left. No one has seen the Knower. It would be a very unintelligent perspective that would in any way, shape, or manner seek to deny the invisible, since the whole realm of effect, I mean of cause, is invisible. You do not see spiritual awareness, but you do feel it. You feel it in yourself when you have it. You feel it in others when they have it. You recognize it when you read about it. You know it when you don't try to think about it. It's a feeling. It's a sort of an inward consciousness and, unless we were taught to deny it, it would be perfectly natural.

One of our great troubles is that we do not live naturally or spontaneously. Most everyone is afraid to be himself. Most everyone is afraid if he likes someone to tell them so, for fear somebody will misunderstand it, probably think it's a proposition of some kind. This is silly. We have so sewed our mouths up that we can hardly articulate our own feelings, and we have so walled our little pigmy intellects in with certain formulas that have but very little to do with life that it's very difficult for that original thing to come forth and break forth in the song that came with us. John Boyle O'Reilly in *The Cry of the Dreamer* said:

*I am tired of planning and toiling
And spoiling and building again.
And I long for the dear old river,
Where I dreamed my youth away;
For a dreamer lives forever,
And a toiler dies in a day.*

About all the world has thought out of the systematically hard-boiled scientific matter-of-fact mind, outside of modern comfort, is the ability to destroy itself. It's quite remarkable. Now, I believe in science, merely because I milked cows when I was a kid and scrubbed floors, helped to make butter, washed and ironed, sawed wood. And it was lucky. People who were lucky had a pump and a sink in the kitchen and didn't have to carry their water. There are not any of you who are antediluvian enough to remember that, but there are people who are still living who remember. They had to prime the pump, and if it was frozen, it was primed with hot water. Sometimes you melted the snow to get the hot water. I never remember having to thaw a cow out before I milked her. That would be quite a proposition, wouldn't it? Well, I'm not one who longs for the good old days to come back, where you arise at four a.m. and worked 'til nighttime, and lit a lantern, and milked the cows afterward. It may be good, but I like to stay in bed later.

Modern science has done a great deal for the creature comforts of all of us, but what has it done to deliver to us that something that enables us to appreciate the universe in which we are living, that makes everything in it come alive and awake and aware and causes the leaves of the trees to clap their hands? What is it that we miss if we depend only on objective methods? That's pretty near the whole works, the whole evidence, the whole thing that delivers us to us—something that the intellect cannot formulate in words but, as Emerson said, let the intellect alone; the heart knows.

Now we call this, maybe, practicing the presence of God. That's what we mean in our language. We call it meditating, perhaps upon God, contemplating the nature of God, thinking about God, but as we discovered last night, God is right where we are and God is exactly what we are—but more. God is an indwelling and an over-dwelling presence, and I suggested to you last night that, in my estimation, the two greatest teachings the world has ever received from the lips of wisdom and the minds of saints and the inspiration of saviors and the deepest thinkers of the ages are, first that the Divine Presence is within me, because it's everywhere. The Divine Presence is undivided and indivisible. God is one. There is nothing unlike God by which to divide God. Therefore, God remains one, a unit whose center is everywhere and whose circumference is nowhere.

In God, there can be no big or little, or hard or easy, or yesterday as something that is not, and tomorrow as something that is not, but only a continuation of the point of perception in which we now function here and now. That is one of the sects of Buddha, called Zen Buddhism, in which the whole endeavor is to find that moment, which is now, which because it is independent of yesterday, severs the tie of yesterday that binds the law of tomorrow to the images of the past and thus perpetuates the limitations we have experienced. Is that clear? That's the whole purpose of Zen Buddhism.

This is something that Jesus understood that they didn't. And the wise of their day, they were probably very good people. They were like our present-day theologians: They are very wonderful people, and there are certain places where things could be tightened up. I often wonder if it's tightened on this side or loosened on that, I don't know. So they said to him—they thought they would catch him in a trap—they brought a blind man. Now they said, "We've got the guy." They thought they had him because he only knew two questions and two answers. They didn't know there was a third one. That's why they fell.

They had Moses and the Mosaic law, which said an eye for an eye and a tooth for a tooth. And many of them had a belief in reincarnation, which is no better and no worse than other beliefs, but a belief only, like people once believed the world was flat. It didn't flatten out anywhere, not much, and so they said, "We've got him." We Jews aren't right; the Hindus must be. Together we know everything, but they had overlooked one point about a little kid who said he and his father knew everything. Somebody said, "All right, son, where is Egypt?" He scratched his head and said, "That's one of the things my dad knows." We call it, passing the buck.

Now they said, "Who did sin, this man or his parents, that he was born blind?" They figured the Jews were right, and grandfather had gouged out somebody's eye so little Abe was born with only one eye. Or in some previous incarnation, he had slipped on a banana peel and broken his journey, and now he has to come back to do it all over again because there'll be another journey and there'll be another banana peel to slip on. It's amazing the vast system of nebulous theory the human mind creates to project a God who is not there and then bow down and worship the illusion. Isn't it amazing? Well, I suppose we all do it.

You see Moses had a time track from grandfather to grandson. The Hindus, or whoever they were, had a time track, that means a sequence of cause and effect a little bigger, from incarnation to incarnation, maybe a thousand years. Now they're hypnotizing them and regressing them, and one remembers when he was a horse and the other when he was the planet Neptune. The third one has not yet awakened sufficiently from his slumber to tell whether he was a mule or a canary bird, but that will come in another chapter. You see, this is a serial story. It's been going on for thousands of years, and the end of the play is not in sight.

So they said, "All right, master, who did sin?" He said, "Let me tell you something, boys, I see what you're up to. I know your time track, but what happened to your little time track and to your just a little bigger time track if I would just take them, smash them together, and there were no time tracks left?" You see what I mean? What if I interfered even with a logical and legitimate and honest-enough series of cause and effect because I don't care if you believe in reincarnation. It can be that way if you believe in Moses. It can be that way but, he said, "Suppose I heal him. What are you going to do then?" Which he did. And so Jesus said to the thief who died with him, "Today shalt thou be with me in paradise."

Now Jesus was a Jew, the greatest of the Jewish prophets in my estimation. So we take Jesus and the great inspiration of Isaiah and the wisdom of Solomon and the heart of Jesus and put them together, and you'll have the very greatest system of emotional thought the world has ever known. Then add to it the intellect of the Greeks, and then you have the philosophy of Christianity, because that's where it came from—the Jews and the Greeks. The man who thought it came out of Ireland was entirely mistaken, completely. And the old lady, as sincere as she was, who at ninety-seven began to study Hebrew, somebody said, "What are you going to do that for, Grandmother? You're not going to live very long." She said, "That's why I'm doing it. I am not going to live very long. And when I see my God, I want to speak to Him in His own language." She was a Boy Scout and to "be prepared" was her motto.

Now Jesus knew something that they didn't know. What was it that Jesus knew that they didn't know, that produced the effect I want to talk about in the practice of the Presence tomorrow night? We talked about locating it last night and contemplating it tonight, or will, if it comes off before I get through. This always is uncertain to me. One of the most inspired spiritual teachers I ever knew was James Porter Mills who wrote *A New Order of Meditation,* which he called "neurotology," and many other books. He had been a physician. I said, "How do you treat?" "Well," he said, "I contemplate. You know, it's like fishing. I throw in my bait and my hook, and I angle. I'm trying to get an intuitive perception, and every once in a while a fish comes along and takes the bait." That's rather interesting isn't it? He was talking about contemplating the Spirit, because he would take a statement—"I am the Christ, the son of the Living God within me. I am the truth. I am the peace of God."—and just meditate on it or contemplate it. In most of his healing work, and he did very remarkable healing work because he was inducing a state that brings this imprisoned splendor and this invisible Presence so close to the surface that It automatically articulates Itself in the form of his desire or the desire of those who asked for help. That's automatic.

Now Jesus, like the Zen Buddhists and like we try to do, must have, to a very great degree, eliminated the liability of the past and the negative probability of the future. This is what the contemplation of the Truth is supposed to do to us. The universe is a government of law and a rule of law and order. It would have to be. Law is necessary, but the Bible says Christ, now if they had been Buddhists, they would have said Buddha or the Enlightened One, frees us from the law. Is the law then of no avail? God forbid. In other words, the law is there, but it is supposed to be a servant. We are not supposed to have to obey the law of our lives. And you and I come to the law of the lives of the generations of the ages that are past. We are hypnotized from the cradle to the grave by fear and doubt and superstition, our wants and needs, our insecurities and anxieties, until we are so pressed against by the prison walls of this false ego that we can hardly breathe. And finally we stifle, and physical death and disillusion come, in my estimation, that the spirit shall no longer be bound to the flesh. It's a happy event in more cases than not. There's nothing morbid about it.

Jesus understood these things, that in this moment by right knowing by right seeing of that which is true or of a truth that makes man free, we are no longer bound to the past. Therefore, the past is no longer binding the future to a sequence already set in motion beyond our control. Isaiah said, "He shall leave captivity captive." To me, this is one of the most glorified statements in the Bible. "He shall leave captivity captive." The law will bind as quickly or as easily as it will free. It's a doer and not a knower, just as electricity will burn the house, it will electrocute somebody, it will toast bread, or do anything else according to the use to which we apply it. That law returns to us by what Troward calls a reciprocal action—that is, it reflects back to us what we have consciously or unconsciously reflected into it.

The law of mind in action, that we use in healing and demonstration, doesn't even know it's being used. If it did, it would know that it didn't have to be used. You don't think the law that produces potatoes has cabbages in mind. It's just a latent possibility. It's impersonal and neutral and plastic, and yet it is creative. Now that is the law of mind, and it's a terrific thing. And we can't escape it, but we can completely reverse our position in it so that that very thing that bound us shall now free us. And if I ever arrived at any truth at all—I know it's very slight, one lifetime isn't time enough to arrive at very much truth, but at least to my own satisfaction—I have arrived at this fragment: that the law that binds is the only law that can free us.

I believe until we realize there is only one law, as there is only one Presence, we shall be fighting. As I remember somebody—and it was a New Englander, that's the way they are—he was contesting a law case, and he lost, and he appealed it. And somebody said, "You're going to still do that," and he said, "I shall fight until hell freezes over and then continue the struggle on the ice." That is the true New England spirit, and it isn't so bad either. But isn't that the way we have done it and we do do it, just because we believe in a dualism, because it looks as though there were a dualism.

I remember the story of Adam and Eve. After God had got things pretty well fixed up and had made all the animals, He told Adam and Eve to sit down, and He would cause all the animals to come in front of them and they would name them. So all day, the animals paraded in front of them. First Adam would give a name, then Eve. Toward night, there comes along a great big, ugly, lumbering-looking thing, and Adam said, "Eve, for heaven's sake, what do you think that strange looking creature is?" She said, "Adam, to me that looks like a hippopotamus." He said, "No, what shall we call it?" And she says, "We shall call it a hippopotamus." He said, "Eve, why do you wish to call it a hippopotamus?" She said, "Because, Adam, it looks more like a hippopotamus to me than anything else." And so she named it that. It's so silly, it makes you sick to your stomach. But that is a good kind of joke.

You see we are, without knowing it, endlessly repeating the pattern of the beliefs of the ages. We are bound by chains of sand and cords of fantasy, with no more substantiality than a shadow that a tree casts and as thin as vapor and as transient as a passing dream. But we make them solid by holding them in our consciousness. I do not happen to believe in any form of dualism. I believe that disease is made out of the same stuff that health is made out of, but in different arrangement. I believe that impoverishment is abundance operating in the only way we permit it. I believe that hell is paved with the phantoms of our fear, and heaven is our highest idea of harmony, but angels are singing in both places. I think that perhaps below, it singes their wings a little, but God causes more to grow that, with our orthodox friends, they shall everlasting burn and only be singed in the process. Isn't that tantalizing? So kind of futile, I mean so silly. If I'd been going to make up one, I would have tried to make up a better one, but so many people have fallen from that one, that the last time I spoke for Catherine Harris in San Francisco, some very nice young man was overheard to say afterward, "This man (Ernest) may have a good mind but he has no religion." Somebody said, "Why?" And he said, "He says there is no hell." Well, there isn't. We don't have to cool it off; it's an iceberg already.

Now wouldn't it be the strangest thing if suddenly we could wake up and look about us, and the crowds would have disappeared and the way would be straight. And then again we look, and it's all muddled. And once we listen, and we hear a song. I was over not long ago to a friend of ours who writes a lot of songs. She said, "Now I want you to listen to this on the piano." I said, "That's sweet." She said, "Well that came to me the other day." I said, "Are there any words?" She said, "Yes, but I don't know what they are." Well, I said, "How are you going to find out?" She said, "Someday I will play this over, and as I play it, the words will be there." I said, "Where do you think they come from?" She said, "I don't know. But that's the way they come."

Beethoven got his symphonies that way. We should get everything that way. Now, why don't we? Because we are not contemplating the one and only Presence in all things everywhere and in the things immediately around us that we thought were inconsequential. I do not see why it is not as important, if there's no big and no little in the universe, to want that which expresses the joy and the happiness of a simple occasion as well as what we call greatness. Who knows that an empire builder is of more importance in the scheme of things than a kid who makes a mud pie and, being tired of it, steps on it and disintegrates it? Who is there among us who has the wisdom to tell us that all of life does not belong to the delight of that eternal or bliss that must exist at the center of everything?

This is what contemplation is for. Now contemplation is a little different from meditation. We do both. It is a little different from the average concept of concentration. I know nothing about concentration. I care nothing about it, not that it isn't good. You don't concentrate reality anywhere. The only thing you could concentrate would be your attention on it, of course. Now why should not our attention be always fastened on the ever-present reality in all of its phases and activities and attributes, from the laughter of a child to the wisdom of the sage, from a bird singing to an orchestra playing, from a little patch of flowers to the panoramic scene of the horizon of a new experience. It should. It should.

But we have divided things up into categories of big and little, rather than adequacies. We have divided up into categories of right and wrong, rather than self-expression. We have imposed a false ethic and morality on everything. When

I'm a talking about morals, I'm not talking about sex. At any rate, this is not Hollywood. A false limitation upon everything, little and pygmy and peewee, and on top of that, offensive and disagreeable and disconsolate. And we stand beside the wailing wall of our own experience and beat our heads against the bricks and think that God is imposing something upon us. Emerson said, "The universe remains to the heart unhurt and only to the heart unhurt, and then in our anguish and our tears, we cry out to that which does not cry, to that which has no anguish, and the only release we get is that release which comes from the explosion of unemotional state, which otherwise would explode us, until finally having gotten rid of it." There is a place open for the transcendence to flow in and a new influx takes place. That's all that experience does to us. That's all that pain, that's all that grief and sorrow can do to us is to temporarily explode the pent-up energy and emotion and feeling and frustration that otherwise would burst the psychic cord and we might die. Not that that would bother me. It wouldn't because I don't believe anybody dies, but the only release that finally comes is when the emotion is spent and perhaps even in physical and mental weariness, though exhaustion is so great that the tension relaxes and that other thing comes in, which always says "peace." Always. Because it is peace.

And so the contemplation is not a meditation to cause things to happen. I believe in that—contemplation is where meditation passes from the meditation upon to the entering into the essence of the thing within, from that which exists externally to that which subsists internally. "In him there was life and that life was the light of men." Contemplation then is not to make things happen. Now meditation may be, and there is nothing wrong with it. You don't make them but you make it possible for them to. Contemplation is the entering into the essence of things. Contemplate beauty, contemplate love, contemplate peace, not that anything has to happen. It's a fluidity, and you arrive at the only thing in the universe that can no longer be resisted—and that's nonresistance.

The power of Gandhi, through nonviolence, and Jesus, through nonresistance, was the same power. They, in nonresistance, discovered the only thing that cannot be resisted. Everything else can.

And so all of our experience may exhaust us to the point where we have not even strength to resist, and in this moment, the influx takes place, noncombatively, nonargumentatively, without struggle "for it is only the finite that has wrought and suffered, the infinite lies stretched in smiling repose," Emerson said. This, I believe, is the meaning of the contemplation of reality. It's an intuition, and one of the characteristics of intuition when it tells us—and this is the way I differentiate between psychism and intuitive perception, myself and others—intuitive perception never tells you to do anything, never. It tells you to be something. It doesn't even do that, but because it is something, it seems to. You see the difference? People say well I had the intuition to buy a certain number of shares of Dupont or General Motors stock. This is not an intuition. It's a hunch and may or may not be right. I'd hate to have to follow anybody who had those hunches in buying stock. You see intuition is not of possession, it is not of becoming, it is of being, it is of essence, it is of feeling, it is of a conviction from the testimony of an interior awareness that so far overlaps, outshines, and dominates the intellect that the intellect is but a weak instrumentality for its office. This is what I think contemplation is.

And then through the contemplation, we are automatically giving back to the law of mind that we had so long struggled to force upon it, but which it never could have rejected because it rejects nothing. We are only finding a new pattern. Suppose you and I had contemplated the abundance of the universe like this. Suppose we sat down on the beach, and think how many grains of sand there are on the shore, or how many leaves there are on the trees, how many fish there must be in the ocean, how infinite is space, how limitless is time, how profound is truth, how abundance is everywhere, until we enter into the essence of abundance and the feeling of right action, not about anything in particular. Automatically all those other thoughts that are in there would reflect relative to themselves into the law of cause and effect and abundance, and in our lives, everything would open up.

Now, I believe in a specific practice, so I'm going to talk about practicing the Presence in this series. But let us be sure we are practicing it from a motivation and a realization beyond that which has already measured out the limitation we seek to become extricated from. It's entirely possible for us to get so tense and so anxious that the very thing we fear is accentuated in the contemplation of the Divine Presence. Rightly understood, I believe, we should have gotten beyond the concept that there are any opposites, that there is anything out here. The universe becomes a liquidity for the period of the contemplation that is. It is a flow; it is no longer solid.

Now, unless you practice this, you won't know what happens. If you do, you'll find out. Lots of people say to me, "Well I don't think it's this way." I say, "Well, let's not argue about it." A man convinced against his will is of the opinion still. I used to try to convince everybody that I met of everything I believed. Most of what I believed then I know isn't true now, but I don't try to convince anybody of anything. I don't try half as hard as I used to to convince myself. There is sort of a good-natured flexibility. If the tree didn't bend, it would snap.

In the contemplation of life, in the realizations of life and love and friendship or success or happiness or whatever it is, all of which must belong to the kingdom of God and ought to be in the kingdom of man and in his experience, there are no opposites. There is no otherness. There isn't some other power contending. Now Jesus and Gandhi saw this, and they stopped resisting the apparent opposites. And because they practiced nonresistance, that which would have resisted, being a solid, only destroyed itself. It hadn't anything to bump up against, so it rattled around until it destroyed its own skeleton and fell into the valley of its own desolation. "I will contend with them that contend with thee," saith the Lord. Now you and I, along with all of our getting and having, all of which I think is good. When I want something, if it doesn't hurt anybody, I think it's all right to have it if I can get it. But beyond all that, since someday we shall quietly fold our tents like the nomads and as quietly steal away, all of us, and no man knows the moment or the hour or the day, nor does it matter. Someday we shall all do it, and it should be looked forward to as a glorious adventure and a liberation of the spirit from the bondage of flesh, but we don't have to be morbid about it or sit around and think about it. We'll never arrive at that divine reaction to it while we contemplate death. It is only life we should contemplate.

"I am come that ye might have life and that ye might have it more abundantly." And as we contemplate the bigness of things and the wholeness of things and the nonresistance of this realization flows out, there is nothing can withstand it. Nothing. And we must have the comfort and the satisfaction and the gratification, and it will come as a proof. One person with whatever you may think God or the truth is, is not a majority but a totality. God is all there is, nothing else. And I do not split God's universe in two and say, "That's mortal; that's human; and that's divine." It is all divine, even though we are reacting to it in a human and in a limited way. We are just not permitting the greater influx, and we must learn to contemplate, to sense, to feel that greater self as Angela Morgan said in "Know Thyself:" "The living one who never tires/Fed by the deep eternal fires.../Angel and guardian at the gate/Master of Death and King of Fate."

Tomorrow night, my brother is to pay tribute to a great lifelong friend of ours, Angela Morgan, the greatest poetess of modern times and the greatest metaphysical poet or poetess who has ever lived. "That inner self that never tires/fed by the deep eternal fires."

We have to contemplate that rock from which we are hewn, that City of God which is eternal in the heavens. We have to contemplate that river, the source of which no man knows; that bread to eat, which if we eat we shall no longer hunger; that water to drink, deeper than the well of Abraham springing up within ourselves unto everlasting life.

Now this is a part of the liberation of our own bondage. Everyone wants things, and I think that's good. There's nothing wrong with possessing things, until the moment comes that they possess you. Then they are an obsession. Then it's time to burn them up and throw them away. The moment anything happens to us that is half as big as we are, we'd better throw it away lest we become submerged. The one and only thing that you and I ever brought into this world with us is that thing that we are. It's the only thing we'll ever take out. Naked we enter, and naked we shall exit, and no person shall go with us to show the way because already within us is "the way, the truth, and the life." We should contemplate until we know. Somebody might say, "How do you know?" When you know, you know, all right. There is no question about knowing. There is something so far beyond the intellect that it's just funny. There is a vision so extensive that it has no horizon. There is a life so eternal that it never enters time.

Now I happen to believe—you don't have to believe it, you don't have to believe anything I believe, you can say it's all nuts, and all I will say is let's open the nut and see if there's a kernel in it. Could be, you know. Who shall know? I believe when we entered this world, a unique individualization of the creative Spirit of the universe entered with us that was never presented before to the threshold of human experience and never will be again. It's that which we are. Socrates called it his Damon. I believe everybody is accompanied by such a presence. I believe it's what we feel, sometimes, almost here continuously, would know if we would let it. An inner guide— that doesn't seem strange to me. I'm not talking about myself. There is such a Self, but the denial of it closes the door against it. "Behold, I stand at the door and knock." The affirmation, the contemplation, relaxedly, without the interference or resistance and the violence of contention, breaks down the iron bars and the prison doors that liberate the Self and let the sun of heaven enter through those windows. Some eternal light shall set the captive free.

Now you and I all are that captive. There is no good and no evil in the larger sense. There cannot be. God is not good and evil. In the larger sense, there is no right and wrong as people interpret it. In the larger sense, to me and to you, there is what is and our reaction to it. And if our reaction to it is a contemplation of love, everything shall become lovely.

Somebody said to me that these people liked me. I said I loved them. I hope they like me. I love them, all of them. I would like to take them all in my lap and rock them to sleep, but that's not good for them. But I would like to, then I would like to wake them up and see them laugh. And then I would like to get down and make mud cakes with them, say, oh well, we are supposed to be so darned profound and philosophical. Let your whiskers grow and take your pants off, and go out and drown yourself then. What sense is there to it? You are never going to beat nature at her own game. If you've got a song, sing it. That's what the birds do. Have you found anything more beautiful, more ecstatic than the song of a bird in early morning or late in the evening? Have you seen a power greater than the wave, or felt an energy beyond the wind blowing in your face? The gates of heaven are open. We are on the threshold, but we refuse to enter. Now this is what I mean by contemplation.

There is a Presence in each one of us in my belief, a unique representation of the Divine wholeness of the universe—just you and just me. This isn't conceit; this is terrific. Just take the time to meet this guy. You'll be surprised; he's there all right. We didn't know it. We are so matter-of-fact and so filled with common sense that it oozes out of our psychic being like perspiration out of our physical bodies on a humid day. So what? I am not fooled by just common sense. In the first place, common sense is too uncommon to find it very often, but beyond this there is an uncommon super-sense, a Divine logic of deduction that knows no process, a spirit of freedom whose natural habitat is the stars and the firmament and the horizon and whose sun never sets. And it's real—and it's you.

Do not believe that you shall contemplate or even too deeply revere the goodness of another. You know nothing about it. Every heart knows its own joy and its own grief. It must bear it and share it. But know this: There is a transcendence in man; they call it the man of the heart, the angel of His presence, the Christ, the Buddha, the Illumined.

Don't think that you and I will ever have gotten into this because Moses or Jesus or Socrates or Isaiah were good men. They were good men. Did darned well in their day. They knew too much to lengthen their day here, and loosing the bondage of that which bound them to a gravitational force by a weight too heavy to carry into the ethers of that celestial region, they cut the bonds that bound them and disappeared. Everybody will go that way some day, but not while we deny it. And so let us see if we cannot—in seeking to emulate, to understand, to feel the Divine Presence once in a while—forget all our needs. What if we starve to death? It only takes forty days. Or choke to death. It doesn't take that long. However, I think it would be very uncomfortable. As far as choking to death, I would just love to have a drink of water.

But so what? What if everybody says you're all wet? Who cares? Who knows? What if we do not possess very much, what are you going to take with you? I've had too many funerals. No one takes a pants button with him. He came in alone;

he goes out alone; but he's never alone. And suppose we get to that place where we don't need anything for a while; things shall then be made up out of our not needing them. This is why the Talmud said, "God will doubly guide the already guided." This is why Jesus said, "To them that hath, much shall be given." This is why Emerson said that a betterment in circumstances follows this new influx. "With all thy getting, get understanding." It's the pearl of great price.

I believe in healing the sick. I believe in demonstrating money if we need it, automobiles if we need them, red shirts, green shirts, and blue shirts, and I bought a grey one and a red one and a blue one just before I came up here, and a brown one. I'll wear the brown one Thursday to celebrate. I think it's nice to celebrate Thursday, because it comes between Wednesday and Friday. There's some great and deep occult significance, because when I was a kid I think they ironed or mended on Thursday, and we had fish on Friday. I don't remember.

It's like the man you know who was going to a psychiatrist, and he went down to Palm Springs and to have a little fun. He found he was having so much fun he called the psychiatrist and said he arrived in Palm Springs, having a wonderful time, what's wrong with me? Isn't it amazing that 90 percent of our time is spent trying to find out what's wrong? Suppose then we take some time among the times of getting and giving and forgiving, all of which I believe in, when we don't need anything, when we don't want anything, but we would like to listen more deeply to a song, we would like to hear that poem, that rhythm in our own consciousness, we would like to, as Walt Whitman says, "I loaf and invite my soul," or as the Bible says, "Be still and know."

Don't ever doubt that what the great and the good and the wise and the exalted have told us is true. They are the only people who had wisdom. They are the only ones who knew. They are the ones to follow.

Let us take time to contemplate that which is beyond time and place, unlimited by space, uncaught in form by some Divine inward exaltation, which I want to talk about this week. And we shall look up, and we shall see a new heaven and a new Earth. Let us do it now.

Infinite and Eternal Spirit within us, which is the only God, the only Power, the only present all-transcendence, infinite in peace and beauty, limitless in love and Divine wisdom: We throw backward as a cloak every want and need, every fear and doubt, look up unto the face of Him who inhabits eternity and look back deep into our own soul and find Him enshrined there—Keeper of the Gate, the Carrier of the Light, the Eternal Good, infinite, indwelling peace within us. We enter into the stillness of that sanctuary where the Lord is in His Holy Temple and all the Earth is still before him. Infinite joy, uncaught ...

[Conclusion of talk not recorded.]

Grace

✣

WEDNESDAY, JULY 10, 1957

In this third evening's talk on our Practice of the Presence, Holmes discusses the concept of grace, which he calls the Divine Givingness. We are neither saved by grace nor have to earn it. Simply by the nature of our births, we are endowed with this Divine Givingness. It is universal and with us always. However, for us to truly know that we have this universal gift of grace, we must practice becoming consciously aware of the Divine Presence, which is always in us and with us.

I also knew Angela Morgan and knew of her admiration for Fenwicke [Holmes] and his wife, who was then living. She was a very brilliant woman and a very beautiful woman. I would like to read a poem she wrote to Fenwicke, inscribed to Dr. Fenwicke Holmes:

His intellect a sharpened blade,
A keen persistent flashing knife
Whetted upon the wheels of life,
His purpose fixed and unafraid
His speech is like an angels' choir
Yet humankind and human sweet
He glows as with celestial heat
The texture of immortal fire
And when his mind is loosed
And runs as lightning leaps along the walls
Oh when his spirit mounts and calls

We soar with him among the suns
Oh prophet soul, oh ardent seer
Oh teacher swept with heavenly rage
Embodiment of youth and age
In you are rounded as a sphere.

Isn't that a compliment to somebody? Moreover, it's no wonder he thinks she is the greatest woman poet who ever lived. He certainly would be very ungrateful if he didn't.

Now tonight I'm talking on the third part of five discussions on the Presence of God. Sometimes I almost hesitate to speak on the subject of the Presence of God because I do not happen to think we go anywhere to find God or that we get anywhere that is away from God or that we look at anything that is not God. I actually believe but do not pretend to understand the full significance and meaning of so profound and yet so delicate a proposition. Carmelita [Trowbridge] was talking this afternoon about the omnipresence, and I said to her afterward, "Carmelita, promise me that before you quit, you will disclose the meaning and nature of the only savior." So I just threw that at the lady and walked away. But she'll do it.

God is in all, over all, and through all, and God is all. What you and I call human is Divine. What you and I call ignorance is merely our lack of appreciation of wisdom. What we call evil is good misplaced. Hell is not hot. There are only two things wrong with it, in my estimation. I think it is a place, first of all, where there isn't any harmony. It might be right here. And I also think it's a place where there is no humor and no wit, where everybody is droll. Wouldn't that be hell? It would for me. Religion is not a long-faced, strange, and peculiar thing. It's the only natural, the most deeply natural, the most divinely transcendent, the most philosophically sound thing there is in the world, and anyone without some religion is a sick person.

Fenwicke was telling me last night something that I haven't figured out whether it was a doubtful compliment or he was thinking of somebody after he heard me. He said something reminded him of a man who went to hear a preacher. Someone said, "How did you like him?" And he said, "Well, he's terrific." He says,

"I never before heard anyone go down so deep, stay down so long, and come up so dry." Now wasn't that terrible? And here I come and read for him a tribute. Well, that's the way it is with life.

Now, I do not look upon the transcendence of God as a peculiar, unhuman or super normal thing. As Carmelita said today, this should be the standard of normalcy for all people. But Emerson said we confuse Jesus with virtue and the possibility of all men. When they said to Jesus, "You're wise, you're good, you are God," he said, "Why callest thou me good? There is none good save one, which is God." When they sought forcibly to make him their leader, physically as well as spiritually, politically as well as idealistically and religiously, he said, "Now you have confused me with what I've been talking about. It is expedient that I go away that the Spirit of Truth shall reveal to you in the innermost recesses of your own mind that which I have been talking about because I have come to reveal you to yourself."

And the Bhagavad Gita says that the self must raise the self by the self. There is hidden in the soul of man the immanence, the transcendence—both. That is, man is both God and man, because God as man in man is man, and there is nothing else you can make a man out of. Where would you go to get the material? You wouldn't.

James Russell Lowell said in his great poem The Vision of Sir Launfal:

Bubbles we earn with a whole soul's tasking,
'Tis heaven alone that is given away,
'Tis only God may be had for the asking.

Grace means the Divine Givingness, that which is given, but we are not saved by grace. Christians thought we were saved by grace. The Buddhists and the Hindus thought we were saved by works. We are not saved by either but only through both, in my estimation. Grace is that which is given; works is that which is earned. Grace is that which by the very nature of the Divine reality, man automatically is endowed with when he is born. He had nothing to do with it.

You know I never have a funeral without saying we believe in immortality. We believe immortality is the principle in nature. Therefore, it's universal. All people are immortal or no people are immortal. And I said always, now imagine saying this at a funeral. It takes, I almost used a word which means intestinal fortitude, so we'll just say it takes courage, but I don't think it takes courage. I always got a kick out of it. I don't mind somebody being shocked, even at a funeral, if he only gets shocked into some slight kind of a resurrection. I always say we are not good enough, we were not intelligent enough, we did not know enough to create our own souls. Who is so stupid to think we're smart enough to destroy it? And it's true.

Grace is that which is given. Emerson said we are beneficiaries of the divine fact. That's the way a philosopher would say it. He says it's a fact from which we benefit. Browning, because he was a poet said, "'Tis thou God that givest, 'tis I who receive." Jesus said, "Fear not little flock, for it is your Father's good pleasure to give you the kingdom."

There is so little that you and I have the intelligence to learn, there is so little that we have the power to create that unless we were beneficiaries of the Divine fact, we couldn't exist because we exist in existence, that which is self-existent, self-impelling, self-propelling, self-energizing. If you and I had to bring an energy with which to energize energy, where would we go to get it? Now that's just another way of saying if you have to breathe life into God, where is the breath coming from? You can't do it. It's impossible. We are beneficiaries. "'Tis heaven alone that is given away. 'Tis only God may be had for the asking." It says in the New Testament, if there had been any law under grace whereby this salvation might come, verily by grace it would have come. Now what it means is this: It says the law was weak but it was strong in that it led us to Christ, who redeemed us from the law. Now this has a reference to what Isaiah meant when he said, "He shall leave captivity captive." It says it is Christ who redeems us; Christ is the anointment. A Jew could accept Christ just as quick as a Gentile if he would no longer mumble in his beard about it. And a Christian could accept Mohammed if he had sense enough to know that there is more than one way to look at God.

We are so stupid and so dense and so thickheaded that even in the vast panorama of the mountains and the ocean here, where all we have to do is to turn around and observe the wonder of an endless horizon, that we put our hands over our eyes and look around and see nothing and how small an object shut out so large a vision. Wouldn't it be funny if we already had arrived where we think we're going, already knew what we're trying to find out and had what we wished to possess? We must have it through grace, which is the givingness of the creative Spirit, which, being all and total and undivided, cannot give without giving all and being omnipresent has to give all to everything where it is, because God does not appear in fragments.

If there had been any law under grace whereby this freedom must have come, verily by grace it would have come. It means this: Even God Almighty or the eternal Spirit or the universal law, call it what you will, a rose by any other name would smell as sweet. I don't care what you call it. Call it Brahma. I wrote something too; I wouldn't repeat my poetry after Fenwicke's. As a matter of fact, I'm getting him to heal some of my sick verses, and he is not doing it in one treatment. But I did say, "Oh, within all things around them/Brahma, light of life divine," a compliment to Brahma, that's all, "shatter all our days of dreaming/Absolve our being into thine/Let us then awake to Brahma...." Oh, I've forgotten it myself. It wasn't worth remembering. Well, it wound up by saying—now I'm very sensitive, if you're laughing with me, that's OK. If you're laughing at me, I'm going home—"Rob the mind of its illusions/Strip the ego naked bare/'til the waiting heart within us/Finds thy presence hidden there. Let us then awake to Brahma that we no more separate be, that the life that seemed divided be not lost but found in thee." 'Tisn't much poetry, but the idea came from reading *Sadhana: The Realization of Life* by Rabindranath Tagore, where he said that nirvana is not absorption but immersion, as an arrow is lost in its mark, "that the life that seemed divided be not lost but found in thee."

If there had been any law under grace whereby freedom must have been given, even God could not invent a mechanical spontaneity. You know there are some things that God can't do. In a Sunday school class—and it had to be in the country or nobody would have appreciated it—the Sunday school teacher said, "All things are possible to God." Some little kid stuck his hand up and said, "No, I know something." And she said, "What?" And he said, "God cannot make a three-year-old colt in five minutes." He can't. I would doubt very much if He could, because God is law. God cannot do anything that contradicts the nature of that self-existent and self-preserving, self-perpetuating thing that God is, and that is why in science, there is no energy known that will destroy itself. That's an evidence of the indestructible One, the same yesterday, today and forever.

Now even God could not have figured out how you and I could be free without creating us in freedom and letting us alone to discover ourselves. And the time, between that and this, is the history of the evolution of man and has broken, as Dr. Trowbridge said this afternoon, "many a barrier and will break many another one, and each time, it will be a new round in creative evolution."

Now we believe in the law of cause and effect, the Mosaic law, and it will be true no matter. It's true in the highest heaven and the lowest hell. Truth doesn't change. It hasn't got a location. But the ways of looking at Truth—"He shall leave captivity captive"—our vision is set toward freedom or bondage. Wherever our vision is set, we're doing the same thing that it is said that Moses did. God took him up in a high mountain. It is our intuition taking us up where we view the world as one vast plane and one boundless reach of sky. And God said, "Your feet shall possess the land your vision rests upon." "As thou seest, that thou be'est."

Emerson said, "We animate what we can, and we see only what we animate." Mrs. Eddy said mortal mind sees what it believes as truly as it believes what it sees. And Jesus, with a much greater simplicity, just said this: "It is done unto you as you believe." And that's that. Something does it, can do it, must do it. There's no question about Its doing it, but Its reaction to us is Its reaction to the way that we have reacted to life. "Believest thou that I am able to do this? Yea, Lord I believe." "It is done unto you as you believe."

Now we're talking tonight about the practice of this Presence. It's very important, but it is important that we shall think now and remember right through that we are practicing to be consciously aware of a Presence that we are now unconsciously aware of. We are striving to find a law of freedom, which we have already found and used as bondage. You will never reverse or change a law of God but only your position in it. "As thou seest, that thou be'est." "As thou beholdeth man, that, too, become thou must—God if thou seest God, dust if thou seest dust."

We are practicing the presence of God consciously. Merely because we didn't know that we were practicing it subconsciously and, in our ignorance, as Job said, "bringing upon us the very things that we fear." We are practicing liberation, not because we are not free, but because we are so free that we have bound ourselves and projected the reason through an unconscious sense of guilt and the thought of a delayed pleasure principle through anxiety psychologically into the universe, and saying, "Well, God is trying us out." And somebody said to me the other day, "Ernest, this came to you to teach you to prove something." I said, "Tell me no such hogwash in my time of need; at least I am still intelligent." I do not believe there is anything in the universe that's trying anybody because if it were, it would be trying itself. There is only one self. God doesn't tempt anybody or exasperate anybody. Our ignorance tries us 'til the day of enlightenment. There is no sin but a mistake and no punishment but a consequence. Ignorance is the only sin there is, and enlightenment is the only salvation.

And now at last, gropingly, seeing as through a glass darkly, impulsed by some desire beyond our own, as blind men long for light, we push forward by an irresistible urge, something lost behind the border, something missing. Go and find it. Something lost behind the border, something missing. Go ye there, it sings forevermore. It will never cease singing. The urge is irresistible and divine and human, pressing us forward and onward and upward. As Oliver Wendell Holmes said:

> *Still, as the spiral grew,*
> *He left the past year's dwelling for the new, ...*
> *Build thee more stately mansions, O my soul,*
> *As the swift seasons roll!*
> *Leave thy low-vaulted past!*
> *Let each new temple, nobler than the last,*
> *Shut thee from heaven with a dome more vast,*
> *Till thou at length art free,*
> *Leaving thine outgrown shell by life's unresting sea!*

And all psychological regression is an attempt to get back into the mother's womb where unconsciously the infant swims in his little pool of liquid. And let us say, he doesn't like it when he comes out into a cold world,

There is something startling about the concept of freedom. There is an irresistible urge attached to it, but there's something about it that's stark and naked and bare. And I can see why Emerson said that no one ever profanes nature. When the fruit is ripe, it will fall. And when you and I are ready for the smallest iota of truth, there it will be as though it had waited patiently at the doorway of our consciousness throughout an eternal year, because it wasn't in a hurry, and it didn't know it was waiting, and it wasn't fussed up, and it wasn't anxious. We have projected our anxiety in our imagination into It. But God is unconcerned about our troubles. Don't tell this to Billy Graham, I beg of you, this sweet, sad soul. Now, I shouldn't say that, it's none of my business. It's what Billy Graham believes, but my God, I would hate to have to believe it, besides I think it's spiritual arrogance, intellectual snootiness, and sheer stupidity. Outside of that, I think it's good. I think it's terrific that anybody can use mass hypnosis. I would love it if we were taking up collections, but I guess your collections came with the lunch. You didn't have to pay for it.

Now, we will say, how are we going to practice the presence of God? You can't stop it. Let's begin to practice it constructively, that's all. Act as though I am and I will be. Now in practicing the presence of God, there are certain things we have to do. We have to identify the immanence with the transcendence. Now I've been talking about the immanence, which is the indwelling God. That's all it means. Here's something: Let's see if you'll guess what it is. "Indubitably, benignity and commiseration shall pursue me all the day of my vitality, and I shall eternalize my habitation in the metropolis of nature." Is there anyone here who knows what that means? It is literally, "Surely goodness and mercy shall follow me all the days of my life, and I shall dwell in the house of the Lord forever."

The saying came from one of my girls, and l have been looking all over the place for her. I spoke at her place the other Sunday, and I'm still enraptured by the music of her choir. It gave me such a thrill and such a vibration, I didn't know if I was going to be able to speak. And if she hadn't gotten up and said a lot of foolish things before I did, to bring me down to Earth, I never could have started. I thought I was going up through the roof. Terrific. Pearl Wood.

Now we have to identify the immanence—God in here—with the transcendent God there. David Seabury has two things he always uses, which he calls identification and instrumentality. He's a good metaphysician, you know. Quimby died in the arms of the father of David Seabury. Did you know that? Well, he did. He had to die somewhere, so why not? After all, to every man his time and place, I presume. This is historic, however. He speaks of instrumentality and immanence. Now that means identification; he speaks of identification and instrumentality. That means identifying this self with that self and, in our estimation, without separating the two selves, causing this to reach further out to that or deeper into itself. So far as you and I are concerned, its expansion neither expands nor contracts that, but draws more of that into it, causing it to expand more and more into that.

She [Pearl Wood] was making a face at me. That's the little devil in here. Everybody says why don't you get rid of it, and I said it amuses me. Why should I lose the most pleasant companionship I have? This is literally true.

If there is an immanence in us, a God immanence and a God transcendence and they are of like essence, as Troward said, the only difference being in degree, then the more we identify ourselves with that, the more of that we draw into this. And that is why it is said, "The higher our universality, the broader our specialization." In other words, the more we see with that vision, the more our feet shall possess. Physically, this is automatic. All this and heaven, too, is what Jesus was talking about.

You see Jesus found no fault with multiplying loaves and fishes when they were hungry. He found the money in the fish's mouth when they needed it to pay tax. He brought the boat immediately to the shore, to the annihilation of time and space as we understood it. He raised Lazarus from the dead, stilled the wind and the wave. And as the last act, said to the thief, "Today shalt thou be with me in paradise."

Jesus found no fault with what you and I call material life because he knew it had no existence separate from God. And let me tell you, if you're looking for a heaven you think you are not now in, how do you think you'll recognize it when you see it? All that this transcendence you heard this afternoon and through this meeting is about is, "Awake thou that sleepest, and arise from the dead, and Christ shall give thee life." We are talking about seeing what we're looking at. Hearing really what we're listening to now, understanding what we are talking about. You think I understand what I'm talking about? Why, I have hardly the slightest idea of what it means. I wish I did but I know it's true—logically true, mathematically true. And by intuition, we hitch our wagon to a star.

God is all there is. How blithe the word. As somebody like one of us was talking, and some Englishman was there—he was quite impressive—and he said to the speaker, a gushing woman, "Now just what do you think your relationship to God is?" "Well," she said, "I'm in God and God is in me." He said, "Oh, I say, how cozy." I thought that was very nice. After all, it's at least comfortably close, and what is more precious than something we can get our arms around? Let's not get God too up or too over, lest we get him too out.

Humanity proclaims divinity; divinity announces humanity. And some kind of a sense or love in you shall break the barrier here and reveal, as the Zen Buddhists say, that which you at first think is real. Then you become abstract; you say it's an illusion. But by and by. ... Bacon said a little knowledge is dangerous. The mountain comes back and maybe even the itch, but the mountain you understand to be the eternal hills of the everlasting God, and you have found out how to scratch the itch, which is a long way along, much farther than anybody believes, because any disease when we get the proper diagnosis is just as well as eliminated from the experience of human race. That is easy enough after we have the diagnosis. Our diagnosis is that the immanence and the transcendence are equal, identical, and interchangeable. "It is not I but the Father who dwelleth in me, He doeth the works. The Father is greater than I, and yet as the Father hath life within Himself, so hath He given it to the son, to have life within himself that whatsoever things the son seeth the Father do, that doeth the son also that the Father may be glorified in the son." They are one and the same.

Then let us identify ourselves with the transcendence, and then let our minds become the instrumentality of that transcendence, and we shall discover everything is subject to that word at the level of our understanding and embodiment of it. It could not be otherwise. Now, if this is true, as was brought out this afternoon by both Carmelita and Elmer Gifford. If you didn't attend his lectures on the Bible, Elmer Gifford knows more about the Bible than anybody else in the Religious Science movement. This will offend some, but it doesn't shame me any because I know very little about it, and since Elmer knows so much, why should I have to know anything about it? It's always been my motto in my life—and it's very good in practical affairs, any businessman will know—never do anything you can get somebody else to do for you. And it's just as well because there'll be something left that you can do better. It will be a very great privilege to hear Elmer and Carmelita. You know it is.

Now, that which they both spoke about, this transcendence lighting this immanence up with this transcendence, interpreting the Universe as a spiritual system now, beloved now, right now, then we shall see the miracle of life take place. But when we do this, as we learned from both sources today and rightly, how shall we hope to bring about the greater transcendence if all we are scattering about are the images of yesterday, which, as Troward said, a neurotic thought pattern automatically repeats itself monotonously throughout life until it is changed. And that's true and throughout the ages. And we're all stupidly repeating what all the world has believed.

Rhonda Fleming, an actress whom you have seen and a friend of mine, said to me one day, "Ernest, you actually speak as though you didn't believe that there was any hell." "Well," I said, "Rhonda, you don't believe in hell." She says, "I don't know. My friends do. One of my friends said they couldn't understand how you could say you don't believe in hell. What shall I say to her?" I said, "Rhonda, just say this to her, Ernest says for me to tell you that when you find it, you'll find that this is the hell you're already in. And then if you'll get out of it/You won't be able to tell your friend to go into it because there won't be anywhere for him to go and nothing in you to project it." Psychologically sound, brothers and sisters in sweet truth. You can't beat it.

Emerson said the truth is past fact. It's like a cannonball. Believe me, we do not teach any sweet, simple philosophy that says "peace" when there isn't any peace. This is the toughest thing in the world to follow. Emerson said it's easy enough in your solitude to do this, "But the great man is he who in the midst of the crowd keeps with perfect simplicity, the sweetness of his solitude." It's no good unless it's right out there in the marketplace selling apples. It's no good unless it's milking a cow. I said the other day to [singer] Peggy Lee, "I bet you never milked a cow." We were comparing. We were both brought up in the country. And she said, "Where do you think I got these big hands?" But she said, "I'll tell you something. Always when I was milking, I kept milking until there was a rhythm to it. Then," she said, "when I got a little older and was working in a bakery, I kept shoving the loaves along until there was a rhythm." I said, "Is that what comes out in a song?" She said "Yes, the kind you hear at the milk pail." Isn't this interesting?

Well, if this isn't the kingdom of God so far as this thing is concerned, then what is it? How are we going to divide the indivisible or separate that which is a unit? You can't do it in the humble things, right here, and in our own hearts. So we want to practice the presence of God, and I don't think that this excludes wanting whatever we want or need or ought to have. But that's very unimportant because we'll get them anyway, if we do the other thing rightly. I believe in both. Troward said something in *The Law and The Word*, which is a wonderful book. It's written to show merely this: The sequence of the creative order starts with absolute intelligence. Intelligence moves upon itself by its own contemplation, and the contemplation becomes law and the law establishes effect. Or, as the Bible said, "And the Word became flesh and dwelt among us, and we beheld it." The invisible of God are made manifest by the visible. He shall count the things that are as though they were not. So Troward said, "Principle is not bound by precedent."

I'll put it this way in my words: Identify the immanence with the transcendence. Find in that upper sphere the prototype that will let down its own shadow from heaven, and you will not be without a rock in a weary land or a shelter in a time of storm. First things first; that's all. I believe in demonstration. I think it's perfectly legitimate.

I remember one time a very sweet and sincere and world-famed metaphysical teacher said to me when I was quite young, I was once like that, "I think, Ernest, you are a very nice boy," a little patronizing. She was about fifty or sixty at that time, and I was a sweet boy and didn't know what it was all about. She had discovered and knew all the answers and did know better than most people, much better than I. She said, "I don't like your teaching that you say you have a right to choose." I said, "No? Well probably it's wrong." I'm willing to admit, you know, I don't know from nothing. I said, "It seems to me — I saw in a Los Angeles paper the other day in the Saturday notices where you had advertised that you were going to speak on the subject 'Living a Life Without Choice.'" Of course, she swelled up but didn't burst open, and she said, "Yes." And I said, "So, did you choose to speak on the subject that you don't choose?" This was too fast for the old girl, and we talked about something else. I'm not going to try to answer it; you answer it.

David Fink said this morning… Isn't he a sweet guy? I liked him so well I gave him a whole set of my records and that cost me money. I don't get them for nothing. They are better than you think or you'd buy more of them. Now, this is a very important thing. The truth does not reduce us to some kind of an inane, speechless, shapeless form of pulp and dust, and it isn't arrogance. Remember, Jesus made the greatest claim on the Eternal of any man who ever lived, and the Eternal responded and said, "You're right, my son, I am everything you say and more." Jesus was the man who broke the barrier because he discovered the spiritual universe hid in what we call the physical. The immanence hid in what we call the transcendence. The son hid in the bosom of the Father, to whom the son is beloved. "Our Father, which art in heaven, hallowed be thy name. Thy Kingdom come. Thy will be done, on Earth as it is in heaven." In other words, Jesus said when the kingdom comes, what's already in here will be out there. It's already here anyway. The kingdom is within you. And he said that then, the without and the within shall be alike.

Now we want to practice, and Troward tells us—and rightly—that since we are dealing with an absoluteness, we shall enter into the consciousness of the absolute in such degree as we withdraw from the contemplation of the relative. Jesus merely said to judge not according to appearances, but judge righteously. "When you pray, go the Father who seeth in secret but shall reward thee openly." And, "Heaven and Earth shall pass away, but my words shall not until all be fulfilled."

How simple it is. Practice the presence of God, not as some far-off divine event, here and now, everywhere. See God in everything. Hear God in everything. Now this does not mean that we stop having fun. This is not a droll religion. It is in some ways kind of a robust and hilarious one, it seems to me. I don't want anything that's sad and sweet. And that sad and sweet smile that says look at me and dies, I don't like it. It's no good. That is not spirituality. That's spiritual anemia, and you'll find very little intellectual rebuttal and very little spiritual embodiment there. There's something pretty vital about a man that can stand before a tribunal of the most military nation up to that time the world had ever seen and say, "My friends, you are only kidding yourself. I alone have the power to take it up and lay it down."

I was telling them last night about the kid who won the race. The judge said, "You were mumbling to yourself. What did you say?" It was a foot race. He said, "I was praying, Lord, you lift them up and I'll put 'em down." Now that's what you call cooperation, and he won the race. His prayer was right. He didn't know it, but he was identifying the immanence with the transcendence. He put his hand in God's and said, "All right, Papa, let's win a race." Why he couldn't have helped but win it. What a lesson. When Jesus wanted to feed the multitude he took the kid, the man of wisdom, who had found out it could be done, and the child of innocence, who hadn't discovered that it could not be done, and when you get the two together for the first time, you will have a spiritual adult. God does not know how God functions or why, or God wouldn't be God. "Out of the mouths of babes and sucklings, thou has ordained praise." Oh, that we might become a child again and yet retain the wisdom of adult thought. That's the whole struggle of our existence.

All the weary, unconscious desire for regression is to get back there, even though we're unhealthy in the mind, to get there, to get to that place of security and safety where again the world is our oyster, and we have something to crack the shell with, and we know the pearl is there that shall be strong and threaded on some pleasurable experience where we go to bed in peace and sleep in joy and wake in a consciousness of good.

I believe that with all of our metaphysical abstractions and philosophic soarings and spiritual depths and the like, all of which I believe in, if I can be a kid again tonight, I'll be completely whole tomorrow morning. The child doesn't know that it can't be done, and there's a long ways from the little kid trudging along singing his song. By John Whittier: "Barefoot boy with cheek of tan/With thy turned-up pantaloons/And thy merry whistled tunes/With thy red lip, redder still/Kissed by strawberries on the hill,…/Outward sunshine, inward joy/Blessings on thee, barefoot boy!" But you know that's it. Now let me tell you every psychological regression, practically all insanity is the unconscious attempt of the human mind, split in its personality by the dualism of experience, to find refuge in a regression to childhood, where he had nothing to worry about. And yet Jesus said, "Fear not, little flock, it is your Father's good pleasure to give you the kingdom." And James Russell Lowell: "'Tis heaven alone that is given away, 'tis only God may be had for the asking."

And so we want to practice the presence of God in everything. God is food; God is digestion of food; God is the elimination of the food, and the best practitioner is the one who has identified his immanence with his transcendence. They are one, equal and identical, and the practitioner now knows that there is no difference between his prayer, contemplation, treatment, meditation or what you call it, and its own action. When you treat activity, see if you can't fix it so there's no difference between the word you speak and the activity it generates. They are the same thing. One is the substance, and the other is its shadow. They are equal, identical, and interchangeable.

And so Jesus had to take the little boy, whose innocence was his power—and Jesus had gone through that and now his wisdom was his strength—and he put the man of wisdom and the spontaneous child of innocence together and, looking up, he gave thanks and broke the bread and fed the multitude. See his example in the front of the tomb of Lazarus. "Father, I thank thee that thou hearest me." This is identification. And, "I know that thou dost always hear me." No quivering of the lips, no stammering of the tongue, no hesitation of the mind, no mumbling, and I know that's unification. Then Lazarus came forth. That's a command and believe me, if Lazarus hadn't got up and come out, Jesus would have crawled in with him. He would have had to. He would have defeated himself. That is not sacrilegious.

Jesus had great wit. One of his disciples's name means "the son of thunder," because one day some of the others got mad at somebody who disagreed with them and asked Jesus to call down fire from heaven—and how human—and burn them up. And it tickled Jesus. Is there any greater humor in the world than when the woman was taken in adultery, and in the only place we have any word of Jesus writing, he stooped over, and he wrote in the sand. I have heard he was writing out all of the sins of the people that were accusing her. That would just tickle me. And he looks up and he says "Boys, you know all the answers, take her out and stone her. God knows, it's coming to her." But he says, "Being gentlemen"—this is sarcasm, very subtle—"being scholars, being doctors and masters of the law, officiating in the temple of the Holy of Holies of the high and only one God of Israel. Of course, you'll have to take your pound of flesh but no drop of blood. Let he who is without sin among you first cast the stone." As hardboiled, as tough-minded, as callous as they were, that knocked them for a loop, because when he looked up they weren't there. He said, "Daughter, where are thine accusers, has no man accused you?" She said, "No one, Lord, nobody." He said, "Neither do I. Go and sin no more."

Now he balances justice. I don't know that he taught [inaudible] as justice, but he said whatever it is you've been doing, if you keep on doing it, probably the same result will be there. That's all. Go out and jump in the water and get wet. Stay on the shore. If you want to stay dry, keep in the sun. That's all. Jesus didn't condemn people, you know, and he said, "Judge not that ye be not judged. For with what judgment ye judge, ye shall be judged and with what measure ye mete, it shall be measured to you again." You are the measurer and the judge and the judgment and the meter-outer and the eater-upper. And you'll have to be the eater-upper and the eater-downer of your own poison until it becomes putrid and you spew it on the road of your experience, until at last you come clean. But he wasn't talking about morals and ethics before the face of the living God, to whom all things are pure. That's all he was talking about.

We have to identify. We have to become an instrumentality in simplicity. How can we expect, if we want a white house to be red, that it will get it red by keeping on painting it white? How can we expect, if thoughts are things, if we don't change the identification of our thought from yesterday that tomorrow will bring any new results? "Look unto me and be ye saved, all the ends of the Earth." I think it's as simple as this.

What an interesting experiment to turn boldly from everything that hurts, from the tears and the sadness, and identify again with that song which the universe always sings, that rhythm which is the heartbeat of the Eternal, the outpouring of that love which forevermore gives of itself, and that peace which passeth human comprehension.

Lover of our soul, giver of good, restorer of life within us, thou eternity living in our time, thou immensity flowing through our dimension, and thou wisdom flowing through our ignorance, "O love that will not let me go, I rest my weary soul in thee, I trace the rainbow through the rain, and feel the promise is not vain, that morn shall tearless be." Infinite and eternal peace, deep calls unto deep, and from the ocean of thy Infinity comes a form of loveliness, across the horizon of our perspective rising with the sun of Truth and filling the sky with light and radiating on the waves, Pilot of our boat, the joy....

[Conclusion of talk not recorded.]

Exaltation of the Presence

✣

THURSDAY, JULY 11, 1957

In this fourth evening's talk on our Practice of the Presence, Holmes discusses developing a sense of adoration of the Divine Presence within us. He makes a distinction between "worship," which implies a personal sense that is being directed toward something outside of ourselves, and "adoration," which relates to the exaltation of the Spirit within us. Along the way, Holmes shares some lines he wrote for his, at that time, future book with brother Fenwicke, The Voice Celestial.

I remember spending one time many years ago with Dr. Einstein. He was so simple that if we had all been children ten years old, we would have had just as good a time as fondly imagining that we were adults. He was one of the greatest intellects the world has ever known, who found a sweetness and a freshness in the simple, in the ordinary, and even in the what we call unimportant things of life. And who shall say what is important and what is unimportant in the cosmos. Emerson said there is no great and there is no small to the Soul that maketh all and from whence cometh all things, and it cometh everywhere.

If we were using the axioms of reason, we would say the Truth is one and indivisible and undivided. Therefore, It exists in Its entirety at any and every point within Its infinity, whose center is everywhere and whose circumference is nowhere. If we were doing it poetically, we would say, as Alfred Lord Tennyson, "Speak to Him, thou, for He hears, and Spirit with Spirit can meet/Closer is He than breathing and nearer than hands and feet." This is why Jesus replied, "Woman, believe me, the hour is coming when you will worship the Father neither on this mountain nor in Jerusalem" but in yourself. It is within you that you discover the kingdom of God.

Our whole theme, as you know, for the week has been on practicing the presence of God. I think one of the interesting things has been the many viewpoints that have been presented of the meaning of the Divine Presence and the practice and the realization of the Divine Presence. It is good that it is that way, because the Religious Science movement is a new form of catholicity. That means "of a universal religion," and it will, as time goes on and beyond my time, because art is long and time is fleeting. It will be, in my estimation, as I looked down the years yet unborn, in many ways. I believe it will take many forms that the Catholic Church has had. Now I'm not talking about its theology. I have no criticism of the Catholic theology, however, or any other theology or religion. I would say but there will be many different orders. We probably won't call them orders, but there will be many different avenues of expression in this great movement. I do not know what they will be, but it is inevitable that they shall be. Just as in the Catholic Church, they have orders that pray without ceasing. Maybe we have been doing that here in treatment. That seems quite fitting to me, to one who likes a life of contemplation and meditation. I think I'm a little too active to do it. I'd probably get the heebie-jeebies about the third hour and jump up and run out, but there are people with greater patience. They will listen longer and more deeply, and if they do, they will hear more.

I think there will be orders where certain phases of this philosophy will be taught, and those particular groups will be noted for teaching certain things with deep appreciation. Now that seems to me a new catholicity, which I think we're forming, exactly what we should expect to happen and what ought to happen because we have only two fundamental propositions from which we shall never depart. Oh, I don't say "we shall never." I never shall. I do not know what somebody else will do. I am not particularly concerned what the future ages will do. The only age I know is the one that belongs to me, here and now, and here and now is the only age there will ever be. The ever present here, the eternal now, and the only evidence you and I will ever have of it is our reaction to it. Somebody might say its reaction to us. That is eternal. Our reaction to it is our salvation, not from sin or future punishment, but our salvation from our own ignorance.

Ignorance and enlightenment stand as two great opposites in the evolution of the human race, and only enlightenment overcomes it—the enlightenment of science, the enlightenment of culture, the enlightenment of music and art, the enlightenment of those deep introspections of the mind where the soul is laid naked and bare to something that is primordial and original and the originator. I believe in this new catholicity that will be formed out of our movement. There will be such orders. They probably won't be called orders. I don't think there will be nuns and priests who do nothing but hide out, not that there would be anything wrong about it, because the power of the Catholic Church is not in its objective activity but in its subjective meditations, out of which flows the objectivity. You can't have hundreds of thousands of people all praying day and night without creating a subjective impulsion that comes out.

But I believe such a new catholicity is being formed, and will be, and that it will be very wonderful. You see there is latitude in our movement for all of these things: obeying the two laws of action and reaction, of presence and principle, of law and order, of incarnation and immanence, expansion, evolution, and transcendence. This seems to be the way the thing happens. I happen to believe that instead of intelligence being the result of evolution, evolution is the effect of intelligence. We can go with the whole evolutionary theory, which has been believed in by the most intelligent of the ages, if we will only realize that that which is evoluting was once involuted. Browning said, "A spark disturbs our clod," and he says we are "a god though in the germ."

Now as my contribution, which is one of many, no better and no worse but different, as it should be because each must present what he feels in the only imagery that reacts to the way he has felt. He must seek to interpret what he sees as he himself has seen it, as an experience and not merely as word imagery. Out of the heart, the mouth speaketh. We spoke on the abiding place of the Presence and concluded that It is everywhere. It's omnipresent. Therefore, It is within and the contemplation of It from the viewpoint that contemplation is a step beyond just meditation, where we enter into the essence of the thing.

In meditation, we think about something, which is good. In contemplation, something thinks in us, which is better. There is an essence to everything, to harmony, to beauty, and to the Spirit. Contemplation is where we just enter into the essence of something. Nothing has to happen, nothing is trying to be persuaded or coerced or shoved around. There are places where that belongs, but we are entering into a deeper listening. Theodore Reik, in the book he wrote, *Listening With the Third Ear*, said that every good counselor and analyst has to listen with a third ear, and that his work is as much intuition as anything else. And I suspect, I'd be willing to bet, that that is at least part of the method that David Fink follows. You couldn't get that thing that is in him that you feel unless this happens, I don't believe. I think it's impossible.

Now tonight I want to speak on the exaltation of the Presence. I would like to read something called *The Awakening*, which I wrote. It isn't very good writing, but it's a very wonderful thought—and I was smoking a cigar one night before I went to bed, which is a bad habit I have. Well, it's better to smoke here than hereafter. Well, it's just as well to smoke in both places. I don't know. I'll take a chance on the next one so long as I enjoy this one, not believing in any God that busts us over the head with a cosmic club. I suspect that our vices and our virtues are more nearly equalized than we realize. I really do, but I wouldn't want anybody to know it. So all at once, I felt like grabbing up a pencil and writing this. It has not been changed, you'll see that. It would have been well had it been.

Now this was written because I was writing some conversation between a man who was having a dream and a Presence that presents Itself to him. And it goes on and on forever, like the book, discussing all the problems of life. And finally the Presence reveals to the dreamer that the Presence is the dreamer. I believe that with my brother's help, it will be a modern Bhagavad Gita. I know that it will because I've read these things, but it will be a Bhagavad Gita for the present day. Probably take another year or two. I started when I went home from this camp last summer, worked on it ever since, and it will take one or two more years. It's just in a formative state, but this is a part of the awakening, for the Presence is telling the dreamer, then, by and by, the dreamer realizes that a transcendent something within him has been talking to him. And the denouement of the whole piece is he looks up and the Presence is no longer there but within himself. He feels a stirring, and I think it will be left that way, as though the idea evaporated in thin air, and let whoever reads it guess what it means. Symbolically, it means the new birth or the second birth. Jesus said you have to be born of a natural birth and then you are born of the Spirit. We have two accounts of creation in the Bible, which says God made man out of the dust of the Earth, and then it says He made him in His own image and likeness. Now these two accounts are there because they ought to be there. One is the man we know, the other is the man who is emerging. And so the Presence says:

> *He has hidden himself in the silence,*
> *He has covered himself with stillness.*
> *His presence is obscured in substance.*
> *He is buried within the deepness,*
> *yet He speaketh not from a distance,*
> *nor is He heard from very far away,*
> *for He is revealed in the substance.*
> *He speaks from a deep inner silence,*
> *His voice is echoed in the vastness,*
> *He is seen in what is most obscure.*
> *He is in the highest and the lowest.*
> *His glory shines in the early sun,*
> *His beauty is caught in the evening twilight.*
> *In the stillness of the night He is felt.*
> *He is one with wind, the rain and mist.*
> *His substance the essence of what's formed.*
> *He is the hidden cause of creation.*
> *The face that inhabits the eternal*
> *is seen in the countenance of His son,*
> *of both cause and effect,*

He is sequence, seen and unseen, the supporter.
Watch for Him then in what is nearest.
He is waiting in silence within you.
He is speaking in the words of your mouth,
but not as shadow without substance
or a dreamer of dreams in deep slumber,
illusion or mirage that is mirrored.
He is substance, not shade of mere seeming.
It is He who ordaineth creation,
the creation that responds to its Lord.

Don't you think that was an interesting thing? I wasn't conscious of its meaning until it was written, and I'm not yet. But as I study it and as I read it and as I think about it, I think it is something that comes to all of us. Most people are afraid, you know, to admit that there might be something that happens that they do not understand, for fear people will think they're strange. Well, we're all strange. We're just different kinds of strange people and don't ever look for or hope to find any human who is perfectly sane. Probably if he were, he wouldn't be here. He would be so unhappy with the rest of us. He would become so frustrated, he would just drop dead. Don't look for any human being who is completely perfect, objectively or subjectively. The Bible says, "Be ye therefore perfect, even as your Father in heaven who is within you is perfect." We are all on the road of an endless evolution. And the end of one round of evolution marks the beginning of another, and on and on, ad infinitum. "Ever as the spiral grew, he left the past year's dwelling for the new." But we are leaving the old house every moment of time. We never jump into the same river twice. We can never do two things alike twice. "Behold, I make all things new."

Now we have discussed that there is a transcendence in the universe and that he who inhabits eternity finds a dwelling place in our own heart and soul and mind. The highest God and the innermost God is one God. We happen to say it this way: God as man in man is man. Emerson happened to say it this way: "The simplest person who in his integrity worships God becomes God." Now we don't need to be afraid of this because there's nothing else we can become if God is all there is. And if God isn't all there is, then there isn't anything. And since something is, whether you call it God or a stick of wood or the truth or reality or what is, or as the Hindu said, "the nameless one," whatever that is, it is both cause and effect and the mediator.

Tonight I am speaking about the adoration of this Divine Presence, and I would like to treat it with a different connotation than our ordinary concept of worship. This is not any criticism of worship. Probably we do not worship enough, but to me adoration has a different feeling. Worship is to something for something and about something that is separate. It is about something that is away from the center of the worship. Too frequently, it has an inclination toward supplication, toward prostration, which we mistake for meekness and humility. Too often its meaning to us is to appease the wrath or to incite the beneficent response of a power greater than we are. Now I happen to believe that there is a power greater than we are, and I don't believe anything else, but I also happen to believe that the power greater than we are is the power that we are. "Who hath seen me hath seen the Father. Believe that I am in the Father or the Father in me or else believe me for the very works sake." Philip saith unto him, "Lord, shew us the Father and it sufficeth us." Jesus saith unto him, "Have I been so long time with you and yet hast thou not known me, Philip? He that hath seen me hath seen the Father."

Emerson said that we have confused Jesus with virtue and the possibility of all men. I am thinking of adoration, not necessarily from the standpoint of worship so much as it is from the standpoint of recognition of conscious unification, until even the self-conscious part of the unification disappears into the unification, which no longer need be conscious of itself, but only needs to be itself. As Omar Khayyam said, he often did frequent the tents of the wise, but evermore he came out ignorant as in he went because they did not know the answer. His conclusion was that he wasn't going to find it from them. He didn't know it himself. He knew of earthly pleasures. He would get a girl, a jug of wine, a loaf of bread, and a song to sing, and go off in the wilderness. "Oh Wilderness were Paradise enow!" He took the best mental and physical equivalent he had for the highest good he had sought and did not find in the tents of the wise. And so he said, "A jug of wine, a loaf of bread, and thou/Beside me singing in the Wilderness/Oh Wilderness were Paradise enow!" Maybe he was right.

Thomas Gray's *Elegy Written in a Country Churchyard* is called the most perfect and beautiful poem ever written, but it's rather a doleful thing. It starts out that way: "The curfew tolls the knell of parting day/The lowing herd wind slowly o'er the lea/The plowman homeward plods his weary way/And leaves the world to darkness and to me." This is where he takes off, and before he gets through, it's pretty tough but beautiful. And in *The Rubaiyat of Omar Khayyam,* the same thing. Now Jesus came singing a song. He said, I know where I came from, I know how I got here, I know why, I know what I'm doing and how to do it, and I know where I'm going and how to get there. And he said to the thief, today you'll be there, too, because you heard something.

Adoration, as I see it, is the exaltation of the Spirit within us. The Hindus called it Atman, somebody else called it Apollo, somebody else called it Ain Soph, the Christians called it Christ. It all means the same thing. The son begotten of the only God and the only son, which is the universal prototype of sonship. We are all members of that one body, and Eckhart said that God never had but one son, but the eternal is forever begetting his only begotten, and he is begetting him in me now.

I believe adoration is the exaltation of that Divine Presence which is in, around, and through immanence, over and above transcendence, but that the transcendence and the immanence are the same thing. The only difference is in the degree. Therefore, I believe that we are all evolving, gradually, slowly, so slowly toward that light that lighteth every man's path to the City of God. We should exalt this Divine Presence, I think. I do not think it asks that we worship it. Now our worship is good because it's our approach to the exaltation. Our song is that, our prayer is that, and that is good. But as these things tend gradually to unite into one great recognition, what is it that we are recognizing and where is the true, the one, and the only savior? We forget, sometimes, that merely 75 percent of the world are non-Christians. Now remember, they are not non-religious. They are not non-conscious or unconscious of the Divine Presence. Their approach is different.

Therefore, we must put together the many ideas and their meanings and discover what Lowell called "that thread of the all-sustaining beauty which runs through all and dost all unite." The common denominator of the universal archetype and prototype of sonship individualized in each one of us, universalized in itself, which is both God and man, in my estimation, at the same time. I happen to believe that this Presence accompanies us through life and that we feel it. And I am not at all sure—now this is just between us, and I don't want you to tell anybody I said this, not until after this talk, surely—I am not sure but the God to which or whom we often pray is our objective and subjective response, to which we feel, which is the transcendent immanence, but is not what we think it is. Would that seem strange? It doesn't seem strange to me.

There is a spirit in man, and the inspiration of the Almighty giveth him understanding. Before Abraham was, I am. Destroy this body and that which I am will raise up another like unto it. If we called it Atman, but we don't, we call it Christ. There is nothing wrong in our remaining true to the tradition of our word if we do not confuse it with a lesser meaning. However, in my mind, I like to think of it as that which I really am hidden behind this veil of flesh, hidden behind this confusion of mind and the psychic turmoil that is our inheritance of the ages, whether you call it the mortal mind or the carnal mind or the collective unconscious or race suggestion or what everybody has believed, I don't care. There seems to be that which would obstruct what already is hidden in the silence within us, and I believe it is the true self.

It is written that there is no mediator between God and man but Christ, Christ in you, the hope of glory, be transformed by the renewing of your mind, by the putting off of the old man and the putting on the new man, which is Christ. And the Gita says the self must raise the self by the self. Jesus said you cannot serve God and mammon. The Gita says, who would enter bliss must first have done away with the pairs of opposites. They are all contending for a fundamental and primal unity that includes all things and excludes none. That is the very essence of our philosophy. It is the very essence of every great philosophy the world has ever had that has this spiritual connotation.

It seems to be the only explanation for those unconscious urgings, those silent strivings, those visions that too often are confused with our psychic experiences and reactions and inner conflicts, but still speak and persist and will not take no for an answer. There is something behind evolution that evolution did not produce or there would be no impulsion to advance. You cannot get out of life what isn't in it. It is impossible.

I believe then that the only true savior is the self, and whether it is coming to psychological self-awareness through counseling or spiritual self-awareness through recognition, I do not care two bits. Truth is true, wherever you find it, and the biggest life is the one that includes the most and sees in everything that which is all things, but caught in nothing, and hears that song the spheres sing and catches the glory of some beauty that, even to the end of its age and its world, blends the last flickering light of today's tinted skies with the first blush of tomorrow morning's rising sun.

What terrific beauty we must be overlooking, what harmony we fail to listen to, because our vision is set on discord. I believe in the adoration of this Divine Presence, in the exaltation of this incarnation, in the songs that we sing to it, the communion we have with it, and I do not personally believe—and I hope it doesn't shock you, and it won't if you think it over—can the self get away from itself? Can a man run away from his own shadow?

Emerson said, "Traveling is a fool's paradise. Our first journeys discover to us the indifference of places. At home I dream that at Naples, at Rome, I can be intoxicated with beauty, and lose my sadness. I pack my trunk, embrace my friends, embark on the sea, and at last wake up in Naples, and there beside me is the stern fact, the sad self, unrelenting, identical, that I fled from. I seek the Vatican, and the palaces. I affect to be intoxicated with sights and suggestions, but I am not intoxicated. My giant goes with me wherever I go."

He is merely saying, everywhere I went, I took myself. So he came home and said, "I tread on the pride of Greece and Rome . . . for what are they all, in their high conceit, when man in the bush with God may meet?" It's the burning bush. At the center of everything there is fire, celestial fire, caught from heaven.

Every bush would blaze if we unified with that central spark that is the cause of all evolution, all advancement, everything we know, everything we shall ever attain. I cannot divorce my concept of the real savior from the Christ, the Atman, the Ain Soph, but these are names that do not mean to me so much as to say I cannot divorce my idea of what a savior ought to be—and I believe must be and I am certain is—with some hidden thing in myself. This is not blasphemy. There is no mediator between God and man but Christ, the Christ within you. If you had been a Hindu, you would have said Atman. There is no mediator between the absolute and the relative but yourself. No man hath seen God. Only the son has revealed the Father, and we are that son.

The adoration of this transcendence in us is automatically the adoration of God. The adoration and the recognition of this Divine incarnation is the adoption and the recognition of God, of the Eternal, the adoration and the recognition in the only place that it can take place—in you and in me. I often say to myself, "Now this is interesting. Don't think I have a split personality, I think I have a multiple personality and that's better." I wouldn't settle for just two when there seem to be so many. I thought the other day maybe I had better go to David and see just what's wrong and I thought, well, maybe I'd find out and I would no longer be happy. Wouldn't that be terrible? Where ignorance is bliss, 'tis folly to be wise.

I thought after I ate a little dinner tonight I'd go up and sort of relax, and I found myself saying out loud, as I changed my clothes from that much talked about brown shirt, it didn't turn out so good. I don't think it was as good looking as the gray one myself. It was a great disappointment to me after I took the pins out and put it on. And I almost took it off and spit on it, but I didn't. That wouldn't be nice; that's an infantile reaction. I have never yet been so fortunate as to have to met one single adult. I am reminded of a story of a little girl who had been naughty. Her mother shut her in the closet. It was too still; the mother was afraid she must be suffocating. She looked in and the little girl was sitting there surrounded by hats and shoes and coats and dresses, scowling. And her mother asked, "Dorothy what are you doing?" The little girl said, "I spit on your hat, and I spit on your skirt, and I spit on your coat. And I am sitting here waiting for more spit."

Now, you know, I'll bet anything when that child grew up, she became a great artist or a great executive. She had sense enough to use such ammunition as she had against the object of her animosity. Psychologically, it was very unsound. Humanly, I wouldn't want a little girl to do anything else because she would become an uninteresting woman when she grew up. I would only wish that energy to be channeled into a creativity that at least was more sanitary.

Now, what's wrong about adoring the only thing that you know knows anything, as little as it knows? Is there anything wrong about it? What's wrong in blaspheming the only thing that you know that the Almighty ever made that at least believes maybe there is an Almighty? I am not sure that our divinity demands that we humiliate our humanity. I put a sign up, "STOP AND LOOK AND LISTEN." I do not think that the Eternal has intended men to be a doormat. It's a false humility that Wilhelm Reich calls a delayed pleasure principle through anxiety, and I think he's right. Well, I wish David were here. He'd explain what this means. I don't know, but it means a mouthful, to say the least.

Did you ever stop to think that if there is a universe, you happen to be the only person you happen to know that you know, knows there is a universe. And if whatever that thing in you that knows anything were not there, there would be nothing there to know anything. There might still be something to be known, but you could never know it. What is more high, what is more holy, what could be more exalted than that self that Jesus proclaimed and every great and good soul has. There is no egotism in this. "Naught is the squire when the king is nigh, withdraws the star when dawns the sun's brave light." I found myself saying this out loud as I shuffled into these clothes that look better but don't feel as comfortable, but not bad. Before ever the world was formed, thou art my habitation. And when this physical universe shall finally be rolled up like a scroll in our imagination, this material universe I mean, and laid on the shelf of obscurity and numbered with the things that were once thought to be, you will be my habitation. That's covering a lot of territory. It was all un-volitional, I said to myself. What am I saying? When people talk to themselves, it's dangerous, but David tells me it's only when they answer themselves that you have to be pretty careful. And when they talk to themselves and answer themselves, they had better be careful. But I went on and on as I was talking out loud. There was nobody there, so nobody knew how screwy I was, and I got a great kick out of it. I said, "I'm talking with God."

Before ever the world was formed, before Abraham was, I am. And when our belief in this material universe, which has no existence—now modern science tells us as a thing in itself—when this material universe shall finally be rolled up like a scroll and numbered with the things that were once thought to be, thou art still my habitation. And I like it. It's strong; it's vital; it's vibrant with life; there is power in it. Before ever the world was formed, before my world was formed, and when I shall leave this world, that which I am shall go as one who casts his worn-out robes away, and saying, "These will I wear today, so putteth by the spirit lightly its garb of flesh and passeth to inherit a residence afresh."

Before I was born, after they shall have laid away that which remains or cremated it, which I believe in, I shall still be. "The sun across its course may go, the ancient river still may flow, I am and still I am."

Now this transcendence, which we adore and worship, if we will, in the beauty of holiness, this transcendence is the immanence within us and when it speaks, it's God. But it doesn't always speak a clear language. It does—we do not always hear clearly because through this psychic confusion of the ages too often the voice must echo out to the intellect and even then be interpreted only, unfortunately, in the terms of our unconscious emotional biases. It's very difficult to get a complete clearance because God is not the author of confusion but of peace. "Peace I leave with you, my peace I give unto you, not as the world giveth, give I unto you. Let not your heart be troubled neither let it be afraid. Ye believe in God, believe also in me. In my Father's house there are many mansions, if it were not so I should have told you."

I wrote something about that: "In thee, oh Christ, thou blessed one/I see both Father and the son/In thee there is one life alone/Eternal sower, seed and sown. In thee I see the promise given/Hope of Earth and crown of heaven. Hope undiminished, vision brigh/Beyond all darkness and the night/I lift myself about the clouds/My soul uncaught by bier or shroud/Shall go beyond Earth's fairest star/To where thy many mansions are." And I think it's pretty good. It's the same thing.

But that's the indwelling presence, the object of our adoration. There was a system among the ancients that taught their students to fold their hands over their breasts and say, "Wonderful, wonderful, wonderful me," and to repeat, "I am that which thou art, thou art that which I am." It's just another way of saying the Father and I are one, yet the Father is greater than I. The eternal presence is the Divine Immanence, the object of our adoration. I can find no true savior outside that incarnation, and since that incarnation must be it in me, as me, that which I really am is my savior. And there is no mediator between that absolute and this relative, between that unconditioned and this limitless, between that eternal beauty and our feeble attempts to paint the picture.

Kipling said:

When Earth's last picture is painted and the tubes are twisted and dried,
When the oldest colours have faded, and the youngest critic has died,
We shall rest, and faith, we shall need it—lie down for an aeon or two,
Till the Master of All Good Workmen Shall put us to work anew. ...

They shall find real saints to draw from—Magdalene, Peter, and Paul;
They shall work for an age at a sitting and never be tired at all!

And only the Master shall praise us, and only the Master shall blame;
And no one will work for the money, and no one will work for the fame,
But each for the joy of the working, and each, in his separate star,
Shall draw the Thing as he sees It for the God of Things as They are!

That's your savior. And Lucy Larcom said:

Into your heavenly loneliness, ye welcome me, O solemn peaks!
And me in every guest you bless who reverently your mystery seeks.
And up the radiant peopled way that opens into worlds unknown,
It will be life's delight to say, "Heaven is not heaven for me alone."

*Rich by my brethren's poverty! Such wealth were hideous,
I am blest only in what they share with me, in what I share with all the rest.*

Here is the Christ speaking and saying what I've been trying to tell you every morning. You've got to get a clearance of forgivingness before you can forgive, because all you can do is to project yourself. You've got to get a clearance of guilt before you can overlook guilt, which is mostly a projection of yourself. You've got to love before you know love. Love only knows and comprehends love. And you've got to see into humanity to discover divinity. He is hid in that which is most obscure. The face that inhabits eternity is in your countenance.

There is no use seeking God afar off, nor in a distant time, or another place, or another country, or even another book. As I have said in that part of our book on the transcendence and in the meditation, "Be still and know that I am" is God, and that which I as an individual am still is that which the universe is in me. "Not I, but the Father who dwelleth within me." Let's stop looking for that savior where he is not.

This is one of the great secrets that Jesus knew. And when they sought to make his physical and mental and even his spiritual being reveal their savior, he said, "No. I shall go away and the spirit of truth will awaken within you and give you the answer and the meaning to the words I have spoken." "I am come that you might have life and that ye might have it more abundantly."

And Tennyson said, in the opening of the greatest poems ever written, "In Memoriam:"

*Strong Son of God, immortal Love,
    Whom we, that have not seen thy face,
    By faith, and faith alone, embrace,
Believing where we cannot prove; ...*

*Thou madest man, he knows not why,
    He thinks he was not made to die;
And thou hast made him: thou art just. ...*

Our little systems have their day;
> *They have their day and cease to be:*
> *They are but broken lights of thee,*

And thou, O Lord, art more than they. …

O living will that shalt endure
> *When all that seems shall suffer shock,*
> *Rise in the spiritual rock,*

Flow thro' our deeds and make them pure.

You will never find Him except there. Don't look for Him anywhere else. He is everywhere. He is hid in the silence of your own soul. Adore Him. He speaks in your own words; let it be as clear as possible. He reveals Himself in the innermost recesses of your thoughts in the long night watches, the evening sunset, the first faint blush of rosy dawn, and in the song of the nightingale, the wisdom of the wise, and the innocence of a child, the mother crooning over her babe, and the babe suckling from the fountain of life which nature has provided, that bread to eat and that water to drink, which is the bread of life and the wine of life and the eucharist and the body and the blood, the substance that flows through Emmanuel's veins, and Emmanuel is God with us. And the highest God and the innermost God is one God. He is in the silence. He is in the obscure, in the evidence, and in everything. There is a transcendence. And the ground upon which we tread is holy, but more holy yet is the human being who alone proclaims the hope, the possibility, the probability, and, finally, the certainty of that divinity that shapes our ends, rough hew them though we will.

Listen to the silence of your own soul, and He will speak. Adore Him, and He will embrace you. Love Him, and you will be loved.

Religious Science

FRIDAY, JULY 12, 1957

In this final evening's talk for Asilomar 1957, Holmes shares some thoughts on the Religious Science movement. He also offers his call for each of the attendees to carry home and to live throughout the year the love and friendship they have shared at the conference, to live from that mystical sense of the living Christ. Note that the Science of Mind Archives does have in its collection an audio recording of this presentation. The first part of this lecture is unavailable in any format.

... Individual expression. Now I've told you over and over that there is no such thing as reincarnation, and Donald Curtis, whom I ought to know very well, he spends a great deal of time in our home, the first thing he says is there is. Now, you see I'm not mad at him and he isn't sore at me, because if there is, I suppose we'll know it in due time, and if there isn't, we won't have to know it. It's like I always say about passing on: If you keep on living, you keep on living. And if you don't, you won't know anything about it anyway. Of course, we think we do.

Now, I do not know of any spiritual movement in the history of the world—modern, medieval, or ancient—that has ever accomplished through an organization a degree of freedom and individualization within an organized body as the body of Religious Science has in the last thirty years. Now this is a lot to say because during this process, there was considerable disagreement. And some come in, and some go out, and some wonder why some came in. And some went out, and I never ask myself why they come or why they went because it's none of my business. I know this, that we have the only spiritually free—to the individual—organization, organized enough to keep it from falling apart at the seams—and it's split several times at the seams—that the world has ever known. It gives promise for the future.

I am not a prophet, else I would wear whiskers. I think whiskers are unsanitary and they itch my face, but I wouldn't be surprised that we might be laying a cosmic egg. It looks that way. It would be just a question of whether we sat on it long enough to hatch out a lot of chickens. Time will prove that. And beyond my time, I wouldn't be surprised if we do. It will be the most remarkable thing in the evolution of spiritual institutions if we do because it was never done before.

Most religions are based on revelation. I suspect revelation because it doesn't ever seem to be twice alike. There is no God who will tell us one thing one day and another thing the next. And one of the first things I discovered in my determination to analyze for the purpose of synthesizing the great religious spiritual aspirations of the ages, of many years ago—and have done it continuously because I am familiar with the great religions of the world and what they stood for—one of my first endeavors was to set down all the revelations of the ages, giving as much authority and validity to one as to another, and letting each speak for itself to see what the facts would prove. And when I found that it was very evident that the contradictions were too great to sustain a unitary cause back of them, I rubbed that out. Then when it came again, it was I who rubbed that out. You know, before I got it all done, the pencil was dull and the eraser worn out. It's interesting.

What I mean was, t'aint what it seems to be now. That's all. There is no God who will tell Jeremiah, "Now, Jerry, you do this," and then tell Isaiah, "Now, Izzy, you do that," which is contradictory to what he told Jerry. Now we may be that way, but let us thank the God that is that the God that's believed in isn't. I always cling to this.

But through all of these, there is a thread of the all-sustaining beauty, and you'll find it in every religion. God is. God is one. Good is the fundamental impulsion of the universe; love is its motivation; law is its propulsion or action.

There is action and reaction. Man does exist in the midst of this Divine dream of celestial being and in some way is hooked up to it and hooked in with it and tied into it. And he did not make it, and he cannot change one particle of it any more than he can create or dissolve a sidereal planetary system. Another thing is certain: Man is in a state of evolution from the lowest form of intelligence to the highest. We see the intelligence in the minerals. We know that it's there. We see the simple intelligence in the animal. We know that it's there. We see the personal intelligence in man. We know that it's there, I mean that it is there. Of course, it's there and at any time might be located. There isn't any question about this. It's inevitable. And beyond man as he ordinarily thinks, beyond personal intelligence, there is another degree of intelligence that he manifests, which is called cosmic. You've read Bucke's book on *Cosmic Consciousness*. If you haven't, get it out of the library and read it. It's one of the few and best authorities on the subject, and it is good.

Here are four distinct levels of intelligence that we know exist here and now. What right would we have to suppose that there is not an ascending degree of intelligence? The Bible says we are surrounded by principalities and powers. Many of the ancients believed and people do, some today believe in planetary gods and things. It's what the Bible means by principalities and powers anyway. Evolution must be an eternal process. There must be beings beyond us, as we are beyond this tadpole, and on and on, ad infinitum, world without end, creation without end, evolution endless, always more and never less, itself that runs through the great spiritual concepts of the ages, and I happen to believe in it.

Now we've put all of these things together. I've spent a lifetime doing it. It's a tremendous job but an interesting one. It's been done as much to satisfy my curiosity, because I had never thought of a church when I began. It's a matter of fact that when friends of mine first wanted me to organize the movement, I ran and hid for six months, more scared than Adam was of God when God came down in the cool of the evening, because it had been hot up in heaven I presume, according to the story. I don't know. At any rate, He came down to talk over the state of the crops and how the animals were getting along and whether there was plenty of water for the tree of life running through the Garden of Eden that watered the tree of the knowledge of good and evil, from which Adam and Eve were told not to eat, and as you know, it was Eve's curiosity that etc. That was terrible, wasn't it? Of course, this is a fable. I wrote one just as good, and I didn't like it well enough. And I gave it to Bill [Hornaday], and he wrote it better enough. Now we're not sure that either one of us had done it good enough, and I gave it to my brother, and he thinks he can improve on both of us. Whether there's any place for that to stop, who knows? But it is a fable that's going in this thing that I'm writing of how we got this way. Where did ignorance, superstition, fear, and doubt, and what the world calls evil come from? Someday it will be done, if we live long enough. If we don't, it won't. I think that's quite certain. After all, there are some things that seem more certain than we thought.

Now, we must not be coerced by the thought that somebody's bible is infallible, whether it's the Jews' or the Gentiles', or the Koran or the Avesta or the Upanishads or the Vedas or the Bhagavad Gita or the Book of Mormon. They all claim to be infallible. Some believe that you must go all in to get saved; others, a little sprinkling or dry cleaning at the top will be just as effectual. Perhaps it's just as good to turn a hose on them. Elaine St. John's son was in the [military] service when he was very young and lived with us for two or three months. The first wedding I had, he was about nine. He turned the hose on the bride and bridegroom as they went out into the yard. I could have killed him and would have if it hadn't have been against the law to murder. I'm not sure it's always a good law. At least, it's inconvenient.

No, there are no prophets other than the wise in our language, but the otherwise also prophet, prophesize. Shakespeare said, "Thereby hangs a tale," and in the realm of revelation, a sad one but one that was quite inevitable. As Carmelita said, we have to step into the abstract with balance; that's what she meant. The Bible says don't listen to all the spirits. They don't always tell the truth. After my mother passed on—she was an old New Englander who lived to be ninety-eight and was completely mentally alert to the last minute—somebody said, "I went to a séance the other night, and your mother was there." And I said, "That's fine. How was she?" They said she seemed quite confused. I said, "You have the wrong woman, you better go back. There must be another Anna Columbia Holmes who answered. That wasn't the one that I knew. She didn't get that way. She had too much sense and nothing has happened to her."

So we have quite a little task, and I would never dare to take on the assumption of it. I can get revelations just as fast as a horse can run. I know what to do to get them. I know how to get them. Now there are revelations that are real and bonafide and genuine. Most of them aren't, because intuition is never about doing things, it's only about being, because it's the impartation of the essence of the nature of the thing. And as it impinges upon the mind of man, it has to interpret itself through his own emotional reaction and his own background. Therefore, we have to study the revelations. We have to be sure they are right.

You see, Religious Science is practical idealism and transcendental realism, and in no way does this lessen the inspiration, the illumination, or the beneficence of its action and reaction. It is, in my estimation, the greatest system of spiritual thought the world has ever known. I know that it is because I have spent a lifetime putting it together. Now, I'd laugh myself to death if I said that I made it up. I can write automatically better than the Book of Revelation. That's saying a mouthful, isn't it? But it's true. That is an automatic writing, like people get them today. You cannot depend on these kind of things—what you feel, what comes though. Anybody can do this if they tried to, if they're a little bit psychic. It's not very difficult. Most people have enough psychic capacity to do it. All great writing is done this way; all great music is done this way; most great art is done this way. There is nothing wrong with it. We just have to be sure that the form comes out.

Now we have something to go by, and I think that we have had the finest spirit, cooperation, a feeling of joy, love, friendship, and agreement—and I don't mean that everybody has to agree with everybody. I wouldn't like that. I don't want everybody to agree with me. I know everyone hasn't evolved to that place yet. I can't expect it, so I'm not disappointed. Of course, I might be surprised, but it doesn't really hurt my feelings. But we have to agree that we are a free people in search of a greater freedom, without license or chaos, than the world has ever known, because that's the way of evolution. And in order to do it, we have to combine the two great realities of life, which is law and order and love, which is the divine principle and a Divine Presence, until one is a continual companion of the other, the eternal servant, until finally our lives become harmonious, happier, and whole.

Now this transcendence we have talked about so much, to some it seems a little confusing, only because it is a little confusing to those of us who have been talking about it. If we knew it better, it wouldn't confuse anyone. You can always impart what is completely clear in your own mind, but where it's a little bit woozy and fuzzy, the wooze and the fuzz will show everywhere you spread it. But let's not be concerned about that. A peach is still good even though it has fuzz on it, unless it gets rotten. Then we throw it away. I'm not afraid of a little fuzz or a little wooze, because nothing great is ever accomplished in a straight line, over and over again, a little here and a little there, trial and error, painstaking, patience, until finally he comes whose right it is, if we wait, if we're patient. If we can get the vision that we are giving birth to some tremendous cosmic event, so far as this world is concerned, have a sense of destiny about it, have a feeling as we go back to our individual homes that continues what we have been doing here, carries it off throughout the year, it will work as a psychic entity and put a background to this movement, which will be terrific, as a movement that heals, that loves, that hurts no one and hates no one; a religion that has infinite tolerance but still knows there is balance and justice in the universe; a religion that knows there is justice without judgment, free at last from the fear and the ignorance and the superstition and the stupidities of the ages that have caused the wars of the world and most of the unhappiness in the world, most of that sense of being alone and that feeling of guilt that so many, many people have, most people, everyone in fact has, born with that, as though we were born sick and had to be healed after we got here into the race consciousness.

And I certainly appreciate your wonderful attention to the talks I have given and everyone else has, the enthusiasm, the love, the friendship you have shown for all of us and all of the teachers who have come here, labored for us. Irma and Dick and the ushers and people at the book table, people who have charge of the building and the dining room, they've all been so very friendly, and we have had such a lot of fun. I feel as though I just got here. It doesn't seem possible. I wish it might go on for another week and that we could have a whole new set of speakers and I could listen to them, because I'm getting tired of listening to us. I don't think we've got spiritual indigestion at all. The spirit doesn't get indigestion. And if there are any ideas that you think you haven't assimilated, forget them. Maybe they're wrong anyway. I mean, we have no final authority. I never pretended to be the final authority. I have never advanced one single authority, one single alleged revelation, one single personal opinion about our movement, since it was inaugurated thirty years ago last February, and never shall because I don't believe in it. Here is the best that the world has to offer. It ought to be good enough for any organization to accept. It ought to be a pretty good place to shove off from to whatever is going to happen next. I feel that way.

I read continuously. Right now, I am reading *The Synthesis of Yoga* by Aurobindo, whom both Tagore and Gandhi consider the greatest intellect of modern India, and a book by another Hindu on the yogi philosophy. Now, I'm not a yogin or a yogi. A yogin is a student, and a yogi is one who has students. And I think that's about the only difference. And the yogin thinks the yogi knows more than the yogin, and the yogi thinks the yogin knows less than the yogi. Sounds almost like the culture they make with milk, but it isn't. It's like a bunch of kids were asked to write what's the difference between a Republican and a Democrat. Now there was only one real smart student in the class, a little girl of twelve. She won the prize because she said, "A Democrat is one who thinks a Republican is all wrong. A Republican is one who thinks a Democrat is all wrong. They both are right." They just couldn't help but give her a prize. She said the whole works right then in her way.

Now I am also reading another thing, which is the psychoanalysis, according to the Jungian system, of the story of *The Pilgrims' Progress*. Now, this is very interesting, if you ever really want to know what and how the Jungian system works in practice. This is a complete analysis of [the character] Christian, of why and how he got that way, and how he got out of it, and what happened and why, according to the Jungian psychology and philosophy. It's very interesting. It's written by Dr. Esther Harding, who is one of America's leading authorities on this subject. It's called, well, I don't know what it's called. It's got a name—adventure or something into the self, *Journey into Self*, isn't it? Is that it? Yes.

Well, now the reason I'm reading these three books at once is I'm afraid if I read just one of them, I might be too influenced by it. You see? I am a New Englander. They do not like to agree with anyone. I said to a friend of mine, he's as stubborn as I am, he says, "I don't believe this," "I don't like that," "I don't think that." I said, "Now wait a minute, wait a minute. If I say to you, you write it out exactly the way you want it, and I accept it, and I read back to you the exact words you wrote, will you accept them?" He said, "I guess probably I would." Well, we're all more or less that way, but I actually, when I am reading philosophy and religion and things like that, I like to read several works that are by different people. It is too easy to coerce our consciousness without doing it deliberately, isn't it? I figure we're all pretty much hypnotized from the cradle to the grave anyway.

The stupidity of our different theologies and not being able to get together because of their silly biases is something to weep about. But since life is a comedy to him who thinks and a tragedy to him who feels, we may take the choice of weeping or laughing. Laugh, and the world laughs with you. Weep, and you generally will weep alone, not because people are unkind, just because they do not know that you are weeping. How strange it is. People are kind, mostly. Sir Philip Sidney said, "If I had the time to learn from you/how much for comfort my words could do/and I told you then of my sudden will/to kiss your feet when I did you ill/if the tears back of the coldness feigned could flow/and the wrong be quite explained/brothers, the souls of us all would shine/if we had the time." And so they would.

There is chord, and a divine one, that rightly struck in every heart, sings in every mind, flows as a cosmic pulsation through every form. We happen to call it Christ. The Jews look for a Messiah. It's the same thing—Immanuel, God with us. That's all they mean. Did you know the Jews had three Adams—the Adam of the earth, the air, and the sky? It says in the New Testament, as in Adam, the first Adam, all die, so in the last Adam, which is Adam, the Adam Kadmon of Masonry or the Christ Adam. All are made alive. The first man is of this earth; the last man is the lord from heaven. This is good Jewish philosophy, and the Hindus called it Atman. In Buddhism, it is the Buddha. You see, Siddhartha was like Jesus. The prince became the Buddha, like Jesus became the Christ, like we might become an illumined person through meditation perhaps or whatever form is native to us. I don't believe there is any set form for anything. Some people do it one way, and some another, and however you do it, do it. There is no one way to find God. There is no formula because someday, we're not going to have to meditate or pray, you know. Right now we need it. The time will come when it will be a waste of time. I've counted my seven times over and over, seven times one is seven. You don't think through all eternity you are going to say, "Our Father, Which art in heaven, hallowed by Thy name." By and by, God will begin to sing in us and say: "Here, look at the spray on the ocean, get out in the sunshine, jump beneath the waves, sing to the mountains, and hear the leaves of the trees clap their hands. Hear the morning stars sing together, and watch the last glimpse of sunset catch up with the blush of early dawn."

No, we're not always going to be so morbid and little and all of these things as to say, "Now I lay me down to sleep." That's good now, but by and by, it won't be any good, any more than voodoo worship is now good. There are no devils. Probably good for people who have to have hell to believe in it, because if they have to have it and they weren't in it, they'd be very frustrated when their feet didn't burn. I think it's probably about the best thing that ever happened to them. Someday, they'll get tired of heat, and then they'll take the heat off. And that's the only way hell is ever going to cool off.

Hell is merely that which lacks the idea of harmony. Heaven is that which has it. Someday we will be so integrally united with the eternal Christ—which won't be Jesus, won't be Buddha, it won't be Moses, it won't be Mary Baker Eddy or Ernest Holmes. It certainly won't be me. If anybody tried to make that of me, I'd shoot them dead right now, if I had to knock them down first, because I'd never hit them if I didn't. That's the way most people go hunting. I have a friend that gets elk, and I asked him, "How much does it cost to get someone to tie it up to a tree before you beat it over the head?" I almost made him mad because he swears he shot it, but I don't believe that he did.

Now you can see and I can see that it will take practice to arrive at the mystical sense of the living Christ, but we must know what we're trying to arrive at. It's the real you; it's the Divine me; it's the Ever-Present One, the transcendence in the imminence in the transcendence. It is wherever we look. Do not separate this search from your own consciousness. Do not take it too seriously. It doesn't come that way. Do not coerce it. Do anything that to you seems good to do, but believe in it, just believe in it. Act as though it is true; it's everywhere.

When I was a kid, I used to know a woman who was then about seventy, and I was very fond of her. And she was a great artist. I'd go out walking in the woods with her, and she would go up to a tree and hug it and kiss it. I didn't think she was crazy, because then she could sit down and paint it beautifully, magnificently. One of the greatest artists of her day. I didn't think it was strange when she talked to the animals. I thought it was strange they didn't talk back in her language. She said they talked back and that she understood them. That doesn't seem strange to me.

There is an interior awareness that opens the gateway to every soul, even as it opens the gateway to the kingdom of God right now, because it will always be right now wherever we may be. We seek the mystical Christ but not the mysterious presence. We seek the mystical sense of a Divine communion. We seek the mystical presence of that which evermore enfolds us in a loving embrace, even while it frees us. Emerson said, "Cast the bantling on the rocks, suckle him with a she-wolf's teat, wintered with the wind and fox, power and speed be hands and feet." He's talking about the necessity that each one shall finally be shoved out of the cozy nest, where he has been fed, into the cold world and shocked by the wind. And wintered with the cunning of a fox, shall finally gain a power and speed to his hands and feet that hastens his journey across the netherlands of obscurity and fear and superstition and doubt into that safe haven of the soul, where the eye views the world as one vast plane and one boundless reach of sky. He was a genius of Religious Science.

Now we come here. We pray together, we think together, yet we are more or less alone. These of us who have the privilege of still talking to people, there are a few people who will still listen to us even after what we have done to them this week. The kindness of the human mind, along with its stupidity, is unbelievable, but its kindness is its great thing. And, you know, there is a great nobility about the human mind to me. People say to me, "Oh, why don't you go away. I know a place out in Oregon or somewhere where you can sit under a tree." I said, "I sat under a tree. It was a very wonderful experience, too." I like it where the traffic is. I like it where the beat of human feet create a collective rhythm that sings to me of the people of the world. Sit beside the road and be a friend to man. And look into this face and that one and some other, and through sometimes the hatred and the fear and the tears and the shame and the isolation, find that common denominator that makes us all tick. And I happen to believe that while it is wondrous to seek the solitude, I believe someday we will have places that will be the genius of our movement, that some church will build a place for this particular form of meditation and some for that. And it will all be good because we are creating a new catalyst, whether we know it or agree with it.

Somebody said last night, "That's a dangerous thing you said." I said, "I am going to skate on even thinner ice because I can swim." It's all right. It has to happen, and it will. But through it all, while I'm here, I'll be out on the street corner. I am not afraid of the noise of traffic. I can give as good a treatment on a major street corner as I can or could in an airtight compartment. And until I can, I do not know how to talk to God. I've got to speak to God in His creation. He has got to reveal Himself to me in life, the way it's lived. This is a practical idealism and a transcendent realism.

Someday there will be people in our movement where perpetual prayer will go on in their church or someplace just like it. I believe in it. I won't be there, but I believe in it. Isn't that funny? Because I'll pray as I run, and when I can't run, I won't be here. To me life is movement, action. How much we lose when we don't observe it. I love people. They don't tire me. It doesn't tire me to talk; if it did I wouldn't talk. Because I talk so much, it couldn't. I'd be exhausted.

There is a mechanics about that, however, and there's something else that you know it doesn't tire you. How can energy devitalize itself? You just try to make it, and see how far you'd get. We do not devitalize energy. We refuse to let it vitalize us, that's all. The Chinese sage said, "Oh man, having the power to live, why will you die?" Someday we won't die. We do now, I know only too well, but we have such a transcendent possibility. We have such a vision before us that it staggers my imagination at times. I don't wonder if we're worthy. Now I know some people that do, and they say, "Well, you're not a humble man." I don't know that I am. I'd make about the worst cuspidor that ever sat in anybody's corner. As a bookmark, I would tear the book apart. And if anybody tried to wipe their feet on me, they certainly at least wouldn't have any shoes left. And I wouldn't call that arrogance. Nature has given us the right to protect ourselves for the same reason it put whiskers on the cat and for no other reason, and that little device on the bat that bounces its own noise back from the wall of the cave so it won't break its own neck in the impact of its flight.

Robert Browning said, "I shall arrive as birds pursue their trackless path sometime, somehow, some day, sometime in God's good time, I shall arrive. Then welcome each rebuff that turns Earth's smoothness rough." Isn't that terrific?

> *Grow old along with me!*
> *The best is yet to be,*
> *The last of life, for which the first was made:*
> *Our times are in His hand*
> *Who saith "A whole I planned,*
> *Youth shows but half; trust God: see all, nor be afraid!"*
>
> *… "Praise be Thine!*
> *I see the whole design,*
> *I, who saw power, see now love perfect too:*
> *Perfect I call Thy plan:*
> *Thanks that I was a man!*
> *Maker, remake, complete—I trust what Thou shalt do!"*

Isn't this a great surrender of the lesser to the greater? He was a transcendent poet. Now we are transcendent realists; we are practical idealists. We believe in the law and in the word, both. More than anything else, I think we believe in the mystical Presence that inhabits eternity and indwells our own souls. Trust yourself more than you would me, more than you would anyone you have listened to. We're all very nice people, but sometimes we get mad and mean as hell. Now I know we say we don't, but I'm too darned smart to believe in that. I see us do it, and I personally am willing to admit it. Lots of people won't because they think it isn't nice. There's nothing you can do to a nice person but to strangle him anyway. Take yourself as you are, because you are going to have to, for better or for worse, right now. This that you are is the only savior you'll ever meet, the only Christ you'll ever know, the only God you can get close enough to. Shakespeare said, "There's a divinity that shapes our ends, rough hew them how we will."

There is no other evidence of the Divine than the human, and only in giving is there receiving. Only in the clearance of guilt and the forgivingness of your own self and the love that there is awakened shall the world embrace you, which is but the extension of the arms that you have put around it. And do not think for one moment that there is a transcendence somewhere outside of your experience whereby your arms shall be around the eternal or the arms of God around you unless your arms are around humanity. There is no such a thing in infinity. If there were, the universe would be a mockery, hypocrisy would be real, and a lie would be equal to the truth. And God Himself would be blasphemed but [as Emerson expressed] nature forevermore screens herself from the profane. Take yourself as you are—good, bad, indifferent, strong, weak, well, sick, ignorant, talented, singing, or sobbing. This is the little boy and the little girl who is going to bed with you tonight, and when you wake up in the morning, he or she is the first thing you are going to meet. And when you pass on beyond the other side, he or she will be there waiting for you. Let us take this vision, this hope. Emerson said, "obeying the Almighty effort and advancing on chaos and the dark," and all the love you have shown me, accentuated as I realized, is very much appreciated. I wish you to know, it has been wonderful.

And now, as we again seek that Divine Presence going on together, loving, being loved, hoping to come back here again—some of us won't. It doesn't matter. We shall be somewhere. I am reminded of something I wrote. It was written for a wedding song:

Let us walk life's road together, you and I,
And love will guide our feet as we go,
Oh my sweet, here and forever, by and by in gladness,

Roses bloom the path we tread,
Hand in hand and heart to heart,
Each of the other's life apart,
'Til time with snowy white adorns the head,
When the sands of earth's brief day have run,
Still hand in hand, we'll go
Where sunset's evening glow, meets the first blush of a new day's rising sun.

Peace, peace be unto our souls. I cannot say peace be unto you. It's too condescending for me. I cannot say, may God love you. It isn't gracious. May we have peace and may we enter into love, for as we have surrendered our soul and spirit to God, we have surrendered our hearts and minds to each other. And one is but the offering of the other, brought to the altar of that sweet communion which blends all into that divine union and that heavenly song which forever sings the stars, rises in glory in the sunlight, sinks into the deep of the infinite ocean of being, and calls unto deep in our own soul, "Awake, awake, awake."

May the peace of that gracious and good God be with us, and that Divine love, which we feel as we embrace each other, encircle us as we encircle each other. May there come to our hearts the song of eternal joy in everlasting blessing. God be with us 'til we meet somewhere again.

Classes on Mysticism

In this series of five classes, Ernest Holmes calls us to create a new form of mysticism within the Religious Science movement, a mysticism connected to the Earth. Throughout the five sessions, he offers his thoughts on what this means and his ideas on how we can bring forth this sense of connectedness to the One.

Mysticism Class One

JULY 8, 1957

Our teaching has a very great deal of mysticism in it, and it should be more completely developed with the realization that mysticism is not mystery, just as intuition is not psychism. Half of the world and three fourths of the people in our field, who should know better, mistake intuition for psychism and think if a person gets a hunch, they must be very spiritual. So most people mistake mysticism for mystery.

Mysticism is not mystery and psychism is not intuition, although many people in our field mistake these. Just as Richard Maurice Bucke said, cosmic consciousness is an awareness of our union with the whole and the unity of the whole, so mysticism is the perception of that wholeness in everything without fragments. When we use reason without fragments, we would very closely approach the axiomatic reasoning of the indivisibility of the unit because there is nothing unlike it with which to divide itself. And that which remains indivisible has to be a total unit, and being a unit and indivisible, that is what they call the perception of omnipresence.

Let's get this clearly in mind: Mysticism is not mystery. Intuition is not psychism. Cosmic consciousness is some degree of a perception of the unity of the whole, the indivisible unity, and it means the unity. Mysticism is the perception of the whole in everything. And in none of these perceptions is there any degree of division at all. What I said this morning about forgivingness is true. I didn't make it up. It not only is one of the true perceptions of the ages and the mystical and intuitive perception of Jesus—because it was true—but it is now verified in modern science, and we find them doing this.

Emerson said, "What is our life but an endless flight of winged facts or events! In splendid variety these changes come, all putting questions to the human spirit." Here is the wisdom in this. Those men who cannot answer, by a superior wisdom, these facts or these questions of time serve them. This is a very great saying. The Bible puts it another way. It says, "We are the servant of the thing we obey." Emerson said, "We animate what we can, and we see only what we animate." Mary Baker Eddy said, "Mortal mind sees what it believes as certainly as it believes what it sees."

This is one of the great wisdoms of Emerson, because he perceived only one mind. And when he says these men who cannot answer by a superior wisdom will serve, that is why Jesus forgave people their sins. You see, we teach a law of cause and effect, which itself is an effect of a previous cause, which has no cause and itself is not an effect. Therefore, all sequences of cause and effect are comprehended within it. Now, we definitely teach in our technique cause and effect. And anyone who thinks he is going to get away from cause and effect merely creates a new sequence of cause and effect. If you passed into what the absolutist think is an absolute state of being, you wouldn't be anywhere at all. You wouldn't be. And if God still is, you wouldn't know it, and so far as you were concerned, there would be nothing to know that God is.

I personally do not believe there is any abstraction in the universe. If there were, we would never perceive it because our perception would be a concretion of that abstraction. It is unthinkable to me there would be an intelligence that knows anything outside of, different from, or other than itself in a continuum wherein eternal change takes place, which is a play of life upon itself, but nothing is being accomplished as purpose. Does that seem strange to you? Dean Inge says that an Infinite purpose is a logical, mathematical contradiction, and the reason for that is that you cannot have an infinite incompletion. It would break up.

Now Emerson said, "A mind might ponder its thought for ages and not gain so much self-knowledge as the passion of love shall teach it in a day." Isn't that an interesting thing? He places love above the intellect and yet he was the most intelligent man America has ever produced.

I am skipping around. I like this. Man is his own star, and the soul that can render an honest and a perfect man demands all light, all influence, all faith. Nothing to him falls too early or too late. "Our acts, our angels are our good or ill or fatal shadows that walk by us still." And the next one, "Cast the bantling on the rocks, Suckle him with the she-wolf's teat/Wintered with the hawk and fox/Power and speed be hands and feet." You see, Emerson said, "An institution is the lengthened shadow of one man. A man should learn to detect and watch that gleam of light which flashes across his mind from within, more than the luster of the firmament of bards and sages." Now I believe as James Larkin said, "The great appear great because we are on our knees. Let us rise." But, we must remember this also: that greatness will not die with us. It has a way of surviving after our ego has shuffled off this mortal coil and can no longer be found, dead or alive.

We must create a new form of mysticism in our movement. We can study as these are four classical examples and there are no better that I know of, particularly Emma Curtis Hopkins and Eckhart. I think Eckhart is the greatest example of a delicacy of feeling and touch in mysticism, a very great beauty. But I think the most robust form of mysticism that I know anything about is Walt Whitman. It is just a robust thing because while Eckhart deals with it very gently, the same thing Whitman just grabs a piece of cosmos and throws it at you, and you can't dodge it. And if you pass through it successfully without getting knocked out, you will know what he is talking about. Otherwise, his language will be crazy. So will Mrs. Hopkins', unless you know what she is talking about. I took her course and it was a great privilege.

One of things Carl Jung said to Bill Hornaday—Bill had the experience of forty-nine interviews with him, and it is almost impossible for anyone to get anywhere near where he lives—Jung said to Bill, "You tell whoever this fellow is who started this thing that no religion can be a success without a very great degree of mysticism in it." Isn't that interesting? He said it is impossible. That is a feeling you see toward the invisible.

How many of you read Alan Watts little book *Behold the Spirit,* where he says unless mysticism comes into the Christian religion, it will fall. I mean, we think it is here to stay, but it has only been around for about two thousand years, and that would be just before breakfast to some of the religions.

So Emerson says that envy is ignorance; that imitation is suicide; that "though the wide universe is full of good, no kernel of nourishing corn can come to him (a man he means) but through his toil bestowed on that plot of ground which is given to him to till." I believe we not only need to have a degree of mysticism come into our work, but I think it has to be a mysticism connected with the Earth. It is nice for us to soar in heaven and let down a few thunderbolts if we feel mean and a few blessings if we think God has His hand on us, but that won't do it. Every man comes original and alone to humanity from the alone and original within his own divinity, and he can't help it. That is the way he is made. And it is only then, as he reveals that thing. But here again, we must be careful that mysticism isn't mystery and intuition isn't psychism, because here is a field for greater illusion, and people speak with madness. We must have the intelligence to discriminate between the two, as it is in Revelation.

I thought when I listened to Billy Graham last Saturday night, that is a sweet guy. And I thought that he is a sweet, wonderful, absolutely sincere guy, and I am sure he is doing good. Then I got to thinking it over the next day, and I still thought he was sweet, etc. Then I thought, let's approach this from the noncommittal viewpoint, without prejudice for or against or emotion, but just thinking he is a sweet guy, which he is. And let's forget all that, and from a noncritical viewpoint because you might not happen to believe it, and let's see what it is under analysis. And do you know what my analysis was? That the greatest spiritual stupidity that can be exhibited by man and the highest form of intellectual arrogance that can be entertained by man is for anybody, sincere or insincere, to believe anybody else is going to a place less good than he. There is no greater intellectual arrogance or spiritual stupidity than this *conceivable* because it deals with eternity. If it only dealt with you falling down and breaking an arm today, that would be a passing event. But when it deals with the eternal verities, there can be no greater stupidity. No greater harm can come to the mind of man.

Now Emerson was free from this. He was so free he said, why drag the dead corpse of the Sunday school across your church? "Trust thyself: every heart vibrates to that iron string." He says so much that is beyond belief. He says, "But the man is, as it were, clapped into jail by his consciousness" (talking about a man who cumbers himself with his own consequences and interests). He doesn't have a genuine independence. "But the man is, as it were, clapped into jail by his consciousness." "These are the voices which we hear in solitude, but they grow faint and inaudible as we enter into the world." He also said, it is enough to do this in the silence or when we are alone but "the great man is he who in the midst of the crowd keeps with perfect sweetness the independence of solitude."

Our religion is a mystical religion, but it is not a religion away from the Earth. It is a religion where the grass grows; a religion that no longer separates physical, mental, and spiritual, but finds action and reaction and actor, one and all, the same thing and here and now. This state of mystical concept to be delivered to whomever comes to us, cannot be delivered except by a non-meanly critical mind. It is absolutely impossible that heavenly discourse shall be spoken by confused people or fools or ignorance. It just can't be done, this kind of a discourse. Now remember, this is what the world is looking for. I recently spoke to two ministers, one a Methodist and the other a Congregationalist. They had just been going to conventions or whatever they have like we are having here. I said, "How did you like it?" And they said it was the most boring thing they ever attended. The people are all nice, but it is all business, all routine. It is how do you do this or cover that, how to make a pillar for this thing. No mysticism, no news from heaven.

We are not liable to bring as much news from heaven as we might either. And the only reason is that we can only bring news from our own consciousness. Absolutely impossible. I don't care how much we strain or how much we know or how many answers we know, in such degree as you and I see something outside of that which is the thing we ought to be looking for, in and at each other, we can have no heavenly discourse. We are dumb.

Phineas Quimby says, I am taking this from "Questions and Answers" and somewhat from "The World of the Senses" and "Christ or Science," [The Quimby Manuscripts] because it is from these three sections that the modern metaphysical movements came, whether they call themselves New Thought or Christian Science. It says that when you have arrived at truth, if you find it attached to a belief, you may know it is not a truth, for it may change. God is Truth, and there is no other truth. Man's God is all the time listening to his prayers and setting off all sorts of trouble. My God does not act at all. He has finished his work and leaves man to work out his happiness according to his own wisdom.

Quimby was not familiar, so far as I know, with the teachings of Ancient India. Troward most certainly was, in my estimation. I read books on India and Aurobindo particularly. Troward didn't get his system from Aurobindo, but he got it from where Aurobindo got his, because they are too similar to doubt it. Aurobindo's "Life Divine" in his section of *The Life Divine* is an elaboration on Troward's "Denouement of the Creative Process" in *The Creative Process in the Individual*. Of course, Troward's was written before Aurobindo's, but it shows they both came from the same source. That is all.

We don't care where it came from. That is where Troward got his. I don't think anybody ever taught Quimby, but there is a question whether he may have known something of Swedenborg in *The Law of Correspondences*. I don't know. He says, my God has done everything. This is no different from Dean Inge teaching that by the process of involution, the soil is impregnated with the spark. Robert Browning refers to it as, "A spark disturbs our clod," and that is what Troward is talking about in the involutionary process—or "the passing" he called it—of Spirit into matter, that matter may pass into form. It is very interesting that this guy worked out a universal matter, too, where he said that spirit is matter in solution and mind is matter in form. But, he said, the two of them he treats as though they are Spirit in its dual aspect. Were the spirit of matter, I mean—were the matter of spirit. I don't see any difference there in Einstein saying energy is equal, identical, and interchangeable. But if energy itself is equal, energy and mass are equal, identical, and interchangeable. What is going to change them other than that which is neither energy nor mass but to which they, as energy and mass being equal, identical, and interchangeable, are as the matter of that which principle is superior to them.

That was the position Quimby took on mind and matter and what he called intelligence. So like the ancient Hindus, his God did not evolve or change. But there was that thing, which they called (Troward deals with it in the first chapter of *Bible Mystery and Bible Meaning*) the involutionary process, because involution precedes evolution and is a spontaneous thing. Evolution follows involution with mathematical precision and is a mechanical thing. That is why we say, and rightly, that I believe this. And when we give a treatment, I think our word falls into a mechanical medium and reacts, but I don't think it knows it is reacting. It knows how to react. But if it knew it were reacting, it might say it didn't want to do it.

In other words, we believe in a Presence and a principle. I think that in the metaphysical field, where they believe in a principle without a Presence, something freezes up inside.

Jesus came into the world not to give an opinion but to bring light into the world upon something that was in the dark. In the spiritual world, there are things, as there are in the natural world, that affect us as much. But these are not known by the natural sense or wisdom, and he is referring to both a psychic thing and what he calls "spiritual intuition." He says the spiritual senses have their spiritual world, with all the inventions of the natural world, but the relationship is not admitted to natural man except as a mystery. There is just as much progress in the spiritual as in the natural world, and the science I teach is the wisdom of my God applied to the senses in the spiritual world. Wisdom is always the same. It is the point of all attraction, and everything must come to be in harmony. And this is the Christ.

Now the whole theory of Quimby, I don't want to go into that but just this idea of his mystical concept of the thing, because Quimby had what he called a "spiritual clairvoyance." I think he had a clairvoyance beyond the average, like Eileen J. Garrett. She wrote me a very wonderful letter the other day. "I have had experiences occasionally like looking through a tunnel, and it seems to be all full of clouds. Sometimes the clouds are very black, and sometimes they are almost white. When they clear up at the other end of the tunnel, you see something. And if you ever do, something happens." I don't know what it means, but I do believe you merely go through a tunnel at the spiritual world. I don't know. I am not talking about the psychic world or the spirit of Annie Rooney. That is different. Annie may be there, but I am talking about something else. I am talking about the medium, if she is there, in which she lives, the originator, and, I suppose, the archetypical patterns and concepts.

You see, in our field, we don't understand these things, but we should feel them. We should sense their importance, and we should feel their presence because, as I said this morning, how can we project what we do not have? And what is everything we think about other than a projection? Because even though, as the Zen Buddhists say, you first say everything is real out here, then you get into their philosophy and say the mountain is no longer a mountain. There is no such thing as a mountain. It is an illusion. But after a while, the mountain comes back. It is there. What you thought of it is gone, but the mountain remains, and it isn't an illusion.

And Immanuel Kant said we are able to perceive what seems to be eternal because it awakens an intuition within us in the medium of a common denominator. We would say it this way: God is in you. God is in me. God is you. God is what I am. God in me sees God in you. God in you knows God in me. This is the way we know things. We could not know each other if there were not the medium of this common denominator.

In other words, there is only one Mind in the universe. Everything individuates from the Mind; nothing is individual to or in the Mind. If we were to suppose something individual in the Mind, it would be separate and isolated and could have no existence. And if it were, it could have no subsistence on that which exists. Physically and psychologically, we subsist on that which exists. Existence is the biggest word in our language. I mean to suppose there is that which wasn't made and didn't make itself and just is, and continues forever but is always active.

Now it is the perception of this through spiritual awareness of the reality of things that gives power to our work, because all the words in the world without meaning won't do anything. We would just be talking to ourselves. This has to come into our work more and more.

Another thing: I chose four things for two reasons and that is this: As our movement evolves and develops, as it grows, which I think it will, I don't know, I am not a prophet, I know if it doesn't destroy itself inwardly—and I have no guarantee that it won't because of the stupidity of all of us, including myself— it would become the next great religious impulsion since Islam. I don't class Christian Science or Mormonism as successful. As they are, they are not big religions. They are not great religions; they are not lasting religions. There is too much in them that contradicts itself. Mormonism has more of an emotional appeal than the other one, because you can baptize people after they have shuffled off this mortal coil, and it still reaches them wherever they are and wets them down good, but doesn't make any sense.

There is very little emotional appeal in Christian Science. And nothing can exist without the emotional appeal, backed by enough reality so that even though it does not interpret it rightly it still interprets it, even though imperfectly. Behind everything has to be the prototype being revealed or nothing is revealed. Now that is the strength of every religion and is why it is the mystical element in religion that enables it to survive, because religion is an intuition. Mysticism is an intuition and inner awareness, without going through processes.

What I wanted to say was: It is hope, and it is only my hope. It would be my hope. I think that unlike other religions that have come upon the scene, very often, I will say almost back to ancient Hinduism, we have no prophets. You know, I make the poorest prophet that ever lived. I don't fast; I don't feast. I don't even practice yoga; I am too lazy. Whatever shall come to me, it is only my system. Whatever is going to come to me is going to come to me while I am walking down the street. It may take longer to evolve that way, but too often "who breaketh through a hedge is stung by a serpent." As Emerson said, "When the fruit is ripe, it falls."

Nothing should be practiced to the exclusion of something else. God's system is inclusive, not exclusive. The biggest life is the one that includes the most, not the least. Who shuts out too much, shuts in too little.

Now it is to be hoped that our religion, if it goes on, becomes a great religion. It is a great religion, the greatest the world has ever known. If we haven't, then the world hasn't known what makes a great religion. If you were to take the ten greatest songs ever sung, you would have an album of the best songs ever written, wouldn't you. But why shouldn't someone else sing another one?

Therefore, we must not shut out the possibility of a future. I think a great and vast literature will grow up around our work, but I hope it won't be a repetition of the few stupid things I have said. That would be bad. We do not want a lot of echoes. If I pass on tonight—the church, they could do it now but I wouldn't let them. I haven't any power to stop them. It would be not by moral but immoral persuasion that I would do it.—If I pass on tonight, they can take everything I ever wrote and throw it in the trash can, and it is going to be thrown there someday anyway. But two things will remain—and only two and whatever goes with them—there is a Presence in the universe and a Power in the universe, and they are not the same thing identically. They constitute a dual unity, the action and reaction and polarity from which all things come, everything, and to which there is no hard or easy, no big or little that can never change in Religious Science. But the way it is said can.

Now we ought to develop many people who know how to say it so well and write it so well that a great literature would grow up around our movement, making it more universal. Now what is our difficulty? I am going to tell you because you are ministers, and I'll be very frank, and this is a clinic. We have to develop this, but there are two things that must be avoided in our talks, in our teaching, and in our writing. One is the unconscious arrogance of the ego that is projecting itself in the name of God with the belief that it has some peculiar dedication that other people do not have. This is stupid. Just plain downright stupidity. And it is arrogant and ignorant. But it is one of the tricks the mind plays. It is called a "projection" in psychology. It is an unconscious defense mechanism. It is an inferiority complex, manifesting its inadequacy to compensate for the fear of its own confusion and rejection.

The other is just plain downright psychic confusion. All of us have got hold of these things. Remember, I have them both, and that is why I know about them. I don't know anything about you, other than what I project into you about myself. So I am analyzing myself to you. Then you analyze yourself to me, and I would say it would be pretty identical and accurate, if you are honest. We are honest the moment we are not condemning ourselves or anyone else. Then we can be honest with ourselves for the first time, and there is nothing wrong with that kind of honesty.

Now if we can do that, we ought to develop a vast amount of literature, which is the most dangerous thing in the world. The reason I would not like to see it done is that I don't want to shuffle off and I would rest uneasy in my grave. I should come back and haunt somebody, if that can be done, if anything ever grew up around what I have just said. Everyone is human and would like to feel they have written something that would last, but the truth will not change. This is very important to me: The last word has not been said; you are not going on my revelation. I am not a prophet. I have no revelations, and if I had them, I would mistrust them. They might be hallucinations, and don't you trust any of yours.

And never let our movement get into that static position intellectually and the dearth of spiritual growth where it thinks everything has been said. And remember this, you teachers and preachers, there is nothing in our movement that restricts anybody. There is nothing in our movement that hamstrings anybody. If they think there is, it is their own stupidity. There is nothing in our movement that is trying to promote anybody. Our movement is the most democratic spiritual movement in the world today, and if you don't know it, it is because you are ignorant of the fact.

I no longer have any hesitation to say these things because I don't care what happens. If it becomes a movement, grand. If it doesn't, it doesn't belong to history. I comment now impersonally. This is true—we are the most independent spiritual organization the world has ever known.

Now let us live up to our independence, but let's not take a power and a privilege or liberty to destroy freedom or spiritual insight, to stupidly hamstring that which we are trying to do, and let us see if it is possible. Now remember, these things don't happen very often in history. We are either a thing of destiny, which the tide of evolution has cast upon the shores of time, that will climb up off the shore and take root, as Emerson meant when he said that a tree starts in a sand dune and gets a little growth and by shedding its own leaves creates the soil from which it is to grow more. (That isn't an exact quotation.) Emerson said the tree takes root in the sand, where there is nothing to nurture it, and after a year it sheds its own leaves and in that way creates its own soil in which it will grow. He likens the things always to the Thing Itself. "Cast the bantling on the rocks/ Suckle him with the she-wolf's teat, Wintered with the hawk and fox/Power and speed be hands and feet." A poetic way of saying the same thing.

Now let us then do this same thing in our own movement. Let us have our freedom, but not destroy it. Let us see if that be the will of whatever is good working out of whatever destiny may be, if it be the operation of such revelation of inspiration or intuition that we have, let us see to it that those who start this thing and give birth to it, that no new bondage shall grow out of a greater freedom. That somehow or other in the evolution of this movement, those things that restrict shall pass away, but with the passing of the restriction, there shall not come confusion. That somewhere in the spiritual evolution of the human race, there might have arrived or there could arise or there ought to arise some group of people in the spiritual field who will have enough mutual respect and admiration for each other to cooperate and, as Robert Browning said, "And with God be the rest."

Mysticism Class Two

JULY 9, 1957

Two of our great mystics were Meister Eckhart and Emma Curtis Hopkins. I never knew him, but I did know her. I took her course, and anyone who would say he had studied with Emma Curtis Hopkins would be misstating the fact. No one ever studied "with" her that I know of. You went, and she talked for an hour, and you left. And you went again, and this happened twelve times and that was it. It is no different, as near as I can remember, from these talks here. I know. I bought her course at that time, and I was more familiar with it then than now. But it was what she imparted that you did get because it was a very definite impartation, in what she did from what she said. At times, it was almost like a wind, a breeze. Are any of you familiar with what is called a "psychic breeze"? You felt something like a breeze, but it was like something alive, animated, not cold, clammy—an entirely different thing.

I believe Emma Curtis Hopkins was nearly eighty years old when I studied "with" her in 1922. She was a very stately old dame. She wore long dresses, and I never saw her without a hat. They say she was never without one; why, I don't know. I went to the door and was announced. It was a beautiful place, a hotel apartment in the old Iroquois Hotel in New York. She would just make a stiff little bow, and with her head, motioned me to the chair. And she sat down and began to talk. It was about ten minutes before I said to myself, "This is the first lesson," which it was. And she talked for an hour, and when she got through, she got up and made a little bow and walked out.

The first four times I went, I didn't know whether she knew who I was. Of course, I was much younger then, and it bothered me a little. This was thirty-five years ago. Now I would be glad if she didn't know who I was, which also is another lie. The lies we tell to show how we deflate our ego are used instead to protect it. Now, about the fourth or fifth time, the old gal loosened up and I used to stay after that and have long conversations with her. She turned out to be very witty and cheerful and sweet and lovable. She was telling me one time about George Edwin Burnell, who was a student of hers. She had a convention in Chicago, and he came in (and he was an absolutist) screaming, "I am God." She said, "There, there, Edwin, it is all right for you to pray you are God, but don't be so noisy about it." She was a very sweet character. It is what you felt and not what she said.

She is the only instance of mysticism that I know about that enables us to tie the mystical concept with the way we use the principle. She was a very profound student of the spiritual classics of the ages.

I would like to call your attention to another bible that is coming out. Have any of you ever seen or read *The Bible of Bibles*? The J. F. Rowny Press of Santa Barbara is reprinting it, and if you don't have it, be sure to get a copy when this new edition comes off the press. There is nothing like it in the world. Mr. Frank L. Riley spent seventeen or eighteen years compiling it, and it is called *The Bible of Bibles: A Sourcebook of Religions*. You can get it from him or from us.

Eckhart says that great harm comes from feeling God is distant. "Man goes far away or near, but God never goes far-off; He is always standing close at hand." Eckhart is the greatest example of the beauty of mysticism that I have ever read. I think there is greater beauty in his writings than in any of the rest. I think there is a robustness in the beauty of Walt Whitman, a virility to it. He says, "I am one with the prostitute and the libertine and the stuff babies are made out of and the foam on the ocean and with the stars and the sun and the moon." I love the virility of his inclusion. It is so strong, and I like great strength in things. And I like beauty, and there is a beauty and a strength in Eckhart, which is sadly lacking in Ernie.

Here is a man who, hundreds of years ago, never heard of modern psychology. But he had a psychological insight through a spiritual awareness, which they all had. I have never yet read a saying of a true mystic that contradicted a single psychological or metaphysical fact. Why is that? Because truth is one body. He says, "If, however, a person is guilty and no confessional is available, let him go to God, acknowledging his fault with great penitence and rest easy on that score until a confessional is convenient. And meanwhile, if he forgets the reproach of his sins, he may take it that God, too, has forgotten." This is no different from what I said, that we can forgive only as we have a sense of being forgiven. "If he forgets the reproach of his sins, he may take it that God, too, has forgotten."

We want to know the reason for these things, and it is very simple. We must remind ourselves that whatever the nature of things may be in life, which we don't know completely, as we see as through a glass darkly, it is our reaction to things that counts with us. And in psychology, they say it is never the experience but the emotional reaction to it that does the damage or the good.

For instance, we can pick up a paper this morning and read that 10,000 Chinese were killed last night, and we say, "My goodness, what a lot of Chinese there are." If someone we love very much is killed, our reaction is quite different. It is our emotional reaction that makes the difference.

If he forgets the reproach of his sins, he may take it that God, too, has forgotten. Eckhart said, be spiritually quite private. He said the reference of ideas to things does not belong to the objective world as far as the spiritual (subjective) man is concerned, for all things are, to him, simply channels of the Divine and the spiritual. You see, if we study Jungian psychology, we go back through the individual and collective unconscious. And we see the reaction of the individual unconscious to the collective and the action of the collective through it. Man is repeating history in his symbols and dreams. You are familiar with the theory that there must be the hero to extricate you, whether it be Jesus or Buddha.

Now like Emanuel Swedenborg, Meister Eckhart saw what we would call the psychic symbols and the spiritual meaning behind them. He says that only when a man is completely weaned from things and things are alien to him, only then may a man do as he pleases with things, free to take them or leave them with impunity. "Seek first the Kingdom of God and His righteousness," as Jesus said. He says that there is nothing in God to destroy anything that has the least being. Modern science knows of no energy that will destroy itself. You see, if there were anything in the universe that would or could destroy itself, the original creativity would be self-destructive. They accused Jesus of this and he said no, that would be a house divided against itself.

Jesus said depth and height are the same thing, there is no great and no small to the soul that maketh all. Emerson said, "And where it cometh, all things are, and it cometh everywhere." Now he said, to be this (he is referring to what we will call the truth), you must become that. To be this, you must become that. In other words, becoming passes out of being. Eckhart taught definitely that there is a consciousness, an inwardness within us which cannot be differentiated or distinguished from God but is God. Then if all creation and God were its best or worst, it could add nothing to or subtract nothing from me. In this way, all the gifts of God are mine, and all being is God to me, in me. There is no other being but God. Now Eckhart saw this, it is interesting thing, although he was a Catholic. He says, "Think only of God and do not worry about whether it is God acting through you or you doing it yourself, for if you are thinking only of Him, God must be acting through you, whether He wills to or not." This is a very profound thing. He is actually saying, if you do speak the truth, there is nothing in the universe that can deny it because there is only one thing that speaks it. He is going beyond, which he clearly saw, the theology of predestination, foreordination, divine planning, and divine purpose. Dean Inge said that "an infinite purpose is a contradiction in terms," by which he means that the Infinite cannot have a purpose without being incomplete. That is why Aurobindo said that everything exists for the delight of God.

In other words, these people know we are not here to be saved. And I believe —unlike most of our metaphysics, which I have often referred to but I haven't for many years; I think it is wrong—you will understand me if I say I don't think we are here to learn. I know we do learn, and the hard way, but what would send us here to learn what It doesn't know? It couldn't be, could it? Now, we do learn by experience, I don't deny it. Emerson said, "The universe remains to the heart unhurt. For it is only the finite that has wrought and suffered, the infinite lies stretched in smiling repose."

Lao Tzu said, "To him who can perfectly practice inaction, all things are possible." Our Bible says, "Be still, and know that I am God. Look unto me and be ye saved, all the ends of the earth." Plotinus said, "A man's work is done better when he faces the One, even though his back is toward his work." This is all mysticism. God must be acting through you, whether He wills it or not. I started to say Eckhart knew something which I say, I should have said. I should say, I say something that Eckhart knew but I said it before I knew him, which says all great minds run in the same direction.

There is no divine will separate from a divine nature. This ought to be clear in our movement, because if it is, we will be the only religious group, outside of a few, that have ever known it. But it is true. There can be no divine will separate from the divine nature. People come to me and say, "What is God's will?" I say, "Don't ask me what God's will is. Try to tell me what God's nature is, and that will be His will. If the nature of God is love, God can only be love."

Now we can believe what is not true; we can only know the truth. I only know of one poet, Edward Rowland Sill, who said, "'T is something, if at last, though only for a flash, a man may see clear-eyed the future as he sees the past, from doubt or fear or hope's illusion free." He had reference to the illusion of hope. It is quite a terrific thing to me. For it is only the finite that has wrought and suffered. He says goodness itself is self-begotten and all its works, for it is the essence of good that it pours knowledge, love, and deeds into the good man.

We often say self-existence is the greatest thing in our whole language. The whole thing is based on the supposition and proposition that we are dealing with self-existence, which makes things out of itself by itself, becoming the thing it makes without any effort. For it is only the finite that has wrought and suffered. In such degree as we put effort into our practice in the demonstration, an equal amount of effort will have to come out, if the universe is in equilibrium. But God, I wish I knew how to do it without it. We are so strenuous, jumping up and down. I don't know that someone else does it. I see someone else do it and recognize it because I am doing it. That is always the way it is.

Its self is self-begotten, when the good is added to goodness. It is still only goodness, except that one is begotten of the other. One begetting, the other begotten, as if it were the child of goodness. There is reality and life in goodness only. And so the good man receives all he is from goodness and in goodness. In goodness he lives and moves and has his being and finds himself. God's giving is my taking, and there is no giving to me until I have taken. This is a great concept. I mean, if the Infinite has surrendered Itself to Its creation, what happens to us is only what we perceive, only as we accept. He said, these agents of the soul being created with the soul are not God exactly, but they must become transformed into God, reborn in Him and of Him so that only God is Father and they, too, become His sons, His only begotten sons.

All through, he [Eckhart] refers to the son, begotten and, as I like to put it, the son begotten of the Only Father, and he said the Eternal is forever begetting the only begotten. He said, "I also say that in God there is neither sorrow, nor crying, nor any pain." Is that any different from Mrs. Mary Baker Eddy saying that as she became more completely aware of the truth, she was less aware of the reality of evil? He says, neither God nor creature, created or uncreated, in his Whole being, life, loving, knowing will be in God, of God, and will be God. He said "both the saints and heathen masters." When he refers to the heathen masters, whenever you hear Eckhart refer to the heathen masters or pagan people or unredeemed with some great thoughts or St. Augustine, he is always referring to the Platonists. Always, because this is where they got the idea of the parallels and the patterns. And the Platonists got it from the Egyptians, and the Egyptians, as far as it is known, came down from the ancient Hermetic teaching, which was given 1,500 years before the time of Moses. And you can trace it right down to the Platonists, where they say (Hermes is supposed to be saying; it was supposed to be a conversation with the sun), know that everything on Earth is a copy of what is in heaven. Plotinus said that even every organ is attached to its pattern or a perfect pattern. And when, by reason of any fact, the organ becomes detached, it gets in pain, and its whole longing is to get back to its pattern that it shall be made whole. And our Bible says to do this according to the pattern shown you on the Mount. These are the prototypes, and you will find continual references here and in Augustine to those ideas.

Here is one: The authorities say—when he [Eckhart] says "authorities" he may or may not be referring to the authorities preceding him, like Augustine, or to the Greeks—the authorities say that the blessed ones in the Kingdom of Heaven know they're creatures apart from ideas, they know their creatures to their common prototype in God. This is long before Kant said that the only way we can recognize an apparently external object is because it awakens an intuition within us in a field of a common denominator. Which is a very involved way of saying, you and I know each other only because we use a common mind in which each other exist. If there were actually individual minds, we couldn't know each other. But the universe, being a unitary system, is so organized or exists in such, and it is so, it is such that there is no individual anything in it. Therefore, all things are individualized from its totality, and that totality presses against everything, all of it. Is that clear? Against a peanut, against my brain, the heart of Christ or the scent of a rose, not any of these things are individual in and of themselves, having an existence by themselves but each being an individualization of the all, has the possibility of eternal evolution, ad infinitum. Now that is what he means by knowing them through their common prototypes. (This was Meister Eckhart.)

The reason I am interested in this is that mysticism is essential to real religion. When I use the word "religion," I always differentiate from theology, as you know. Theology may or may not know mysticism. All religion, like all art, is born out of the mystical sense of things. It has to be. And that is interesting because religion and art are the only two things that have outlived the ravages of time, and they are both intuitions. Now an intuition is merely the impact of the Invisible on the intellect and will and emotion, but in religion, that impact is continuously It. And that is why every age has had a religion but has interpreted itself naturally, in necessity, in the channel through which it came. And that is why there are attached to all religions things that ought not to be in any religion, including our own. But it does seem to me that Religious Science should, ought to, and must, and I have no doubt, will create sort of a modern type of mysticism, a new form of mysticism. It will be a new form. Its essence will be identical because it has been throughout the ages.

Inge said Plotinus was the king of the intellectual mystics of the ages. I think in Plotinus and Plato, we find something more nearly like Emerson, or in Emerson something more nearly like them, because I think that group of thinkers was the greatest line of intellectual thinkers the world has ever known—and that in no place does it crop out again to the extent that it did in Emerson. I think there is not much between, I mean in the same class of Plato and Plotinus, until you get right down to Emerson. There may be, but with my little knowledge, I haven't found it.

We find here in Emma Curtis Hopkins a mysticism that is more nearly applicable to our need. We will have to create a mysticism that will go with our need. I don't know just what it will be like. Very frequently when I speak, I know I have said something that will be it, not all of it but would be a line in it. It is a sense, a feeling toward the Invisible, and it is only when the consciousness is open to the Invisible and aware of the Invisible that it takes place. I don't know how you would describe it. How would you describe that you suddenly look up, which I have done, and you see the universe filled with an infinitesimal mass of little not atoms. I don't know what they are, just packed completely solid, but it isn't solid at all. It is light. Light is diffused, but it tends to white light not yellow light. Another interesting thing about it is that it is falling, it eternally falls, but instead of falling on things, it falls into them, through them, flows right through them. How do you account for it? You can't, but it is not an illusion. It is real.

We can give a name to a transcendent experience, whether we call it a celestial vision, it is perhaps; it is looking and suddenly seeing something. It is entirely different from the psychic thing. We are familiar with that, and we know the difference. There is a vast difference. As a matter of fact, 3,500 years ago when Patanjali was compiling the wisdom of ancient India, he shows how you have to get through the physical and psychic before you can emerge into that other thing.

Now we have to create a new form, and I expect we would find a better pattern in Emma Curtis Hopkins. It would be more adaptable to our needs, I think, than anything else because she understood the metaphysical approach.

She understood treatment. She understood all these things. She understood the what you would call "stirring up the ethers." In *High Mysticism,* she states, "Call to the Lord of Life and Glory beyond the bars of human sense, and all the living fountains lying deep in thee shall quicken into stirring streams, and all the pent-up wisdoms that inhabit thee shall leap to meet the Universal Wisdom, shining forth as the sun with the glory of their father." That is pure mysticism. And she continues to say, "But Thou! O Highest Original! art forever, and the manna Thou givest for the calling of Thy name, is radiant beneficence scattering and yet increasing, 'til the world is alive forever more! The High and Lofty One inhabiting Eternity is above the pairs of opposites, good and evil, life and death, spirit and matter, therefore His ways that inspire us as we look toward Him are not our accustomed ways." This is a very terrific saying. The High and Lofty One inhabiting Eternity is above the pairs of opposites, good and evil, life and death, spirit and matter. You will find the whole theme of Emma Curtis Hopkins is a very simple theme: As you look, It responds; therefore, look up and not down.

I referred last night to her saying that there was a race of people who produced some of the greatest prophets the world has ever seen, but they looked at a valley of dry bones. She was referring to the Jewish race. I had a friend a number of years ago, a young rabbi, and he was starting a synagogue. And he had just fitted up his office and wanted me to come and see it. And all over the walls were the pictures of these Jewish people with their shawls pulled up around them, fleeing from horror. And I looked and said, "My God, is this all you can afford to get? Let me buy you some pictures that won't make me sick when I look at them. Why do you do it?" He said, "This is the history of the Jewish people." I said, "It will remain the history of the Jewish people, if that is where your vision is." This is a tragedy, a race tragedy. That is what she refers to, but I didn't want to say it last night because we do have Jews and they might misunderstand it. She also brings out, as long as they look at the crucified savior, they will see the resurrected Christ in terms of limitation of the crucified savior. It is impossible to escape it.

She understood that the High and Lofty One inhabiting eternity is above the pairs of opposites, good and evil, life and death. Jesus said you cannot serve God and man. "Look unto me, and be ye saved." The Gita says you have to do away with the pairs of opposites before you can enter into what they call "bliss." Hopkins says, speaking of a prophet and decree to be the healing and strengthening and illuminating of all the people whom he may look upon or who look upon him, she says, deep believers in punishment are unconsciously drawing it. If we would transcend our limitations, we must look above them. And we always believe in what we look toward, and we draw what we believe in. All the prophets drew punishment. You wouldn't expect a gal like this to say that, would you? All the prophets drew punishment. Isn't that interesting. Why? Because their visioning was divided. They drew also salvation, you know. But why? Since they walked in the fourth dimension (she is referring to someone else), and no prison walls could hold them and no iron jaws could destroy them and no former ignorance or common birth could restrict them. She transcended all of them because she did not happen to believe in reincarnation, but she believed we are bound by our beliefs.

You will find her whole theme to be where your vision is set. What does it look like to you? It will always respond the way you see it. And that is why I said last night that the second part of the thing I was talking about in the transcendence and the imminence is logically an outgrowth of the first, that there is freedom, and if there is an imminence, which can only come from the transcendence or it wouldn't be there. In other words, we only live because God lives in us. Then that within us is that which is there and what that part of it becomes. It, in no fragments, sees what is, therefore to that which seems greater than we are. "It is not I, but the Father who dwelleth within me, the Father is greater than I, and yet as the Father hath life, so hath He given it to the son to have life." It is the same life. The words that I speak, they are spirit and they are life. That is what I want to bring out when we come to the practice of the transcendence, that theoretically there shall be no difference between the word we speak and what it does, that we shall not separate a sequence and delay a conclusion in time because we have unconsciously created a stretch of time which, still in the future in our own mind, can never appear in the present in our own experience.

This is the kind of mysticism we want to create for our own movement, so people can understand and explain. Therefore, we create part freedom and part bondage. She says the science of God reveals all science. All that we as yet know of the Maker of the universe is the practice of His Presence.

I said, at our opening probably, God is love. If God is love, which we believe, I don't know it just because the Bible said God is love. You know it only if your arms are around somebody. Love only knows and comprehendeth love. We don't know that God is peace unless we are at peace. We have a beautiful theory. It is probably a correct one, but we don't know. Our motto is "to know is to do and to do is to know." These signs shall follow them that believe.

She saw that so clearly, all that we yet know of the Maker of the universe and, I believe it is, all we will ever know is the practice of His Presence. And I think that is what Jesus knew. She [Hopkins] was terrific.

To the true mystic, the upward looking and the in-breath of heavenly atmospheres are volitional and scientific. She is here hooking up the two things I said at the beginning of our talk. I do not know what will happen to the Religious Science movement; I am no longer personally concerned. I was awfully worked up about it at one time, and it was like Emerson said, he goes into a political meeting or big argument and gets all worked up and goes out into the field, and nature says to him, "Why so hot, little sir?" And Shakespeare says of Romeo, "A little pot soon boils." So one day I realized both these things. There is nothing in the Universe we can fool but our psychological self; it is foolproof.

For the way of life, wrote Solomon, is above the wise, and he may depart from hell beneath. The secret that sin tells to the wise is that by vision toward matter and mind and their laws of pleasure and pain, we get caught in the wheels of destruction, but by vision toward the High One above are the pairs of opposites we are charged with: independence of matter and mind. There is but one commandment issuing from the giver of Almighty health, and that one commandment is, "Look unto Me, and be ye saved, all the ends of the earth. Beside me, there is no Savior, for inbreathing winds of unceasing strength from above where the inner eye seeks the Author of strength, who giveth all men liberty, even unto unbreakable omnipotence." She had a peculiar style. To the true mystic, the upward looking and the inbreathing of heavenly atmosphere are volitional and scientific.

That is why I said the other night, whatever happens to this movement, should it progress, much will change. Everything I have written will be thrown in the trash can someday unless people who are then in it become stupid. It is open at the top. But two things will never change and never have—and that is the self-existence and the self-emergence of law and order, and person and Presence, principle and power of feeling, and reaction of affirmation and what follows, and it is in my estimation polarization between these two, not positive and negative as such, but parts of a creative whole—one with volition and the other with action. It is the Ark of the Covenant, Joaquin and Boaz, cause and effect. It is the law of polarity. In my estimation, there is nothing in the universe but action and reaction, nothing. Now this doesn't exclude anything. The action is spontaneous; the reaction is mechanical. That is why she is tying science as law into the feeling as love. And Robert Browning said, "I spoke as I saw. I report, as a man may of God's work, all's love, yet all's law."

Let us meditate on that. And let us know that deep within us, in the living wellsprings of our being, beyond the pairs of opposites, good and evil, mind and matter as dualism, and beyond the limitation and fears and beyond the faith, just as beyond the doubt, and beyond the hope, and beyond the height of our earthly vision, that which is without dimension and deep within our own souls shines an eternal light. And in that light, there is no darkness. That mystic light, which envelops everything we contact, heals and blesses everything we touch and brings life or death and joy for a song. Eternal Spirit within us, blessed life and infinite peace, everything that denies this we deny, everything that affirms that living Presence, we announce. And all the past, whatever we believe it may have been, and every negation is wiped out, and there is no past. Every expectation of the future is wiped out, other than the affirmation of the Presence, which says, "Behold, I make all things new." Infinite beauty, harmony, and rhythm, where everything fits together in a form—that beauty is our own soul and the depth of that infinite peace, in which all motion takes place without moving and everything is effortless. We abide, and in that love that merges and flows through us as stream with stream to find a higher level by its own action, we surrender. Not to some abstract love of God, which has no meaning, but to the warm pulsating rhythm of the feet upon the pavement, and the horses' hoofs, and the roots of the grass, and the song of the lark, and the wild power and surging strength of the waves, the freshness of the wind, and the dew and the rain in our face, and the warm embrace of each other. That is all we know about it, and if back of that there is more love, we welcome that by whose eternity and in whose immensity we have even an equal affinity with all that is. And all that is is delivered, and we accept the gift, even as we give it back in joy to that high and lofty One who does inhabit eternity and finds a dwelling place in our own heart and mind and soul, for He is all.

Mysticism Class Three

✤

JULY 10, 1957

[Holmes read part of the story of *Wayfarer*, part of *The Awakening*.]

Now from Emerson's *Circles*: "Our life is an apprenticeship to the truth that around every circle another can be drawn, that there is no end in nature but every end is a beginning, that there is always another dawn risen on midnoon, and under every deep a lower deep opens." This is in line with the teaching of the octave, the occult teaching of the octave, and why, symbolically, Jesus was resurrected Monday morning, which was the eighth day of the old week and the first day of the new week. As Isaiah said, take a little of seven and a little of eight, because in ancient numerology of the sacred numbers (I am not thinking of it as a fortune-telling device), seven stood for the completion of a series, and eight becomes one, which is the beginning of a new series. That is why we have the seven days in the week and seven branch candlesticks and in the old Mosaic law, the statute of limitation was seven years.

This is why Emerson said, in another place, "We wake and find ourselves on a stair; there are stairs below us, which we seem to have ascended; there are stairs above us, many a one, which go upward and out of sight." It is the teaching that every stair in evolution is a reproduction of the one just below it and a reproduction on a higher scale and a reproduction on a lower scale—if we can use higher and lower—of the one just above it.

"Still, as the spiral grew, he left the past year's dwelling for the new." Oliver Wendell Holmes catches that vision there, and always the end of one series is the beginning of the other in a cosmic evolution of sequence. As the Hermetic teachings said, "As above, so beneath; as below, so above; what is true on one plane is true on all." These are what he referred to in that mystical saying.

Emerson said, "There are no fixtures in nature. The universe is fluid and volatile. Permanence is but a word of degrees. Our globe seen by God is a transparent law, not a mass of facts. The law dissolves the fact and holds it fluid." If you will read Emerson's essay "Experience," you will get pretty much get what he had to say. I should like to read this one, at the beginning of "Experience:"

The lords of life, the lords of life,—
I saw them pass,
In their own guise,
Like and unlike,
Portly and grim,—
Use and Surprise,
Surface and Dream,
Succession swift and spectral Wrong,
Temperament without a tongue,
And the inventor of the game
Omnipresent without name;—
Some to see, some to be guessed,
They marched from east to west:
Little man, least of all,
Among the legs of his guardians tall,
Walked about with puzzled look.
Him by the hand dear Nature took,
Dearest Nature, strong and kind,
Whispered, "Darling, never mind!
To-morrow they will wear another face,
The founder thou; these are thy race!"

Isn't that terrific?

There is no fixture; God sees in his transparent law. And again, Emerson said that we see the universe as solid fact, God as liquid law. And the Law of Mind, "the law dissolves the fact and holds it fluid." Is that any different from the thing I marked here in *The Quimby Manuscripts*? So far as I know *The Quimby Manuscripts* are the most original books in the world. It make take another hundred years for people to know it. Here is a guy—no one told him what to say. I think he is terrific. Quimby speaks of mind in the ordinary sense of the term as a substance, a substance which can be changed, in which thoughts are sown as seeds. Mind is put in contrast with intelligence or wisdom—mind is not intelligence or wisdom, according to Quimby—thus, intelligence is said to possess an identity or reality that mind does not have.

Remember, we treat with mind, and Troward did more. In this sense, as neither person, place, nor thing of itself, it is a medium. Troward said it is indeterminate, impersonal, plastic, present. It knows how to do, but it doesn't know that it is doing.

It will be necessary to give the reader some idea of what is suggested in the following article, headed by "Mind Is Spiritual Matter," in which Quimby said, "I found that by the power of my own mind, I can change the mind of my patient and produce a chemical change in his body, like dissolving a tumor." Mrs. Eddy converted this as: "There is no life, truth, intelligence, nor substance in matter. All is infinite Mind and Its infinite manifestation, for God is All-in-all." There is no life, truth, or intelligence, or substance in matter, divinely authorized, uncontaminated by human hypocrisies.

The word "mind" is not the substance, only the name of a substance that can be changed. The key to Quimby and to Christian Science treatment and all modern metaphysical treatment is so simple that, as Quimby said, "The mind is matter in solution, and matter is mind in form." But there is a superior wisdom to which this form and this formless is as the matter of spirit. That is the key, because in that practice, as I want to talk tonight, you already know it. The key to the whole thing is not that the disease is a—this is important—not that a disease or a situation is a result of a mode of thought. It is a mode of thought. The more you think about that, the more you will get a key to all spiritual mind healing that is consciously used with a definite technique.

In other words, there should be no difference in our treatment between the thought and what it does, because what it does is what the thought is. The nearest comparison would be in physics, in Einstein's statement that energy and mass are equal, identical, and interchangeable. The world makes mind intelligence. I put no intelligence in it, but make it subject to intelligence.

Now, of course, Troward hadn't read Quimby, and Quimby hadn't read Troward. I don't assume that Troward had read Quimby. Troward had a very similar concept, except he dealt with mind in the subjective state. That would be what this man would mean. I call the power that governs mind, Spirit. I think this is confusing. But you will see, I recognize the wisdom superior to the word "mind," for I always apply the word "mind" to matter but never apply it to the first cause. Have you read this passage before? It is one of most significant in Quimby. It is in *Mind Is Spiritual Matter*, on page 180. He says, "I always apply the word mind to matter, but never apply it to the First Cause. Mind is spiritual matter. Thought is also matter but not the same matter, any more than the earth is the same matter as the seed which is put into it. Thought, like the seed, germinates and comes forth, like a tree, in the form of an idea. It then waits, like the fruit, to be eaten. Illustration: A thought is sown in the mind while asleep or ignorant; it grows and comes forth. Disease is what follows the disturbance of the mind; this mind is spiritual matter." To him mind has a dual aspect of liquid and solid or temporary solid, and disease is what follows the disturbance of the mind or spiritual matter.

Then he says, "Weight, like mind, could never set itself in motion. But being set in motion, it is called mechanical power. So is mind, set in motion, spiritual power. Truth works by laws, like mathematics; error, like chance." I said this morning that we can believe what is not so; we can only know what is so. Truth is the only thing that can be known. Isn't it because what ain't so, ain't?

Disease is what follows an opinion. It is made up of mind, directed by error, and truth is the destruction of this error. The mind, being matter under control of the spirit, is capable of producing any phenomenon. That is remarkable, I think.

Question from Don C:
Ernest, will you repeat that about mind not having anything to do with first cause? Would you explain that a little further?

Remember how he is using the word "mind." Emerson uses it a little differently from what we do. If Troward had understood our terminology, or if it had been applied such as the way Troward did, he would be speaking of mind here, as Troward speaks of the universal subjectivity—a substance to be molded. But I think, better than Troward or better than anyone else, Emerson put the idea that mind as an idea and mind as the form are the same thing, because only thought could dissolve thought. In other words, the form is a thought. It isn't a form separate from a thought. Thought does not operate upon the form.

If you ever read *Christian Science Simplified* by Herbert W. Eustace, he gave a wonderful explanation. You don't spiritualize matter or materialize spirit. In other words, there isn't something unlike operating upon what is unlike itself. But like is operating on like. So to this idea of mind, he never refers to is as the first cause because Quimby believed in what he called a superior wisdom, the mind of Christ or science. Where you will find most everything that is in *Science of Being* and *Science and Health*, he supposes a superior wisdom that governs mind.

Now let's get back to Emerson and the universe. "There are no fixtures in nature. The universe is fluid and volatile. Permanence is but a word of degrees. Our globe seen by God is a transparent law, not a mass of facts. The law dissolves the fact and holds it fluid." That is no different from what I have just read from Quimby. Emerson says, "In the thought of to-morrow there is a power to upheave all thy creed, all the creeds, all the literatures, of the nations, and marshal thee to a heaven which no epic dream has yet depicted. Men walk as prophecies of the next age. ... The life of man is a self-evolving circle, which from a ring imperceptibly small, rushes on all sides outwards to new and larger circles and that without end." This is one of his great essays, "Circles." That passage should apply pretty well to what we are doing.

In the thought of tomorrow there is a power to upheave all the creeds. He said also to beware when God lets loose a thinker on this planet, then everything is subject to being changed. Oh, here it is, "Beware when the great God lets loose a thinker on this planet. Then all things are at risk. There is not a piece of science but its flank may be turned tomorrow; there is not any literary reputation, not the so-called eternal names of fame, that may not be revived and condemned. The very hopes of man, the thoughts of his heart, the religion of nations, the manners and morals of mankind are all at the mercy of a new generalization. Generalization is always a new influx of the divinity into the mind." That is on page 171 of "Circles." It is one of Emerson's great sayings; it would go with the other saying. I have read this book for twenty-five years, just as I have the one on Quimby, so I can use them.

Question from Paul:
Emerson uses mind the same way as Quimby, doesn't he?

I thought it was the same way, at least he used this thing as a liquidity. He said, "An institution is the lengthened shadow of one man, and all history revolves itself very easily into the biography of a few stout and earnest persons." Troward said, "This is a generalized statement of the broad principle by which Spirit expands from the innermost to the outermost, in accordance with a law of tendency inherent in itself. Without the element of individual personality, the Spirit can only work cosmically by a generic law, but this law admits of far higher specialization." Do you remember? In his *Law and the Word*, which is one of the things I want to use tonight to show that at any time a new sequence of cause and effect is set in motion and, as he said, "Relying on the maxim that Principle is not bound by precedent, we should not limit our expectations of the future." But Troward dealt with the universal subjectivity as a creative agency, which, while it is a mind stuff and a substance stuff and a plastic, impersonal, and neutral stuff ready to be operated upon, it is exactly like the soil in the ground. It is intelligent to do but doesn't know it is doing. It is creative but doesn't know that it is creating but it cannot initiate anything. I think Quimby had the same idea there.

And that is basic to our thought. Now, we are initiating a new religion, in a sense. I think it is a new religion. People often ask me, what makes you think it is right? And I certainly don't think it is right because I had anything to do with it. I didn't write it. I wrote about what has been taught, and I think had sense enough to discriminate between the intuitive and the psychic. I don't know and sometimes wonder. I am not the writer and not original, but these thoughts that are gleaned from the ages must constitute the highest truth that is known, or else no truth is known.

But remember this, you who are leaders: There is nothing in our setup that perpetuates anything I ever did, because if some of you don't do something better, then our cause is hopeless. So far as the world is concerned, it is a bauble, a ship that passes in the night. It is a light that is good but not good enough.

Out of this should evolve—but here is the danger. Most people mistake liberty for license and unity for uniformity, and both are wrong. The danger of our movement will not be in its teaching, but in the freedom of its teaching. And I wouldn't give a nickel for it if it didn't have the freedom. And if it wants to shatter itself on the rocks of experience, it is none of my business, and I can't help it. I used to think I could. Out of this may or may not evolve, in the next hundred years, what the world really needs. There is nothing else known in the world today out of which it can evolve. It won't be up to me; it will be up to you guys, whether you pull it apart and put it together again. And that is your business.

Always remember this and never forget it: We have fallen heir to the heritage of the ages, and we need not be ashamed of what we teach or of what we believe because if we are, then shame be on the intelligent of the world throughout the ages. This I would not accept. Evelyn Underhill said the only knowledge we have of the kingdom of heaven has come through the consciousness of man. Therefore, she said, the mind should swing between prayer, contemplation, and action. We are not a religion that believes only in prayer and contemplation.

I think if we could all be shocked until there was nothing left to be shocked out of us, we would start with almost a balanced mind. But we are so filled with emotional prejudices and intellectual biases that it is almost impossible for anybody to think straight, and Jung carries this way back into the collective unconscious and shows how the prototypes of thought have come down through the ages. We are born hypnotized and, believe me, mostly we stay hypnotized.

Out of this movement can come what the world is waiting for, but it isn't just the meditative movement. It is the meditation that leads to action. It is a meditation that will find in action merely the physical correspondent of the psychic fact, which is its physical correspondent in execution. Is that clear? It doesn't seem very clear to me, yet I know it is true. It is just what I read from Emerson and Quimby, and we will put it in our language and say there is no difference between the thought and the thing. The thing is the thought as the thing, else thought couldn't affect it.

Now if that is true and we swing between prayer, meditation, and living—you see to us, all the systems of retiring from life to serve God or be good are beautiful but false—we have no criticism of them. But anyone who knows anything about the way the mind works and emotions work knows that every one of those who goes to a convent or to the side of a hill and digs a hole is a sick man. I don't care how much he serves God with it. He can't face life or he would be out there facing it. Do you believe this?

You know, that is one of things we have to do. Someone says, let's have a retreat, and I always ask, "What shall we retreat from?" I want us to stay with the field and advance. Some of these people often say to me (with this spiritual snootiness), "What is the background for your movement?" And I always say, "Thank God, the only background our movement has is what ground we leave behind as we advance into the foreground." That is good, very good.

Now let's get to Meister Eckhart. He was a Catholic priest who was excommunicated two hundred years after they discovered what he had been talking about. Jean Racine said, "Life is a comedy to him who thinks, a tragedy to him who feels." And it is so very true. It is an axiom in psychology that it isn't the experience but our emotional reaction to it.

Christ in you is the birth of God in you. This is quite a thing for a Catholic priest to say. He says this takes place in the sinner as well as the saint, for both have the same Being at the core of their being. Walt Whitman said about the prostitute, "I will reject you when the wind no longer blows."

Speaking about the new church, I want in the vestibule, or whatever you call it, a bust of every great religious leader and a few of the great thinkers, from Zoroaster down. This is a universal religion. We have gathered it from every source. And what do you suppose I want the inscription under the bust or whatever it is of Jesus? I want: "Neither do I condemn thee." I think it is the greatest thing he ever said. It is so cosmic, so universal, so all-inclusive, and it is the greatest tribute I think we can pay to Jesus. Someone will find something else that has to do with salvation, but nothing is lost but a lack of an idea of harmony. To the Jews it will be, "God is One. Hear, O Israel, the Eternal God." Emerson, it will be, "There is one mind common to all individual men." And if any of you think of just one line from any of the great ones, let me know because I am trying to work on it now.

Well, here is the saint and the sinner and he says, when one turns to God a light at once begins to glimmer and shine within. I want to read you something about the light that I have written. This is not a word imagery; this is mysticism. It is not a poem; it is not blank verse. It is a description of an experience. I want you to think of it from that viewpoint.

"He causes the sun and rain to come alike on the just and the unjust." When we get our little peewee egos punctured, and get over that misery, and take a new step in evolution, and it is possible for people like we are to see beyond this theological bunk that is spread over the world and discover the seed of perfection nestled at the heart of all things, you will find it in the saint and the sinner. The only difference is that most of the saints were not very interesting. I said to Adela the other day, "There is no God who knows anything about virtue or viciousness." And Emerson said that when virtue is conscious, it is vicious. I love that.

Effort can neither explain nor bring this light into being. It is beyond the intellect; it just can't do it. Every attempt to explain it will cause confusion in the intellect. There are certain things we are going to have to learn to accept. We don't claim to have all the answers. I won't waste my time on anyone who thinks he has all the answers. Emerson said it in a nicer way. He said that when he meets a new man, he hopes to find a lake to swim in, and he finds only a puddle in which he may wade.

More often, they are swept back into the ocean of their being, unrevealed. I think here is one of the troubles our with our revelations. I believe in revelations because revelation is the intuition speaking to the intellect, but it looks at what is between that makes it almost impossible to get it. Then the intellect is liable to explain it in the light of its desire, conscious or unconscious, so we get all these crazy things, like Mormons baptizing people who have gone on and Catholics praying them out of limbo.

Now he quotes from St. Augustine—this is Eckhart: "There are many people who have sought light and truth but they look for it outside themselves where it is not. When one turns to God, at once a light begins to glimmer and shine within. I know more than I was ever taught." Isn't that an interesting saying? And the same is true of God, who sees everything in Himself.

I believe this. See what you think of it. I do not believe there is any God that knows you beyond your ability to know yourself. This is no way limits God. I do not believe there is any abstraction in the universe that knows itself. I do not believe there is any God or intelligence in the universe that knows anything that happens, other than Itself, as though it were happening to It. You can't have division, and we can't deny everything we don't like just to save our own intellects. Eckhart again: "God sees everything in Himself. It is by reason of this fact that we are made perfect by what happens to us rather than by what we do. It is necessary that God should both be active and passive in order that He may know and love Himself."

Whether he knew it or not, this goes right back to the original Hindu philosophy. It is exactly the way Aurobindo states, that "everything exists for the delight of God." I like that idea. That He may know and love Himself in the soul. And the soul may know as He knows and love as He loves, for it is for this reason that the soul is more blessed by what is His than by what is its own. And for this reason, its blessing depends more on what He does than on anything we can do.

I think that is pure mysticism. What we plant in the soil of contemplation we shall reap in the harvest of action. Begetting our spiritual counterparts, eternity is above all ideas or images. These are mystical sayings. Relax, and let God operate upon you. But when a person has a true spiritual experience, he may boldly drop external disciplines.

One of the troubles with this guy Eckhart was he said if they were all right, they wouldn't need priests, confessions, or anything. All of these things we will say are for the uninitiated. And be sure you read this, what is called *Eckhart's Trial: The Defense*. The defense is where he defended himself in Rome, and it has about fifty pages. It is one of the most subtle forms of reasoning ever put into print.

Mysticism Class Four

JULY 11, 1957

I want to call your attention to a new book, *The Oxford Book of English Mystical Verse.* It is very good. I just draw your attention to it. And also I want to read you a little of something I have written. It speaks about "gods creating man with freedom of will to continue their plan, but concealing the secret of life and freedom deep in the center of man to be left to the time of his waking, that even the gods did not purpose or plan when they ignited the clod and waited."

You remember James Russell Lowell says, "Every clod feels the stir of might/An instinct within it that reaches and towers/And groping blindly above it for light/Climbs to a soul in the grass and flowers." That would be good Hindu philosophy of the mind that sleeps in the mineral, waves in the grass, and wakes to simple consciousness in the animal and self-consciousness in man and God consciousness in the upper hierarchies, all of which I happen to believe in.

But buried deep in the chambered dark, they have planted the seed of perfection. Walt Whitman said, "Enclosed and safe within its central heart/Nestles the seed perfection." Some poet said:

> *To sleep in the mineral, wave in the grass and follow the leopard to its lair,*
> *To wake in the consciousness of man by endless sequence of cause and effect,*
> *Through time and timeless, whichever endures,*
> *Extant the stars and planets above,*
> *And follow the galaxies out in the air,*

And starting again in the reaches of time,
Continue the cycle without any end,
From the less to what is more, ever ascending,
Each round of creation in fullness of time,
Giving birth to another but greater
And forever the cycle continues.

That is pure Hinduism. Do you recognize it? That is good mysticism but not good poetry.

Here is another one:

From life's constant inner urgings to know the why, the what and how,
From its ceaseless asking, surging, there is no final proof but thou,
If logic wise and wisdom fair should unite nor stand alone
They would find the Sphinx's answer,
That which sows was never sown.
"Who am I?" addressed to what it is that sows,
You alone shall make reply for only you the sower knows.
This the secret of the ages through all one enduring plan,
The fire of heaven caught in atom, celestial essence caught in man,
The gift of God to all on earth,
What nature brought at earliest dawn, the seed of life that came with birth
Is uncreated and unborn,
For cause has neither why nor what,
Original, it stands alone from its own being
Putting forth sowing, itself was never sown.

That isn't good poetry but it is mystical and deeply philosophical.

The theme of this is self-existence: The seed of life is uncreated and unborn, sowing itself was never sown. These stand alone. And I have often said over and over that "self-existence" is the biggest word. We have to conceive of that which was not born and cannot die. We have to conceive of that which is self-existent. It isn't even self-cause—that is just another way of saying God didn't make God; God is.

It is very difficult for us to conceive of a causation that nothing caused. But since something is, we have to conceive of it. That is why the first axiom of truth and reason starts with a self-evident proposition: "Truth is that which is," and an axiom is a self-evident truth or a truth so evident that intelligence cannot deny it.

Now we will get down to Emerson. He said, "Why drag about this monstrous corpse of your memory, lest you contradict somewhat you have stated in this or that public place?" "These are the voices which we hear in solitude, but they grow faint and inaudible as we enter into the world."

I think that is interesting. Trust your own emotion. "In your metaphysics, you have denied personality to the Deity; yet when the devout motions of the soul come, yield to them heart and life, though they should clothe God with shape and color. Leave your theory, as Joseph his coat in the hands of the harlot, and flee." This is a very great mystical concept because Emerson did not believe in an anthropomorphic God. You will find the same thing in the section of our textbook under the "Perfect Whole," which I think most of our students overlook because they get caught up in the first part. But it is all in there.

Someday in another fifty or one hundred years people will catch it and know what it means. It is mathematically and logically certain that since there is no individual anything in the universe—because if there were, all things would be isolated—all things are individualizations of a totality of things and essence. Therefore, it is mathematically certain that since no two thumbprints are alike, no two individuations of the Infinite can or ever were or ever will be alike. Imitation is suicide; unity is not uniformity; multiplicity is not division; universality does not mean impersonality.

It is necessary if people really want to think things through, which very few people seem to want to take the time to do, that they understand these things. In our system of thought we have the most exalted concept of the warmth and color and personalness uniquely personal to each one of us I have ever seen put in writing, anywhere. And it is all in that section.

Emerson says, "A foolish consistency is the hobgoblin of little minds, adored by little statesmen and philosophers and divines." He says, "Misunderstood! It is a right fool's word. Is it so bad then to be misunderstood? Pythagoras was misunderstood, and Socrates, and Jesus, and Luther, and Copernicus, and Galileo, and

Newton, and every pure and wise spirit that ever took flesh. To be great is to be misunderstood." (I like that because it praises my vanity.)

He said, "Men imagine" (you see, I imagine he is talking about me, and so do you, and it won't do you much good unless you do) "that they communicate their virtue or vice only by overt actions, and do not see that virtue or vice emit a breath every moment. There is a great responsible Thinker and Actor working wherever a man works, that a true man belongs to no other time or place but is the center of things. Where he is, there is nature. Every true man is a cause, a country, and an age."

Emerson continues on to say, "An institution is the lengthened shadow of one man. In that deep force, the last fact behind which analysis cannot go, all things find their common origin. For the sense of being, which in calm hours rises, we know not how, in the soul, is not diverse from things, from space, from light, from time, from man, but one with them and proceeds obviously from the same source whence their life and being also proceed." Isn't that remarkable?

You see, Emerson understood that the unity of all life is an indivisible unity and permits of no fragments. "The simplest person who in his integrity worships God, becomes God." There is nothing holy but your own soul. We must take Jesus with virtue and the possibility of all men. "Whenever a mind is simple and receives a divine wisdom, old things pass away; means, teachers, texts, temples fall; it lives now and absorbs past and future into the present hour.... Whence then this worship of the past?" Although he knew so much about antiquity, he had no very great reverence for it. But he knew more about the ancient teachings than any other American up until his time and probably with a deeper appreciation than any American of any time or any man in Europe whose thoughts I have ever read. Peter Ouspensky may have.

Emerson said, "These roses under my window make no reference to former roses or to better ones; they are for what they are; they exist with God today. There is no time to them. There is simply the rose; it is perfect in every moment of its existence." This is from *Self-Reliance*.

I had something here from Quimby I wanted to read On Mysticism or Christ or Science, from which chapter, and there was a great deal of what came out as Christian Science, is at least very similar. Let us say, has the same odor.

To know God is to know ourselves, and this knowledge is Christ or truth, and he says the use of it is the Science of Christ. Once Quimby called it "Christian Science," not that we care or that it matters to us. We don't care where anything came from or how it got there. All we want to know is, is it true? I was thinking last night, we are a new form of Catholicism. I wish our people—that means the leaders; the public knows nothing about it; they take what you give them. They say it must be right because you tell them—I wish our leaders could see what a new form of catholicity really means because a lot of them are crying, like everyone in every organization does. We all do and might as well admit it. In a new catholicity, there is room for everything that is right. The Catholic Church has one hundred different orders in it. The Anglican Church has, too, but they all dovetail in one final agreement, without which they would not have existed or come into being or subsisted.

Carmelita said yesterday she thought it would be a grand to have a sanctuary where people would go and pray and do all these things off in the woods. And I said, "That is good, and I happen to know two people who heard you, who have plenty of money and could do it as far as money is concerned and probably would be very glad to." There is nothing in our system against anything like that. If someone wants to go down the road, carrying a cross and singing "Nearer My God to Thee," I don't care, if they will only know that there are two fundamental truths you can't get away from: There is nothing in the universe but action and reaction, nothing, and the polarity between the two, nothing.

The action is spontaneous combustion of an infinite personalness, which we do not comprehend: God. The reaction is law. There isn't anything else because all relationships are established by this. There are two pillars in front of the temple of Solomon. They are the law and the word, represented by the Ark of the Covenant of the Mosaic law and order, because Ark means a vehicle containing the life principle and the Covenant, the eternal laws of God that cannot be broken.

We are a new catholicity. If there is anything that would be distasteful to me, it would be the idea that anybody ever thought that I or anybody else ever wanted this thing to be tied down to what I or any other one person ever said. I would be the one who would burn up my own writings before anybody else could, myself.

Just as I would be the first one to destroy any organization that tried to perpetuate another superstition or, because of the stupidity of the people, would try to exalt another person. I don't believe in it.

Instead of your happiness being in the world, the world's happiness is in you. Why couldn't we evolve something that would take into account all of these things, give credit to them, give plenty of room for them, give our consent to them. And if somebody wants to erect a great big cross over their cathedral, let them do it. If anybody wants to take the bread and wine, let them do it. But let them explain what it means. It has nothing to do with salvation. It is not the body of Jesus; Jesus didn't leave any body. He is the only guy who got out without leaving an undertaker's bill for somebody else to pay, the smartest of them all. But let us do it intelligently, as free people cooperate for a definite purpose, rooted in the cosmos. If there will ever come that vision to the world you will see something happen.

Now, let's get back to Quimby, who found out what nobody taught him.

<u>Question from Don C</u>.:
May I ask a question? Lots of times someone will say, "But this isn't Religious Science." In an individual case when a person is endeavoring to reach this catholicity and explore what is true, you said there is room in the movement for anything that is true. Many times people say, "Well, that isn't Religious Science." Isn't that a limitation?

Yes, I think so. Someone came to one of our teachers one day and said, "We went to a séance last night, and the medium read from *Science of Mind* magazine." They thought that was terrible. I said, "Get me the name of the medium. I would like to send her a deluxe edition of our textbook." And then I thought of a story of a family that prays, and they are all down on their knees praying. And when they get through, little Johnny went over to his father and said, "Jimmy had his eyes open, looking around when you were praying." And his father said, "How did you know, Johnny?"

And God says, "Where are you, Adam? Who told you you were naked?" A sick man is like a criminal cast into prison for disobeying some law man has set up. I plead his case; and if I get the verdict, the criminal is set at liberty. If I fail, I lose the case, and his own judgment is the judge. His feelings are his evidence. If my explanation is satisfactory to the judge, he or you will give me the verdict. This ends the trial, and the penitent is released. You are all familiar with that, but it is very interesting to me.

There is one thing that neither Mrs. Mary Baker Eddy nor Quimby explained. They announced, but they didn't explain it. Troward did explain it, but from Troward we do not get quite enough of what it means. There is no such thing as your subjective mind and my subjective mind or the subconscious or unconscious mind of psychology. They have no existence whatsoever, and yet everything happens as though it were true. It has no existence as an individual thing. It is merely the reaction to an individualization in a neutral field of creative possibility, now by identity attached to that individual and through instrumentality flowing through it. Does that make any sense? What I am saying is this: If it takes four sacks of meal to fatten a lamp post, how many potato peelings will it take to shingle a barn? It is a mathematical proposition and very difficult. I never got it figured out.

There is one common field of reaction of law to our identification with anything, causing us to automatically become the instrumentality of its operation. There is no such thing as your law and my law. There is the subjective state of our thought in a common medium. Now individually and collectively (Jung, collectively), the psychiatrist analyzes these reactions and thinks he is analyzing an independent individual mind, not realizing that if he were, he couldn't get at it. We can see an external object only because it awakens an intuition in a common denominator in our own mind, which merely means this: You and I look at the mountain. We both see a mountain, and the mountain is not an illusion. We both see it because the mind that sees it, the mind that put it there is looking at it. Emerson said history is a record of the doings of that mind on this planet and that we can interpret history only in this light, for there is one mind common to all individual men.

Jesus called this truth the Son of God. Peter called it Christ, but the people's ignorance compounded the two and called it Jesus Christ. Isn't this rather an interesting thing. On page 197 of *The Quimby Manuscripts*, Jesus called this truth "christ" and "truth." Jesus called this truth the son of God; Peter called it Christ. "'Thou, the Christ, the Son of the Living God,' and Jesus said, 'Upon this rock I will build my church and the gates shall not prevail against it.'" The people's ignorance confounded the two and called it Jesus Christ. In another place, he [Quimby] said, "People have confused Jesus with virtue and the possibility of all men. To suppose that Jesus performed a miracle is to suppose him ignorant of the power he exercised, and if so, he was just as much a quack as those he condemned." Quimby claimed Jesus knew what he was doing.

Mrs. Eddy thought of this by saying, "The only thing faith should do to us is heal us of faith" because, she said, this is done by understanding and not faith. I knew a Christian Science practitioner once who was friendly enough to talk to me and she said, "What do you teach?" And I said, "The truth, so far as I understand it." And she said, "Then you must teach Christian Science." And I said, "No, I differ in many ways." And she said, "How can you teach the truth unless you are teaching Christian Science?" And I said, "Where does the truth come from?" "Mrs. Eddy's revelations told of God." And I said, "What happened to God then?" She happened to have wit enough to see.

He [Quimby] said, "What Jesus did never belonged to this world. He didn't talk about any kind of a religion; it talked to itself. Itself was its life, and its life was the healing of the sick and distressed." I think that is one of greatest things Jesus said because, to us, the treatment is the thing and there should be no difference between the treatment and what it does, in my estimation. And that is why I think no treatments can never be alike because there can never be any formula for treatments. It has to be a spontaneous combustion.

He said, "Christ never was intended to be confused with the man Jesus. He is in us and a part of us, and to know ourselves is to know Christ and to preach Christ is to help each other out of our troubles, destroying the enemy that has taken possession of us." You see his old theory: The explanation is the cure. Christian Science is that, if in your argument, the balance of this is on the affirmative side, that it will produce the result. All you are doing really is to inductively and deductively argue to that which listens only deductively and cannot hear inductively. That is all you are doing.

He who expects God to leave science and come down to ignorance and change a principle for a selfish motive to please Him is either a knave or a fool. A desire to know God is a desire to know ourselves, and that requires all of our thoughts to come into this happy state of mind that will lead man in the way to health. This is a science and is Christ's prayer. Emerson said, "The simplest person, who in his integrity worships God, becomes God."

Now let's get to Eckhart: "The opening of the door and the entry are simultaneous." Isn't that interesting? He is talking about opening the door to spiritual perception. This is what I was talking about this morning, that the opening of the door and entry are simultaneous and this, to me, is self-evident in all the psychological facts. That is all they are trying to do. But they [Christian Scientists] are trying to do it one way, and we are trying to do it another. And all either of us are trying to do is trying to get rid of the interference in between, which they call the conflict.

Meister Eckhart said, "For if there were any void under heaven whatever, great or small, either the sky would have to draw it up to itself or bend down to fill it." Isn't that interesting? You see, it is a continuum, a very interesting thing.

There is a beautiful love poem called "The Lady of Seville," which is very mystical. This young traveler comes along, and the lady is leaning over the balcony. And there is a river here. And she leans down, and he stands up in the stirrups and kisses her. And then he starts to go on, and she liked this pretty good and said, "Come back," and he said, "No, I am on the road." And she asked why, and he says, singing to her:

> *The river forever flows singing along,*
> *The rose on its bank bends her down to his song,*
> *And the flower, as it listens, unconsciously dips,*
> *And the rising wave listens and kisses its lips.*
> *But why the wave rises and kisses the rose,*
> *And why the rose bends to those kisses,*
> *Who knows, who knows.*
> *And away flows the river, but whither, who knows.*

Isn't it beautiful? And I don't know why I think of it here.

Everything stands for God, and you see only God in all the world. Nothing else. Eckhart perceived the Omnipresence as it is; modern metaphysicians try to perceive it as it isn't, are very liable not to perceive it because they are separating the human from the divine—and there is no such thing, the good from the bad, their type of virtue from my type of vice. And they don't know that saints and sinners all have hearts and livers that you couldn't tell apart. Just stupid, which is the only sin there is.

I speak of love. He who is caught by it is held by the strongest of bonds, and yet the stress is pleasant. He [Eckhart] speaks of it somewhere else as a sweet bondage. Isn't that a beautiful expression? There, in the innermost core of the soul, where God begets his son, human nature also takes roots. There, too, it is one and unanalyzable. Anything that might appear to belong to it and yet could be distinguished from it would not be of that unity. You couldn't make a better statement of what you and I believe, if we really believe in unity. Here is a Catholic priest in the 15th century, and he continuously refers to that which is unanalyzable. You see, all that science does is to analyze the way things work. They don't know. They don't know how; nor do we. All inquiry into the truth is to expose how the truth works and to suppose from this exposing that it must be of such a nature. That, I told you, Gandhi said in the last part of his life. Truth is God. God can be only explained from what happens. But if we start with the idea that God is Truth, then all our preconceived opinions or what we think is truth are attributed to God. Isn't that a terrific distinction? Did you know there is a record of Gandhi's voice?

Eckhart said, "To seek God without artifice, is to take Him as He is and so doing, a person 'lives by the Son' and is the Life itself. Life is its own reason for being. I live only to live." Isn't that interesting? He had gotten beyond our coming here to get our souls saved. He had got beyond it in his thinking of sin and salvation in his own mind. He had to conform somewhat to Catholic church. And to say that "a man lives only to live" is no different from Aurobindo saying that the manifest universe exists for the delight of God, which I think is a beautiful concept. I live only to live.

Now the orthodox will say, we live to save our soul and avoid hell—and raise a lot of hell while we are doing it. Very funny. Stupidity is a strange thing. But in our field, how far have we gone beyond that stupidity? Every day someone says to me, "This has come to teach us an experience." They better shave the Old Guy up there. They have only curled his whiskers so far; they haven't really given him a clean shave.

It is time that truth came—clean, unadulterated, and real. There is nothing "trying" anything in the universe—and never was and never will be. If there were, you would have a universal law that is self-destructive.

I admit, we learn by experience, tragically and in pain. But what do we learn? Only that the tragedy and pain exhaust themselves, both physically and mentally, and you are so reduced that finally through this method you might get quiet long enough to let in some influx that had never really gone out. I think we do learn by experience, most certainly, and I know I do—and it is a tough way to learn it.

Eckhart said, "Why live? I live only to live! And that is because Life is its own reason for being, springs from its own Source and goes on and on, without ever asking why, just because it is life." That is pure Religious Science and what little Ernie teaches. It is beyond all theology, all sin, all salvation. It is beyond the renunciation and denunciation and reincarnation of Eastern philosophy, the anathema of the Judaism Decalogue, and the silliness of modern theology, that hasn't sense enough to know smoke goes up a chimney.

"Life is its own reason for being, springs from its own source and goes on and on without ever asking why, just because life is life." I said to you the other day, "If you could personify God and say, 'God how did you get this way, where did you come from, what are you?' There would be nothing to respond. You would be speaking into a vacuum or void." Because, if the inexplicable explains itself, that what we call now the inexplicable is like the Hindu said: "If you give a name to it, it isn't that." That is what they meant in saying, "That which cannot be explained therefore must be accepted." Now in our field, our field calls for just as much surrender as the old theology, but it is a different kind of a surrender. Troward says it is "a surrender of the lesser to the greater intelligence," and I think that is probably good.

"God asks only that you get out of the way and let Him be in you." Let God be God in you. You give up to Him, and He will give up to you. When both God and you have forsaken self, what remains between you is an indivisible union. The axioms couldn't have done it any better. Have any of you studied *Axioms: The Book of Health and Science*? All of you ought to. It is Burnell's book. I think it is the best. It is all in my *Your Invisible Power*. It is all in there because I copied it out of Burnell: "God is nearer to me than I am to myself. Man is not blessed because God is in him and so near that he has God but in that he is aware of how near God is, and knowing God, loves Him. Man is not blessed because God is within him. He is blessed." But Burnell is trying to explain this: "He is blessed only when he recognizes what is within him." Isn't that rather remarkable?

"To see God aright is to know Him alike in everything. The soul that is to know God must be so firm and steady in God that nothing can penetrate it, neither hope nor fear, joy nor sorrow, love nor suffering, nor any other thing that can come in it from without." As I told you, Edward Rowland Sill said, "Though only for a flash, a man may see clear-eyed the future as he sees the past; from doubt, or fear, or hope's illusion free." The illusion of hope, he refers to it here.

The Gita says you have to do away with the pairs of opposites. It is not inside of time, it is of it. "It compares with speed beyond belief, the force of heaven is outside of time and yet time." (I don't know what this means. I knew what it meant when I marked it, but now I don't.) "He says God is within, we are without. God is at home, we are abroad." Emerson said something like it, only he said, "Traveling is a fool's paradise. Our first journeys discover to us the indifference of places. At home I dream that at Naples, at Rome, I can be intoxicated with beauty and lose my sadness. I pack my trunk, embrace my friends, embark on the sea, and at last wake up in Naples, and there beside me is the stern fact: the sad self, unrelenting, identical, that I fled from. I seek the Vatican and the palaces. I affect to be intoxicated with sights and suggestions but I am not intoxicated. My giant goes with me wherever I go." Isn't that interesting?

Here is Hopkins: "Call to the Lord of Life and Glory, beyond the bars of human sense, and all the living fountains lying deep in thee shall quicken into stirring streams. And all the pent-up wisdoms that inhabit thee shall leap to meet the Universal Wisdom, shining forth as the sun with the glory of their Father. He that seeks me identifies with me. He reigns with me. He lives as my life, He strengthens as my strength, He understands as my understanding. What I Am, He is. He calls upon my victorious name, and whatsoever He does prospers, reminding mankind of my ever-present, ever-friendly, ever-available supremacy. The angel of His Presence accompanies every man. It is his kingly Self. Two are ever in the field. One shall be taken, the other left. It is the closeness of the Ain Soph, the Great Countenance of the Absolute, above thinking and above being, which the Hebrews called Angel of God, the Brahmins called Divine Self or Stately Soul, the Christians call Jesus Christ." She says that attention is the secret of the success of all combinations. We combine with what we notice. We produce something worthwhile by combining with the angel of God's presence.

Let's review that a little and have a treatment.

As I said, Emerson probably had the greatest intellect since Plato. In my estimation he did. He knew what the Hindus taught and the Buddhists and the Muslims and the Christians and the Jews, but you know there is nothing in literature or religion anywhere, until Quimby began to teach, followed by who or what. As the mystic said, "If I love you, it is none of your business. If I recognize the truth, I don't care who else brought it."

There was nowhere in the history of the world, 'til this guy came along, wherever spiritual truth was consciously and definitely applied with a technique. Now they are discovering in the modern metaphysical movement that this is true. We want to take everything out of psychology and philosophy and theology that it has to give, but never, never be timid about your own self-possession. Don't be afraid of your own belief. Don't think that because the ancients didn't teach it and modern science may not announce it and some people may say you are crazy, that it is not true. A man said to me the other day that he is going to see a psychiatrist, and he told him he was going to hear Ernest Holmes, and the man said, "It is all damned nonsense." And he asked me what I thought of it, and I said, "The man doesn't know what we teach. If he did, he'd like it. If he doesn't, he can't help it, and it is damned nonsense to him. I believe what he is doing because

I understand it." I know what I am doing because I understand it, and I happen to understand where the two come together.

We are a modern renaissance, but we are not a reformation. We are evangelists; we are not reformers. We are not concerned whether anybody believes what we believe or not. We are happy if they get any good from what we do. I would like to find out if Billy Graham—that sincerity, that sweetness, which he certainly has, and that simplicity and that is a good hero for me; the rest I would like to forget—if he knew me, would he find just as much in me as I find in him that he would love, too?

I think it should be our genius to know that and to know it among others particularly. I don't think it is so important right now what the reaction of the world is to us because there is a great deal more reaction in the world than we can handle right now, ten times as much, for a lack of leadership. All that matters now is what is our reaction to it and to each other in what we are doing. That is all that we need to be concerned with for the next fifty years. And should it happen that it worked in line with a certain impulsion and a certain consistent rhythm, a religious concept will be introduced into the world that will revolutionize it. Should that happen to it which has happened to all the New Thought movements—I have known the great leaders for fifty years—it will shatter itself on the rocks of experience, and the tide that brought it in will wash it out because it will have proven itself unfit to meet the need of that particular period in evolution, which is trying to cast up eternity on the shores of time long enough to interpret the nature of reality to the age in which it acts.

Such little wit or wisdom that we have, we surrender to the idea, the big idea, the great idea, the cosmic whole, the perfect Christ, the living God, unseparate and inseparable from ourselves, begetting within us the only begotten, singing in us the song eternal, living in us the light that lightest every man's path. And as we listen, we hear Lord God of truth and peace and wisdom and love.

Mysticism Class Five

JULY 12, 1957

I would like to go on with the idea we talked about on Quimby yesterday, a little more of the concept of how he worked and what he taught, because out of what Quimby did came Christian Science and the New Thought movement. *The Quimby Manuscripts* is one of the few original books in the world. It is certainly the most original book I have ever read. It is possible there is not another single book in the world as original as this because Quimby was not taught what he taught, or if he was, there is no way of discovering it. Some think he may have read some of Swedenborg, particularly his *Law of Correspondence*.

There is no deviation in the Christian Science or modern New Thought field or our own to the method he used in "Techniques of Practice." It is the same thing. You will find in there the same thing as Mrs. Eddy's system, on page 410. He calls it his explanation. There is no other place in any literature in the world where the reference is made like the ones we talked about yesterday and today.

He says, "God is with us, even in our speech. You know, I have tried to prove that mind is spiritual matter, and if I have proved that, I will now show you that matter is life. That is the idea—mind is spiritual matter—and that is the basis. Mind to me is not wisdom but spiritual matter" (page 231). You see, as in our own field, someone said, "What is our idea of mind as different from Spirit?" There is confusion in our field about it. There is confusion in the field of Christian Science about this. There is confusion in everybody about it. There is confusion about what is the difference between mind and soul and spirit. So, let's admit we are confused about it and try to straighten ourselves out, but without any criticism.

One of most difficult things—and I have practically made up my mind that it is impossible; therefore, I have released it as a problem to me—is to have a lot of highly intelligent people like we are and strongly individualized as we all are. I see very little that happens between when a little girl becomes an old hag of twelve and a little boy becomes an old man of thirteen until we pass through a lot of experience. There is a great period of unwisdom there, because the spontaneity of the emerging thing is stifled, and the experience hasn't brought wisdom enough to have people very interested. I am more interested in young people and old people than I am what comes in between. There is more there to talk to.

I am not sure it is possible to take such a highly individualized group as we are, as nice as we are, and get them all to agree on any one idea long enough to let anything happen. All you can get out of grief is its emptiness and pain. I am going to wait very interestedly but not impatiently to see what you will do with it. Meanwhile, I would like to see if we could understand what we are doing.

I know so much about how the human mind works. Someone says, "You better study how the Divine mind works." This is the only thing that interprets the Divine mind. You can soar all you want to, but you are going to light. And the trouble isn't the distance you fall, but it is hitting so quick when you get there.

Quimby said, "Mind to me is not wisdom but spiritual matter." This is the background of all spiritual mind healing with a technique, whether it is Christian Science or anything else. Mind is spiritual matter, and here then we must say that we probably treat of mind in a dual aspect or a singular or a unitary thing. I have thought a great deal about this, and it is in our textbook. If there is what we call "a spirit" or if there is what we call "the Spirit," the only thing that will be aware of it in us, to know that it is aware of it, will be what we call our conscious intelligence. Therefore, whatever the Spirit is in us as our spirit, it is our conscious awareness. Do you think that is right? Then let's call that the aspect of mind that is objective rather than subjective, conscious rather than unconscious, although unconscious is a bad term.

So let us think of mind as Quimby is mentioning it, as that which can be changed, and, in our field, as mind in its subjective aspect, which is merely the way that intelligence operates or that a creative principle reacts to intelligence, which as Troward says, is not volitional. But to Quimby, mind is not wisdom but spiritual matter. And you see, even Quimby supposed what he called a superior. He says, "Let mind then embrace all matter of the human and brute creations, as the word matter embraces all animate substances. Then the soul will represent wisdom that creates from inanimate matter into manifest atoms." Now we have confusion in that statement.

We have the same kind of confusion we have in our work that all theology has, all philosophy has, all metaphysics, and that is the confusion of having, as Plotinus had, an absolute, a spirit, a soul, a mind, a matter. We have a spirit, a soul, and a body, and we don't know what we mean by soul at all, anymore than theology knows what it means by the trinity. I have never had one single intelligent answer because there is always one part of it that they say something about that has no meaning. It is nothing. And that is the soul part. That is probably why I am so confused over it.

I particularly asked Bill [Hornaday] to find out from Jung what his concept of that was. And his concept of it and the Plotinian and Platonic is nearer, because it is from that I got the idea of soul because it is from that. Christianity got it from the Greeks, you know. It really originally meant the feminine side of life, the Holy Mother that conceives and gives birth. It is about as near as we can come at it. But when Quimby treated mind as this fluidic thing, which in its superior wisdom takes hold of, he has not differentiated either between the mind, which is the matter, and the wisdom, which is also another phase of mind that manipulates the matter, has he? You still have a confusion here. How confusing it is to try to get out of confusion.

What is it that is not wisdom, God, or Spirit and not matter, and yet can be changed? He is trying to explain what I don't understand. It is matter held in solution called mind, which the power of wisdom can condense into a solid so dense as to become a substance called matter. Assume this theory, and you see how man can be sick or get well by a change of his mind. That is an interesting statement; it is on page 234. It is one of most interesting of all his statements because he asks himself the question we are just asking: What is it that is not wisdom? It isn't God; it isn't spirit and not matter, and yet can be changed. It is matter held in solution called mind.

Now when he says, "I change it by a superior wisdom," he is really saying there is a mental stuff which is subject to another mode of mind, which can change it—the mental stuff and the mode of mind that changes it. Now I will introduce a superior wisdom, and all he is doing is raising the attention of this thing that he has called the other thing. Is this at all lucid?

It is very important if we want to understand the origin of this thing, because we have to suppose—because I have tried to put this together with Plotinus and Plato and with our idea of spirit soul and body and in the Bible—the idea that the other ancients, because they have all had it. Isn't it the same thing Troward said in his "Self-conscious contemplation of the Spirit"? Yes, but here is still the greatest confusion in our whole field. I don't mean Religious Science. I mean the whole modern New Thought movement, because we are very liable to suppose a human mind that goes in search of a divine wisdom, rather than to suppose there is only one mind that perceives the divine wisdom. It does not become divine because it perceives it; it becomes better acquainted with truth.

In other words if any one of you or all of you understood as well as I do the action of conscious and subconscious and emotional states and unconscious projections coming back as revelations and intuitions, and then if you believed that there is an upper layer influencing a lower layer, you have not accounted for the fact that there is only one of whatever it is with different aspects. And I will tell you right now, this is where the New Thought people, all of them including ourselves, are pretty well mixed up.

I say it is of vast importance to the world, for if it can be shown that mind is spiritual matter, it will be seen that mind is under the control of a wisdom possessed by man, so that wisdom acting upon mind changes it and destroys the error and brings man to the truth. Now here we have what Mrs. Eddy said:

"The human mind alone suffers and is sick and the Divine mind alone heals it." But there is no such thing as the human mind and the Divine mind. If there were, one will not find the other. There are only different aspects of the same mind, and here this mind condenses into matter, and here it comes up into what we call spiritual. But it is only one; it cannot be two. There cannot be two of anything in the universe and that has to include every fact, whether we like it or not. (I detest snakes but they are in there somehow, and what in the name of God He did it for, I don't know.)

To suppose mind is wisdom is as false as to suppose that power is weight. Now this is a contradiction because mind is the only thing that can suppose the wisdom that mind assumes is not the mind that takes the form of the matter and the liquid and the fluid.

Question from Mollie:
Would we be dividing ourselves too much to speak of our subjective or unconscious mind?

Well, Mollie, I think what the psychologist analyzes, what he calls our subjective or unconscious, has no existence. It is reaction in a field of creative intelligence to our thinking. Our own conscious thinking, to me, is the action of whatever the Spirit is, whether we know it or not. What else can it be? I don't think it can be anything else, otherwise we become split personalities by causing this thing to reach for that thing and only this thing can recognize that thing and only like can know like.

Question from Mollie:
What about knowing hate?

We have to include this. One of the finest things Aurobindo ever said was that one of our troubles is that we have tried to attribute an impossible morality and ethics on the universe, because it is too small. It is only an incident. It is just negative use of the same thing; it has to be the same thing.

Scientific man sees through matter, which is only an error acknowledged as a truth. It is an error acknowledged as a truth. But what I am trying to bring out now is to save dualism. I mean to save us *from* dualism, in that what we call the human is merely the way we are using what we call the Divine. Otherwise, we will have a split personality. There isn't any question about this in my mind, not at all.

Our life is in our senses, and if our wisdom is in our mind, we attach our life and senses to matter. But if our wisdom is attached to science, our life and senses are in God, not in matter, for there is no matter in God or wisdom. Matter is the medium of wisdom. This led to my discovery, and I found that my real senses (now he is beginning to separate) are not in my body, but that my body is in my senses. And my knowledge located my senses according to my wisdom. A man who knows all this is in wisdom with all his senses and his life. If we can show that man's senses can act independently of his natural body (*Scientific Demonstration of the Future Life* by Thomas Jay Hudson was the basis of that) and it was the basis of extrasensory perception that they can reproduce all the activities of the organs, of the senses without using the organs of the senses. You have whatever you may call it independent of that. And in *The New Reach of the Mind*, it is taught that it leaves no trace as brain cells. You no longer have any use for the brain. We always thought we had use for it.

If we can show that man's senses can act independently of his natural body, if it can be shown that man's wisdom is not of matter but of God, we will divide him into as many senses as is necessary for the scientific world. That is a very interesting saying, I think.

In other words, Joseph Banks Rhine says, why should we limit senses to the five? There may be a million senses for all we know, and I believe that is true if we are dealing with Infinity. We ought to know that this is the source of modern spiritual mind healing.

I prophesy that the time will come when men and women shall heal all manner of disease by the word of their mouth. You see, Rhine believed just as Jesus did. "The words that I speak unto you, they are spirit and they are life, the words." I believe that, too. I don't see what else it can be, do you?

When people think they have a disease, which I know they have not, I do not ascribe it to their imagination but to the fact that they have been deceived. Mrs. Eddy said in one place, "This is more than imagination." Now, but to the fact that they have been deceived will lead us into the idea of the collective unconscious, the Jungian mind, the carnal mind, the mortal mind, the sum total of human thought. And this is something I have always held, and I think it is one of greatest mistakes we can make in our field, is to try to locate, we will say, your error, or your sins have produced this. Whether you call it error or sin or negation, it is neither person, place, nor thing; cause, medium, nor effect; and doesn't belong to anyone, but it is an impersonal human thought force operating wherever it can. Wherever the seed falls, something grows.

Don't you think we ought to take that viewpoint to get away from the harshness of this? I almost said it, so we'll get right back to my text. One of my troubles is I despise intolerance. And I sometimes think you ought to hate your own intolerance. Why don't you take it easy? I hate intolerance more than anything else. Ignorance is all right, it may excuse nobody from its effects, but ignorance is ignorance, and who is ignorant? Intolerance is vicious, and it is always masked in religious things in the nature of "God" to relieve the tension of the one who is intolerant and projects that which appeases a need unmet in some other way. As I said this morning, most of the saints were neurotic. That will shock most people, but even the Catholic Church now says they are going to analyze.

Give man the knowledge of one great truth: that man is constituted of two different principles—wisdom, which is seen in science, and error, which is seen in matter or in opinions. The latter is governed by no principle known to man—this is interesting—but is simply the action of cause and effect. But man who sees only the phenomenon puts wisdom into it, yet the cause is not seen. Mind, like the Earth, is under the direction of a higher power, which is subject to wisdom. The world calls this God. Everyone who knows that ideas can be sown in the mind like seed in the ground and that they will grow and bear fruit, the cause of both are unknown, but to the world above matter, they are known. To wisdom, these facts are ideas, but to matter, they are solid truths.

Remember where we read the other day that Emerson said, "The law dissolves the fact and holds it fluid." Quimby is saying the same thing. He never read Emerson, of course. This was written before Emerson wrote that, I guess.

Every disease is the invention of man and has no identity and wisdom, but to those who believe in it, it is truth. And how true that is. There is a bread, which if a man eat, he shall be filled. And this bread is Christ or science.

The basis of Dr. Quimby's theory is that there is no intelligent power, thought, action, and matter of itself, that the spiritual world to which our eyes are closed by ignorance or unbelief is the real world, that in it lie all the causes of every effect visible in the natural world, and that if this spiritual life can be revealed to us. In other words, if we can understand ourselves, we shall then have our happiness or misery in our own hands. And, of course, much of the suffering of the world will be done away with (page 319). And this is what the author of this book says about him, the one who wrote this, says you know—you know this was a brother of David Seabury. You all knew that, I am sure. Quimby died in the arms of the father of David Seabury and also the father of this man, Dresser. Dresser edits this, *The Quimby Manuscripts,* but Dresser's father was David Seabury's father. They didn't have the same mother.

Here is something entirely different. This is the most delightful mysticism probably in the world.

All of God's efforts are directed to reproducing Himself. Aurobindo says creation exists for the delight of God. There isn't any difference, is there? I believe this. There is no cause or purpose in creation as theology explains it. Inge says purpose is contradiction, mathematically and logically, therefore, it would be spiritually. He is saying the same thing. All of God's creation is to delight God. All that nature can do comes to an end with the making of form, color, and being. Thus, the work of nature ceases, but as it does so, it reappears in the work of the intelligent soul. This is quite a remarkable saying. The ancients said that nature unaided fails. Quimby has explained this better, more on the line that the Father hath life within Himself, so hath He given it to the son to have life within himself, that even a modern social reform that is rightly instituted is not separate from the originating mind but is merely the continuation of it at its level.

This is why Emerson said, "The ancient of days is in the latest invention." And he said, "Every invention is an intuition, and the development of every technique is but a series of intuitions." And I think that is a very interesting thing because we would have to put the whole thing together. If somebody strings beads, God is stringing the beads, and then God is going to count them. Then God is going to sing the rosary and listen to it. Then God is going to sing and go out and dance because He likes to sing and dance. I know from having worked for so many creative artists that that is the way it works, if you can do it. They will sing and dance, all right.

He says, in which God is pure and self-creating, there is no reason for being. Because if there could be a reason, then there would be a reason underlying the unitary God. Now, let me do it this way, because this is a point I have made so often, and it is misunderstood. I don't feel I am getting to be a misunderstood person, remember that. Creation has no reason for being, God has no reason for being, Creation has no reason for being outside of self-expression. If there could be a reason, then there would be a reason behind the reason. What he is saying is this: When you arrive at self-existence, do not try to explain it further. That is it. Things flow out of it. The first inquiry into truth is, "What is reality?" The next is merely, "How does it work?" And the third is, "Let it work." Everything flows out of a self-existence that stimulates itself into action by its own imagination or, as Plotinus said, "If I were to personify God, I would say I do not argue, I contemplate, and as I contemplate, I let fall the images of my thought" into what he called an indeterminate stuff, of which he said, nature is the great no thing but it isn't nothing.

He is begotten in the now moment and today. All begetting is in the now moment and today. Only the One is at rest in Itself, receiving nothing from without. There is your self-existence. There is your peace. Augustine said, "For Thou hast formed us for Thyself, and our hearts are restless 'til they find rest in Thee." The man who stops with the enjoyment of a symbol never comes to its inward truth, for all of these deities refer to one and only one truth. Thus, to get no farther than the symbol is to be kept from the one great truth. The symbol, other than as an artistic thing, should disappear as a substance is known.

Furthermore, there are people who are hindered by too much dependence on repentance and confession. That can be true. It is like people who are always afraid they are not good enough. Truth is to be found within for this reason. Do not cling to the symbol, but get to know the inner truth. To seek the spirit of God's truth is to be in spirit and truth. We were created only for God, the delight, not to get saved, not to have a purpose, not to accomplish a purpose and bring something or a gift to God that he didn't have, but to express the life that God is; that is why we are. There is no reason for being other than the expression of being. And you can take it right down to this: There is no song unless it is sung and no dance unless it is danced. Is there a sermon unless it is preached?

Meister Eckhart said, "The Eternal Wisdom said about Itself, 'He that created me reposes in my tent,' who withal is uncreated, for God is unborn wisdom." Isn't that a beautiful saying? He who created me rested in my tent. This goes on until even our debt is killed. He speaks of the desert of solitude, where the eternal Father teaches in His own being. The person who is thus within God's knowing and love becomes just what God Himself is. The person who is thus within God's knowing and love becomes what God Himself is. Emerson said, "The simplest person who, in his integrity, worships God, becomes God."

And he says, "for He and God are a unity," thus one becoming the real person for whom there can be no suffering, any more than the Divine Essence can suffer. He did not teach a suffering God. Emerson said, "The universe remains to the heart unhurt." God is already with us and we are united with him. And our union in each individual is unique and has nothing in common with anything else. That means objectively, as we would say. He understood that there is individuation but no individual anything in the universe. And because there is no individual anything, all individuations have the whole universality behind that particular individuation, as though if you were sewing on a button or painting a picture. All the thought and time and attention, power and presence of God is concentrated in the sewing on of that button and to nothing else in the universe, nothing else. And all time in the timeless is concentrated and all space, just in sewing on that button. Someone will say, "Suppose somebody else is sewing on a button?" Here is where the differentiation between individuation and individual comes in, to show that the totality of the indivisible universe is at any and every point in its infinity having no circumference. This is what these great people have seen, and this is what has made them great.

That person is both God and man. It is unique. Thus, in God all things are equal and are God, for He is this identity Itself. All things are in God and equal in God. Emerson said, "There is no great and no small to the soul that maketh all, and where it cometh, all things are and it cometh everywhere."

Eckhart said, "The eye by which I see God is the same as the eye by which God sees me. My eye and God's eye are one and the same, one in seeing, one in knowing, and one in loving." That is what I was trying to say the other night, that the two greatest teachings in the world or the two great ideas of the greatest single teaching are right there. What I mean is, I didn't make it up. Troward mentions it. They have all mentioned it. It is said right here: "The eye by which I see God is the same as the eye by which God sees me, my eye and God's eye are one and the same. One is seeing one and loving." Therefore, as Troward said, the point of saturation is never reached because of the Divine incarnation in me, the imminence, and this sees the transcendence. The transcendence flows into the imminence, back and forth, and one is the other. But this is the way it operates in us.

If anyone owned the whole world and gave it up as freely as he received it, God would give it back to him—and eternal life, to boot. All this and heaven, too, and as free as he was before he existed in this now moment. Like to like is the condition of unity. All time is contained in the present now moment, a blossoming of the Holy Spirit, in which the soul loves God. One of the apostles writes, "This is my beloved son, in whom I am well pleased." The second writes, "This is my beloved son, about whom everything pleases me." The third writes, "This is my beloved son, in whom I please myself." Whatever pleases God, it is in His only begotten son. And whatever God loves, He loves in him. Therefore, one should so live that he is identified with God's son and so that he is that son. Between that son and the soul, there is no distinction. That is the same as saying that the highest God and innermost God is one God.

As long as one clings to time, space, number, and quantity, he is on the wrong track. To say that God created the world yesterday or tomorrow is foolishness, for God created the world and everything in it in the one present now. Indeed, time that has been passed for a thousand years is as present and near to God as the time that is now. It is still one birth. To seek Him and apprehend Him in His uniqueness and abstraction, in the desert of solitude, is seeking Him in the essence of His being.

Contemplating the creature, God gave it being. And contemplating God, the creature received Its being. Contemplating the creature, God gives it being. And contemplating God, the creature receives Its being. It is terrific. (Someone said that Ernest Holmes said the same thing on a certain page in a book, and Ernest says he probably got it from a different page. And he doesn't care where it came from.)

God is intelligence occupied with knowing Itself. That is saying a mouthful. God is intelligence occupied with knowing Itself. The now moment gathers all parts of time unto itself. All things have a common prototype in God. God is neither being nor goodness, as such. God is neither good, better, nor best. To say that God is good is to falsify Him, as much as it would falsify the sun to call it the dark. This is almost like the Hindu saying, "The moment you give Him a name, it isn't that."

God imparts Himself as He is in Himself. He gives Himself to the limit of the capacity of him who is to receive. You don't have to do anything to God. I say that intelligence draws aside the veil and perceives God naked, stripped of goodness or of being or of any name. Thus, the being of angels depends on the presence of the Divine Mind in which they behold themselves, like a morning star shining through the cloud mist. Every creature is on its way to the highest perfection. God becomes as phenomena express Him. That is rather interesting. The difference between God and the Godhead is the difference between action and nonaction. That is the polarity.

Well, we have to quit.

PHOTO ALBUM

Ernest Holmes at Asilomar

Scenic view at Asilomar, looking from the meadow to the ocean, Pacific Grove, California

Holmes with Asilomar participant

Holmes and Minister Rosalie B. Fowler of Redlands Church in 1957 (now known as Center for Spiritual Living Redlands)

Holmes and Pete Robertson

Hearst Social Hall at Asilomar, Pacific Grove, California, circa 1950s

Holmes with a family at Asilomar

Holmes talking with Asilomar participant

(left to right) Louise Hornaday, Bill Hornaday, Hazel Holmes, Ernest Holmes, Arthena Fostinis, Jack Fostinis

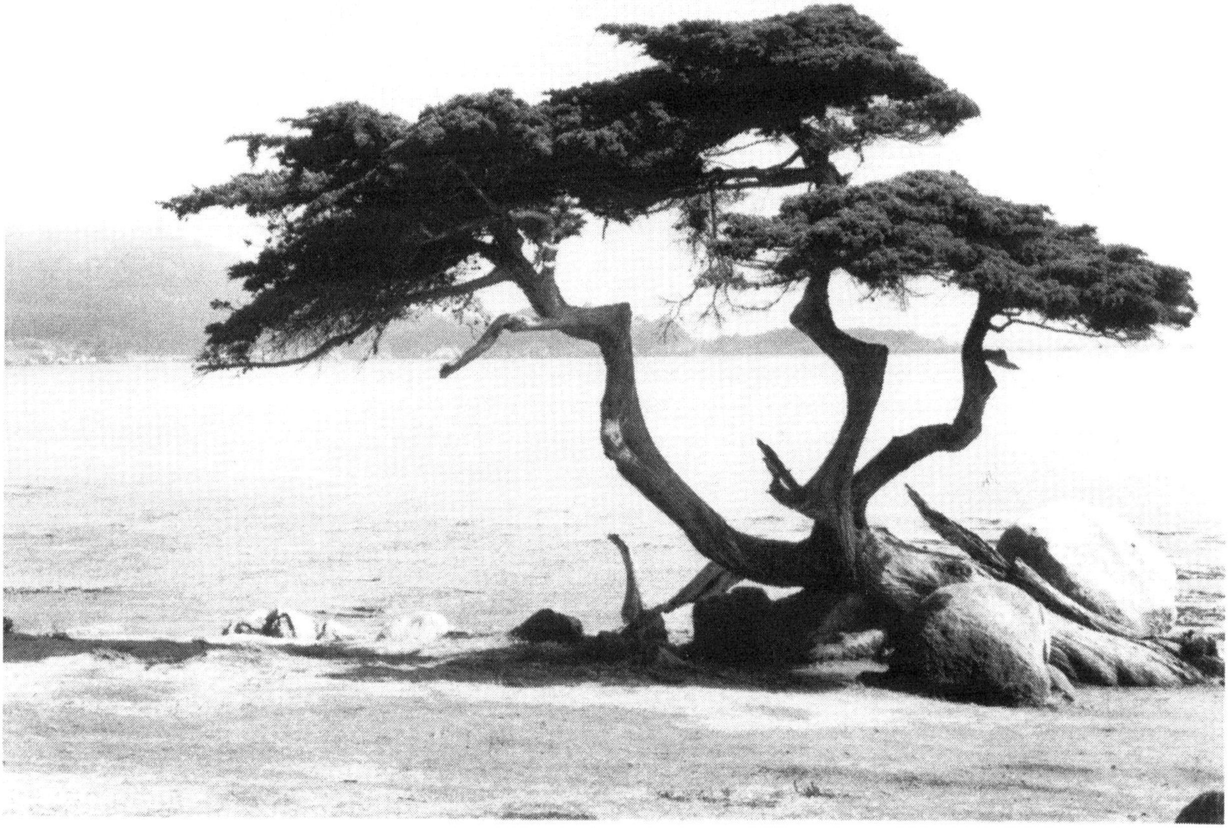

Holmes in dinner discussion with participant

Holmes with musician Richard Froeber

Holmes at Asilomar, Pacific Grove, California

Posing with participants

Holmes at Asilomar, Pacific Grove, California

SECOND ANNUAL

SEMINAR of LIFE

SPONSORED BY
DEPARTMENT OF AFFILIATED CHURCHES
CHURCH OF RELIGIOUS SCIENCE
ERNEST HOLMES, *Founder*

THEME:
"Living in Spirit and in Truth"

July 23 - 30, 1955
ASILOMAR
PACIFIC GROVE, CALIFORNIA

Three pages from the 1955 program, the only year for which we currently have no Holmes transcripts

ASILOMAR

JULY 23 – 30, 1955

STAFF

DR. ERNEST HOLMES: Dean and Founder
REV. LORNIE GRINTON: General Chairman
REV. BARCLAY JOHNSON: Camp Manager
MRS. BERYL BARBER: Registrar

PROGRAM COMMITTEE

Rev. Lornie Grinton
Dr. William Hornaday

Rev. Craig Carter

Rev. Barclay Johnson
Dr. Carmelita Trowbridge

CHILDREN'S ACTIVITIES	Rev. Mildren Hill
YOUTH ACTIVITIES	Rev. Norman Lunde
	Mrs. Norman Lunde
	Mrs. Adela Rogers St. Johns
MUSIC	Dr. Irma Glen, Chm.
	Rev. Donald Kelsey
VIGIL OF PRAYER	Dr. Carmelita Trowbridge
MINISTERIAL WORKSHOP	Rev. Barclay Johnson
PRACTITIONER'S WORKSHOP	Robert Leonard
	Mrs. Patricia Turnbull
JUNIOR CHURCH WORKSHOP	Rev. Donald Kelsey
NATURECRAFT	Mrs. Mary Geiger
ART WORKSHOP	Mrs. Louise Mock
RHYTHMIC RELAXATION	Mrs. Nusi McClellan
RECREATION	Dick Leo
LIFE GUARD	John Cummings
USHERS	Rev. John Turk, Chm.
HOSTESSES	Mrs. Edith Breest, Chm.
BOOK DESK	Mrs. Lucille Benedict
	Miss Geneva Lasley

MONDAY
July 25, 1955

6:30	RISING BELL	
7:00	SUNRISE SERVICE	The Dunes
	Rev. Iris Turk—Youth	
7:50	FLAG RAISING	Flagpole
8:00	BREAKFAST	Crocker Hall
9:00–9:20	MORNING MEDITATION—Dr. E. Holmes	Merrill Hall
9:00–10:30	CHILDREN'S ACTIVITIES	Ocean View Room
9:25–10:45	YOUTH ACTIVITIES	Merrill Hall
10:30–12:00	CHILDREN'S SWIMMING	Pool
9:30–10:30	WORKSHOPS	
	Ministerial	Hilltop Living Room
	Practitioners	Guest Inn Living Room
	Junior Church Teachers	Lodge Living Room
	Art	Merrill-Backstage
	Naturecraft	Merrill-Backstage
9:30–10:30	RHYTHMIC RELAXATION	Scripps Patio Room
9:30–12:00	NURSERY	Scripps Living Room
10:45	MEDITATION MEETING—Rev. L. Grinton	Merrill Hall
11:00	LECTURE—Dr. E. Holmes, "The Science of Mind and Inspiration of Spirit"	Merrill Hall
12:30	LUNCH	Crocker Hall
1:15–3:00	YOUTH SWIMMING	Pool
1:30–3:30	CHILDREN'S NATURECRAFT	Ocean View Room
1:45	MEDITATION MEETING—Rev. K. Bryson	Merrill Hall
2:00	LECTURE—Rev. Craig Carter, "Spirit and Truth in All Religions"	Merrill Hall
3:00–4:30	ADULT SWIMMING	Pool
3:30–4:30	LECTURE—Dr. W. Henry McLean "Jesus, the Master Teacher"	Merrill Hall
3:30–4:30	CHILDREN—Fun to Music	Ocean View Room
4:30–5:30	QUIET TIME	
5:45	PRAYER FOR WORLD PEACE	Flagpole
	Rev. A. Michael	
6:00	DINNER	Crocker Hall
7:00–7:30	SING SESSION	Merrill Hall
7:45–9:00	CHILDREN'S ACTIVITIES	Ocean View Room
7:45	MEDITATION MEETING—Rev. N. Lunda	Merrill Hall
8:00	LECTURE—Dr. William Hornaday "The Truth Has No Horizon"	Merrill Hall
9:00	DISMISSAL OF CHILDREN TO PARENTS	Ocean View Room
9:15	DANCE AND TALENT SHOW	Merrill Hall

Asilomar

For those of you unable to attend Asilomar, this report cannot take the place of the experience but may serve in its way to bring you some of the highlights and "fix" your determination to attend the next.

The week began with a new dedication in the Chapel. Dr. Gifford and Mrs. Gertrude Keller opened the vigil of prayer in a simple but significant ceremony that was dramatic in its implication - that was powerful not so much in what was said, but in what was left unsaid. The element of potential was not limited in any way, but was left to be realized by the consciousness of each individual present.

From the opening of the Prayer Vigil to the closing by the sea, this was the tone of the week - the unfoldment of the maturity and consciousness of the individual.

The nightly talks were beautifully started by Dr. Irma Glen who continued during the week to bless us all each evening with the poetry of her musical talent and the beauty of her presence. Never were evenings so wonderful.

During the day the workshops were busy bringing to the attention of Laymen, Ministers, Practitioners the ideas that have proved to be successful in Churches of Religious Science everywhere. We all received something new in whichever workshop we attended. All were well attended and in their own way inspirational as well as informative. Stronger Churches in all Departments will be the result of the attention given during this time.

The lectures just before noon were the finest heard at any time anywhere. They covered the field of Maturity on all levels and each speaker gave all of his or her understanding to the subject at hand. Again all of us in attendance found something new to walk with each day - something new to consider and to implement in our living. There is no measure to the ultimate good each individual obtained from the expressions of Dr.'s Johnson, Clark, McHenry, Hefferlin and Hornaday.

A high point in the week were the informative talks given on metaphysical interpretations of the bible as given by Dr. Gifford. Surely at some point in the future we will be privileged to have them repeated.

No less inspirational were the sessions on Treatment as given by Dr. Wayne Kintner. A new insight into the technique of affirmative prayer was offered to each who was drawn to this "class". What a tremendous life this man gave our thoughts.

Each day was highlighted by the evening talks given by Dr. Holmes who expanded and yet summed up the points given during the lectures preceding him. Truly we were blessed beyond our ability to comprehend the blessing at the time. Never has Dr. Holmes been better than he was during this time as he shared his keen insight into the Truths of the Ages with us each night.

The youth with their vitality and display of life, the children with their activity and wonderful venturing into our life at Asilomar, the Talent Show, the Prayer for Peace, the wonderful social evenings and the visiting and sharing - this was Asilomar - 1959.

From September 1959 Affiliated Churches of Religious Science Newsletter

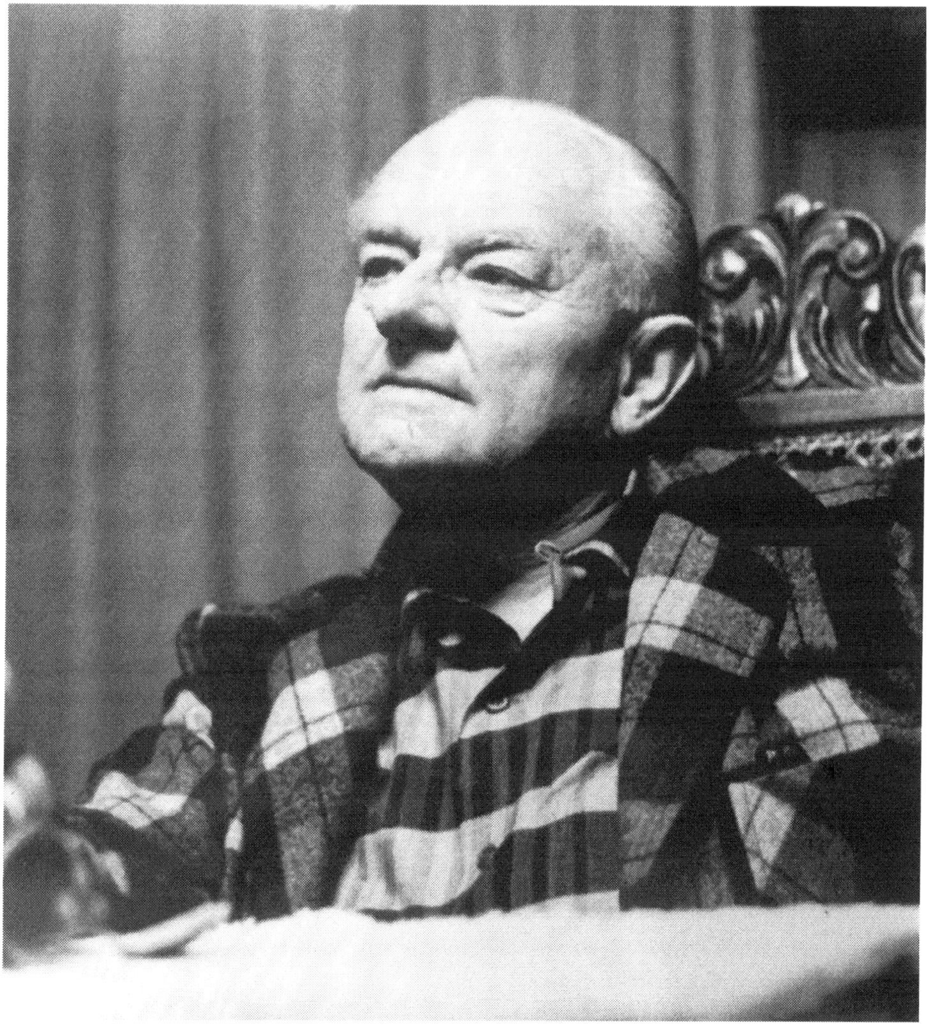

CHAPTER 4

1958

Oneness

Fear Is Faith

MONDAY, AUGUST 11, 1958

Dr. Holmes's theme for his series of talks at Asilomar in 1958 was Oneness. In each of the lectures, he brings forth concepts that appear to us as opposites but that are, in reality, the same essence, two sides of the same coin. In this first lecture, he spoke on how our fear is actually tied to our faith. When we fear something, we express faith in the manifestation of that which we fear. Similarly, Holmes points out that the human mind can only affirm something to be true, although it can be negatively stated. He then goes on to tell us not to worry if we are using affirmations or denials, but only to examine the words we use and their meaning.

We are engaged in something that isn't the answer to destiny. It has to do with you and me, only in so far as we are privileged in our lifetime to take part in the beginning of one of the new religious impulsions of the ages. There has not been, since the time of Islam and Christian Science, a new religious impulsion given to the world that is worldwide. Religious Science is the next one, and the greatest of modern times, and the greatest of all times because it incorporates the greatest spiritual philosophy the world has ever known. That is the Christian philosophy, which itself incorporates the intellectual concepts of the Greeks and the emotional concepts of the Jews and goes back to the hermetic teachings of ancient Egypt. I would say that Religious Science is a combination of the spiritual philosophies of the ages, a synthesis of the great thoughts of the ages.

Not long ago a member of our state board of education sent word and asked if I would write twenty-five words describing what Religious Science is. He said there were so many people talking about it everywhere they went, and he wondered what is this new and strange thing and what does it mean. And it must contain twenty-five words. I wrote it in five minutes and haven't changed it:

Religious Science is a correlation of laws of science, opinions of philosophy, and revelations of religion applied to human needs and the aspirations of man.

Just twenty-five words, and isn't that perfect. We are going to have it put it on all our literature. The reason I used the words "revelations of religion" is because that is accepted by the world, but you and I would use the word "intuition" because we know there is no true revelation other than through the self, the immediate perceptive faculties of the mind. But revelation is a better word to use for the average person. I'll say it again: Religious Science is a correlation of laws of science, opinions of philosophy, and revelations of religion applied to human needs and the aspirations of man.

Now our theme this week is Oneness. We have come from many churches, and we have new churches, and we welcome them all. Every minister in our field meets with great success if he knows what he thinks he knows, and if he understands the meaning of what he says, and if he does what he means. That is something. In his poem "Life and Song," Sidney Lanier said,/"For none o' the singers ever yet/Has wholly lived his minstrelsy....Or lived and sung, that Life and Song/Might each express the other's all." And Richard Eugene Burton said in his poem, "If We Had the Time":

If I had the time to learn from you
How much for comfort my word could do;
And I told you then of my sudden will
To kiss your feet when I did you ill;
If the tears aback of the coldness feigned
Could flow, and the wrong be quite explained, —
Brothers, the souls of us all would chime,
If we had the time!

The minister of Religious Science has to know the meaning of love as well as law, of the Divine Creative Presence, as well as universal responsive principle. Then he has to be able to put them together, as one is a complement to the other. The law is a servant of the word; the word is the servant of the eternal Spirit throughout the ages. Both are necessary, and each belongs, and each in its place is a part of the teaching of the dual unity of that Presence and principle, which is the basis of our work. Every practitioner must have it.

Now very few people understand the meaning of Religious Science and very few people in our field understand it as well as we ought to. I know I don't. I often say, "I would give anything and all I have, if I only knew what I believe." Wouldn't you say the same thing? We believe something terrific.

Now the next thing is to know, "Ye shall know the truth, and the truth shall make you free." Religious Science is free from superstition and the awe of theology. "The great appear great because we are on our knees" [James Larkin]. Let us get up and act as though we were grown ups. There are no prophets other than the wise. Even all the Bibles that were ever written were written by people just like you and me. We are not in awe of anything.

People frequently say to me, "What is your authority?" I mean well-meaning people; they wish me well. I always say the authority of our word is in what it does. We ask no background for our work other than what we leave behind us when we advance into the foreground of the universe, to that broader horizon, and there is no other. There is no law in the larger life but that your own soul shall set it under the one great law of all life. Now, we must be careful not to become dogmatic over the little we know, not to create another closed system that shall be the wonder of the world for a little while. My brother and I are writing the greatest spiritual epic since the time of the Bhagavad Gita. He has written most of it. It doesn't seem like it belongs to me.

I come here, and you are so sweet, and I love you so much. And you are so kind, and I appreciate it, but that is personal and what we do is entirely impersonal to me. Entirely impersonal.

I have been thinking during the last five weeks while speaking for Bill Hornaday, here is an audience of well over 2,000 people in the middle of a hot summer.

And I asked Reginald Armor if it is a good audience, and he said it is terrific. And I said, "I hope they won't be sorry they came." I tried to follow what I have always followed, never to convince anyone of anything because we have nothing to sell. I have never used any method; it is the only thing I knew enough to do when I started. I remember the first funeral service I ever gave. I had only been to two or three funerals in my life, so I got all the books from my brother and other books, but none of them were right. And I asked myself, "What shall I do?" I didn't know what observations to make over a corpse. And finally I worked on it and said to myself, "Why do you believe this man is not dead?" Answer that to whomever comes, because words mean nothing unless there is a meaning. And I did that.

The undertaker said, "What religion is this?"

And I said, "It is no religion."

He said, "It certainly is," and asked where I got it.

I said, "I made it up."

I had a service thirty-five years after that for Hamlin Garland, the great author. And a cultured, white-haired gentleman came up to me afterwards and said, "Dr. Holmes, I wish to tell you I have listened to funeral services all my life. This is the first one I ever liked." I said, "I thank you very much." And I turned around to go away and thought, well my gosh, if a man is as sweet as this and he certainly looks like a gentleman and a scholar, you might want to be decent to this man. So I said, "Would you be kind enough to tell me your name?"

He said, "My name is Goodspeed."

And then at last something clicked, and I said, "You wouldn't be the Dr. Goodspeed who wrote the version of the New Testament?"

He said, "I am afraid I am."

I thought then that the great don't have to sell themselves, do they? They are sure of themselves.

He said, "It is the best I have ever heard."

Now the only point I am making is this: I have never changed that method at a funeral, and this is just what I have been preaching for forty years, and it is right on this new record, which just came off the press, called, "You Will Live Forever."

That is what we do in our field. We only teach what we know; the rest are words. Our teaching is from the intellect, partly, and the heart, more. There is a feeling that goes with it. There is the self. James R. Lowell said:

In whatso we share with another's need,—
Not that which we give, but what we share,—
For the gift without the giver is bare,
Who bestows himself with his alms feeds three—
. . .
Himself, his hungering neighbor, and me.
And for a god goes with it and makes it store,
To the soul that was starving in darkness before.

Love. Givingness of the self. But we have a great teaching, that is the unity of all life, as you heard this morning; that is our theme: the Oneness of everything.

When I was told what it was, I arranged four topics that I knew as little about as anyone else, but they would be so wonderful if we could get something out of those topics. "Fear Is faith": this is on the oneness of apparent opposites. I am going to stay on this theme all week. Fear is faith, bondage is freedom, etc. In all the metaphysical fields, our own included, we are very liable to try to divide the indivisible and say God is up there and I'm down here, or there was a power in Jesus different from the power in Abraham Lincoln, or there is an absolute over there and here is a relative, or here is something that is hard and there is something that is easy. Now the great thinkers of the ages have not taught this. Emerson said, "There is no great and no small to the soul that maketh all, and where it cometh, all things are and it cometh everywhere."

We try to divide the indivisible. We are never successful. We think there is a fear, and we think there is a faith, and we think there is a hard and an easy and an affirmation and a denial. Now since the beginning of the modern metaphysical movement, which started, as you know, more one hundred years ago with the investigations of Phineas Parkhurst Quimby. And we will slide over his history because it does not matter. We waste our time worrying over the little things, when if we would get them out of the way, the big things will come along.

We sweat blood contending against an adversary who has no existence outside our own imagination, and we do not remember, with Lao Tzu, that all things are possible to him who can perfectly practice inaction. We do not remember, with Jesus, that there is a nonresistance that cannot be resisted, or with Gandhi, that there is a nonviolence that cannot be violated. Why? Because we are dealing with pairs of opposites: good and bad, heaven and hell, big and little, right and wrong, righteous and unrighteous, spiritual and material, absolute and relative. And now it grew up in the New Thought movement. As Quimby has said, "Mind is matter in solution, and matter is mind in form." But he said there is a superior wisdom, something I call a superior wisdom, which dominates this whole thing and to which what we deal with as mind and matter, which is a dual unity to which this is the matter of the Spirit.

Now Einstein much later said energy and mass are equal, identical, and interchangeable; and scientifically, that is pretty much what Quimby was saying philosophically, because what you see and what you don't see flow back and forth, from the transparent back into form and back again into an invisible formless. But they are the same thing. And so Quimby said, "Mind and matter are what we will call intelligence and the form they take is the same thing." Unless we understand this, we shall never understand the basic principle upon which the whole modern New Thought and metaphysical movement is built, whether it is New Thought, Divine Science, Christian Science, any of them. They all like to feel they are a little different, but their differences are only accentuated by their similarities or it wouldn't work at all. Two and two is going to make four; a rose by any other name will smell as sweet.

The belief in duality… I told a group in New York last week, the new religion will come when science is no longer materialistic, philosophy is no longer dualistic, and theology has gotten rid of its superstition and is no longer afraid of the universe in which we live. Because, of all people on Earth, the theologian is more scared than the pagan. I think probably he is better off with his fright because he is more intellectual, and he suffers more greatly. But it is true. It is a sad truth, isn't it? It is a self-evident one.

We are free of the shibboleths as well as the anathemas and the denunciations of the theologies, redeemed at last from doubt and fear and hope's illusion. Religious Science, if it follows the simple precepts upon which it is based, will be that religion in which science is no longer materialistic—it is rapidly coming in science—in which philosophy is no longer dualistic—so we will say they are idealistic and materialistic—and in which theology is no longer afraid. Jesus said, "Fear not, little flock, for it is your Father's good pleasure to give you the kingdom."

Life is a gift. We didn't earn it. Humanly speaking, we are not good enough to have made it or bad enough to have destroyed it. Robert Browning said, "'Tis thou God who giveth, 'tis I who receive."

So there came up the affirmations and denials, and there has been a great argument: Shall we affirm, and shall we deny, and shall we build up faith, and shall we counteract fear?

I would like to start this series of talks with a little explanation: The human mind can only affirm, but it may do so negatively. I can say, "I am happy," and we will say that is an affirmation. I can say, "I am unhappy." That is still an affirmation, but it is negatively stated. I can say, "I am afraid." We will say that it is negative. We can say, "I am fearless." We will say that is positive. It is positive and negative, but it is just an affirmation. If we can get it in our mind that the human mind may only affirm, it cannot do anything else. So we have from Quimby a series of affirmations and denials. It flowed over into Christian Science. It flowed over into the Unity movement. Both Fillmore and Cady, in the first two sections of their textbooks start with affirmations and denials, and also Emma Curtis Hopkins where she speaks of the great affirmation and great denial. What are they trying to do?

What they are trying to do is all right, and I am not criticizing I am just trying to point out that they are all—and we, too—using a method of straight affirmation to arrive at a conclusion about something. And we may call it a great affirmation, the great denial, doesn't matter at all what we call it. If I say, "God is all there is," then that is an affirmation. If I say, "There is nothing but God," I am saying God is all there is. If I say, "There is nothing but one," that is an affirmation.

If I say, "The universe, being one, cannot be divided. It is indivisible, undivided, therefore it exists in the totality." That is an affirmation. But if I say, "There is no such a thing as nothing," there are two ultimates; that is a denial, but it is all the same.

The mind may only affirm. Therefore, let's forget whether we are affirming or denying during this series of talks. I don't care how we do it, so long as we arrive at a few simple conclusions, intellectually, as a basis for clear thinking, and spiritually, as a foundation for clear thinking, because the universe is more than a principle of mind or a law of mind in action. It is a living presence, an infinite personalness, a divine responsiveness, a universal wholeness, and something that presents itself to each individual in an individual way, filled with warmth and life and color and blessedness. And there is a voice that speaks from eternity and time, at all times.

Fear, then, is faith used as fear. And it is just as powerful as faith used as faith, except in those instances when faith is used as faith, it is stating its faith in the immutability of a law and a principle, which is self-evident to the highest intellectual conception and deepest... . Oh, this is getting all balled up. I don't understand it myself; it is crazy. What I am trying to say is making the thing very simple: It doesn't make any difference, you know; you have no one to convince but yourself. We may believe what is not so; we can only know what is so. That is definite. People believed the world was flat. Now that belief was an affirmation of a flat world, but the affirmation didn't flatten out a round world. Therefore, there are certain affirmations that, while they are still affirmations, don't do anything because there is nowhere for them to go. And still, they are affirmations. Now whenever anyone affirmed that the world was round, he was telling the truth, whether he understood it or not. The world was round. One day someone was so convinced of it that he sailed around it, and he couldn't have done that if it had been flat.

That is why I say there are certain affirmations that, because they are consistent with reality, they affirm the truth, will have to have greater power than affirmations that might be placed as denials, which are affirming that which is not the truth or that which is less than the truth. Is that clear? All words must have some power. Remember, you can only affirm, even though you make it a denial. You can only affirm. There is nothing else you can do. That is settled. God speaks only in affirmative language. "I am that I am, beside which there is none other."

I was thinking the other day, and I got to playing with an idea that I spoke to a friend of mine. And I said (we were driving down to Palm Springs or someplace), "The universe can never say no." He said, "Is that so?" I said, "Yes." And he said, "What do you know about that?" And I said, "I don't know about it." And within two or three days, one night at home, I sat there for four hours and figured it out: God speaks only a universal language, interpreted to each one of us out of Its generic nature, as that which we are, just as one universal man, of which each is a member. That universal man is generic, which means cosmic.

So don't wonder whether you are using affirmations or denials; wonder only if what you say has a meaning. Some words will have to have all power. The word we speak will have a power commensurate with, identical within the likeness of the exactness of as much as we have embodied in spirit, of that which we have articulated in the form. Because the correspondence of the parallel will be in the mirror of the law.

These things are so very simple that we are very liable to think we have to get all worked up and use a language that no one understands, and we are apt to do that for lack of simplicity. Let us reduce our thought to the utmost simplicity but keep it absolutely tied back to a unity, which will not be divided, which by the nature of its truth remains solid and steadfast. And we will never do it while we say fear is one thing and faith is another; big is one thing and little is another; the infinite is one thing and the finite is another; the human is one thing and the Divine is another. There is no such thing as the human and the Divine. God is all, over all, in all, and through all, and there isn't anything else.

I always say heaven is lost not for a lack of a location but only for the lack of an idea of harmony, nothing else. The universe in which we live, being timeless, isn't going anywhere. The universe, being a changeless omnipresence, has got all of it right here between your two fingers. Evolution, being the result of involution, is merely the awakening of instrumentalities to their office and their relationship to essences. I'll say it again, and think about this for a long time, because that is really something. Evolution is an awakening of instrumentalities to the essence that is already within them, pushing out for self-expression; that the universe, whose whole creation exists for its own delight, may delight itself in everything that it does and sees in you and in me, that which it knows itself to be, without effort.

And so we arrive at the conviction that what we are going to do is not hard. It isn't difficult to understand the truth; it is absolute simplicity that has eluded us. If we were to say, "I am afraid I could not heal a cancer or a blind man," which I suppose we all are more or less, then we have affirmed something that no one can un-affirm but ourselves. *But* if there were nothing in you and in me that saw a blind man as blind, he would look at us. If there were nothing in us that saw a paralyzed man when we walked by, he would get up and say to us, "Let's go in here," and he would go in first.

Why? Because that is the nature of reality. I don't know why. Would God have particularly blessed us? I don't think so. Does God bless children who aren't afraid? Sure, because there is a pressure against everything to express itself. And you may know and I may know that back of everything there is, if we will forget the dualism, there is the self-insistent persistency of a gentle urging in an irresistible pressure that nothing can resist. "Yea, before the day was, I am he and there is none that can deliver out of my hand: I will work and who shall hinder it?" That is a perception of that we may know. That is why I say our authority is in the word. You and I may know that since a certain thing is true, if we state it according to our convictions, it will manifest itself as it reflects itself into a new law of cause and effect, which is its servant, of the spirit. We shall never do it, or only to a very small degree, unless we gradually lift our methods of legitimate affirmation and denial to at least a realization. No matter how we speak this principle, we are still affirming that which cannot be resisted, because just as sure as we are here, the ages have proclaimed evil. Now it is a pretty terrific thing if out of 154 psalms of the most glorious literature on Earth, you can only get about 400 lines, with eleven words to a line, where there is no negation. It shows how difficult it is to speak in an affirmative language. Same way in Isaiah and all the prophets.

Someone came to me and said, "I am trying to find God. Where shall I find Him?" There is a beautiful tree outside of my office, and I asked if he could see that tree. And he said, "Yes." And I said, "Why don't you say, 'Hello, God?'" He said, "Why, that is material." I said, "Is it? What do you mean by material?" He said, "I am looking for something spiritual." I said, "Wouldn't you be terrifically surprised if that tree were it?" I would love to have explained to him that since the tree actually exists, no matter how much he denies it, it won't wither up, and if it does, another will grow. Someday he is going to have to accept that tree as a spiritual reality. What will he have left? Nothing but his belief in a material universe. There never was a material universe and never will be. But it doesn't matter how we arrive at that; matter is Spirit, all a part of one stupendous whole whose body nature is with God, the soul.

Well, he came back later and said, "I have been thinking about what you said." And I said, "What do you think about it?" And he said, "It is terrific, and it is true." And I said, "Let me tell you something. You have been studying for about ten years to find the spiritual universe. How do you like it?" He said, "It seems awful low." I said, "How would you like to sit on a tack for the next ten years and just say, 'Nuts'?" He said, "That would be stupid," and I agreed with him, and the tack would never complain. So I gave these silly things to him until he finally said, "I see what you are trying to do. You are trying to tell me this is it." I said, "This is it, and you are it, and I am it. We are talking about it, and it is good." And he discovered the spiritual tree. We say there is an obstruction because we say it is material, matter. It is something that opposes Spirit; it is so dark and came under the wrong star.

Now don't forget, in our science, one man with God is a majority and a totality and a universality and an infinity and an absoluteness and an immutability, all rolled up in one, in such degree as he speaks the truth. But he couldn't expect it to be if what he speaks is not so. Let him forget whether he is denying it or affirming it. It doesn't matter. If I say there is no darkness here at all or if I say it is all light, I have said the same thing. Let's forget that but know the light. "And ye shall know the truth, and the truth shall make you free."

And let us know that the responsibility is in the Divine Presence and the law of good. We—because of our fear and our mad pawing and screaming, thinking they are helping the universe to be round—all tiredness, all exhaustion is because we are pitting affirmations against denials as though they were opposites: energy against non-energy, inertia against energy, good against evil, right against wrong, high against low, big against little, and screaming our anathemas and praises. And they both are spoken to an illusion that we worship, thinking it must be God.

And so as we start out, let's start with this thing, this oneness. There is only one of whatever it is. There is nothing else besides "God is." And let's see if this week, we cannot get back to the absolute simplicity of it. You are a practitioner. You may not know it, but you are. If you believe what I said, you can't help from now on being a practitioner because you are at least going to be changing enough thought to see if something won't happen. And that is all that practice is: seeing if something changes. We do not breathe the ethers into space; we do not control gravitational force to bind the sun and the moon and the stars together.

I heard a lot of talks when I was back east about "healers," and I said I would like to correct something in my own mind. I said, "Let us take another viewpoint." We do not have healers. We don't have anyone who has a healing power, any more than we have somebody who has electricity. The response of the universe, even as healing, is absolutely impersonal to us, but it personifies the moment we let it in and it becomes personal. And the son is born through the mystic marriage. The laws of the universe know to do; they don't know they are doing.

So now let's not say any more; let's this week stop saying, "Do I know enough? Am I good enough? Have I understanding enough? How many more classes do I have to take?" and start out with this simplicity: Is my method right? I want to dissolve the illusion that your method could be wrong. It can't. It is only what your method leads to. Your method can't be wrong if, with complete nonresistance, you accept the universe and announce that you are a spiritual being and affirm the supremacy of that. All that is left then is to build up that inward awareness of what the substance means.

What does good mean to me? What does love mean to me? Are my arms actually around the universe? What do truth and beauty mean to me? It is in that silent meaning, in my own consciousness, from it alone, that power is born out of the stillness. And I have come to learn that you and I and everyone, by the very nature of our being and nature and constitution of the reality in which we are emerged and freedom toward which we point, we too slowly falter.

It is a psychological and emotional morbidity that winds itself around us as a serpent and ensnares us and encoils us in the slime from which we are so recently emerged in evolution, as though it would pull us back into some dark and black matrix that has no existence outside of our own imagination. And now I have learned that every man will be alone until he is not lonely. He will listen to the silence until it speaks. He will look into a dark abyss until it becomes illumined. And he will die continuously until he resurrects himself. There is a self—cryptic, hidden, illumined to us, expansive to itself, never moving—which is absolute, primal, going to do what it may and promise and must, not just to a few practitioners and a teacher for which all creation awaits, this groaning and travail, but to the child. And Jesus said, "Suffer the little children, and forbid them not to come unto me: for of such is the kingdom of heaven."

Now let us seek that kingdom in the quietness of our own heart, in the solitude of our own mind, this stillness of our own spirit, and in the love we bear one another, as we embrace each other, look long and earnestly into each other's eyes, and see there the fire kindled in heaven, listen to the heartbeat of each other and humanity, until we hear the great rhythm of the universe, resounding in us. Lord God of heaven and Earth, infinite and eternal and ineffable beauty, we are that which Thou art and Thou art that which we are. Now and forever more. Amen.

Bondage Is Freedom

TUESDAY, AUGUST 12, 1958

Dr. Holmes continues with his theme of Oneness. Here he explores another set of apparent opposites that in reality are interconnected: bondage and freedom. Holmes reminds us that we experience bondage to the degree that we identify with the finite world and our perception of its apparent limitations. When we shift our attention to the limitless infinite, we shift into a greater degree of freedom.

I was thinking probably the highlight of our convention was reached last evening. It was a very wonderful thing to me that last evening, the calmness, the deliberateness and assurance and poise with which our youth group spoke and treated. Someone said, "I guess they just repeated a lot of things they are familiar with," and I said, "No, Everything that was said was spontaneous, and it would have been impossible for them to have said it the way they did if it had been repeated." You can always tell. That was a spontaneous thing.

Now I happen to believe that the universe is a living Presence. I happen to believe there are beings beyond us as we are beyond tadpoles. I believe in expanding manifestation from a unitary basis. God does not evolve, but we do. We evolve or unfold, in my estimation, because there is already involuted or incarnated, or put into us, a spark that impregnates the mundane clod and a pressure that is insistent, dynamic, calm, unhurried but persistent. Robert Browning said, "A spark disturbs our clod."

I happen to believe that we are not one in, or with God, but one *of* God. Now there is a big difference. If we were one *in* God, there would be something in a totality that is unlike the totality. If there were something *with* a totality, there would be a separation between the totality, which we shall call the truth. And if we are one *of* a totality, as some of the ancients said, whose center is everywhere and whose circumference is nowhere, then we are a part of that totality. Now don't worry where this leads us to; and if it sounds crazy, it doesn't matter.

There is a super logic in the universe. If there weren't, we wouldn't get beyond the tadpole. There is the self-existent universe. No one made God. Nothing made the law of God. There was never a time when it was not. It didn't begin, and it won't end. That is why infinity is described by a circle, which begins everywhere and ends nowhere, like the boy who gave his girl a ring and said, "Darling, this is a symbol of my love. It has no ending." And she passed it right back and said, "This is a symbol of my love. It has no beginning." They were both right. So always infinity has been described by a circle. That is why one of Emerson's essays is "Circles."

The first circle is an eye, the next is the horizon, and so on, ad infinitum. It is why everything in the universe moves in circles. Einstein tells us that even time, light, and space bend back upon themselves because a circle is the only movement that can be eternal. And any movement that takes place within the internal, changeless reality will have to be out of like nature with it because it emanates from it and cannot contradict it. If it did, that slight movement out of variance with the whole would destroy the whole.

We have to understand these things because we are metaphysicians. They will be simple if we stop thinking they are hard. If everything in the universe moves in circles—and it does—from the atom to the whole sidereal universe, then Jesus was right when he said, "Give and it shall be given unto you: good measure, pressed down and shaken together and running over, shall men give into your bosom." But you and I have to know that men cannot stop pressing it down because everything is an agent of the infinite and belongs to the infinite. That is why Emerson said, "Words are finite organs of the infinite mind."

Now it is essential that we understand that you and I are not just in God, or of God, or with God and the truth, implying a separation and a division. The truth is a complete totality. That is another way of saying that God is all there is. The truth is a complete totality and cannot appear in fragments because it is not broken in parts, because there is nothing with which or by which or through which to divide, unlike itself. Hence, it remains indivisible. And because it is indivisible, it exists in its totality at any and every point within its infinity, simultaneously, instantaneously, changelessly, and eternally.

Let's just briefly go over this because we are thinking out some propositions that, after we think out of the intellect, we will have to feel with the heart. Emerson said to let the intellect alone, the heart knows. And when that divine moment comes, leave all of your theories, as Joseph left his coat in the hands of the harlot, and flee.

Now you and I exist. We are or we couldn't say we are. We are then necessarily a part of the coexistence and self-existence of God, or we wouldn't be. Lest we become conceited, all of these things we have called God are silly. There is no such God as the God people worship. If there were, it would be worse than it looks, much. Because you and I belong to the universe in which we live, we belong to self-existence. And self-existence has projected itself within itself that it might enjoy itself.

This is quite different from saying that we are here to work out our salvation with fear and trembling or that we are here to glorify God. Neither one is true. God is not trying to prove anything. God has nothing to prove. God is God. "I am the Lord and there is none else, there is no God beside me." We are here because God must be expressed. We are the delight of God. We are what God knows Himself to be, manifest at the level of what we know ourselves to be.

Our subject tonight is that the limited is the limitless as the limited, but the limitless is not limited in what looks to be limited. This is terrifically profound or very silly. I have thought all my life about it. The world has spent all the ages thinking about it. What you and I believe is the culmination of the hope, the aspiration, the longing, the endless ages of saying, "Why, why hast thou forsaken me?" The whole search of mankind is to find security somewhere. In this world, there are certain things that are called security, but beyond that the whole search of man is to be made whole, because he isn't happy until he is. St. Augustine said, "Thou madest us for Thyself; our heart is restless, until it repose in Thee."

Everything in the universe is a spiritual thing, a spiritual idea emanating from a spiritual pattern. There is no such thing as a material universe, as people used to think of matter. That which the universe projects is the universe, manifested within itself, because it is the nature even of the ultimate reality to manifest itself, to behold itself, to experience itself, to enjoy itself, to glorify itself, to proclaim itself. That is what is back of the libido and the id of modern psychology. We call it a divine urge. That is why an artist paints, a singer sings, a dancer dances, and chipmunks gather nuts, the fish swim, and you and I are here, and why Jesus was crucified, and Socrates drank the hemlock bark, and the little child says, "Now I lay me down to sleep." It is because there is an incessant demand, urge, emotional craving for self-expression, and we say, a feeling, a pure desire at the center of everything to express life and to live. Jesus said, "I am come that they might have life and that they might have it more abundantly."

Now remember, the universe is a spiritual system. It is alive; it is awake; it is aware. Arthur Young in 1741 said, "God sleeps in the minerals, awakens in plants, walks in animals, and thinks in man." And God consciousness and cosmic consciousness in the upper expanding, out-swinging, upward spiraling hierarchies was right. And even as staid a man as Dean Inge was, the greatest student of Platonism probably of our day, said that it does not seem strange even to think that planets were individuals, because everything from the infinitesimal to the infinite expresses, according to its own nature, the reality of that which is the ultimate nature of all nature, because it is the ultimate that is in the simplest fact. And that is why Emerson said, "There is no great and no small to the soul that maketh all, and where it cometh all things are, and it cometh everywhere." We think of the big and little, the much and the more. The universe doesn't, because it is an infinite unity expressing itself. It must and does express itself in infinite variety, but unity does not mean uniformity. It is one of the philosophic errors. Communism—their error is that they do not know that while everything is rooted in one, all things individuate from the One. We must suppose an infinite cause but not an infinite purpose. God isn't trying to go anywhere; there isn't anywhere for God to go. God isn't trying to accomplish a purpose that did not exist.

We believe—and I mean, I believe—there isn't a single fact in life that has to be denied in order to affirm a complete and superior faith. Not one. All we have to realize is the universe is an infinite, living presence forever expressing itself, and that which is expressed is itself expressed as itself. That is why I said: God in man as man is man. Jesus said, "The Father and I are one." That is simpler and, therefore, more profound. The simpler you can state it, the more profound it will be. Profundity is simplicity so self-evident that the mind that is always accustomed to trying to find causes for the causeless, gets confused in the effects of the simplicity of the cause that is, itself, the effect. That is true, but I don't think it is clear.

One of our great troubles is that we get so consciously profound and have so little sense of wit about it and aren't quite flexible enough to not resist the mental fact; that we get all caught up and think we have to look strange, act strange, and have a sort of faraway look to say a stone is a stone. Now the infinite then, which is limitless, is also what we call the finite, which appears to be limited. But the finite that appears to be limited is merely the infinite projecting at whatever that is—a blade of grass.

There is nothing that has to be denied in the universe of reality. It has come to me very plainly in this past year. I have been reading a lot about Zen and I think it is wonderful, but I said to myself, "Why do people have to get so caught up in so many words to say such a simple thing?" And I read so many books, and they are terrific, but after I got all through, I thought they are all caught up in words. And then I read it again to try to find out what the guy meant. Sometimes we look for the needle in the haystack; it wasn't even there. It is there in this profound system, but all they are trying to say is that eternity is time and there isn't any time. If we can catch the split second of the eternal now, where the future is no longer bound to the past through a sequence of cause and effect or a chain, then today will be free from the thralldom of yesterday and the fear of tomorrow.

Now the Apostle John said, "Beloved, now are we the sons of God and it doth not yet appear what we shall be: but we know that when he shall appear, we shall be like him; for we shall see him as he is. And every man that hath this hope in him purifieth himself, even as he is pure." A mystical thing, but not mysterious. He is saying: We are what we are going to be, now. Whatever we are going to be we are now. The imprisoned splendor, beloved now, and we don't quite see what we are going to be, but we know that when he (that is, "it") shall appear, we shall be like him for we shall see him as he is. He is here. He will appear when we see him as he is. We will have to see him as he is before he can appear. Our seeing him as he is and his appearance will be instantaneous, simultaneous, universal, homogeneous, instant, and perfect when we see him as he is. This is the whole theme of Emerson, Hopkins: "Where is your vision set? What thou seest, that thou bee'st." "If thou loves not thy brother whom thou seest, how canst thou love God, whom thou dost not see?"

The universe is a spiritual system governed by two laws. Emerson said that they played this familiar tune over and over again. I believe in the law of parallels: as above, so beneath. In the invisible, which Jesus called the kingdom and the Platonists called over yonder, there is a pattern for everything that is here, but not a purpose, as though God were trying to accomplish something.

The old dreary, miserable theology of sin and salvation is nonsense. There isn't anyone good enough to have sinned that much, and if he did, he certainly doesn't know enough to get out of it. He wasn't bad enough to have made the mistake and will never have intelligence enough to correct it if he made it. I think it is colossal egotism for anybody to think you could ever be that good of a sinner. I certainly wouldn't have that much imagination. There is no sin but a mistake and no punishment but a consequence. But that doesn't mean we can play fast and loose with the universe. There is the universe's justice without judgment, because it is in equilibrium; it is in balance. "Therefore, all things whatsoever ye would that men should do to you, do ye even so to them, for this is the law." This is a promise.

What has all this to do with the subject tonight? It *is* the subject. Bondage is freedom, merely because we have mistaken freedom for something that is opposite to bondage. Jesus said, "Ye cannot serve God and mammon," and the Bhagavad Gita says you must do away with the pairs of opposites before you enter bliss: good and evil, big and little, right and wrong, heaven and hell, God and the devil, I'm right and you're wrong. All these things are finite concepts, and are like all finite concepts, being intrinsically drawn from an essence of infinitude, as every concept must be, else it has no existence. It is just as someone said, "There has to be someone at home before you can think at all."

Every limitation we have, every bondage we have, proclaims the freedom we would obtain if we reverse not the law of bondage but the way we are looking at it. I thought, What is illusion and what is reality? You and I must never be in a position of just denying what we think is unreal and affirming what we think is real, until finally we play a psychological trick, which is an escape mechanism, on ourselves and begin to deny everything we don't like and affirm everything we do. And suppose we were wrong.

The next generation of Religious Science ministers won't have so much to do to untie the knots that ignorance and fear and superstition have too tightly tied and unfurl that flag of freedom, which is without fear, in the universe in which it floats, and like a child who is no longer afraid to look at the stars and say, "Hello, God." Know companionship with the infinite and no tie to the finite. We loosely say God is love, but how do we know unless our arms are around each other. People say, "You are so sentimental." So what? I would rather go to hell and be happy than to be unhappy in heaven.

So, I thought something is wrong. I know there is a greater reality than I see, yet I do not deny what I do see, for fear that in denying it, I will deny what I don't see. And my criterion of judgment is very finite, and I may be denying the wrong thing. And I have watched so many metaphysicians do that. I find it a very bad thing to do, and one becomes very arbitrary and then gradually they get that set look of determination. You and I have to settle all these questions for ourselves. I can't tell you anything, and you can't tell me a thing, but we can talk to each other and, by listening to each other, put together what little each knows. And each will know a little more than he did before we met in this communion of Spirit. There are no prophets other than the wise. No one is saved but the man who is no longer unhappy. And if any soul were lost, there is neither a saint nor a sinner who would look for it. I wiped my slate of theology years ago and made one I liked better. You must create, and might as well create, the God you like because they were all created by human beings.

But the God that is, being so insistent, appears morning, noon, and night outside the doorway and inside it, and knocks on every man's consciousness, and being so insistent, will not let us go. As the man who is insistent enough, Jacob in Genesis, said, "I will not let you go until you bless me."

So I got myself straightened out this last year about illusion and reality. This is what I want to talk to you about. And if it is right, it doesn't matter whether anyone accepts it or not; and if it is wrong, it isn't right and no matter who believes it, it won't make it right. What you and I believe has nothing to do with the truth, but the truth might have a lot to do with what we believe. If we believe in whatever is true, then the power of the truth will flow through that belief. Otherwise, how can it? There is no channel.

I made up my mind the ocean is real enough out here in Los Angeles, California. It is not an illusion. You and I are not illusions, yet there is something about us that doesn't seem quite right. But at least, if we realize we are not all there at the same time, there is something divine about it, because in realizing we are not all there, we are realizing there is something that is there that doesn't appear. I claim every analyst and psychologist and one who orients and puts together the mechanism of the mind, whether he accepts it or not, starts with the simple fact that there is a mind, and when you get it put together, it will automatically function all right. That is all he can do.

I got to thinking about this, and this is what came to me: You know each one of us has a word imagery that satisfies him. So I thought, I cannot deny one single fact. I thought, I will not permit myself to deny one fact. I dare not; it gives me a split personality if I do. I have to put the whole thing together to satisfy myself, and I believe you have to, too. You see, as a movement, you are not expected to believe because I believe it.

So I came to this conclusion: We see it through a glass darkly. An ocean is an ocean; a tree is a tree. You and I are real; the piano is real. But someone will say, "God didn't make it, man made it," and there is your division again. How are you going to divide the indivisible? Experience has drawn a curtain, some kind of a veil, between the reality that is in all things and our perception of the thing in which the reality is. The illusion is not in the thing but in the way we look at it. This I can understand. I can't have a universe of illusion because I can't have a God of illusion. You know, this is terrifically significant. I have never in my life known a man who condemned others without unconsciously condemning himself, and he has expressed the hurt of his own self-condemnation by projecting it onto others and getting the relief of the tension, just as a pipe has a safety valve to release the steam.

So the reality is here, but I have hung a screen between myself and it, and upon the screen, against which the outline and shadow and substance of the objective reality reflects itself, beyond my vision, seeking to reach and gain my attention and acquiescence. "When we see Him as He is," and I am projecting upon this side of my screen that which sees only as through a glass darkly, "not then face-to-face." The illusion is my projection against the face of reality. The face of reality has never changed. Therefore, if I can remove the screen, which is a subjective creation of my own unconscious reaction to life, I shall see Him as He is—and that is everything. Lift the veil, draw the curtain, wipe off the mirror, doesn't matter what you call it or how it is done; then freedom will no longer appear as bondage.

I can only project myself against the screen of my experience, and it will reflect a form out there so that even the form—which is perfect, it doesn't change, but I don't see it perfectly—it will never change. We see freedom as bondage. It is the only bondage there is. Now in trying to unsee it, remember this: You and I, in our spiritual so-called manipulations, most people don't know what we are doing. The awakened ego has the right to be glad but never arrogant. We believe in egoism but not egotism. Egoism says, "How wonderful is the work of God, even in myself." The ancients used to sometimes tell their disciples to fold their hands over their arms and say, "Wonderful, wonderful, wonderful me." Now Jesus said, "He that hath seen me hath seen the Father." "The Father that dwelleth in me, he doeth works, for my Father is greater than I." He also said, "I am the way, the truth, and the life."

Jesus made the greatest claim on God any individual ever made, and you and I are making the greatest claim on the universe we have ever made. And since all psychological and emotional frustrations are the result of not reaching the goal of our desire, we will be the most frustrated idiots who ever lived if we don't continuously do better. Why? Because we have asked for more, believed in more, and expect more. The more you expect, the more you can be frustrated. Isn't that right? We have to clear the track back to reality.

In doing this, do not try to materialize Spirit, because you can't do it. Do not try to spiritualize matter, because there isn't any matter, and if there were, you couldn't spiritualize it. We neither spiritualize matter nor do we materialize Spirit. And we do not concentrate; we do not compel; we do not wish; we do not will. Our treatment is not a daydream. It is such a persistent nonresistant attitude toward reality that it shall finally come whose right it is. By some divine interior awareness, which Plotinus said all people have but few people use, we know these things. When someone teaches us what we are going to learn, he is merely removing a part of our veil temporarily, that we can see what we were already looking at, because now we are recapturing an inner vision for a greater reality.

We are not putting opposites against each other. We do not bring a good power to combat an evil power. There is no such thing as an evil power in the universe. There is not something opposed to freedom. All freedom and extension of the infinitudes, of all the categories of the infinite, are not limited by our finite concepts. We shall never contract the infinite. We may expand the finite, by some soul-stretching, mind-stretching, intellect-stretching. I have learned to call it that and have tried in some of our groups to do it—I mean, stretching your mind, causing your intellect to take itself to the doorway of your intuition, that it may receive a new mystical, spiritual influx, which will still be perfectly rational. Jesus and Plotinus and Socrates and Emerson were not crazy. They more nearly approached a normality and a psychological emotional balance than any other people who have ever lived. We are crazy, from that standpoint. The Chinese sage said, "Oh man, having the power to live, why will ye die?"

And so I am convinced that we are looking at the reality. Now don't rub anything out. All we have to change is that little illusion in our own mind. If there were ever an answer to prayer, it was according to the law that responds to all things, because finally, in the universe, there can be nothing but action and reaction, the polarity between it. There can't be anything else. It is impossible, in my estimation.

But we do see as through a glass darkly, "But we know that when He shall appear, we shall be like Him, for we shall see Him as He is." Now remember, He is there, and we are like Him. He will appear, but He can't appear until we see Him as He is, and then He can't help it because we are like Him, because we are that.

Ernest Hemingway said, "I am thee and thou art me and all of one is the other." This is a message the great and the good and the wise have ever known; the otherwise have guessed. Those who were less wise even than the otherwise have laughed and doubted the sanity of those who see, and yet by some interior awareness—because a blind man longs for light—have groped even in their unbelief for that wholeness which is only of the soul and the mind and the spirit, is never ill.

This is the whole theme of Emma Curtis Hopkins, of all mysticism, and of Eckhart. Eckhart is the greatest example of the simple sweet mysticism. Plotinus and Emerson are the great examples of the intellectual, and Platonism of the concept. Jesus combined both. He spoke as the great prophet and as a child. "The wind bloweth where it listeth but canst not tell whence it cometh and whither it goeth. So is every one that is born of the Spirit." Now I have begun with some of our groups what I call mind stretching. It isn't anything weird or peculiar; you don't have to take any pills. Emerson said, "For it is only the finite that has wrought and suffered, the infinite lies stretched in smiling repose." He also said, "Spirit is matter reduced to an extreme thinness: O so thin!", and, "We are begirt with spiritual laws which execute themselves." Now you and I don't have to create a law or shove it into being. The word is greater than the law. The law is a servant to the word. It is a reaction out of what we call the soul, or feminine, or neutral, or creative mind principle, just names given to thought, that when you speak the word, it at once becomes the law of the thing whereunto it is spoken. That is all it is. Jesus justly said, "Heaven and Earth shall pass away, but my words shall not pass away." So darned simple but so profound.

We may consciously stretch the intellect or the mind through identification with our largest concept, until finally when we think of our smaller concepts, they have increased in the light of the larger because our vision has been set on something bigger, if there is big and little, which now entertains a greater activity. Oh, this is all balled up. Now look, if all the fish in the Pacific Ocean laid eggs and all the eggs were to hatch, all the land would be inundated; the ocean would raise up, so I have been told. I knew a woman once who had an abundance of money and hard times came, and she said she went to the ocean and thought, How many stars there are, how many grains of sand, how many fish, how much of everything, so much, so much, so much. And before the day was over, she was able to demonstrate abundance because she was able to change her thought. You see, the curtain was there, and on this the curtain was her experience of want and lack and limitation. But just on the other side was the pressure against all of this abundance, just as Jesus multiplied the loaves and fishes and brought the boat immediately to the shore and found the money in the fish's mouth and raised Lazarus from the dead, because he looked through the curtain that men or perhaps he had drawn for himself. "When we see him as he is, he will have to appear," implies the universe can never say no to itself. Angela Morgan said in *Know Thyself*, "The living one who never tires, fed by the deep eternal fires, angel and guardian at the gate, master of death and king of fate!"

We may stretch the mind through the imagination, the feeling, the thought that consciously stretches the intellect so it says how many grains of sand; what is man that thou art mindful; everything is so big; so much goodness in the world; how much beauty; how terrific is the love we know—gradually leaving behind the lesser which was the bondage converted into the freedom. And that freedom isn't intended, I think. It is meant that it is instinctive in the nature and constitution of the universe. And I believe it is just as easy, if we knew it, to get it as to be limited. I don't believe the universe denies anybody anything.

When Jesus told the story of the prodigal son, he was telling the story of the ages, the struggle of evolution in every man's life. And when he said a certain man had two sons and, one of them said unto him, 'Father, divide unto me the portion which is mine,' he divided it unto him. And he went into a far country and there he wasted his substance on riotous living." Now, why didn't the father say, "Look here, don't go over there. They will steal all your money." He didn't. He said, "Oh my son, I can't get along without you."

Whenever you get self-righteous, just stick up a sign that says, "Stop, look, and listen." There is no dualism in the universe. There is nothing but God. The universe is a spiritual system. Substance and everything that is back of what we call supply—the universe, the air, every blade of grass—the trees give it out, we breathe it, we exhale it. There is nothing but riches in the universe. There can't be anything else. We interpret it. If we want an undershirt, all right. If we want it to be red, who cares? God made that color, too.

The image of eternity is engraved upon time. The boundless concept of the infinite presses against the finite. The abundance of the universe so flows that out of its flow we draw our limitations, and there is never any dualism anywhere. Never, not for one split second. And that is why the father didn't argue with the son. And he said, "I'll get up and go back home," and he was filled with self-condemnation. But the father saw him afar off. This is what Troward calls the reciprocal action between the universal and the individual. As we turn to it, it turns to us. Because we are turning to it, it is turning to us at the level of our turning to it. Don't ever forget that, for it is one of the great secrets of our own mysticism. "What thou seest, that thou be'est."

And so the son throws himself down and says, "I have done all these terrible things," and papa but didn't argue. Plotinus said that if I were to personify the infinite, I would say, I do not argue, I contemplate; and as I contemplate, I let fall the forms of my thought, that mirror of that which he did not say was an illusion but [inaudible] that had no mind of its own. You see, God didn't say, "Where have you been? Where is the money I gave you? Why are you sick? It serves you right." This is what God did not say; this is the father. But he did say, "I haven't seen you for a long time and I am happy. So let's go in and have a bath and rest and then have a party." Jesus is talking about God and our human relationship to the infinite, that which withholds nothing from the infinitude of its limitless store. "For it is only the finite that has wrought and suffered, the infinite lies stretched in smiling repose," Emerson said.

Our poverty enriches us, if we understand it. Limitation proves the infinity, and bondage alone is freedom because the universe is one system and only one. Let us stretch our imagination. Let us stretch our intellect way out against the horizons of our previous experience. And in the golden glow of the setting sun of that which is passing, let the glories of the day reveal its course, and come back against the eastern sky—a light with hope and many colored hues of the rising sun, coming across the mountain to spill its light and warmth into the valley and wake the desert lands into the newness of life—and bring hope to man.

Ineffable spirit, eternal good, forever love, infinite peace within us, which is God: I am that which I am; Thou art that which I am. And all of our yesterdays are winnowed out into the winds of heaven, and all of our unborn tomorrows shall become pregnant with hope, alive with expectation to give birth to a new harvest. And today, we shall rest in peace.

Beloved of our soul, lover of our soul, we embrace you. And we know that embrace is everywhere. Our arms are around the world and stretch out to the universe in confidence and in peace, in the joy and expectation of the more glorious concept of the now, filled with the air, alive with today. Oh, blessed peace within us, we are one and all the substance there is. We no longer resist, nor do we attack that which seems so little and which has limited us. We dissolve it in the glory of a new dawn. "O living will that shalt endure/when all that seems shall suffer shock/rise in the spiritual rock/flow thro' our deeds and make them pure."

(Alfred Lord Tennyson, in his poem "In Memoriam")

Time Is the Timeless

WEDNESDAY, AUGUST 13, 1958

In this third part of Holmes series on Oneness, he explores the interconnection of our experience of time in the finite world and of the Timeless, the Infinite. Holmes tells us that time is the plaything of the Timeless, a way for us to measure our experience in the finite world.

[Preceding Holmes's talk, his brother, Fenwicke, read the poem "Alone."]

I am so glad you have heard this poem by my brother. And there are lots of books back there for sale, and I thought how wonderful it would be to buy these books for Christmas presents. Christmastime is just around the corner, and there is no better gift than these books or the records or a subscription to the *Science of Mind* magazine.

I wanted to read a little of the book that my brother and I are writing, because it refers to time. It is about a man who has a dream (a long dream, five hundred pages) in which he talks to a Presence, which finally turns out to be himself, but in which all the spiritual wisdom of the ages is recapitulated. [Then another part of "Alone" was read.]

Now our subject tonight is "Time Is the Timeless," and I have chosen the apparent opposites because there are no opposites in truth. The whole miserable mess of negation, that since time began has spread itself around the world in the name of God and religion and philosophy, is false. This is a great claim to make.

Someone asked me the other day, "Who made up this religion?" And I said, "I did, a lot of it." They asked what right I had to do it" I said, "No right." They asked, "Why did you do it?" And I said, "Because I didn't like the others." Someone made them all up, somebody wrote every bible. God never had a private secretary or a typewriter. And you and I have just as much right to decide what we wish to believe as Moses did or Jesus or Socrates or Emerson, and we might be just as nearly right, and being a New Englander, I am quite sure I am. Why shouldn't I be? Somebody has to be, and if somebody has to be, I would rather it would be me because I am so handy to get at it to find out what is right. I said to someone at dinner that by Friday night, we shall all be so confused, we shall probably have to be taken home or retained in questionable places.

No one knows what sanity is because the few sane people we have ever known, like Jesus and Socrates and Emerson and some of the great poets and artists, these are the only sane people who have ever lived. And they were so far from our sanity that they call them geniuses, which they were. We called them God, which they were. And as Emerson said, "Christ is … confounded with virtue and the possible of man."

"Christ … is confounded with virtue and the possible of all man," and that is right. Now, you and I are emancipated from the thralldom of the ages. We do not care who wove the net that we were caught in. We do not care how much authority is in it. All ecclesiastical authority is an assumption of the intellect and emotion, devised in ignorance and fear, but sometimes I think with malice, as well as with prejudice.

You know if you can knock a guy out and make him believe he is lost, you can sell him a pretty good bill of goods about being found. But I feel more like the North Country woman who came over here and was very religious and a little superstitious, and the usher was going up and down the aisle saying, "A dollar for the Lord?" And she didn't put in anything, and he said, "Don't you want to give a dollar to the Lord?" And she said, "I do," and he said, "Why don't you?" She looked at him and said, "I'll give it to him myself. I think I'll see him first." Maybe she was right. Who knows?

So you and I are redeemed from the bondage of the fear, the ignorance, and superstition of the ages. We really are. There is nothing in the universe to be afraid of, as such. There is no one who knows any more about himself than we do, and just because an endless, weary, and monotonous repetition of beliefs has been repeated throughout the ages, it does not necessarily make them right. It is not true to say that 40,000 monkeys cannot be wrong, so peanuts must be good. That is not good logic.

Now Troward said that a neurotic thought pattern repeats itself with monotonous regularity throughout life. He also said that a psychological repression is a group of highly charged thoughts, feelings, and ideas, so deeply repressed in the unconsciousness that they cannot be brought to the surface, either by an act of will or through the imagination, and, he adds, where they are remain in a dynamic state, by which he means they are buried alive. And they are kicking around, and it is this kicking around that is what is meant by the inner conflict.

This inner conflict is the thing that takes place in the individual mind, between the push of what they call the "it" or the "id" and what we call the "divine urge," through here and the push back out there. And this creativity that starts here doesn't get here into self-expression, and because all energy returns to its own source automatically, that which rightfully should go out into creativity, whether it is painting, or singing, or dancing, or whatever it is, anything that explodes the desire into action relieves the tension of the creativity, which itself is the greatest thing we possess. But when it doesn't do it, it goes back and stays in here. And the reason for it is that in the time track etched out of time— which man has created and it has a reality in experience, I don't believe in denying anything, time may have no existence in itself—it has existence in our experience.

St. Augustine said that time is attention, recollection, and anticipation. Dean Inge said time is a measure of events in a unitary wholeness. And I said time is any measure of experience. It means the same thing but more simply because I am not philosophically inclined that way. I like to know what I am talking about, but it seldom happens, so every once in a while I get surprised.

Time is that which is and is not. It is not an eternal verity. If it were, the Timeless would get caught in time and would then become the servant of time.

But just the reverse: Time is the plaything of the Timeless. Like creation. Creation is necessary to a creator because a creator who didn't create wouldn't exist. A consciousness that is not conscious of something has no reality. An actor who never acts has no reality. An absolute unexpressed has no reality. And if there is such a thing as a complete and absolute abstraction in the world, neither God nor man would know about it, because in the act of the knowing, it would become a concretion.

So it is necessary that the infinite is expressed. Just because it is infinite and because we partake of the nature of the infinite, it is necessary that we are expressed. All repression, which is the cause of 75 percent of all accidents, all of these things are the results of the lack of the flow of the Original through us, maintaining Its originality into expression, which is Its expression in us, as us because God in man as man is man. And the discovery is made only by man.

Now the whole process of evolution is to wake up to this, to arrive at this without conceit, without arrogance, without strutting around and saying, "Look at me," and, "Drop dead," and without getting so holy that we are no longer interesting. It is something warm and colorful in whatever it was that painted the sunset tonight. There is a terrific grandeur in the strength of the waves and the wind. There is something alive and awake and aware. This ocean is teeming with life. The very air we breathe is filled with life. The planets are alive. The universe is a living universe, and you and I are conscious and aware of it.

I wish to take this concept of Freud, which is scientific and has been proven. I am not a Freudian psychologist, but I will tell you this: We want to gather all the truth we can from everywhere and put it together to find out what we ought to know. And if we will do this, we will know what is known, and then we will be able to go on somewhere else on a broader basis. The more completely one analyzes and universalizes, the more perfectly he can specialize through synthesis. What you and I know, and what the world could know today, would be taken from all the great thinkers and experimenters of the ages because as Plotinus said, "Knowledge has three degrees—opinion, science, illumination." By illumination he meant what we would mean by religion or revelation. These are the only three ways; that is why I put in this definition that the laws of science and the opinions of philosophy and the revelations of religion or intuition, that there are no other ways through which we gather knowledge.

Now if we take the best the world has had throughout the ages and put it together, always studying to discover a psychological trick the mind plays on us, which is axiomatically taken by saying where there is an emotional bias, there will be an intellectual blind spot. Jesus said it another way: "If the blind lead the blind, both shall fall into the ditch." In an ordinary analysis, if the analyst, for instance, had hated his father and the one being analyzed had, but the one who was doing the analyzing had never got a clearance from his own rejection, when the analyst comes to the place where he ought to be able to uncover that the one being analyzed hated his father, he can't see it because in seeing it he would have to reveal that in himself which caused him to hate his own father. If the analyst saw it, they would both be healed.

I believe it works the same way in us. I believe if a tubercular person would treat a tubercular person and heal him, the first one would get well himself. You can't give what you haven't got. Now this is interesting: what unredeemed areas in our mind, what emotional biases? The first one is our unconscious sense of rejection. The first law of the ego is that it must not be rejected. That is axiomatic. The first law of the libido is that it must have an object. These are two basic laws fundamental to our whole human nature, and if so, back of them are great cosmic forces, which of course are not repressed. But there is a cosmic reality or, as the poem said, a prototype in the invisible for everything that is the visible. And if it is true that man must create or die and love or die—physically, psychologically, but not spiritually—and if it is true that the individual endlessly and monotonously repeats over and over his neurotic or unhappy inclinations, it is equally true that the great universal negations of the human mind are merely a collective neurosis, endlessly repeating itself in the human mind en masse.

We are hypnotized from the cradle to the grave, en masse. There isn't any hell, but look how many people believe in it. There isn't any devil, but think how many people are scared of him. We didn't have to get reincarnated to live this life, but think how many people believe in it. The stars do not control us, but think how many people believe they do. Therefore, even the one who reads stars says that they incline but do not compel. What laws the human mind has built up that go round and round in a little time track of our unredeemed lives, until we are born believing them. And we do not know why we believe them, and because we have the emotional bias to believe them, if anyone contradicts them, we are scared for them and for ourselves and for the world. We are horror stricken. That is why Emerson said, "Let us know the truth. Draw a straight line, hit whom and where it will."

These are neurotic thought patterns chasing themselves around in the little time track of an unredeemed experience, first individually and then collectively, until finally even most of the bibles of the world have been more or less influenced by the neurosis of the collective group of the whole human race, seeming to write an inspiration but mostly as psychic revelation. It cannot be possible that we are referring to the same God, and yet Jesus said, "He that dwelleth in the secret place of the Most High shall abide under the shadow of the Almighty." And then he turned around and said, "Thou hast also given me the necks of mine enemies." That is the kind of a God to have if you have an enemy, because when God puts his heel in somebody's neck, they will at least know they have been stepped on. No question. And yet Jesus saw through this.

Now this is time borrowing from eternity and the Timeless and enough reality to masquerade as though it were a separate entity from the whole thing, and it puts on a show. Emerson said, "The universal nature, too strong for the petty nature of the bard, sits on his neck and writes through his hand." Sometimes that inspiration comes only from the psychic field. Anybody can remember anything that ever happened to anybody who ever lived if and when and to such degree as he gets into a vibration of that individuation in the psychic envelope of this planet. And countless sages will pick it up and describe it. I am not saying these things were not true; I am saying they didn't necessarily have to be true. You can hypnotize a person and put him into a trance with the suggestion he was Julius Caesar, and because we enter that vibration, we are in a timeless field from which nothing erases itself, but from which things can be erased. And it will repeat itself over and over, and if the person is clairvoyant, he will see Julius coming in and out of his palace. He will see the servants serving him wine. And if he is clairaudient, he will hear their conversation.

Now all these things seem impossible because they are so spectacular and so startling. So it is we could see Emerson surrounding someone if he had been reading Emerson or Jesus. Why do we think the pictures the artists draw of Jesus make him look like a Swede instead of Middle Eastern? Because this is the way it started, idealizing it. The first little time track was made, and it was added to and added to until finally the emotional bias reached out into the unformed ages, and chained and nailed down the possibility of the future when it came to being rational about this particular thing. Jesus didn't start it; somebody else did.

Now this is of great importance because you and I believe that time is not a thing in itself. It is merely the individual use that we are making of an eternal possibility, which is the Timeless, but which is forever giving birth to time and space to accommodate the conditions and situations and creations that are instinctive in the nature of its thought. Now what I mean by that is this: All creation, as Troward said, in the law and the word, starts with pure intelligence —intelligence acting as law, intelligence moving as word, word acting as law, establishing fact, fact being revealed, but everything invisible from the intelligence, the word, and the law. And you see nothing until it appears. The things that are seen are not made of the things that do appear, and he shall count the things that are as though they were not.

Every time you and I think in what we call time, we create the time and the situation that goes with it and the condition inherent within the thought when we think it. That is why Troward said, "Principle is not bound by precedent." It is new and spontaneous creation, whether we know it or not. We actually create out of the Timeless that which is still the Timeless enacting time to dramatize Itself, experience Itself, and take delight in Its own doing.

If you turn to the first chapter of Emerson ["History" in *Essays*], he said, "There is one mind common to all individual men. Every man is an inlet to the same and to all of the same." He said, "This human mind wrote history and thus must read it." He said that human history is written by the mind that reads it and cannot be explained on any other basis, because human history is a record of the doings of that mind on this planet. Here is a thinker. "The simplest person who in his integrity worships God, becomes God," Emerson stated.

Imagine the sweep of a man who can say of all human history—he doesn't say it is just a fable that has been told; he knew too much to do that—even history is a living, pulsating thing reenacting its past in the present by precedent, until it is changed by reversing the action of the time track that created it. Every time you give a treatment, you do that. Every time you say, "It doesn't have to be that way," you intercept, short-circuiting a time track so that it can no longer be effective, definitely and deliberately. And every time you initiate a new chain of causation in mind, you are creating a new time that it shall accompany a new experience unbound, unprecedented, new, spontaneous, springing from apparent nothing into apparent something, because all of creation is but an outward manifestation of an inward fact or creator.

Every time this is created automatically, everything is set in motion to provide the conditions necessary, just as when the world was created in the mind of the creator, for that creation goes on. That is why Troward said "in this time track," and he is right. Every creation carries its own mathematics with it, every creation. It is not bound by precedent. And that is why you and I can sit down in our own little time track, but we have to free ourselves from the beliefs that are in the time track of the ages, which is never a thing in itself. It is never an entity. There are no psychic entities self-propelled. They are all compelled by a force extraneous to them, whether we call it a spirit obsession, theory of reincarnation, the influence of the planets, or just because it is another time track created by an individual.

Now the Jews believed the sins of the parents were visited on the children, unto the third or fourth generation. And they believed it. Out of the Timeless, they borrowed enough energy to create a little time to supply their needs, so that for a few generations it would work in a vicious circle. The Hindus believed in the same thing, but they extended their time track. They said it is from incarnation to incarnation. It was no different. And so they invented reincarnation —the intrinsics of it, the fact that neither they nor anybody else could know anything about it and the limitless contradictions of how they operate. Now I am not saying reincarnation isn't true. It may be, for all I know. I don't happen to believe in it. Therefore, I am prejudiced against it, and consequently I can't think straight about it. I am now exemplifying what I meant when I said that if you have an emotional bias, you will have an intellectual blind spot. And it is true. But I am like the wife of Job; I shall not curse God and die. I happen to believe there is an integrity in the universe and in me, and, as Job said, "Though after my skin, worms destroy this body, yet in my flesh shall I see God and mine eyes shall behold God and not another."

He put himself up against the whole anathema of the ages, the whole Jewish and the whole Hindu faith and every other faith, monotonously repeating over and over again, on its time track, just like any neurosis, until the person no longer talks but then the neurosis talks. And there isn't an honest psychiatrist in the world who will condemn his patient, no matter how screwy he is. He always says it is the neurosis and not the neurotic.

Someday in science, when we synthesize its values, it will give us a better religion than we have now. In the beginning of man's unconscious rejection, in the Bible it starts off by saying God came down and said, "Where are you Adam?" And Adam said, "I jumped behind a bush, God." And God asked, "Why did you hide?" Adam answered, "I am naked." And God answered Adam, "Who told thee thou art naked?" This is one of the great revelations of the Bible.

Someone came to John the Baptist and threw himself down and said, "What shall I do to avoid the wrath to come?" And when John answered, the man kept on crying, just as we do now, louder and longer and harder. And the time track emphasizes and reemphasizes, with monotonous regularity, the emotional bias of a sense of unconscious condemnation that will not let the world go. "I came to proclaim that the kingdom of God is at hand." And yet man is so interwoven with the infinite, our nature is so unified with the totality of reality, that out of its freedom we borrow our bondage.

And so the world unconsciously projected the God of vengeance, and to appease the vengeance, the God of mercy and the God of hate, and because it had more good than bad, the God of love and the God of punishment. And because it had more hope, always hope springs eternal in the human breast, it created the light that shall overcome the darkness. But a bunch of the sad-eyed brothers and sisters, who had very little spiritual vitality and a good deal of animosity and meanness, stopped and began to project their own little meanness, dirtiness, "un-redemptive-ness."

I said to one of the greatest writers in America not long ago, "My God, what a terrible area in your mind there must be that is unredeemed, that you condemn people so." He jumped up and said, "This is something I can't take," and I said, "You don't have to take it. It is mine and I'll take it back, but I'm willing to loan it to you."

The big rumpus they had up in heaven, and the originality of that idea, and they threw the guy over, and he fell like a flaming sword. This means the descent of the divine spark impregnating the mundane clod with an involutionary impulse, that will cause it someday to spread and grow by an evolution, until it returns to the source from where it came, individualized, a god among gods. That is the teaching of the ages. That is why Robert Browning said, "A spark disturbs our clod." That is why he says, "to receive what a man may waste, desecrate, never quite lose," in that great metaphysical poem "Saul." And so the ages that followed created a God that had no existence but the time track of the Timeless, where we borrowed from the Timeless that which gives birth to time, and time is not an illusion, but it is necessary to our experience. There are some things even God cannot do. He cannot make a three-year-old colt in five minutes. We say all things are possible to God. It is not possible for God to do anything that contradicts God, and that is why Tolstoy said that there is freedom within the laws of inevitability. God could not be hate without destroying God. God couldn't be fear without destroying the universe.

Now there was once one of the greatest races of people who have ever inhabited this planet. They gave us the greatest line of emotional prophets the world has ever known, even as the Greeks gave us the greatest line of intellectuals. But there was a certain soberness, and they thought of themselves as a downcast group of people. And if they created such a time track evolving around their natural spirit that it has come right down to this day, you couldn't convince them of that. They say, "You are critical of us," but that has nothing to do with it. I am not critical of anything or anybody, but we are redeemed.

Much of this doesn't have to be this way. Why? Because new truth makes ancient good uncouth. What limited us yesterday frees us today. The absolute is the relative. The infinite is the finite. As we were discussing, the Timeless is time, but we borrowed enough to create our little time track and put them together. And out of our own unconsciousness, our sense of guilt, we projected a cosmic assumption. And most of it was a lie. Now what are you and I are going to do about it? We are going to reverse it.

First of all, our intellects and emotions must become convinced. There has been a good deal in the New Thought movement of trying to heal people, which I believe in. There is nothing wrong with this. If I have a pain, I want to get over it and will do most anything I can to get over it. But here we are playing effect against effect, pretty much, and that is all right. But somewhere there is a timeless that overlaps, overshadows, interspaces, interferes, and controls every one of our time tracks. But we can never do it, individually or collectively, until we individually and collectively see through the time track and know it is an effect and not a cause.

It does not matter how many people believed in it, that has nothing to do with reality. It doesn't matter if everyone on Earth believes in it, it still is not true. Jesus knew a time track beyond the Jews and the Gentiles of his day, and they said, "Who sinned, this man or his parents?" because he was born blind. They thought they had him stuck; this is all they knew. The Jews knew of this time track, grandfather down to little Moses. The Hindus knew of this one from way back in the dim past that no one could remember, and they shoved the thing back so far. And you don't solve or explain any problem by shoving it so far away from you that you can't see it.

Jesus knew this. Maybe there is an overlapping of time and space where what went out, when it gets back will carry back with it all it took out. And maybe it didn't take so long to carry it out as we think, and maybe it carried it back before it sent it out. And if it did, you might be a dimension in the universe where a guy could jump in the saucer on the planet Mars in the morning and have lunch with us in the afternoon. I don't know how he would get here.

Now, Jesus did not argue with all of these people at all. He had another kind of time track and knew things were all right. And he said to the blind man, "You are all right." Where was the karma? Jesus did not repudiate differences. One of the greatest things Aurobindo said was that the transcendence does not reconcile, it transmutes. And Jesus was transmuted, time into the Timeless, but he did not destroy either time or the Timeless. He just wove the whole thing back again into its cosmic reality, and right then and there, created a new sequence and a new chain. Maybe Buddha was right. He is supposed to have discovered the law of cause and effect through which imprisoned souls are bound. Maybe he was right. Maybe Moses was right when he said that is the way it works. I don't doubt it. I am sure Jesus was right, and I think I know what he did, which I am going to talk about Friday night. I am just saying the same things in a different way, to see how confused a person can be without having to find out. As long as we are not violent, we are safe in having a lot of fun.

Jesus didn't say the multitude could not be fed. He knew they would starve to death if they didn't get fed. He said, "Sit them down, and I will feed them." He didn't say Lazarus has been dead for four days. He looked up and said, "Father, I thank Thee that Thou hast heard me." He was listening to something beyond the man who was dead for four days. He told his disciples plainly, the time track of Lazarus on this Earth is ended as people count it, but I am going to take a new one to him. And then he looked up, and with no quivering of lips, said, "Lazarus, come forth." He had command of the situation. He understood that all things manifest are subject to the invisible. Jesus knew it didn't matter who believed what or how many believed which. It didn't make a bit of difference.

Then he created a new time track and reversed the old. And this is what you and I do every time we give a treatment. The Timeless enters time, as the uncreated enters creation, and God becomes His own creation. That which is the Creative Impulse may know Itself, understand Itself, behold Itself, enjoy Itself, delight in Itself, and that is why you and I create. And someday, without violating the laws of the universe or the integrity of the intelligence of the eternal, every one of us.... This is what Troward meant by the creative process, what Aurobindo meant by Gnostic man, what is meant by Christ, Buddha, all of them, the enlightened. It is what Isaiah was talking about when he said, "When he ascended up on high, he left captivity captive." Until you and I leave captivity captive—without resistance, without violence, not even denying it perhaps, but flowing through it, some higher essence, some finer force, all permeating, all penetrating—we shall still be stumbling around in the old time tracks, which were never a thing in themselves but appeared to be, and the law of their being, which was created when they were made, self-sustaining until the day of their dissolution. The morbidity of theology and the denunciation of the Jews, with their greatest of all prophets, and the renunciation of the Hindus and the Buddhists, the most sublime philosophy perhaps the world has ever had, did violation to the soul of man and did circumscribe and desecrate almost the spirit of the Almighty, until someone came, saw through the warp, and lifted the curtain of obscurity, created a dome more vast, and by that law, which is bound was freed.

The Relative and the Absolute

THURSDAY, AUGUST 14, 1958

Here in this fourth talk for 1958, Ernest Holmes calls us to view the relative and the Absolute not as separate things but rather as two aspects of being that are interdependent on each other. As Holmes states, we cannot have the Absolute without the relative and vice versa. Through the process of involution, the Absolute embedded Itself within the relative and then left it, through free will, choice, and the process of evolution, to return to its source.

NOTE: Preceding his evening lecture, Holmes made the following comments as part of a practitioner ceremony.

We are idealistic. We are transcendentalists, realists because we believe that we can use a spiritual law or a mental law in spiritual work for any legitimate, concrete purpose. Now, I consider two main offices that are essential. Everything else revolves around the two concepts I am mentioning: The teaching of the Presence and the practicing of the principle. These are essential. The world is no longer going to say that it is fed while it is hungry; there is no reason why it should. We teach the divine Presence and use the universal principle. And unless some sign follows our belief, we have no justification in its assertion. Not any. But some sign will follow.

I was talking to one of the boys just before dinner, and he said, "I wasn't sure when I came here but now I have proven that this works." So I called over three more kids about his same age and said, "Tell them how to give a treatment." They knew anyway, but I wanted to hear what this guy had to say about it. He starts right off and tells them how to do it, because he told them what he did, when he did it, and he knew what he did was all right because it worked.

Our movement will rise or fall, and it will rise on what happens to the people in it, not what they talk about, not how loud they scream. It will depend entirely on what happens to the individual life and what happens to those who come to our practitioners and leaders for help. I do not consider physical healing or the demonstration of money to be the principal office of Religious Science. Of course, it is essential.

Our movement depends entirely on the practice of our science. People must have a deeper, mystical, spiritual sense of reality. God must be more real without superstition, more intimate without dramatization, more personal, infinitely more personal, without mawing and pawing. God is personal to everyone, which I wish to demonstrate tomorrow night. Therefore, you are the most important group of people we shall ever have. Practicing, teaching, proving, so that other people shall see us. We have nothing to sell, no one to convince, and if, as a result of your work, someone is happier, has a deeper sense of abiding peace and assurance, a certainty of the universe, and is emitting something that everyone feels and knows, then all the better. You will be practicing a transcendental realism, and if as a result of what you do, some practical good occurs, you will be a practical idealist. If someone has a greater sense of security in the universe for himself and a sense of God, you will be practicing true religion. If someone has a broader-gauge intellectual viewpoint of the universe, you will be practicing philosophy. If you know and he comes to know that the law of action and reaction governs all things dominated by the Spirit, you will be practicing the finest science the world has ever caught up with. And through it all, you will never treat anyone but yourself.

You will never influence anyone. You will never try to win anything, other than the joy of knowing that there is something in the universe which responds directly to the approach of the individual for the purpose for which he identifies, something that is good and wonderful and true and all together lovely. And, my friends, you will never do this through cold intellectualism. You will never do it through just making statements that are true. You will do it only when that which is the truth makes a statement in you that cannot be refuted. You will do it as you feel your way back to that central flame, which is the living Spirit within yourself, and as each lit the candle of another here in this beautiful symbol, your light will light the candle of those who come to you. And then, and only then, will they be able to say one thing: I know that whereas I was blind, now I see.

The audience, the ministers, the practitioners join with me in this dedication to a great, high, and holy purpose, and together, all of us dedicate this group of practitioners to the love of God and the service of man, to the joy of their own souls, and to the delight of the Spirit.

EVENING LECTURE:

The substance of these talks is collected in a little book I wrote called *Your Invisible Power.* It is the only four ways I know of that spiritual truths have ever been presented to the ages. And another little book, *What Religious Science Teaches,* gives us, as briefly as possible, the sources of Religious Science. Everyone in our movement should have it. And there is another book, called *The Bible of Bibles: A Source Book of Religions*, that every student of comparative religions, ones interested, should have. It is the only book of its kind in existence. It has more in it that will lead to comparative thoughts in religion, what all the ancients taught. It is all in that one book.

Now our subject this evening is The Relative and the Absolute, and I would like to make a few more brief remarks before I say anything, and that is this: We shall never understand any spiritual philosophy unless we can conceive, in some degree, of the necessity of there being a self-existent life in the universe, which was not created and which did not create itself. The mind you and I use is very finite, even though it is the Infinite as the finite. We have a limited use of the limitless possibility of what we are using in our own evolution. But we have to, without trying, encompass the Infinite, which we can't do. And it would be terrible if we could, because if we knew everything there is to know and had to live forever, that would be hell.

There has to be a self-existent life. Nothing made it. God didn't make life; God didn't make law; God didn't make God. The word we use for God means self-existence, the truth, or that which is. "I am that I am, beside which there is none other," the first axiom of truth, and all we have been studying this week are axioms of truth in a very abbreviated, simplified, and easy to understand form. Everything we are talking about is axiomatic, that is, conclusions based on propositions that sanity cannot deny. That is what axiomatic reasoning means. It does not contradict the intuition because if we had an intuition that contradicted the axiomatics, one or the other would have to be wrong. The universe will never contradict itself. Fact and faith will never collide. If they appear to, we must reexamine the fact or examine the faith more carefully, always.

Baptism never had anything to do with salvation. As a matter of fact, the original baptism had nothing to do with salvation at all. They just said that water is the symbol of Spirit, and we are putting the water all over because Spirit is all over. "In him, we live and move and have our being." The Lord's supper had nothing to do with eating the body and drinking the blood of Jesus. It had to do with the solid and liquid of the universe, in much the same way as Einstein's theory that energy and mass are equal, identical, and interchangeable. The invisible things of God are made manifest by the visible, or as Alexander Pope said, "All are parts of one stupendous whole, Whose body Nature is, and God the soul."

Now part of these things I have just told you, I made up. And you will say, "What right did you have to make them up?" Somebody made all of them up, don't kid yourself. Somebody made all of them up, and the somebody who made them up was somebody like the somebodies who are right in this room. But some of them didn't have as much brains as we do, and I'm glad. I am the most modest man who ever lived until it comes to announcing a truth, because it is none of my business. I didn't make it, and I can't change it. There are certain self-evident propositions of the universe that sanity cannot deny. What we call God is the truth. What is self-existence? In the Greek Catholic Church, when they use the word God, they say self-existence. I am that which is. Now you and I have to suppose that self-existence or we wouldn't be here. We have to suppose it is all there is. The truth is that which is. There is not the truth and something else that contradicts the truth, no matter what it is. There just isn't. There cannot be, and yet that which appears is not illusion, but our interpretation of it can be largely illusion. We have to suppose it is the nature of reality to be thus and so.

Now I would like to explain that there are no divine plans, there are cosmic patterns. A divine plan and a divine purpose is a climax. It is like a line that begins here and ends there. Infinity is described only by a circle. God has no plans to become something that God wasn't before He started to get to be what He wanted to become. There is no such God. Being Itself is endless of days, It is omnipresent, It is indivisible, all of It is everywhere, but it is the nature of truth—God, reality, self-existence—to express Itself.

It doesn't matter who tells you, "Why, it is the nature." They don't know. What is is. Why is life? There isn't any reason why life is. It is, and that is where you start. Science never explains the why or the what but only the how. That is all a scientist can explain or all he tries to. He discovers a principle that is so. This principle exists that God may be glorified in Jesus. That is the theology of Christianity. But the Muslim said, "There is no God save Allah, and Mohammed is his prophet." The Mormons say it was all revealed to Joseph Smith when the angel whispered something. God did not get Mrs. Mary Baker Eddy up in an attic and say, "Now Mary, you got it," and yet they all think He did. And He did reveal Himself or Itself to them in such degree as they listen deeply enough to whatever it is that works inside a man's mind, beyond the range of his intellect and higher even than his mathematics, but some of divine interior knowingness, which Plotinus said all people have but very few people use.

You and I have to suppose an Infinite Cause then, which is forever expressing Itself because that is the way It does, I believe, for Its own delight, for Its own self-expression. I suppose that an Infinite can't help creating. This is my theory because I see creation everywhere, everything, from the infinitesimal to finite. The child making mud cakes, is it any less important than somebody building the Empire State building? In some process of time out of the Timeless we discussed last night, they will both wither and turn to dust and blow away and the place will know them no more. And that is right because the only thing that is constant in the universe is change, a change which takes place within the changeless. We have to suppose that because of the divine nature of reality. And don't let anybody tell you why God is God. We may always thank the God that is, that the God that it is believed in isn't, because then it would be as bad as it seems to be.

We must suppose that it is the nature of reality to incarnate, to flow from being, out into becoming, just for the joy of its own movement. And we must suppose, I do not pretend to understand this part of it or any other part of it. I am talking about something I do not know anything about but I believe in it or I wouldn't be wasting your time. It is so darned simple that it seems hard to understand. What we have been talking about here is very simple, very simple. We just have a bigger idea that we want to introduce to things and people. It has been a great concept of the ages. We must suppose that eternally the living Spirit incarnates. I am not speaking about incarnation in you and me. In everything, it incarnates and impregnates. Let's say, forever the womb of nature is impregnated with divine ideas.

That is why Emerson said that the Ancient of Days is in the latest invention and why Meister Eckhart said, "God never begot but one son, but the eternal is forever begetting the only begotten." We must suppose that it is by the impartation of its own inherent life through incarnation, and as James Russell Lowell said:

And what is so rare as a day in June?
Then, if ever, comes perfect days;
Then Heaven tries earth if it be in tune
And over it softly her warm ear lays;
Whether we look, or whether we listen,
We hear life murmur, or see it glisten;
Every clod feels a stir of might,
An instinct within it that reaches and towers,
And, groping blindly above it for light,
Climbs to a soul in grass and flowers.

And Robert Browning said, "A spark that disturbs our clod." We must believe because everything acts as though it were true, and it is, that this spark that all the great philosophers of the ages have referred to as a process of involution, which means the passing of Spirit into form through the process, which always precedes evolution. And evolution always follows involution with mathematical precision, backed by immutable law, impulsed by the nature of reality, which is love and self-expression.

All the deep thinkers who have ever lived have taught this. It is simple as that. Therefore, we must suppose that the involution is a part of the nature of reality. There is buried in the clod, we will say, now this means everything; everything is impregnated with the universal nature and set on its journey of eternal evolution or unfoldment, already endowed and equipped with what I want to talk to you about tomorrow night, which gives significance to human personality and which alone makes the significance. Otherwise, it would have no significance whatsoever, that which was born in the morning and passed on before the sunset.

It is a different destiny than that, because eternity has endowed time with the ability—consciously, uncaught—to be loosed into eternity and remain an individuation of a universality without destroying the unity from which it emerged or separating from each other the diversities that have emerged. I don't exactly know what it means, but I know it is true, because I know two and two make four. These things we have to accept. They are not my opinions, and I didn't make them up. The great and good and wise and just and intelligent and intuitive and thinkers of the ages have believed them. And that is why I believe them, because if there is any news from the kingdom of God, this is where it has come from, just as we say if there is any news from the nature of electricity, study what is known about it, and these things we do.

We must suppose there is incarnated in us, from the lowest to the highest, from the smallest speck of dust to the archangels, if such things exist. I happen to believe in an evolving, upward spiraling, outward swinging, eternal evolutionary process, which never retraces its step. This reaffirms what I said last night. "Truth, crushed to earth, shall rise again; the eternal years of God are hers; /But error, wounded, writhes with pain/And dies among his worshipers." (William Cullen Bryant)

One of the great tragedies of the human race is—it pertains to and surrounds the highest and greatest good the human race has ever had, and that is its spiritual convictions—because it has projected a finite form upon an infinite mirror, and looking at it, has mistaken the form it projected for the reality and realization of the substance that caused it to project any form at all, since he has never left himself without a witness.

There is and must be incarnated then in everything not only that which makes it what it now is, but that which will make that thing what it is going to become forever. A prototype, a something that has a persistence and a constant urge back of all things, and tomorrow night I want to tell you what I think it is going to do. And I think it because all of the greatest thought it. It must be axiomatically certain; that is, it is rationally certain, it is logically certain. And since evolution is a process that history reveals, it had to follow an involution, which was less mechanical, and perhaps a spontaneous emergence setting in motion, in time, those laws I spoke of last night, which are automatically created every time you and I think. The laws pertaining to what we think about are now set in motion and would work until they produced what is thought. But we neutralize not law but this particular vibration in it, just like planting a seed and going out and pulling it up. Therefore, there is a divine pattern in you and in me—inviolate, absolute. It is perfect, complete; it is now. And all of it is here now, and we must next realize that an infinite, undivided, and indivisible cause does not create by projection or reflection. Now let me qualify projection. If by projection you mean the essence of its being beyond the circumference of that being, that it shall behold itself apart, it can't do that, otherwise God would take a cosmic knife and cut His own head off. You cannot divide the indivisible. I am saying this: There is no God who can create outside His own essence. There is no God who can make anything outside of His own Self. There is no God who can reflect or project anything away from Himself. It is impossible. There isn't any "away from Himself." This is not my opinion; that is just the way it is.

Now the truth is what is. I haven't anything to do about it; it is not my business. The world was round when they thought it was flat, but because it was round, the first guy who knew it went around it. People like Buddha, Moses, Jesus, and all the great prophets lived not in a different world than other people. They lived in the same world, but they looked at it differently. Therefore, they experienced it differently. There are laws within laws, ad infinitum, and each will parallel the other on a higher or lower level of expression. That is why Emerson said that we are born and we realize we are on a certain step and there are steps above us and beneath us. And Jesus said, "In my Father's house are many mansions." And Hermes said, "As above, so below; as within, so without; as the universe, so the soul." The law of correspondence and parallels, doesn't matter what you call it.

Now there is no possibility that any Infinite Power projected Its essence outside Itself. If It projected it, it was a projection not apart from Itself or outside Its own essence or the boundaries of Its own infinite personalness, because, strange as it may seem, you and I believe in and our system teaches the most exalted concept of the personalness of God that has ever been put into print. There is nothing in any bible that is to compare with it. Someone said to me the other day, "It is pretty bold." And I said, "Have you read our section on the perfect whole? It is the most exalted concept of intimate personalness with universality and infinity that was ever put into print." I just gave to it the words. I got the ideas from the great but, "The great are only great because we are on our knees, let us rise!" This is where the soul makes its great claim upon God, but it must make a true claim because God doesn't honor a liar. Of course, God doesn't know anything about liars, but Emerson said, "God screens us evermore from premature ideas," and, "When the fruit is ripe, it falls."

Let's say God doesn't project God outside of God, but God manifests God in God for God's delight, just as you and I would sing or dance. We don't have to step outside ourselves. And God can only make things out of Himself. And since God, or the truth, or what is, is undivided and indivisible, all of it appears everywhere. Consequently, back of every individuation is a universality surging to be and become that individuation as even the God or the Absolute. Just as if It spent all Its time and concentration on you and on me, that is what is back of personality and individuality, something terrific. This is the meaning of Christ.

Now the next thing I would like to establish is that there can be no absolute without what we call a relative, and all we mean by a relative is that which is in a certain relationship to an absolute. By a relative, we do not mean something that is separate from an absolute, something detached from it. There is no absolute that can reflect anything but the absolute. What else would it reflect? There is no possibility of an absolute reflecting or extending or projecting a relative without itself becoming the relative and without establishing the relationship in law and order and evolution of the relative as itself, not evolving but expressing through what you and I call evolution. This, the great and the good and the wise have held. Nobody could have thought all these things in a lifetime.

I have to stop and say to myself, "What does this mean?" Don't worry, it is going to be all right. Let's relax. Someday everyone will have to know what I am talking about before they become whole. You cannot get wholeness out of fragments of infinity. No kind of wholeness comes out of a fragment. The relative is the expression of the absolute at the level of the relative. The absolute cannot create a relative out of relationship to itself, different from itself, other than itself, apart from itself, or opposed from itself, or separated from itself. It is impossible in an undivided and indivisible universe. All that the relative is is the absolute proclaiming its absoluteness. Now, that is what is back of law and order. That is what ought to be back of every treatment we give, for the treatment is spontaneous, like involution.

I just forgot—that thing (the microphone) works wherever you go. How stupid can we be? It has taken me four nights to discover I could move. It shows that bondage is self-imposed by a law that works.

The infinite can only project the infinite. The infinite can only reflect the infinite. The infinite, being undivided and indivisible, cannot reflect or project fragments of the infinite, but it can project individuation, ad infinitum, without limit. Each one of which can expand through eternity toward infinity with no point of saturation, because it will never exhaust eternity, because every time it thinks, it will create the time for where it is and the law that goes with the time. When it thinks in a broader scope, it will go deeper and higher, and so infinity is forever manifesting what we call the finite, which is merely the infinite in manifestation as the finite. We will never get anywhere in thinking we affirm the absolute by denying the relative. It is like having a cup with only an inside and not an outside, or a stick with only one end, and that would be very confusing because you wouldn't know which end to grab hold of.

Now that I know I have freedom, I want to be where I am comfortable and with what simple things cosmic truths can teach us. There is no such thing as a relative separate from an absolute, and there is no such thing as an absolute separate from the relative. It is necessary we understand both positions or we can't say they are the same thing. They would be apart unless they were instantaneous, simultaneous, and eternally conjoined by the nature of reality, which, without changing itself, has change within itself that its life shall not be an eternal monotony. If you and I had to live forever without movement or imagination, we would be dead. Life is action. Therefore, it is the nature of reality to express. It is the nature of that which is expressed to be the absolute as the expression, but still conditioned by it, subject to even its own absoluteness. The master is greater than the servant, always.

In our treatment, it means that in our treatment, and in such degree as it is in accord with the law of being, what happens will be relative, depending on our essence of absoluteness. This is why Jesus said, "Heaven and Earth will pass away, but my word will not." There will come an authority in our word when we gradually wake up to realize what is the meaning of authority and why. You can stretch your intellect until your imagination takes you across the chasm between the absolute and the relative, and still the absolute will not become relative, the relative will not become absolute as separate entities. But the absolute will be eternally giving the relative back to itself to play with, the playthings of the Eternal.

God is full of fun, else you and I wouldn't laugh. James Whitcomb Riley said, "As it's given me to perceive/I most certin'y believe/When a man's jest glad plum through/God's pleased with him, same as you." The authority of our word exists to the degree that it is either consciously or unconsciously stated, and I think mostly consciously should be if it is conscious, with an absoluteness beyond the word, but making the word subject to the absoluteness, so that the creation may be withdrawn when we no longer need it. You are not wearing the same clothes you wore last year.

And so the absolute, now this means the truth, what it is, it means God. What is back of your treatment is the consciousness in you giving the treatment. It is God; there is nothing else it can be. You are made out of God, and I am made out of God, and the only difference is in just enough of the outline for the articulation of the unique individuation of a universality, which is eternal. This is the very nature of our being, since as we said, a denial is an affirmation and an affirmation might become a denial, because the mind may only affirm. And since there is no bigness and littleness in it, and since time is eternity, and eternity is time, and the absolute is the relative, and the relative is the absolute because it is expression, its mode of express, it is certain, completely certain, that this play of life must take place eternally, that there is right now incarnated in you and in me, of a necessity, absolute essence, absolute law, and absolute manifestation.

We may not be doing very much with it right now. We are at that process of evolution that brings up another point: I believe all limitation is freedom, as you know. All relativity is absoluteness. All time is eternity. All noes are yeses, and I believe one other thing, which I am impelled to accept and do not try to rationalize, but I believe it is intelligent to accept it, and that is: I can't tell you why it is so, every great religion has said that it is so, but mostly I think they intuitively feel it, but mostly they misinterpret the intuition. We can do this because psychicism can confuse our intuition; it seems as though this thing is done and then left alone to discover itself. Probably that is the only way it could transpire because we could not have an automatic or just mechanical spontaneity. Our Bible calls this period "The Fall," when Adam was made. This is an allegory. The preacher was telling the story and said, "Adam was very lonely, so God put him to sleep and made Eve. And he looked up and said, 'Hello, where did you come from?' And she answered, 'It doesn't make any difference where I came from. Here I am, and that is enough.'"

This contains infinite logic. The universe cannot be explained, it can only be accepted. Its *what* and *why* have no existence; and its *how*, science, philosophy, and intuition may come to understand. Aurobindo calls this "the period of ignorance"; we call it the fall and the redemption. I like the thought of a period of ignorance. As William H. Carruth said, "A fire-mist and a planet, a crystal and a cell/A jellyfish and a saurian, and caves where the cavemen dwell/Then a sense of law and beauty, and a face turned from the clod/Some call it evolution, and others call it God."

One thing is certain in my mind: When that divine consummation took place and the face was turned from the clod, no arbitrary or compulsory process of evolution went on after that. Jesus said, "My Father worketh hitherto, and I work." All nature, the Bible says, "For we know that the whole creation groaneth and travaileth in pain together until now." I believe—and it is what I want to explain tomorrow night—what happens when it happens, theoretically. All of them taught it—the great, and listen only to the great, when they speak a language of love and unity, evolution and unfoldment on the sure basis, backed by an immutable law, impulsed by "a love so limitless, deep and broad that men have renamed it and called it God" (Ella Wheeler Wilcox).

Infinite person becoming you; infinite presence flowing through you. But if man is to be spontaneous, like the prodigal son, he has to make the return consciously, because the ultimate of all reality and realization in the universe is not the abstraction of a dead identity lost in a nirvanic stream of howsoever pure waters of Spirit. Rabindranath Tagore said that nirvana is not absorption but immersion. And he is right. It is rather to produce that thing which shall contain the potential of all things, and in their infinite variations of manifestation forever ascending, the much and the more of life. And so I believe in the process according to its nature, not by the will of God or the purpose of God. God doesn't plan things, God *is* things, and there is a vast difference. Plans are finite; purposes are finite. Cosmic patterns are as eternal as the Infinite and as inexhaustible and indestructible as the mind of the Eternal.

It was necessary, then, that that period, whether you call it "The Fall"—I don't like the fall and redemption. The fall and redemption through salvation are two ends of one morbid stick that you can't beat any truth out of at all. They are the projections of morbidity and fear and doubt, the dark corners of the mind, but it means this, which is all these talks are leading up to this thing I want to discuss tomorrow night: All evolution is something that takes place where time is a plaything of the Timeless, where the freedom is so great we may deny the freedom and by freedom hold ourselves in bondage to the day of liberation. Where the relative will stick us with its relativity until we see through that which we now look through as a glass darkly and behold absoluteness of the relativity, and the freedom of the bondage, until at long last, wherever we look, whatever we see shall declare the glory of God and the kingdom of heaven now and the immutable law of being, which is a servant of the eternal Spirit throughout the ages.

Don't be afraid of relativity because those who deny the relativity merely create a different kind of relativity. It is impossible not to. They would cease to exist if they didn't. If it is a better God, that is fine. "Naught is the squire, when the king's at hand, withdraw the stars, when dawns the sun's brave light." It is given to you and to me to know the mystery of the kingdom of God and to understand the deep thoughts of the ages; and to come, at long last, once and for all, to cut that knot of ignorance and of fear and of superstition that has bound us hand and foot in a self-imposed prison, until at long last, some light from an inner source rises across the horizon of the darkness of our night and the despair of our souls. Something sings, "Build thee more stately mansions, O my soul/As the swift seasons roll/Leave thy low-vaulted past/Let each new temple, nobler than the last/Shut thee from heaven with a dome more vast/Till thou at length art free/Leaving thine outgrown shell by life's unresting sea". (Oliver Wendell Holmes, "The Chambered Nautilus")

Infinite and Eternal Spirit, absolute and relative, big and little, up and down, over and across, and every color of the rainbow; light of the morning star, the sunset's glow, children at play, the innocence of life, naked and unafraid; God of all people, of saints and sinners, who are just the same, each groping forward as an infant crying in the night: Consciously and definitely we now place our hands in the outstretched hand of the Infinite, and all fear is gone, and all loss is swallowed up in gain, and all failure in victory, and all death in eternal resurrection of a jubilant and a beholding soul. James Whitcomb Riley said in "A Hymn of Faith," "O Thou that doth all things devise/And fashion for the best/Help us who see with mortal eyes/To overlook the rest."

The Finite Is the Infinite

FRIDAY, AUGUST 15, 1958

In his concluding lecture for the week, Holmes humbly states that this "is the only important talk I shall have given this week," but he acknowledges that all the other talks have been leading up to this one. He set the stage on the previous nights for us to better understand that the things we see as opposites are really united in the oneness of the Divine. Now, he calls us to use the power of contemplation to increase our sense of identification with the Divine or Spirit so that we may "storm the kingdom of heaven and break down the gates" and in our own way, each become a mystic.

Thank you so very much, Gene [Rev. Gene Emmet Clark]. That is about the sweetest thing that ever happened to anybody, because love is the lodestone of life, without which there is very little in life worthwhile. I have certainly enjoyed, more than ever before, this wonderful assembly, getting together, this seminar. Probably I have had more fun out of it than anyone else. I am particularly grateful and wish to express gratitude to all of you for the courtesy you have shown in listening to rather abstract and not-too-interesting concepts, but concepts I feel have come down to us from the ages, and the patience you have had to listen. I have particularly enjoyed the love and sense of friendship I have felt from all of you, and I know it will go on throughout the ages. I love you; you love me; we love each other. And that is as it should be.

I consider Religious Science the next great spiritual impulse of the ages. It comes rarely. There hasn't been a major one since the time of Mohammed.

This may surprise you. There have been a few new religions, but they are not destined to do what Religious Science will do. It has the elements not only of success, which seems rather mundane and material, but it has the elements of substantiality. It has the thing the world needs when faith becomes more or less on the wane and when the attempt to restore it reverts to the idolatry, the superstition, the fear, and the ignorance of the Middle Ages. It will never work.

And so evolution has brought forward something that answers the demand of the age in which we live. We happen to be living in this age. We are grateful it came while we are here. We inherit the great thoughts of the ages, and we believe if there is any spiritual authority in the world, it will have to be drawn from those great men and women whose lives proved they knew something that other people didn't. And when we stop and look and listen to them, we, too, hear something. And what we hear is not an illusion; it is the greatest of all realities. This is Religious Science, to which is added the modern touch, embracing modern science, psychiatry, psychology, and all the new things that have happened in the last thousand years in the world.

That is as it should be. We are the religious impulsion that has come to the world. Somebody might ask if that is a criticism of the New Testament. Not at all. Emerson said, "For every stoic, was a stoic but in Christendom, where is the Christian?" Now a stoic, a little East Side boy, asked his father, "What is the difference between a stoic and a cynic?" And Papa said, "I will tell you. The stoic is the bird that brings the baby, and the cynic is where they wash him." But we are talking about a different stoic and not a cynic. A stoic is merely one who has to be shown. We have stoics, in a certain sense. You see, Jesus didn't invent his religion; Moses made one and gave it to the people and said, "Take it." Jesus lived in years afterward, and they tried to remember what he said, most of which he may or may not have said, and created a religion to go around a historic figure. Both are good, and they were all of the same race, a great race. They gave the world its greatest prophecies of feeling we know of, as the Greeks gave the world the greatest prophets or philosophers of intellectual conception.

But what happened afterward was too bad. Provisions are being made that we shall never get into any set form, ever. No one will ever be able to say that I ever thought I was a prophet. I shave twice a day, and prophets must have whiskers. And I don't like whiskers at all. I have had no revelations. I don't see things. Now we have written something I want to read you a couple of pages from, which is a fictional thing written in blank verse and free verse. It is a story of man who went to sleep, and as he went to sleep, he began to think on what is the meaning of life and what is it all about. He then read the fable. You will recognize in this small section what we have been talking about this week, the hidden cause, which because it is an undivided wholeness, must of a necessity be omnipresent. Take an apple: The apple is omnipresent in the apple. There is nothing in the apple but apple, and all the apple is in the apple, and all that is in the apple is apple, and the apple will remain just one apple unless something cuts it in two. And still, all of the apple will be where the apple is.

God is one, undivided and indivisible. All of God is wherever we think. That is simple enough to understand. But if all of God is wherever we think, and if we think all of God is where we think when we think, this we cannot help. We didn't put the ocean out there, and we don't make water wet. Consequently, we find, in the long process of evolution since time began, that process which gradually pushed everything forward, evolved the human being to the place where the human being got up on his feet and looked about and said, "I am not that. I am something else because I can recognize this. I am different from my environment."

Now in the arbitrary processes of evolution, as we discussed last night, it has done that for endless millennia. The day that this divine consummation took place, everything would have to await man's cooperation for his further evolution. I think that is very simple. In science, we know that all new things discovered existed in the potential of the universe. We could say of them, "Before Abraham was, they were." All progress is a result of our conscious union with nature, discovering the laws of nature and using them, and nature never seems to say no, except for those times when we go contrary to her laws. She doesn't say no but her yes is kind of messed up because we are not using the laws right. Her yes isn't mixed up, ever. We are mixed up. Therefore, we don't get a clear, definite thing.

And so in science, they experiment and experiment. Now you and I are spiritual scientists. We are not just mental scientists, you know. We don't sit around holding thoughts to get over the itch. We don't want to just get a thin dime, for fear we won't get breakfast. Josh Billings said that if you want to see how much you are missed, stick your feet in a pail of water and see how big a hole is left. That would deflate our egos and perhaps shrink our big feet just enough so we won't stumble over them anymore.

The universe surrenders itself to everything in it. We believe our word is acted upon by a spiritual power, a mental cause, an absolute and creative law, which returns to us or to those things or persons with which our word is identified, that which will represent the high point of our meditation and acceptance. That is our whole principle. This bunch of youngsters know what we are talking about, just as well as you and I do. They just use different words. We believe in this. Now then we believe there is an Absolute Power, which operates upon our word. We don't put creativity into it; we take it out, because it exists in the universe.

Suppose we believe—and this I consider the greatest single spiritual teaching the world has ever had. And so far as I know, it has been given by great spiritual philosophers of the ages and great religions of all ages, without exceptions and illusions. From Zoroaster, all of them, all the great poets, we find this thought, that there is something that responds to us at the level of our consciousness of it, knowledge of it, embodiment of it. It is what Troward meant by the reciprocal action between the universal and individual. It is what he meant by the dénouement of the creative process. It is what Aurobindo meant in what he called gnostic man—that means man of wisdom. It is what the great have taught, what the Bible means when it says, "I shall awake in His likeness." Now the Old Testament is crammed full of it, and the New Testament is, too. But the stupid people who only read the Old Testament and the equally stupid people who only read the New Testament are both so stupid—they can't be any stupider, and there can't be anything more stupid than this kind of stupidity. Why, in the name of God, anybody will refuse to admit sugar is sweet, whether they find it in a dustpan or in a sugar bowl, is beyond me. It is one of the great tragedies of the ages, that every religion getting some good from it and proving some point, because all of them have been mostly right. They should swear that where they are wrong, they are right, too, and destroy their own philosophy inwardly, not knowing everything in our universe is growing and expanding.

There are no Jews and no Gentiles, and no black and no white, and no big and no little, and no good and no bad, and no right and no wrong. Heaven is lost merely for lack of an idea of harmony. And hell is peopled with discordant images of our own morbidity. And we are privileged apparently to move back and forth at will. The greatest single teaching of all the ages is so simple that when I tell it, it will be hard to believe it. All we have talked about this whole week, all that I have I said, is to lead to this one thing, because I have been giving you what are called the axioms of reason, a system of thinking so self-evident that human intelligence cannot, in its integrity, deny its validity or refuse to accept the automatic conclusions that its mathematics and logic lead to. You can't do it. It is impossible.

And it is this: Since the universe is indivisible, all of it is where you are, all of it is where I am, whether we know it or not. All of its creativity is at the center of our thinking, and this is why our thought is creative. We don't put it in; we take it out. Always, we take it out, but we take everything out of life. We don't lay an egg; we don't make a garden. We set a hen and plant a garden.

But we unite our personal equation with the universal principle. We unite our finite personalness with an infinite, at first seemingly impersonal, but when we unite it consciously with something that contains the warmth and color of the universe, and it wrote every book that has ever been written and will write every book that will ever be written. Somebody asked me today, "Can I write a book?" And I said, "Certainly, if you can get out of the way long enough. Of course, everybody can."

There is only one author; there is only one singer, only one dancer; but you are that one. You say, "How can I be that one?" How can you help being that one, individualized as you? You and I have to be God's idea of Himself as what we are. Emerson said, "The simplest person, who in his integrity worships God, becomes God." He means the more we consciously unite with that which is the Truth, the greater receptivity to it, the larger opening to receive it, the more it flows through, the more power and truth and beauty flow through us. But the wonder of it is, to me, that since no two of us are alike, we are individuals, even the Infinite will come to you and to me in a different way from anybody else. That is why Emerson said, "Trust thyself, every heart vibrates to that iron string," to that spark of that light by which man is truly man, that spark of genius that flashes across your own consciousness. And listen to it. This is not insanity.

Emerson was the greatest intellect of modern times and called by many one of the ten greatest thinkers who ever lived. This man was not a screwball by any means, nor was Socrates, nor Buddha nor Plato nor Jesus nor Moses nor the great prophets of the ages. They were smart people. They may have cried over the troubles of the world, but they drew from an invisible source, an unknown river. And we may be certain that it is real. But if this is true, then the next great thought to consider: God is personal to each one of us and infinitely so. In our abstractions, we don't call God a principle and sit on a cake of ice and say nothing hurts us. People who think God is only principle and law amuse me. You know, God is warmth; Spirit is colorful; the universe is filled with light, a voice that speaks from everything: running brooks, stones, trees, animals, moon and stars, desert and stillness. And you can listen to the stillness until it speaks to you.

Now the theory is, and it is correct, that since these things are true and the age of probation has passed whenever any man recognizes it, because now he is going to consciously cooperate even with the Infinite, that the Infinite may more completely flow and extend to him. He will first have to agree that it is so. I did not make these things up. I am glad I didn't, because if I had, I wouldn't have believed them. We seem to go forward two steps and slide back three; but we will get there.

It comes to you as an individual. You have to believe it. Why? Because the universe is a thing of thought and, as I told you before, affirmation and denial are the same thing because you can only affirm. I can say, "Well, there isn't any such God. The kind of God you are talking about doesn't exist. It doesn't happen." That is an affirmation and shuts it out. "Eyes have they, but they see not." But you can and I can and all of us can, and we shall see. What happens, It is like a mirror. It looks back to us as we look at It, because our looking at It is Its looking at us at the level of our looking at It.

This is the greatest single truth the world has ever known. I want you to prove it to yourself. There is a mirror, and I am holding up my hand, and in the mirror is the form of my hand. And I look at it and say, "How did that get in there?" And I try to scratch it out. But this is an indestructible mirror. You can't destroy it. You can't wipe anything out of or off it. There it sits, like this sphinx, and grins, and there is my hand. And by and by, I wonder how did my hand get out here, and I think my hand is stuck out here. And that is a neurotic thought pattern, repeating itself over and over, reflected in this condition. Then, by and by, I realize I can pull my hand back, and I look, and my hand isn't there. Then I can stick out my foot, and it will reflect that, or a stick of wood, or dynamite, or a piece of gingerbread, and a fool, and a wise man, and they will grin right back. It doesn't even say, "You put me there; and if you don't like me, take me away." Nature never argues. This is a law of nature.

Then I begin to work and study and say, "Yes, whatever I want, I can put there." Now I have an awfully good time putting things there to look at the reflection, because I discovered a law of reflection from a cause, which is the image mirrored in the law. Then I say, "This is it!" The *summum bonum* (the highest good) of all evolution. But it is only the beginning. These are the playthings. We want our little tin automobiles and our little whistles and our ham sandwiches, and there is nothing wrong with them, but we can only eat so many ham sandwiches and ride in so many automobiles.

So, by and by, we begin to think, "I would like that mirror to work automatically for me. I would like to have everything that is good and beautiful and love and friendship, as we all ought to have, but I don't want to have to be always holding my hands up to the mirror. I am getting tired of it." Then we begin to discover something else goes with our science, through contemplation and meditation, and that is what I am now going to call "identification" with the Infinite, through stretching the will and the imagination, and doing it consciously.

This is the only important talk I shall have given this week, and it probably will sound so simple and like there is not much to it. But it is all leading up to a simplicity so great that, as Jesus said, it is like the kingdom of heaven, but nobody would believe it. We begin by identification through contemplation to identify ourselves with that which is beyond us, but which really is already within us, but hasn't come out of us in a kind of reflection. Now this is called mysticism. The greatest examples of it intellectually that I know of you will find in Platonism and in Emerson. This is an intellectual concept and a wonderful one. The greatest emotional and feeling and colorful you will find, of course, in the great poems that are mystical and in the works of Meister Eckhart, whom I admire above most of them. It is a feeling toward the universe. It is a spiritual sense of things, which does not deny or discount the physical. It doesn't say you haven't got a heart, or lungs, or a liver. It says if you have them, then why shouldn't they work all right. If they don't, we haven't returned to the divine pattern that sustains them. It is a system, a little beyond meditation, for things that make things happen. Now I believe in that, for healing and for every purpose. I believe in it just as much as when you go to the grocery store in order to get what you want, and when you plant a garden, plant beets if you like them, and don't plant cabbage, if you don't like it. There is no reason why you should.

We want something beyond that. The human mind is never going to be satisfied with littleness. It is always feeling the wonder and the lure of the unknown, and that is what causes all progress. Always it is saying, as it looks out to another horizon, "Something hidden. Go and find it. Go look behind the ranges, something lost behind the ranges. Lost and waiting for you. Go!" (Rudyard Kipling). And it says it to itself, I don't care whether you are fourteen or one hundred, a person who doesn't have this is dead. He doesn't need a psychiatrist, he needs an undertaker because he is through.

We are so born, so constituted that there is something in us that has such an irresistible urge to do and to be that we cannot stop it. And that is why this philosophy is the greatest thing on Earth. By contemplation through meditation, by consciously stretching the imagination and the will and the imagery, it is not hypnotism, it is not a trance, it isn't mental suggestion. You are alive, conscious. I don't want to get anywhere unless I know how I get there. I want to know what happens on the way, every minute. The universe in which we are living is intelligent. Stretching the imagination means gradually to identify ourselves with that which up until now has been way beyond our experience. Suppose we identify ourselves with beauty, so that we see and sense that everything in God's universe is beautiful. Now at first it is words only, but by and by, beauty surrounds me. Everything must be beautiful in its own light. These trees are beautiful. Beauty is everywhere, and we identify ourselves with the infinite beauty.

I have probably done more work for creative artists than most people in our field, because I have known, loved, and appreciated them very much. And I always work for them this way. The singer cannot help singing; the dancer cannot help dancing. All the beauty, all the rhythm I identify with in the universe, I know their nature to be. You see, we think of it, we believe in it, we contemplate the essence, then we identify our contemplation with someone who wants benefit of it. And at the level that we have reached in our contemplation, we have passed it on to them automatically through a creative medium that we have discussed and which doesn't know big or little, hard or easy, time or space, absolute or relative, affirmation or denial. That is why we talked about them axiomatically. We have wiped them off the slate of our necessity, our karma, our anything, and said, "As of now, we are free with the freedom of the living Spirit."

Identification means to contemplate. Now contemplation is just a little beyond our ordinary sense of meditation, just a little more than saying, "Now right action is coming to this person." This is all right, nothing wrong about it, and it will work. We use it, and we should, but identification is not about peace. It is entering into the essence of peace until there is no longer anything confused and no longer anything that has to be gotten rid of. That will help you, if you do it, and then if you want to help someone else, you will identify your work with them. We identify ourselves with the living Spirit. Now this is what I think happens, I can't swear it is going to happen, this is what I believe happens, this is what I think, and I have plenty of reason to believe it happens. And if it seems rational to you, you try it, and I think you will come to believe it is what happens.

I think there is only one of whatever there is. Call it God, call it truth, call it a principle, call it anything you want. But believe it. There is something in the universe and in you and in me that is absolute. It knows no otherness, knows no opposition and has none, knows no interference, knows no resistance, knows no violence, and flows through everything because all that it sees is the clear track and the perfect way and the infinite harmony, and it forever sings. I think we have to be glad to do this. And I think, as Barclay [Rev. Barclay Johnson] said this morning, we have to know there is nothing in the universe that holds anything against us. I think we have to know there is no past from right this minute. He shall count the things that were as though they were not, and no one will ever do this for you but yourself. There is, fortunately, no one in time or eternity who has the power to save you but yourself. The self shall raise the self by the self and, "This above all: to thine own self be true, and it must follow as the night the day, thou canst not then be false to any man." Well spoken by Shakespeare, the bard of bards.

To you and to you alone, to each one of us, uniquely presented. God will never come quite alike to us, nor to someone else as He does to us. You are a unique institution in the universe. But because we all live in the one Mind, we see, know, appreciate, meet, and commune with each other in the medium of the one Mind, the one Spirit. That is all there is. And each one of us individualizes all of it, but only at the level of his comprehension. We cannot contract the Infinite, but we may expand the finite.

Contemplation then sees this happen: I am that peace; I am that joy; I am that power. It is why the ancients used to say: "I am that which thou art, thou art which I am." It is why our Bible says, "Do this according to the pattern shown thee on the mount." "I will lift up mine eyes unto the hills, from whence cometh my help. My help cometh from the Lord (that is the indwelling God), which made heaven and Earth." The God that is making our liver right now made heaven and Earth, and He knows how to make livers pretty good. Isn't that interesting? He just naturally knows how to lay an egg, and we don't because He laid all the eggs that were ever laid. Only the Creative Principle could have ever entered into its own creation. There is no creation outside of It. You and I are centers of Its creativity at the level of our own perception, identification, and instrumentality. By that I mean, as we identify ourselves with It, we become the instrumentality for Its essence, and even given to somebody else, this is the cup of cold water we have to give. You know, if the wellspring were one we had dug, we could never give it. It is greater than the well Abraham dug. It is greater than the Niagara or all the mighty falls or lakes or rivers or oceans on Earth, for it is the living sea of cosmic light and life, with love, stirred ever with action, animated with movement, in which a thousand million histories have been written across the pages of their brief time. And the Timeless goes on to create the whole. "Behold, I make all things new."

This is the great, the divine possibility inherent within each and every one of us. Robert Browning said, "A god though in the germ." And yet nothing will ever force it on us. Nothing. It never has. You see, Abraham did not have an automobile, because he didn't know how to make an automobile. God did. But the moment someone came along who had the idea of how to make an automobile, it was projected through his mind the blueprint, the mechanics, and the mathematics that could result in nothing else but the automobile. They didn't know how to do it; that is all. They weren't bad; they weren't cursed; they weren't punished; they weren't limited; they weren't working out some miserable karma or some evangelical fool who had hurled his own guilt at them for the release of the tension of his own anguish. God bless him, but he didn't get it, or he wouldn't still be crazy and screaming. The neurosis has not been healed.

Now, I just said a mouthful. Because when the neurosis is healed, that will be that. And it will be rolled away like a scroll and numbered with the things that were once thought to be real and no longer bedevil God's beautiful creation and beset it with the works that are written in horror and from the sense of a martyrdom, that no universe ever imposed upon itself, because He willed nothing to you that He hasn't already willed for Himself. We are His delight. We may not act like it; we may not believe it; and yet here we sit as someone who is blind. Someone might come along and say, "This is it." How do we know? How do we know but there are another whole set of laws inherent, there is a body within a body to infinity. Science believes it. And we in our spiritual science are not going to be so stupid that we say you can't raise the dead, you can't turn the water into wine, you can't multiply the loaves and the fishes, you cannot tell Lazarus to come out. It would be pure stupidity. And only the One who knows He can will. He spoke as one having authority. The prophet of old said, "Awake, thou that sleepest, and arise from the dead and Christ shall give thee light."

Now that is what we are practicing. It is good to practice a simple beginning, but now those of us who have studied—remember, this is a continuing study—we all want to go on further. We all want to learn the fundamentals. This is all we can teach. We can teach you how to give a treatment. We can teach you how to preach a bad sermon and read badly and fall on the platform. We can teach that, all right. It is very simple. But who is going to teach somebody what beauty looks like? You will never find anyone who can teach you what harmony feels like. You'll never find anyone who can tell you what the silence will say to you. You will never find a thinker outside yourself. Never. It is impossible.

And how fortunate that, at long last, we have discovered that there are certain things we must teach ourselves. Listen, beauty will speak. Listen to strength, and it will come. See it; claim it; believe it as though the Almighty brought it in Its own hands and bestowed it. And the heritage of heaven, it shall be brought to you, "and the gates of hell shall not prevail against it."

Ella Wheeler Wilcox said in her poem, "Illusion":

God and I in space alone
and nobody else in view.
"And where are the people, O Lord," I said,
"the earth below and the sky o'er head
and the dead whom once I knew?"

"That was a dream," God smiled and said,
"A dream that seemed to be true.
There were no people, living or dead,
there was no earth, and no sky o'er head;
there was only Myself—in you."

Now this is not solecism, this is not egotism we are talking about—not about the physical or even the mental. They are all here; they are all necessary. We need them, but we are talking about that thing that most people do not believe in. And if you and I sit on the shores of time, the dream will pass by. It does not make any difference that all the world shall say no to our simple ideals. The world has fooled itself. You have nothing to convince at all, nor can you convince it of anything. You have nothing to sell the world nor need to. But should one person go down the streets of this beautiful city and there were a hearse going by with a corpse in it, and you stopped it and said, "My friend, get out and walk," and he got out, they would know it in Moscow within six hours. It would be continuously broadcast for years, that a Divine visitation, the mother of God or grandfather of God or some near or distant relative had visited Carmel, California. Wouldn't that be nice? Now that is all right, but if we believed it, then our belief would do something.

What would have happened is that something in you had listened to life until it could no longer get dead. Something in you had listened to life until it had resurrected everything that ever got dead. And when that which appeared dead came near, it sprang into the newness of life because the all creative genius of life itself has come full orbed through you.

That is where your soul will make its great claim on God, and do not think it is an illusion. Don't even argue with anybody. Try it; prove it. "'Prove me now herewith,' saith the Lord, 'if I will not open you the windows of heaven and pour you out a blessing, that there shall not be room enough to receive it.'" Who has ever believed enough? Who has ever accepted enough? Who has ever embodied enough? Nobody, and the few who have, people have worshiped almost as God.

Now this is the genius of our movement, that step by step, as it has in classes and meditations and contemplations, shall forever more seek to storm the kingdom of heaven and break down the gates, which were never placed there by any deific hand but by the stupidity and ignorance of men's minds, so that when someone announced it can and shall be, it may sound crazy. But who cares, and what difference does it make? Somebody is going to do it. Some group of people are going to stretch their will and imagination and intellect until the dome of heaven opens and, symbolically, angels ascend and descend in a heavenly chorus, "Holy, holy, holy, Lord God Almighty. Holy, holy, holy, Lord God within you."

This is our challenge. This is our privilege. This is our opportunity. Somehow, out of the depth of the universe, some great demand is being made upon us. I know we shall answer it in joy, through laughter and singing, not by tears, not through sadness. We no longer wish to resurrect the dead in morbidity. Now, we wish to so chant the hymn eternal that there shall be no dead or that we have come to give the world life and joy and peace and happiness. And I know it shall be done.

CHAPTER 5

1959

The Basis of Religious Science

Personal Responsibility

MONDAY, AUGUST 10, 1959

In 1959, Ernest Holmes presented his final series of Asilomar talks. In them, he describes the overall series as being about what, in his view, is the basis of Religious Science. He describes his first talk, "Personal Responsibility," as a foundation for the talks to come the rest of the week. He sets the stage for what is ours to do by first describing the spiritual process of involution and evolution, examining a core belief that a self-knowing Reality embedded Itself in Its creation and left it alone to discover itself and its source. As expressions of that One, what then is our personal responsibility? Holmes tells us that our role is to discover our Divine Source, to express our creative abilities, to be at peace, to live in joy, and to personally identify with the Divine Essence within us.

NOTE: This talk begins following a brief presentation by Ethel Barnhart about opening an accredited grade school associated with Religious Science and under the auspices of California Independent Schools. She said this was "part of the cosmic pattern of Religious Science and part of the very lifeblood of Ernest Holmes."

This is really a dream come true, a wonderful thing that is happening in the Religious Science movement, a progressive movement. I will tell you just one other idea I am interested in, which you may not know about, but together with some friends, we have organized what is to be known as and is legally now known as The Holmes Commonwealth for Boys and Girls, which will be for all children from any age to eighteen from broken homes, and they call them delinquent children, although there are no delinquent children. You will hear more about this later. No one knows what might happen in this group because later, as this moves along, I will ask everyone in our movement to support it with some kind of membership. And I know all of you will.

You see, we have to put what we believe into practice. We are not doing something in a corner, something exclusive, something where we say, "Bless my son, John, and his wife, me and my wife, we four and no more." That is a very small blessing, but we have an expanding consciousness.

Now I have chosen a series of subjects for my evening talks that look very commonplace but they are very uncommon, if I can get them in place. And because of the limitation of time, I am not going to try to logically prove anything I am going to say. I am merely going to announce to you that which I believe, that which the great minds, the great spiritual seers and sages and saviors and enlightened saints of the ages have taught, which constitute the root and fundamentals of all the great religious systems of thought that have ever been given to the world. Whether they are Judaism, Hinduism, Christian theology, or whatever. There are certain essential occult or esoteric—which merely mean hidden—beliefs, facts, oppositions, suppositions, and theories that govern the great teachings that have come to the world. I happen to be familiar with most of them, and so I am going to assume, not going to try to prove theoretically, logically by argument, or by quotations.

I want to start right out as though what I say is true. Whether it is true or not, I think it is. It has been believed in by the great, the good, and the wise.

Now if we do this, we will save time, and you can argue it out with yourself. And you don't have to accept it, because it is different a little. Not different from what you and I believe, it carries it just a little farther into the realm of what we will call self-existent cause. Tonight will be the foundation for the other four talks, and they will also reveal to you what you probably already know, but in a consecutive series, what in my estimation Religious Science is based on. And it will dovetail very well indeed with what Elmer Gifford said this morning.

You see, Religious Science is nothing I made up. No one person ever made it up. We do not know who made it up. I do not know where much of the philosophy I believe in came from, since I have read so much and studied so much for so many years and thought so much, with always an endeavor to synthesize a vast analysis and put together those things that must flow out of self-evident facts; such as, if the universe were not a unity, it would be a duality, and if it were a duality, it wouldn't exist because it would destroy itself. It is very simple and self-evident, but the vast conclusions that flow from this are quite different from the conclusions that would flow from the supposition that there is primarily a good and an evil. Now there is no evil in the universe. Even that which we experience as evil is merely good as it presents itself to us and passes through us into our own experience, that we shall learn from that experience what is constructive.

I would like to start out and make a few marks on the chalkboard. I am talking tonight on our responsibilities, our personal responsibility, and I want to go forward with the assumption that we have three levels of responsibility: first, to the nature of reality as it self-evidently must be, not what you and I think it ought to be. We put all the words in God's mouth that are written in all the bibles that were ever written. "Thus saith the Lord." Who said the Lord said thus and so? Some man like we are, some better and some worse. We put all those words, and we say, "Thus saith the Lord." Now there are certain self-evident truths that we don't contradict. They have to be true or there wouldn't be anything. What is, you see, when I speak of responsibility tonight, obligation, and duty, I am not telling you what you ought to do. I do not know what you ought to do. How could I? You do not know what I ought to do. You couldn't. You are you; I am myself.

But if I say there must be a responsibility and an obligation to the nature of the universe as it exists, if we wish to get along with it, that would be true, wouldn't it? If water is wet, when we go in the water, we will get wet. Isn't that so? What is the obligation imposed upon the rose other than to bloom? What is the obligation imposed upon the beauty of the sunset tonight other than to be beautiful? What is the duty or responsibility imposed upon gravitational force other than to hold things in this mundane plane in place by inexorable laws, which belong to the nature and constitution of the reality of the self-existence, which they serve? I don't think that means much.

What I am trying to say is this: There is no God who made God. God is self-existent. "Before Abraham was, I am." There is no God who made law; law is self-existent. We have to suppose a universe that is a living system: alive, awake, and aware, everywhere, not just somewhere. We have to suppose that the universe is a government of law and order, which law and order precede from its own nature and maintain its own nature. We have to conceive that we must be some part of it else we would not be here and that everything that appears to proceed externally and enter into our consciousness is something outside coming in or something inside coming out.

If we proceed on the basis that it is something outside coming in, we won't get anywhere because there won't be any "in" for it to come to. There would be no one at home. If it rapped on the door, there would be no answer. We have to proceed then that all evolution, all unfoldment is from within out, that there is already something within us, externally, for some reason, which we must accept, which unfolds, and by a series of the process of gradual awakening to what it is, becomes what it awakens to. I said I wasn't going to explain anything, but in the New Testament it says, "Beloved, now we are sons of God, and it doth not yet appear what we shall be, but we know that when he shall appear, we shall be like him, for we shall see him as he is."

Now let us interpret that in our language. It says: Now look here, beloved. We are the sons of God, right now. We are not going to become the sons of God. We were the sons of God; we are the sons of God; we shall forever remain the sons of God. It is none of our business. We can't help it, and we must accept it. It is our obligation, our duty, our responsibility imposed upon us by the nature and constitution and order of the self-existent reality that we have to do it. We are the sons of God, and it doth not yet appear what we shall be. We haven't seen what it means to be the son of God yet. We have only dreamed a dream, seen a vision, heard the silence speak, and reached out a little—or in—and discovered what appears to be an unfolding and ascending reality through not the evolution of truth, but the awakening of our own consciousness to something that preexisted that awakening.

Somewhere I wrote something that said:

Rob the mind of its illusion,
Strip the ego naked bare,
'Til the waiting heart within us
Finds thy presence hidden there.

All process of evolution is not a process of something coming out of nothing, but of something showing where nothing appeared. It isn't something being made out of nothing. Even God does not create something out of nothing; God manifests what God is, and we call it creation. It doth not yet appear what we shall be, but we know that when He shall appear—He is sure to appear—we know when He will, we shall be like Him. We are already like Him, for we shall see Him as He is. And we would say, "He is there." And He will appear when we see Him as He is. His appearance will be simultaneous and instantaneous with our seeing Him as He is. This is what Jesus called knowing the truth. Truth is not a process itself, but a revelation. Its operation through law may be a process, but the oak tree is in the acorn, and the chicken is in the egg, and God is in man.

Now I would like to start with an assumption that all the great and good and wise have believed in (you know the microphone won't work until you use it the way it works), and yet how many of us expect God to change His nature to suit our whim? I am going to draw a circle, which represents infinity because it has neither beginning nor end, and the ancients said it is that whose center is everywhere and whose circumference is nowhere. This has always been represented as the life principle. Now we will assume, theoretically, this is the boundary of the universe. Of course, it hasn't got any. Now every action and reaction is going to have to take place in this circle. I am going to say this. I am not going to try to prove it, but it is what the great and good and wise have taught, and if we have any way of getting truth at all, it will be from these people. It will not be from dogmatic opinions of someone who is trying to substantiate a position that was never right anyway.

You see, we think that logic will conduct us to the truth. There can be no greater error, because unless the logic is on the right premise, the more perfect the logic, the farther away we will get from the truth. If we assume the universe is dual, then we have a place for a devil, hell, purgatory, limbo, and whatever other nonsense goes with it, and it is logical, because the thing is fighting itself. If we assume there is a fundamental dualism, you will have a good and an evil, and the good will always be trying to overcome the evil, and the evil will always be combating the good. This is what is the trouble with the great religions: There is no such thing as good and universe in the universe I am going to talk about. But don't say I said you can do as you want and get away with it.

We have to assume the nature of a reality that is self-knowing. God is a power that knows Itself. We have to believe it is the nature of God to express God's nature, don't we? You cannot have an Infinite unexpressed mind; you cannot have a God without having an awareness; and you cannot have an awareness without having a thing that God is aware of being in accord with law. So this is the teaching, and this will unmix much of our theology. Any theology based on dualism is not true; and we have a lot of dualism, too.

Now we have the great teaching of involution and evolution. Troward starts his book *Bible Mystery and Meaning* with this, and it is the very fundamental premise of the whole Hindu philosophy and Christian philosophy, because it is in the Old Testament and is the substance of the teaching of the prodigal son. This is the story of every man and what is called the "passing of spirit into substance" or the descent of the spirit from the very topmost part of itself down— now remember, there is no up and down in God, but we have to use expressions —the passing of the Spirit through law into substance prior to the passing of substance in form through law and all for the purpose of the delight of God. The whole creation exists for the delight of God, for the expression of God. Beauty is its own excuse for being.

Our duty, our obligation, our responsibility to be true to the nature of God is to understand that nature and, as far as possible, live in harmonious accord with its laws. That is the beginning place of all wisdom, but our trouble has been that we have tried to make the Infinite finite, contracting It rather than expanding the finite. In other words, we have created a God after our image, rather than discovering the image of God already created within us, that it may give back to God that which we are, because the descent of the Spirit is the basis of the whole teaching of the divine sacrifice. It wasn't intended to be morbid. It has nothing to do with a sadistic vicarious atonement. It had only to do with necessity, that all the Creative Power and Wisdom shall express what It knows Itself to be.

Now in psychology, they say the libido is an emotional craving for self-expression back of all things, the repression of which leads to psychoneurosis, the unexpressed life. God is not neurotic. We would amplify this and say there is a Divine urge. It makes the singer sing and the chicken lay an egg. It makes us adore It, because It is adoring Itself. We are talking not about this little squeezed-up ego out here attached to the body and the mind and the emotions. We are talking about the Self giving Itself to the Self for the Self, by the Self, in the Self to experience in joy and take delight in the Self. Man is that delight. "Who hath seen me hath seen the Father, but the Father is greater than I."

Now through this process of involution—the exalted, the supreme, we call it God, the absolute, truth, doesn't matter what we call it, let's just say God—it is the nature of God to express. Now remember, this is the teaching of the wisdom of the ages. No one knows where it comes from, and everything works as though it were true in application. Everything, without exception. This is what has been called the self hid within the self, the secret self, the absolute self, that self of freedom hid within the self of bondage. The bondage has been called the ignorance and the loosing of it, the enlightenment. That is why Emerson said that ignorance is the only sin there is and enlightenment the only salvation. In this great process of involution, which I think eternally takes place, it would have to because God does not think up new principles and laws nor does He invent new ones, but eternally thinks up new manifestations in the principles and laws. And Divine Presence cannot vary. It never changes from eternity to eternity, hid within all things, evolved in silence, beauty, wisdom, will is that which makes the cycle move, unmoved, immovable, and still. At the center of the silence is an activity so intense that there would be no mental or physical instrumentality that could measure it. It would be so elusive, but because it is a nonfrictional activity, because it is a noncombative activity, because it is a nonviolent activity, it cannot dissipate its strength and its action, but finds delight in its own movement. It is true.

The resistance, the strain that is back perhaps of most physical disease and tension, is our unconscious resistance of something which of itself would be all right if it could pass through to us, as it is meant to. Consequently, all or 85 percent of all diseases, we are told, are a result of the restraint of that action of creativity, thrown back upon itself into what is called a repression. Unable for the energy to escape into the explosion of self-discovery and manifestation, the law that binds the ignorant and frees the wise is working. That is the karmic law, the law of cause and effect.

We will say, "Here is the imprisoned splendor. Here is where Walt Whitman said, 'nestles the seed perfection.'" Here is what Jesus referred to when he said, "Be ye therefore perfect, even as your Father, which is in heaven, is perfect." "I have said, 'Ye are gods and all of you are children of the Most High.'" But that which is involuted— nobody knows the answer to this, no one has tried to answer it, but it seems this way— the answer will be a theory. And it is buried so deep in its own ignorance that it doesn't know itself. Whether we like it or not, I believe it is true because every advance in science is an advance in the discovery of something that has existed before the discovery was made. Hid in everything is the possibility of all things. Hid deep in man is divinity because God is here; man is God here; there is no man outside of God different from God, other than God, apart from God, or away from God, because there was nothing to make out of God, to make that which that was not God when it got made. The form, the shape, the color, the tone, the individuation. That is why we say everything is an individuation of God, but no thing in itself is an individual separate from God.

It is basic to our belief that Divine Presence exists as a person, hid within us as a presence revealed through Atman, Jesus, Buddha, all of them. That is what they were. That is what they knew themselves to be. Now this thing, reaching its lowest level, this is called being thrown into outer darkness. This is Lucifer thrown from heaven, like a flaming sword landing in the mundane clod and impregnating it with that spirit, that spark, which as Robert Browning said, "to receive what a man may waste, desecrate, never quite lose." A divine spark ignited at the altar of a cosmic fire, a flame in the process of its own unfoldment, that innumerable, limitless, infinite variation of the One Self shall return to the One Self, having established the right relationship with the One Self, separate without being separated: one with God, that God may enjoy the variation of infinite inherent potential possibilities of His own self-expression, like a singer who sings more than one song. Isn't it beautiful?

Now, I fail to find in anything so grand a concept as this: that I am enfolded in the arms of God. This is literally true. As Barclay Johnson said this morning, Religious Science teaches the most exalted concept of the personality of God ever put into any book in metaphysics at any time, by anyone. I don't say that because I put it in. I put it in because it wasn't out. Now, down here at the lowest rung, the lowest level is what has been called the mind that sleeps in the mineral, waves in the grass, wakes to simple consciousness in the animal and self-consciousness in man and God consciousness in the upper hierarchies because there are beings beyond us as we are beyond tadpoles. We have to accept this; it is a part of our theology. God is a presence hid within that which seems imperfect and incomplete.

As the Bhagavad Gita says, the self must raise the self by the self, and the Christian adds through grace or the givingness of God. But the Christian theology mostly has had God as a self separate from ourselves, and there is no God separate from the self of you or of me. It is impossible that there shall be any duality in the universe, no matter what appears. No matter who says there is, there isn't. There is no dualism. God is all there is, and there isn't anything else.

What this thing is involuted, put into, is its nature to start the process of the journey of the soul back to the source. The whole story of the meaning of the prodigal son (all evolution) has been taught by every great religion in the world. We are in the process we call a process of becoming. Being passes into becoming, but the becoming is not in the becoming of what was, not in the being through a process of awakening. All evolution is an awakening to what does not evolve but what unfolds from its own involution. It is already there. "When he shall appear, for we shall see him as he is." Every step in advance is, as I want to say later, that the next steps in advance we shall have to make ourselves. Why? Because the moment the evolving thing, which only appears to be evolving, has produced an instrumentality that perceives itself, that moment by the law of its own nature it will not go further without conscious cooperation with the principle and the Presence. "My Father worketh hitherto, and I work."

I want to get back to our obligation to It, to us, and to the universe in which we live. What is our obligation to God? We haven't any obligation as duty to God. We have no obligation as the pathway to salvation to God. We have nothing to contribute to God. I do not believe we can tell God anything. But whatever the Divine nature is, if we are going to be true to what our nature is, it will have to be true to what that nature is. There isn't any judge in the universe, but there is balance. Therefore, there is justice. There is no God beating us over the head with a cosmic club.

What is our duty, our obligation, our responsibility to God is to be like God. We haven't any other, not as duty, not as obligation, not as responsibility, but from the same motive of joy and delight that the Eternal has spoken Himself into being through us and beholds forever more His own countenance in us. But the very moment that we have arrived at the perception of that, we have become conscious partners. We have entered into a divine partnership that will never cease. "And whatsoever things the son sees the Father do, that doeth the son also, that the Father may be glorified." This is conscious cooperation; this is the great adventure of the soul; this is the limitless possibility, eternal expansion, forever.

Our obligation to God is to be like God. This we cannot avoid. This is the givingness of God through the expression of Himself, to the delight of Himself, to the love of Himself. It is a part of the nature of the cosmic order in which we live. More than any other person in science, Carl Jung proved this archetype has existed throughout the ages and had to be brought down from the cosmos itself. It is a self-evident proposition. And so our obligation is not one of burden. Our duty is not enormous. Our responsibility is not weighty. What is the obligation of a rose but to bloom? The bird must sing, the dancer dance. This is our obligation, but since God is one and undivided and indivisible and within us, our full obligation cannot be given back. We cannot give back to God what He gave to us until we give it back in the same way He gave it—it is impossible—not as separation, not as isolation, not as otherness but as that which perfectly fits into the cosmic scheme of that divine pattern, which is absolute beauty, absolute peace. Our obligation, duty, and responsibility to whatever we think God is, is that we shall be at peace, that we shall be filled with joy.

"I am come that you might have life and that you might have it more abundantly." We haven't the duty to redeem a lost soul. We don't have a lost soul. Our obligation is to discover the nature of reality and, insofar as the present state of our own evolution, to live in accord with it and in absolute independence of the opinion of the world. "Who told you that you were naked?" "The just shall live by faith." I have never met a person and never shall, who, having forgiven himself and gotten rid of his own unconscious condemnation of himself, would even know how to frame the words to deny somebody else the privilege of being all right.

It is an obligation to live in accord with that divinity, as Shakespeare said, "that shapes our ends, rough-hew them how we will." And we may and without fear. There is nothing in the universe to be afraid of. It is an obligation to not deny the world or want to get away from it—there is nothing wrong with the world—but to live in it in harmony and peace. Insofar as we may say, if God is love, it is certainly our obligation to love and to be lovable. If God surrenders Himself as a sacrifice to Himself and gives Him back to Himself as His atonement for Himself, which is the only eternal and correct teaching of the cross and the crucifixion, there is no other way that makes any sense. The self hung up on the cross, which the self created, and took the self from the cross and redeemed the self. It is all in you. That cross is you. That rosary is your own life. Count the rosary beads over, one by one, and at the end, a cross is hung. Not morbid but the joy of the union of the tree of life upon which the Father and the son are eternally sacrificing themselves to the Self for the glory and the delight and the beauty and the song and the laughter of the Self.

Jesus was the only one who was happy enough because he wasn't afraid. He was the one. Just imagine, he didn't have to be a banker; he found money in the fish's mouth. He didn't have to catch the fish; he multiplied them. He didn't have to own a bakery; he multiplied the loaves. And he didn't have to have transportation; he brought the boat immediately to the shore. This is the end, the aim, the denouement of all evolution, that whatsoever things the son seeth the Father do, that shall the son do also that the Father may be glorified in the son, in the delight of His own being, the joy of His own expression, the light of His own eyes, and the song of His own heart.

This is the most exalted teaching the world has ever known. This duty we have to the self, because the self must be raised by the self. This is the obligation, responsibility—not ponderous, not heavy, not burdensome, but a song of emancipation. It is a joy of the soul beholding itself, the Oversoul of the universe as that soul, and with it comes the great emancipation from the thralldom of the psychological emotional and psychological ego, which we have created, not that they are wrong. They belong to the evolution. They will be there, that we shall no longer attach the ego to the self with this, which seems so little, so meager, and see the abundance. For instance, look out across these sand dunes, how many grains of sand are there? How many fish in the ocean? Etcetera. They are infinite, limitless, but we are identifying ourselves with the meager. Where is our vision set? It is the duty, obligation, responsibility of the self to free the self.

To identify all this with God, Longfellow said [in "The Builders"]:

Build to-day, then, strong and sure,
    With a firm and ample base;
And ascending and secure
    Shall to-morrow find its place.

Thus alone can we attain
    To those turrets, where the eye
Sees the world as one vast plain,
    And one boundless reach of sky.

This is Religious Science and the savior whom Jesus, Buddha manifest. We belong to the Christian faith. We are a Christian religion, but we are more than that, for the Christian religion itself derives much of its grandeur from that which was the product of antiquity before there were ever any Christians. Jesus drew from the teachings of those who were before him. It doesn't lessen him in caliber and stature, but rather melts into that larger concept.

It is your duty and mine, if we have one, to identify that Over-Self with this, and we can do it only in such degree as we see Him as He is. He is not poor, not weak, not sick, not forlorn or forsaken. He is a glory of magistry and might, presence and power, beauty and light, and a song of triumph in father and mother and son. This Over-Self we must identify with.

Remember this: Religious Science is an adventure of the soul. It is an adventure of the expression of that capacity inherent and latent within us, ready to come forth into the glory and beauty and splendor of our own becoming, as law. We are the enforcement of the law and order of the universe, as individuations. We are the manifestations of the supreme Self without division and innumerable cells without separation, that the multiplicity shall explain and live in and on the unity, and the unity shall find complete self-expression in the multiplicity. We are not poor or weak or unhappy. We are on the progressive pathway of an eternal evolution, on that eternal dawn of a blossoming soul, which shall ever see light.

Self-Existent Cause

✤

TUESDAY, AUGUST 11, 1959

In his second talk of 1959, Ernest Holmes describes the Religious Science belief that the Power that made the universe made everything out of Itself. Hence, It was a "self-existent cause." He contrasts this to other religious beliefs that see God as a creator who exists separate and apart from Its creation. Holmes tells us why Religious Science makes this assumption and its implications for each of us and our lives.

You and I assume that there is a self-existent cause in the universe that made everything out of Itself, by the process of Itself becoming what It makes, that It may behold Itself in Its own works, not to Its glory, as though what It makes must adore It, but to the delight of Its own soul, that It may experience what It is in what It does. There is no God who needs our glory, our congratulation. We need to glorify God; God doesn't need to be glorified. Who is there here who can tell the Pacific Ocean to be any wetter than it is? The united intelligence of the human race will not create a rosebud. Jesus said, "Which of you by taking thought can add one cubit unto his stature?" And then he turns right around and tells them to take thought, believe this, believe that, believe something else. That is why this paradox is devised, because positions are correct. We do not put energy into energy. If we had to energize energy, where would we get the energy with which to energize? We take energy out of the atom, put in there by the universe. We shall take Divine energy out of the human atom when we discover that the human atom is not a fragment of the Divine but a unique representation of the totality of all there is, everything from a blade of grass to an archangel.

We have to assume a self-existent cause, something that was and is and will remain. Nothing created God. God did not make God. God did not make law. Law is God or the operation of God. We have to assume a self-existence that is equally distributed throughout time and space; time, which is eternal. We have to assume that it is equally distributed everywhere and that while it exists everywhere and is not in fragments, it is one total and complete unity. Therefore, if we exist—and we must exist else we couldn't even deny it because there wouldn't be anybody at home to say anything—but if this unity and this totality exists at all, it exists not in a fragment of itself, because you could not take a pair of cosmic shears and dismember the Eternal. It would be impossible. All of God is everywhere. "Whither shall I go from thy spirit? Or whither shall I flee from thy presence? If I take the wings of the morning and dwell in the uttermost parts of the sea, even there shall thy hand lead me. If I say, surely the darkness shall cover me, even the night shall be light about me." "Yea, though I walk through the valley of the shadow of death, I will fear no evil, for Thou art with me."

This unconditioned absolute, this complete, exists in its infinity and its entirety and indivisible wholeness in all of its being at every point within its being, self-knowing. But that which is self-knowing is self-executing. Accepting not only the self-existence of the Divine Creative Spirit, we must equally accept as energy and intelligence and force and a creativity commensurate with this divine imagery, with this divine imagination, with this divine purposiveness. Now God hasn't got a purpose as we understand purpose because God is complete. God isn't trying to go where God has not been. God is eternally manifesting and everlastingly manifesting new things. "Behold, I make all things new." There is no ennui; there is nothing static. Therefore, we must have an eternal change within an infinite and eternal changelessness. It has to be that way. This was called the "divine Maya" by the ancient Hindus, and the Buddhists had another kind of a Maya, which was an illusion. But the divine Maya was the logical manifestation or imagery of God, or the play of life upon itself. It is quite natural that it should be that way because the creator must create, the singer must sing, the dancer must dance.

It is necessary that you and I accept these things, not because Religious Science teaches them. Religious Science teaches what the greatest thoughts of the world have discovered, what the greatest minds have believed, what the most intense rationality of conductive and deductive reasoning has arrived at, and what the great intuitions and illuminations of the world, when they were free from the hallucination of psychic things. If you put all this together, you will have the only guidepost to truth that can be known to the human mind.

That is why Richard Maurice Bucke analyzed fifty or sixty cases of consciousness and found the common denominator, the thread of the all-sustaining beauty that runs through all and unites all. There is no question in my mind but that common denominator running through these people of the different ages, telling the same story, declares the truth to us about our relationship to life. As Elmer Gifford said, there is nothing to be afraid of. The talk this afternoon was an exposition of the theology of Religious Science. My talks are because while we have thrown all other theologies out, we jumped out the window and grabbed them back in and took the best out and called them our theology. Religious Science is the first absolutely emancipated theology the world has ever known. Most of the doctrine of Christianity came from somebody who didn't know Jesus. The writings of Jesus were recorded forty to sixty years after what he said. You try to remember tonight what I said last night. I haven't the slightest idea myself of what I said, and it doesn't matter.

Therefore, rationality, intelligence, and sanity compel us to put up a sign before the gateway of the intellect in the beginning of our adventure, a sign which says: Stop, look, and listen. Aaron Burr said human law is that which is boldly asserted and plausibly maintained. Sigmund Freud said a neurotic thought pattern repeats itself with monotonous regularity throughout life. Joseph Jastrow said one of the greatest troubles in analysis was what he called the "inertia of thought patterns," which argue to us as though they were entities. And the world says there has always been war and there always will be. That is a collective neurosis based on a sense of fear and a need for punishment. But if tonight there were a universal clearance of all the fear, there would never be another war because there would never be anybody to fight. It is the only way it will ever come to be. It will be held in abeyance through fear, we hope. There is where fear may be salutary.

There are many devils you know and the devils besought Jesus not to cast them out. This is the argument of every human mind, the argument of the prodigal son on his way back home saying, "I am no longer worthy," and yet it is an interesting thing. When he left the father's house, the father didn't say, "Where are you going?" And he said, "There was a man who had two sons. And the younger of them said to his father, 'Father, give me the share of property that is coming to me.' And he divided his property between them." And yet he didn't say, "Where are you going?" or advise him not to go there. And when he came back, the father didn't ask, "Where have you been and what did you do with your money?" God never argues. There is nothing in the universe that is against anything in the universe, because if there were, the universe wouldn't be here. You cannot have two universes; you can only have one.

Therefore, there are no adversaries and no opponents, so all we have to do is to be sure we have discovered the truth. The religion of Religious Science and theology is, of course, a combination of the teaching of the Greeks and the Jews, just as theology is. According to Dean Inge, it was 75 percent Greek and 25 percent Jewish, a combination of the impositionalism of Palestine and the immanentism of the Greeks. And all that means is this: a combination of overdwelling God and indwelling God. And the mystic says the highest God and the innermost God is one God. And Jesus said, "Who hath seen me hath seen the Father," and Emerson said, "Who in his integrity worships God becomes God."

Now I don't want you to believe anything just because I believe it. I am the most surprised person in the world that there is such an institution as a Religious Science Church because I never planned it or wanted it and fought against it for many years. The only reason I ever permitted it was because there was no other way to spread it. We are all missionaries. We are a Christian philosophy, but not necessarily what is accepted as a Christian theology because the Christian theology is what was added to the teachings of Jesus mostly by people who didn't know what Jesus was talking about.

You and I have to differentiate between what is and what isn't. The universe is one system, a living system. There isn't any heaven, any hell, literally. No devils. There isn't any of this nonsense that fundamentalism teaches. So I say, I thank the God that is, that the God that is believed in, isn't. There is nothing in the universe to be afraid of, and Elmer said when that experience comes—and he has had it and I know what he's talking about and he is right—don't get scared anymore because you know. Wouldn't it be funny if Emerson and Plato were examples of what everybody ought to be and the only two individuals that even approached being normal intellectually, and if Robert Browning and Alfred Lord Tennyson were among those few people who had the normal imagination, and if Jesus and Buddha were perhaps the two most outstanding cases, possibly with Moses, of people who had a sane viewpoint about God? Wouldn't that be funny?

Now we had to believe in that self-existence cause. It is easy to believe in it. It is so simple, you laugh at it, but the implications are so terrific, it is hard to believe. We are a Christian faith, a Christian philosophy that believes in the teachings of Jesus, but not necessarily the theology as now presented of Christianity. We believe in the theology of the Jews, the theology and philosophy of Hinduism. We put them altogether, and we say this is what we know about God.

It is necessary. And this is not my opinion, and I have no opinion about truth. The truth is what is. It will stand on its own feet and reveal itself. No one has to be a champion of it. Jesus said, "Heaven and Earth will pass away, but my word will not" until all be fulfilled. So we have this magnificent concept in Religious Science, borrowed from the ages, to which we shall bring more illumination and enlightenment, which understands the reality of a self-existent cause and a law that backs the will of the Spirit. The law and the word—this is why you find these symbols in every Masonic temple—the mechanics and spontaneity, the thought and the way it works, love and the law. Browning said, "I spoke as I saw, all's love, yet all's law."

We are talking about the law tonight, and law is the most unsentimental thing in the world. If we jump off the roof, we will land with a sickening thud, and gravitational force will not be hurt. There is an impersonal law in the universe. This is the law we use when we give a treatment. If it weren't a law, it would be a caprice. And our subject is justice without judgment. Elmer Gifford this afternoon gave a magnificent talk on what I call the cause and effect of sin and salvation, saying there is no sin but a mistake, and no punishment but a consequence. Emerson said that there is no sin but ignorance and no salvation but enlightenment. The ancient Hindu said man is born unconscious of who he is and, through a process of evolution, comes to discover himself. Everything is self-discovery, and that is true of every science. This they called the "Age of Ignorance," and we might call it "The Fall." The enlightenment we might call the redemption or salvation, the sin and salvation, the reward and punishment, but this impersonal law that every great thinker has told us about is a part of the dual basis of our whole philosophy—the presence and the law, the masculine and feminine, possibly, the thing that works and the way it works, and then what it does. It is the basis of our whole philosophy and practice.

The Presence is conscious, alive, awake, aware. The law is intelligent and creative but not aware of its own creativity. They are making robots that can compute and do all kinds of things, based on statistics that are fed into them. They will never make one that will write a Sermon on the Mount or a sonnet of Shakespeare or paint the Blue Boy. There isn't any danger of this. They will never make a mechanical machine that knows it is a mechanical machine. Some people say that nothing is impossible to God, but I don't think even God denies His own nature. There is an involution and evolution, a time to sow and a time to reap, but the law is impersonal. It is a judge but doesn't know it is a judge. It measures out justice but doesn't know it is measuring out justice, any more than gravitational force knows it is holding us in place. It is exact and its exacting. "'Vengeance is mine,' sayeth the Lord." We have to believe in such a law because it is the servant of the eternal Spirit throughout the ages. In the New Testament, it is said, "For the law was given by Moses, but grace and truth came by Jesus Christ." Yet Christ has redeemed us from the law. Now remember, "Christ" means you; it doesn't mean Jesus. This is our theology. We believe in the divinity of Jesus, and we believe in the unity of Christ in all humanity, lifting all humanity to the level of the divinity of Jesus and in exactly the same way. It could not be otherwise.

Here is a law that knows how to do, but does not know that it is doing. It is weighing out the balance of everything through action and reaction, which probably, in the ultimate, alone exists in the universe. Action and reaction is probably the only thing there is—action being conscious intelligence and reaction being subconscious or unconscious intelligence. Plotinus said, "It is a doer but not a knower." Troward called it "the universal subjectivity," Mrs. Eddy, "the divine principle." It has been called the womb of nature, the soul of nature, the feminine side of nature. It has been said that Eve got fooled, and then she fooled Adam, because it is like the subjective and objective faculties and the coercion of the conscious and unconscious, backed up in modern psychology by the axiom that wherever there is an emotional bias, there will be an intellectual blind spot. We are faced with such a law in the universe. It is here. It brings to us or withdraws from us, but the law is a servant. It is a thing without a soul. It is a doer but not a knower. The garden does not know it is making potatoes, but it knows how to make them.

Moses brought us the law, but Christ, through grace, redeemed us from the law of Moses. Is the law then of no avail? God forbid, for if there had been any law in the grace whereby men must have been made free, that, verily, by grace such a law would have been given.

What does that mean? It is one of the deep teachings of the Bible. We will put it into our language. It says this: There is a law in the universe and Moses taught it. It is a good law and a true law, but it is an impersonal law. There is a Presence in the universe, a divine and loving Father, and Jesus taught that, and he was right. They were both right. And Moses said, "God will raise up another like unto me." And Jesus said, "As Moses lifted up the serpent in the wilderness, even so must the son of man be lifted up that all who believe in him must not perish but shall now enter into their immortality and begin to sing the songs of immortality and not a funeral dirge." He wasn't talking about the salvation of the soul. Jesus never referred to the salvation of the soul. He knew it wasn't lost. And that is wonderful because if it were lost, it would have to be lost in God, and like the prodigal son, the soul was never lost to anything but God to itself, until of its own volition, it turned to the Father.

Now, the teaching is this: As the Hindus and the Buddhists say, salvation is of the self; the self must raise the self by the self. The Christians say salvation is or should be our grace. They are both right, but each is only half right. Religious Science comes in and unifies these two teachings because they belong together, and both Jesus and Moses knew it. And we say law is necessary that the universe shall be coherent and chaotic, and grace is necessary because all creation is the givingness of God. But there couldn't be any law of grace whereby God could have made a mechanical spontaneity or a spontaneous mechanism. The only way that individuation and personality and the warmth and color of life could be produced by the process of unfoldment was to impregnate the mundane clod with a Divine spark, and let it alone to discover itself. The process of that discovery is its ignorance. The thing it discovers is its enlightenment. What it discovers was always there. The law that seemed to inflict bondage and pain and sorrow and fear and impoverishment and death was merely acting in accord with its own nature, as it reacts to ignorance, for karma is the law that binds the ignorant and frees the wise. All laws may be used that way.

Now the law of grace is the givingness of God, if we need any. We believe in both aspects of the law because we are pseudo Christian, Hindu theosophical New Thought-ists, spiritualists, redeemed from all the bondage of all of them. And we rolled it all up in a ball and called it Religious Science, and that is why it is good and why it will get better all the time. Nothing can be left out when God has made the pile complete.

The arbitrary process of evolution must stop the moment man becomes self-aware, and that is the dawn of human history. He looks up and sees he is different from his environment. He is a man. He is something else, but he doesn't know what he is. He stumbles around half conscious. It doesn't matter. But gradually the enlightenment comes, and each new truth he gains immediately responds to him. But from that day on, nothing can be arbitrarily imposed upon him by the universe. The old law of balance will keep on working, the law of justice without judgment, the law of cause and effect, the law of sow and ye shall reap, give and unto you shall be ye given. "Judge not that ye be not judged; with what judgment ye judge, ye shall be judged." And remember this: "Condemn not that ye be not condemned, because with what condemnation ye condemn, ye shall be condemned." It is the greatest thing we could know. Harmful gossip is wrong judgment. Bearing false witness is wrong judgment. Accusing everybody else of everything is wrong judgment. Criticism is wrong judgment. And let me tell you another thing: The only thing you and I can see in another is what we have projected, because if it were not in us, we would not project it; and if it were not in us, we couldn't see it.

Emerson said that truth is like a cannonball, but we dare not deny that hard fringe of the law, without which nothing could be here. The world is bound by a law of freedom, which has been used wrongly in its ignorance, so that even our Bible says we are born in sin and conceived in iniquity. And we shall live for seventy years and suffer greatly and die, and after that, go to hell. It is not a very sweet outlook. Religion is a tough thing, but I don't believe in anything but God, and that makes me happy.

Remember, it isn't that we have to go out and cut somebody's throat to be a murderer. We are a murderer if we would like somebody's throat to be cut. This is one of the subtle teachings of Jesus. It isn't enough to steal from somebody's pocket; we are a thief if we would hurt him. This is why Shakespeare said, "Who steals my purse steals trash, but he that filches from me my good name, robs me of that which not enriches him and makes me poor indeed."

We are caught in the law. The Hindus understood this law and called it karma. Moses understood and taught it, and Jesus understood it as the law of cause and effect. Now the Jews knew about their karma. Let's you and I call it a time track that monotonously repeats itself, like a neurotic thought pattern in the individual and in the race, over and over and over again. The generations come and go, falling prey to the same illusions. The world is not round; the world is flat. If we sail out here, we shall go overboard. Someone else comes along and says it is round and proves it is round, but it was round all the time. He discovered it was round and it was always round, the same world. And so it is with everything. It is new to us but not to itself.

The Hindus worked it out in their sadistic way, I think a little more tough than the Jews, because they said the sins of the father were visited on the children to the third and fourth generation. The Hindus had worked out the most melancholy of propositions. You are born over and over and over again, and each time you suffer and what a mess. They were both wrong. Now Jesus comes along and was always talking about his joy and how happy he was and he was drinking from a well that never ran dry and had bread to eat they knew not of. I don't think he was a sad person. Sure enough, he suffered physical pain for a few hours to prove death has no sting and the grave no victory. It took this much of a great man like this. It takes an awful lot to appease a big appetite. You and I would be satisfied to walk on the water. But Jesus said, "The biggest thing I can do is to show all these people they don't have to be afraid. I, if I be lifted up, shall draw all men unto me." And he was right.

So they said, "Who hath sinned, he or his parents?" Had to be one or the other. This is one of the unique things that goes with Christianity and with our beliefs. Jesus forgave them their sins; he short-circuited the time track. It doesn't matter how long ago it happened. If some of you want to believe you have lived here a thousand times, that is all right with me. If some of you want to believe it is only three generations, that is good. But I am not concerned why this man was born blind; I am going to heal him. And this was a new thing in the world.

This is the spirit of Religious Science, too. We do not care what happened yesterday. The time track can be short-circuited, and the moment it is, it hasn't any existence. Not the slightest. Where does nothing go when something comes in? Where does the dark go when the light comes in? And, "The light shines in the darkness, and the darkness comprehendeth it not. I am the light of the world."

Every time you give a treatment, you short-circuit the time track of that disease. I knew a nurse during the flu epidemic who started to have the flu, went through all the symptoms in six hours. Everything that belonged to the logical evolution of this disease, she experienced and got over it in six hours. She shoved the time track together. Jesus just split it in two. This is what we do in a treatment, but we cannot do it by running around that particular track of time. Therefore Jesus said, "Neither do I condemn thee." If you don't want the same thing to happen again and again, stop doing what you are doing that caused it to happen. But I don't condemn you.

The seamless robe, the ring which symbolizes the unity, right in a split second, simultaneous with turning of one was the turning of the other—this is what we have to expect when we give a treatment. We short-circuit the time track. Justice has been done without judgment. A new kind of justice and a new kind of judgment will take place on a different kind of basis. The Divine withholds nothing, gives everything through grace, surrenders all through the surrender of the self, hangs Itself on the eternal cross of Its own glorified union to redemption of the world, and resurrection of everything that is little, to everything that is greater. But there was involved in that a creative act, the image of eternity, of infinite being and life. So we break the time track and create a new one. Man cannot forget that celestial palace, always, as St. Augustine said, "Thou hast madest us for Thyself, and our heart is restless until it repose in Thee."

There isn't a person living who doesn't remember that celestial palace whence he came. You cannot forget. And somewhere and someday, we look up, and there is a light substance eternal, falling so fine, and you think it will drift across the sands of time and enclose all objects, only to discover it falls through them. Infinite, infinitesimal, lighter than light and brighter than bright. You can look right through it like you can look through a pane of glass. This is the Divine stuff of which we are made, made gross by the fear and dullness and stupidity of our own ignorance until the monotonous neurotic thought patterns, repeating over and over again, almost slay the world with that thought which Browning said, "what a man may waste, desecrate, never quite lose," is destined to go on; "all that is at all, lasts ever past recall." The rest of it lies in karma and reincarnation and sins and anthems of theology of their day. And all devils and demigods the imagination can conceive, to bedevil that which should be a fair haven for the soul, paradise, paradise so close. And we are so blinded and afraid of life that we don't know it brings its book every day and gives us a new one.

There is nothing in the universe that can forgive you until you forgive yourself and everybody else. We are all included. The old law of cosmic cause and effect will grind our utmost farthing until he comes whose right it is. This is justice, final judgment like in that happier land of self-realization, where fear is fled and superstition is gone, and the soul is singing a hymn of praise and not a funeral dirge. But we shall have to reenvision everything. The law will serve us. If you plant peanuts, you will reap peanuts. That is justice. Tear them up and plant corn, and you will get corn. The justice was the judgment wherewith you planted. The tearing up was the act whereby you changed the sequence of your own cause and effect and broke down the time track of the ages, built on fear and superstition and doubt and uncertainty and horror of the unknown.

Now we have to be born again, out of all that fear and into the heritage of the glorious sons and daughters of God, reenvisioning, rethinking, re-knowing, re-saying. Love everything else in the stillness of the night when the soul listens, the silence speaks. Let it sing a song, for there is ever a song somewhere.

We shall have to reverse the old time track consciously, definitely, breaking it down as the truth hammers away at apparent resistance until finally He comes. Then the dawn breaks. And across the hilltops, chariots of fire cast the glory of the warmth and color against our tents of isolation. And we look up, and He appears, the risen Christ, the glorified Atman, the illumined Buddha. Here at last, we behold the image of the Eternal One. And all the old time tracks and old sequences and old impoverishments shall have fled, and in its place glory, peace and power. And we sing, eternally, "Holy, holy, holy, oh most holy Lord God Almighty."

Nonresistance

WEDNESDAY, AUGUST 12, 1959

In his third talk of this year, Ernest Holmes offers his take on the topic of nonresistance and its role in Religious Science. He reminds us that the universe belongs to each of us, as we are individualizations of the one "self-existent cause." As the universe expresses itself through form and time, we feel a divine urge to express our unique talents and gifts. However, we often create barriers (though false beliefs and psychological repressions) to the flow of the universe expressing itself though us. In other words, our free will allows us to resist being in the flow of the Divine givingness. Holmes tells us that the only thing we ultimately cannot resist is nonresistance, that at some point we will let go and let God flow through our lives naturally and perfectly. When that occurs, we will transcend the limitations of identifying ourselves as only these physical beings existing separate and apart from the rest of life.

Our subject tonight is really "nonresistance." It is going along with life. And because of the nature of the two previous talks, we don't know what will happen in the next hour. At least I don't. Technique without temperament is as futile as temperament without a tongue. If we listen very deeply and particularly, together we will develop in what India they call "darshan," which is something that happens between a speaker and his audience. Something goes from a speaker, and the audience picks it up, and it comes back up here, and it goes back and forms a triangle to each person in the audience. And unless it takes place, there has been no real communication with an audience. When there is an entering into a rapport, something happens that is beyond either the audience or the speaker. So, with your indulgence, I will change the subject tomorrow night and the next night, because I see it might fit better into the way this seems to be formulating itself in our consciousness as we go on with these lessons.

Thinking is the most difficult thing in the universe and, particularly, to think straight and to synthesize our thoughts and out of a vast analysis create a unification of facts that justify the fact. Religious Science is not looking for facts to prove a theory. It is trying to work out an adequate theory to justify and explain the facts it has discovered. That is the only way any philosophy ought to be established. It is the only way any science is established. We are not looking for facts to prove something we fondly believe in. Columbus was not looking for facts to prove the world was flat; he knew it was round.

We know we are living in a spiritual universe. It is a spiritual system. It is alive, awake, and aware, all over with equal intensity. So tomorrow night I want to speak on the universe or infinite. It belongs in its entirety to each and every individuation of itself. Emerson said, "The universe remains to the heart unhurt." We do not believe there is an individual anything in the universe. If there were, it would be separated from the source of its own being, which is a universality. The universe cannot create infinite variations of individuals separate from itself, but because it is infinite and ever present, it can create innumerable individuations of the entirety of itself, in multiplicity, remaining in unity and without division. And that is the secret of the ages.

I was thinking today, we get all our knowledge either from science or philosophy: philosophy, which is opinion; science, which is fact; revelation, inspiration, intuition, which is another realm. All the knowledge the human mind has comes from one or a combination of these three sources. There is no other place it can come from. This difficulty in understanding a unitary universe—one universe, the difficulty in getting over dualism, whether it is spirit and matter, or whether it is good or bad, or God or something, or mind and matter—it will be overcome the instant we perceive that the transcendence is the imminence, and that the imminence is the transcendence. All that means is this: Jesus said, "I and the Father are one, for my Father is greater than I; he that hath seen me hath seen the Father. Believe me that I am in the Father and the Father in me, or else believe me for the very works' sake."

It is only when we realize that that which we are evolving into is merely the outgoingness of that which we are evolving out from, that we shall understand the meaning of involution and evolution. Only when we understand that every man is rooted in God, not as something separate, apart, or different in essence, but as identical in essence but different in degree, shall we understand the meaning of the nature of the Divine incarnation, which was a historical event in Jesus but was also another historic event when you were born. It is that which some of the ancients called "the one who is awake within the one who sleeps." It is what I referred to when I said, "The divine transcendence is hid in the inward imminence." Robert Browning speaks of it as "that imprisoned splendor," and it is why Walt Whitman speaks of it when he says that "at the center of everything nestles the seed of perfection."

The philosophy of Religious Science—keeping faith with the great thoughts of the ages, understanding the teaching and the meaning of the great thinkers of the ages, synthesizing the great spiritual systems of the ages—has discovered what I did not discover but we have and shall continue to discover, what is the greatest spiritual teaching the world has ever known or they would all be wrong. Truth doesn't belong to anyone. How could it? How much gravitational force do you own? It is given alike to everyone, equally distributed through space. Isaiah said, "Whosoever will may come."

So I want to speak on the thought that all of the universe belongs to every individuation in it and to you—all of it, not part or some or a little of it, but all of it. The universe has form but not size. It expresses in time as a sequence of events and unitary wholeness but never in duration, because all of it, in its infinite possibility of any form or size we think of, is inherent in a raindrop. And eternity is merely time extended, like an accordion, to fit the needs of expression of whatever is expressing. But to the universe, time and space have no existence. They have an existence as form and experience, but not as separation and duration.

We are not denying either time or space. We are merely giving a place where it can lay an egg.

The truth has nothing to do with what you and I think it is. We are only fortunate if we can think a little about it, the way it works, and I suppose that is all we do. The human mind creates an image, which endlessly and monotonously repeats itself like a neurotic thought pattern, and because we see it and experience it, we believe it. And because we believe it, we create an idol out of it, whether it is human or a paradox, allegedly divine. And we worship it, and then we are afraid of it and recoil from it. Carl Jung has recently said that at times of great stress, the collective mind demands some help from heaven. An interesting concept.

So, we build up and build up, only to find that what we have built up falls apart. No adhesion, no cohesion. And out here, we see nothing but change and decay. Because there is a transcendence and an imminence, there is always a witness. God moves in circles His wonders to perform, merely because a circle is the only movement that can be eternal. And this is probably why everything from revolutions at the center of the atom to vast planetary and sidereal systems move in circles. And this is also why Troward could say, scientifically, that a neurotic thought pattern will repeat itself with monotonous regularity throughout life. It is on its own time track. Over and over and over again, it plays this tune, this neurotic tune, this psychological repression.

Now I want to prove that nonresistance is the only thing that cannot be resisted and demonstrate that nonviolence is the only thing that cannot be violated in the universe. Jesus merely announced it when he said, "He who takes up the sword will perish by it." Emerson said [in "Brahma"]:

If the red slayer think he slays,
   Or if the slain think he is slain,
They know not well the subtle ways
   I keep, and pass, and turn again.

I would like briefly to refer to a few psychological axioms that are self-evident truths, which all the different schools of psychology, analysis, etc., in the world accept. None of them reject what I am going to talk about. It is said man is born out of the unconscious and by some irresistible thing, which they call the libido or an urge. And the libido is defined as the emotional craving for self-expression back of all things, the repression of which leads to psychoneurosis, which means 75 to 90 percent of all disease, according to medicine, and 85 percent of all accidents, according to experiments at Presbyterian Hospital in New York, and according to the man who said the will to live is all disease, and another man who said all disease is a result of strain.

The libido, at any rate, is an emotional craving to express. They say it comes out of the id. That makes it equal to the id and to whether you and I believe the thing we are talking about. We would call it a divine urge. Jesus referred to it when he said, "The spirit seeketh such."

Whatever we call it, there is an irresistible urge to create, emanating from and passing through man. It is an energy; it is creative; and it will not be thwarted. There isn't anybody living who can thwart it. There isn't anybody living who can change it. There isn't anybody living who, through denying it, would remove it. It would still be there. Our affirmations and denials do not create or erase realities. They only establish our individual relationship in something that we didn't create, like we change our position in gravitational force.

This is designed to come forth in the explosion of self-expression and energy. It's creative energy. It has to get from there to here and to express itself through us, and if it doesn't, like all energy, it just bends back on itself. It is the nature of all energy to return to its source. This is why it is said that at the core of every neurosis there are certain things that are put there by this creative energy, because a psychological repression is a group of highly emotionally charged thoughts, feelings, and ideas so deeply repressed into the unconscious that they cannot be brought to the surface either by the will or the imagination. It is fundamental to all these things. Therefore, they devise all kinds of methods to get them out. Here they are, and here is where the inner complex, the confusion takes place between the pressure of the urge there and the repression of the urge here, shoving it back where it raises in there the thing we don't believe in.

It is as simple as this, but no one believes it is that simple because we want everything to be hard. We want it to be a mystery so it can't be explained. We believe only a few people have it, so we can idealize them. And because of our sense of unworthiness, we condemn ourselves. This morning Elmer [Gifford] told us Jesus said, "Love your neighbor as yourself," and you are your neighbor's neighbor. Never forget that. There is nothing wrong with you, nothing wrong with your neighbor but the error of false conclusions attached to us in a universal field, which acts as though the error were truth and impersonates it over and over again.

We believe this—first of all, in an up-push from the universe that we call involution—every bible teaches it. It is a necessary conclusion; the passing of Spirit into Its own form, into Its own image, containing Its own measure and all of it. And then the evolving or unfolding of that thing into the evolution of what we are, up through the ignorance into the enlightenment, where we call it the conscious mind, which—we never forget; we teach and rightly—is the spiritual mind because it is the only mind that knows it is a mind. It is going to be hard to accept this because we want the Spirit to be way off from anything we can ever reach every day. We will never understand unity until we know that God has passed into everything and is everything and stimulates and animates everything, and through everything is projecting other things for the delight of Its own creativity, for the expression of Its own imagination, for the gratification of Its own will. But of course this will, this creative imagination, is always constructive, and there is nothing to oppose it.

We believe this divine spark, a spark which is, as Browning said, "to receive what a man may waste, desecrate, never quite lose," comes up through but carries with it from this ignorance and through this unconscious and, as Mrs. Eddy calls it, the mortal mind. The Bible calls it the carnal mind, and all it means is what everybody has believed. It has to get through all that to get up to our self-awareness in exactly the same way; if we were dealing with psychology, the inner urge and all repressions must be brought to the light of day to be seen, and then the avenue is cleared.

What has this got to do with the theory of nonviolence? Because every psychological repression is based on a resistance to the flow of that which ought to be expressing life, beauty, happiness, prosperity, it ought to be painting a picture, singing a song, etc., giving to the universe. But it must come up through and express, or the very energy of the most sublime thing will block its own passage. This means there is something in us now that is nonresistant. Psychologically, we are resistant. Physiologically, we are resistant. There is a spiritual principle and a spiritual Presence within us that does not resist anything because It doesn't have to. But between that and this, the world has built up so much denial of that and created so many devils and hells and fallen angels and so many things that say it cannot be, that man is not worthy, that man has fashioned a weapon with which he has almost slain himself.

The nonresistance of the universe, the nonresistance of truth, the nonviolence of that nonviolent and nonresistant principle within us that dominates everything, controls everything, governs everything but must—because of our nature and what it is doing through us—leave us alone to discover ourselves. And as I said last night, from the date of that self-discovery to whatever is going to happen ever, there will have to be a conscious cooperation, as there is in every discovery in life, in science, and in everything. The truth is always there.

Nonresistance is the only thing that cannot be resisted. Nonviolence cannot be violated. But whatever we resist, on the level of the resistance, we shall hold the psychic image, and the physiological corresponds in place, as though it were held there by inexorable laws of its own being, which it is, until we non-resist it. This is a law of nature, and we cannot change it. That means this: The neurotic thought patterns—whether is impoverishment, the fear of God or of each other, the thought that I love someone and they don't love me—could we non-resist that? The outgoingness of love? We would have to bring back ten thousand persons perhaps more worthy of our affections than the one who has rejected us and, resisting, blocked. Whether you call it the libido or the divine urge, it doesn't matter what you call it. There is that irresistible pressure that will not be blocked, and it goes in here, as Troward said, where it remains in a dynamic state. He meant by that, it is buried alive.

Now it is always based, according to Karen Horney, on four things, four psychological and emotional factors: rejection, guilt, insecurity, and anxiety. It is the core of every neurosis—rejection, guilt, insecurity, and anxiety, all of which are built up out of nothing. Remember, all thought patterns and all time tracks that the mind of man has created are creations of sand, not cemented together, which the first wind can blow apart. They are fluidic. Emerson said that we see the universe as solid fact; God sees it as liquid law. You could not give an effective treatment, as I said last night, until whenever you did it, you canceled out, you broke up a time track that is holding the error or whatever you want to call it in place—whether it is impoverishment, confusion, sickness, or whatever it is, the foolishness of the fear, the morbidity that fundamentalism has taught people, out of the ignorance of their own unconscious sense of guilt. And I haven't any sympathy for it at all. I do not believe I have to believe in a devil because it is unkind not to believe in one. This, to me, is crying tears of hypocrisy. There just ain't no evil in essence in the universe, and everything you and I experience that is any form of evil is merely that thing flowing through us in the wrong form because of our ignorance, and we haven't given it any other form. That is what practice is, a transcendence.

You will discover in treating people, if you will spend a little time forgiving them their sins, healing them of their guilt, removing their anxiety, and giving them security, 75 percent of all their troubles—and maybe more—won't be there, because they are built on this kind of a timetable or chart. But a friend said last night that there is a Jewish proverb that says only when we speak from the heart do we speak to the heart. Isn't that a wonderful saying? Love only knows and comprehends love. Jesus said that if you want to know this doctrine, do it, because it is only as we reach out beyond that which is resisting, that there is nothing to resist. The transcendence, now let's call that spiritual awareness, does not deal with a resistance in the field of multiplicity and the clash of opposing forces vibrating at the same level of consciousness. Here are two icebergs. They will come together and crush the Empire State Building. The sun comes out and does not resist the iceberg; it is just a different degree. The iceberg cannot resist the sun.

Two of the greatest things in the Bible are where God was supposed to come down in the cool of the evening and talk with Adam, and Adam discovered he was naked. And God said, "Who told you you were naked?" This self-condemnation, the resistance, this thing that blocks the Divine, it blocks the beneficent and magnificent of the increase of the incarnation that can only come through our own volition because we are now individuated. It is all man's doing, and all of its laws are written in sand. The only record we have of any writing of Jesus was when he wrote in the sand, soon to blow away, because Jesus knew the laws of life are liquid and that there is nothing permanent but change, even in that which in Itself does not change, the great play of life upon itself.

Again in the New Testament, someone comes to John the Baptist and throws himself down in the dirt and asks, "What shall I do to avoid the wrath to come?" God reveals things by the heart, through the heart by the intellect, and the intellect tries to reason them out and see if they make sense. But it always feels them because there is always an up-push of the witness. It is givingness because its whole reason for being is love. But our receivingness is not equal to its givingness, and because our receiving denies its giving and does not build a habitat which is like it, it rejects it, resists it, and even love turns to hate. And that is why the psychologist says they are so close together, it is hard to tell them apart.

The emotion is fundamental. What we do with it changes that which is an equal energy, and it turns feeling into emotion. Feeling is at the center of everything, intense feeling, all the feeling of the universe, back of everything. So John said, "I didn't tell you you had to do something to escape the wrath to come. I came to preach that the kingdom of God is at hand." Now the transcendence must not deal with the wrath because God isn't mad. The transcendence does not deal with disease because God isn't sick. The transcendence does not deal with impoverishment because God isn't poor. The transcendence does not deal with unifying things because God is unity. We deal with these things. And while we deal with them on their own level, we merely hold that level in place and create ten thousand more devils and, seeing it and experiencing it, say it is the will of God and "whom the Lord love, he chastises." Stupid—"what fools we mortals be" (Shakespeare).

Now it is 100 percent true psychologically, and if we are going to discover the nature of that truth metaphysically, we must simplify it. Truth is God. And we shall discover that that urge, no matter what it is to do, it is all good, all play of life upon itself. Unless it proceeds from a field of unity, it builds up an apparent duality, believes what it sees, sees what it believes. And Mrs. Eddy said it right when she said, "Mortal mind sees what it believes as truly as it believes what it sees." And Emerson said, "We see what we animate and animate what we see." It just means this: While we deal with a problem of disease and the unhappiness and impoverishment resistantly, at the level which creates them, we shall enforce them, and the last state of that man will be worse than the first.

We have to get up here. The sun does not resist the iceberg, and the iceberg cannot resist the sun. We haven't power to split the cosmic path. We may only make our journey—temporarily unhappy, very momentarily, just for a moment—in eternity long enough to learn better. This is what we need to know. We believe in spiritual mind treatment. It is not mental suggestion or holding thoughts. It is getting a new viewpoint that discards the old automatically. The transcendence does not reconcile the difference. It does not change the difference. It operates above it and completely disregards it.

Now let's get to the practical side. We deal with the transcendence applied to the needs of life—where we need it, when we need it, while we need it, whatever it may be. There is nothing wrong with being happy and well. There is nothing wrong with having abundance and enjoying life. There is nothing wrong in loving and being loved, because we believe God is love. It was on this basis that Jesus multiplied the loaves and fishes and resurrected himself from the dead, because he sang a hymn of life and not of death. He saw the abundance and not the want. He saw the wholeness and not the unworthiness. And he didn't resist it. He didn't fight it or argue with them. He said that it is true on the level where it works. He said, "No matter how many eyes a man has put out, if today he is willing to put his own eye out and give to his neighbor, he shall for the first time in his experience receive eyesight. Look up, see and behold, the son of man cometh." He said it doesn't matter how thirsty he has been or how dry and arid the country. If he knows it and believes it, there is a well of water within him springing up unto eternity from which, if he drinks, he will never thirst again.

And Jesus introduced that which the prophets of Israel and others sang about, the glorious teaching of the transcendence and our nonresistant identification with it. There is no other name whereby we shall be elevated to that beyond our previous experience. And Jesus said, "I have meat to eat that ye not know of."

On the level of conflict and resistance, there shall be many dead, until somebody comes who sees not the corpse but the living form, who, looking up, beholds his face only. The transcendence and triumph of the spirit over every apparent material resistance is brought about and consummated only and when and if our own vision looks out beyond that which has created the fear. And no man shall raise the corn or grind the grain or bake the loaf that shall sustain your life. No man. Because the transcendence is hid in the imminence in you and in me.

And the glory of the kingdom of God shall come to each one of us only in the dawn our own consciousness and in perfect peace. This is our discovery of that which is lost. Beyond the border of our human ignorance, where the trail runs out and stops, and in the beauty of this thought and grandeur of this concept, know this: The savior you have sought has never been away. He is what you are. For looking up and within, we shall behold his face.

Evolution

※

THURSDAY, AUGUST 13, 1959

Ernest Holmes's fourth talk of 1959 centers around the topic of our spiritual evolution. This is a subject that has been woven into all of his previous talks this year. He begins by citing some of the oldest sources influencing Religious Science, such as the Hermetic teachings. From these early days, we have been presented with the idea that while there can be only a unity within the universe, it can be experienced as the variety in the multiplicity of expressions. Our Divine Source embedded Itself (or involved Itself) in Its creation and left it alone to express its creative urge and use its free will to evolve back to its realization of its source. Religious Science offers ideas and tools for navigating this spiritual path.

We speak about the mind that sleeps in the mineral, waves in the grass, wakes to simple consciousness in the animal, to God consciousness in the illumined, and that there must be, in the process of evolution, beings beyond us as we are beyond tadpoles. Our Bible speaks of it as principalities and powers. This is a part of our theology, part of the belief of Religious Science, that we are all on the pathway of an endless evolution where we shall evermore become more and never less ourselves, where each step in evolution will be a sequential, logical, inevitable, and irresistible step from a lower to a higher. As Oliver Wendell Holmes said, "Still, as the spiral grew/He left the past year's dwelling for the new."

The greatest teaching the world has ever known is Religious Science because it is a combination of the thoughts of the great, the good, and the wise throughout the ages, synthesized, modernized, made understandable and practical, teachable and usable. Nearly 1,500 years before Moses, Hermes, the Hermetic teaching, was given. It informed a great part of the teachings of Moses and most of the teaching of Pythagoras and practically all the teaching of the greatest intellectual minds of philosophers the world has ever known, which were the Greeks.

The Christian philosophy, the original concept of Christianity, was based entirely on these truths. The book of Genesis is a story of it. All the teachings of Jesus are based on this. Most of the great poets, most of the great philosophers all taught it. Emerson taught it. It was believed in and has been taught by all the great and deeply illumined souls the world has ever known. So when people wonder if we have any reason for believing the things we teach, we can refer them to these great scholars, because most people's eyes are closed. It has taken the world nine thousand years to realize there can be unity and variety in multiplicity without division, and it is one of the great philosophical problems of the ages. How can one become many without dividing itself? And that is a very interesting thought, and it has never been answered intelligently by most theology and never once by the theology of fundamentalism, which is complete ignorance and complete stupidity; I shouldn't criticize it, but it is stupid.

Now the greatest philosophical error here is that the premise is wrong. The starting point is wrong. If you have a God of unity up there and a manifestation of variety of many here, how is the God there going to unify the many here with the God there? He isn't. That is why it never got put together. It is only when you realize the God there and the God here is the same God, that this great philosophical and theological problem is solved once and for all, in such a complete symphony that a child can understand it. It isn't hard to understand at all. Once you admit that the Creator must, of a necessity, become Its own creation because there isn't anything to make creation out of, you have God plus nothing out of which to create. And God plus nothing leaves nothing but God. God is all there is, here, there and everywhere. God as man in man is man. God in the tadpole is the tadpole. This is no slur on the Almighty. We have infinite variations in everything. This is how it is that your life is God.

I would like theoretically to establish the proposition. This is basic to Religious Science, this is what we believe: that every individual is a unique representation, a unique individuation of a universality. For a couple of illustrations, this represents the life principle, the divine Presence, and everything that exists within It, by It, of It, on It, and with It and is It, as that thing. But It is always more than what It does. That is why our statement says, "God is more than creation, but God is creation and is not exhausted by creation. God is the soul of the universe, embodied and embedding everywhere in everything."

We believe in this. By a process of evolution, the divine incarnation that has taken place, not by our own volition or will, has implanted an impulsion in everything in the universe that compels it to evolve. That is clear, isn't it? More and more and more. That is why hope springs eternal in the human breast. That is why there is an irresistible urge back of everything, which we discussed last night, which psychology has discovered and calls the libido. It doesn't matter what you call it. Man is born to create. And that is why it is that when the creative impulsion of a desire to express life fails to find the explosion of self-expression in action, as the seed fails to bear fruit, the energy of it goes back with itself and creates the psychological confusion, conflict, complex, suppression, and repression, and probably 90 percent of all diseases, accidents, and everything else. It is now known that 85 percent of accidents are unconsciously invited because the person cannot see his way through. Dr. Arnold Hutschnecker, who wrote *The Will to Live,* said everyone unconsciously chooses the disease from which he is going to die and when he is going to do it. And I don't know whether that is true or not.

The next thing for us to remember is this: that the impulsion, the divine urge, the spark that Robert Browning said, "A man may waste, desecrate, never quite lose," that thing that pushes all evolution forward, upward, and outward is the original creative urge. It is God. It is that thing that has touched us with life. And since everything individuates—that is, everything is different while it remains the same—there has to be at the center of everything a unique representation of God that will never be reproduced, because we have no hesitation in describing to the Infinite the infinite possibility of limitless manifestations of the entirety of Itself without division. This is what Jesus understood and from this that he spoke of a transcendence he called a unity. "The Father and I are one."

Now we know in our metaphysical practice—and this is the key to it, the secret of it and the law of its being—that the Infinite flows down to a point of differentiation. This is the point of our objectivity and objective experience, environment, and body. This represents our everyday life, the intellect, and everything. We find that starting from here—we go through here and want to get up to there—this is pure Spirit up here. This is what analysis does; it clears the track, and it is all the same thing. Truth is God. And that is Emerson's theory of parallels. All of the great have taught it and all parables of Jesus were drawn from nature, because, he said, "You look at stars and say it will be a good day or a bad day tomorrow. Why don't you look at spiritual things the same way?" There is no law in physics you won't find in metaphysics backing it, because the universe is one system. When we go into metaphysical practice, we don't suddenly slide from cosmos into chaos. We don't suddenly slide from intelligence into something that is not intelligent. We become more intelligent.

Now there are two ways, in our theory, of doing this. In here is the collective unconscious, what everybody has thought, which keeps pure Spirit from coming down here. It is as simple as that and as profound. We have one method, which we call the argumentative method, whereby we start here and deny everything until our denial builds up an affirmation to come through here. This is what we call practicing realization, which means the transcendence, and because this cannot resist, through realization, realizing man is pure spirit and that is all there is.

Now all this represents everything in the universe. It might be a buttercup or Buddha or a monkey, and into each of these differentiations is being poured what? The Infinite, unobstructed, undivided, a totality, a completeness, an allness of God. And thereby, we establish that the Infinite is actually devoting Its entire time, thought, and attention to every one of Its manifestations because it is Its nature to do that and to be it. Therefore, we establish that back of the thought of each one of us is all the power there is, all the presence there is, all the life there is, all the intelligence there is, and all the love there is, too.

We are so used to separating God from what we are, and what we are from God, that we go somewhere to find God. When I stop to think of the intensity of life in the most minute thing, I am not afraid of action. It isn't that way at all. The universe is a living system. It is alive, awake, and aware. It has an irresistible desire, impulsion, and necessity of expressing itself. And it is interesting, recognizing that most of all of our diseases are built on stagnation, inaction, and a lack of circulation, because if we had circulation, assimilation, and elimination, we wouldn't have any reason to be sick.

The ancient Chinese said man has three bodies: physical, mental, and spiritual. The physical cannot be well unless the mental circulates through it. The mental cannot circulate through the physical unless the spiritual circulates through the mental. We have established an even physical circulation, and that it is impossible unless there is an emotional balance and a right mental circulation, and that is psychosomatic medicine. And we come along to add one other word and call it spiritual-psychosomatic medicine and add the numa to the soma and the psyche. That is the spirit-mind-body relation, and we come up with spiritual mind healing, which does not deny either the stagnation in the physical or mental body, whatever it may be, but it affirms the supremacy of the spirit.

Now all the things I have said about the Infinite being at the point of the finite are self-evident propositions, axiomatic. We can't help it. We didn't make it that way. We have to accept it. The truth is what is, not what we think it is. Jesus said there is a truth that shall make you free. And when Galileo was compelled to repent and say the world is not round, he thought, for their stupidity, he would say something he knew was not true because it didn't matter. So that is the way it is with truth. Emerson said that truth is like a cannonball: a hard, cold fact. We must face the fact of truth and at the same time receive the divine effulgence and ecstasy and beauty and warmth and color of the Spirit back of the law because we deal with a combination of presence, power, principle, the law, and the word, Joaquin and Boaz, the big foundation of the whole teaching of our Bible, the New and the Old Testament, and every other bible that was ever written, the mechanics of the universe, the law of mind in action, the divine Presence and the universal Spirit: God in me. Now we have to add one other thing. The universe is a combination of the divine self-knowingness, God, the living Spirit, personal to each one of us, I think. And I think it is uniquely, warmly, colorfully personal to each one of us. We have the most exalted concept of the personalness of God that was ever put into print, if people will understand it.

We don't say God is a principle. You cannot merely intellectualize a feeling. On the other hand, one need not deny the other. We have to have both temperament and the law of the universe that governs everything, the Spirit that ordained everything. And we have to have them both in reach of our consciousness, if we are one with eternal verities of the universe. Therefore, it is necessary that there is a law of creation, which is the servant of the eternal Spirit throughout the ages.

Self-existence, coexistence, that means eternal existence with God. The Spirit is God the law, but the law is the servant of the Spirit. The law is absolute. Jesus said, "Heaven and earth will pass away, but my words shall not pass away," and the psalmist said, "O how love I thy law! it is my meditation all the day."

The law is impersonal. The impersonal, the word: What do we deal with? Therefore, if we wish the highest, the most complete, and most effectual use of the law, we shall find it only by practicing the transcendence of the present. There is something that cannot be resisted. There is an altitude of thought that nothing can deny. And every practitioner knows this. There is an altitude of transcendence, and some days you get better results than others. It will always be when your thought has transcended the lesser condition.

All these things are now, not by and by. Time is the plaything of the timeless, of eternity. It has no law to support it other than the law of eternity. It has no duration other than that which is perceived. You can be very sad and disconsolate and forlorn, and quietly sitting by yourself and forgetting this, rise into a place where it becomes dissipated without antagonism, just as the ice will melt before the sun. But you and I have to know, we have to prove every step of it by demonstration. We need nothing else. I never did believe that because we can heal people and demonstrate prosperity and all that sort of thing—all of which I believe in, and it can be done—but I never believed that was the main object of our work. But I believe it is good. No one knows your thoughts but you. The thing that intrigues me about our philosophy and its practice isn't that it heals somebody, but that because it could heal somebody, because it can heal one person, it can heal everybody. It isn't just the act of accomplishment. There is nothing wrong with the loaves and fishes. Jesus multiplied them, nothing wrong with them at all. But the thing that is fascinating is that there is something that can do it, and you and I understand it and, to some degree, know it and, to some degree, can practice it.

Every Religious Scientist must be a practitioner or he is asleep at the switch. But know this: If there is some power in every thought, there are some thoughts where all power resides in its fullness—the transcendence, the spiritual realization, I don't care what you call it. It is only the ideas we assimilate that will ever become a part of the body of our thought. There are some thoughts that have all power, but they are thoughts that have risen with conscious union with the Eternal, above and beyond the field of conflict.

I say the universe exists for the individual. This is not solipsism. Solipsism says, "I am that there is." It has nothing to do with that. I am saying we are not identifying the psychological or the physiological ego with the thing I am talking about. We are talking about the Self, as there is only one Self, the Self, that one of the ancients. Upanishads or Vedas said, "the One who is awake within him who sleeps." The old Jewish prophet, the Apostle Paul, said, "Awake, thou that sleepest, and arise from the dead, and Christ shall give thee light." We call it realization, spiritual realization, or transcendence, and we aim at all times to speak from this. But I want you to see the logic of it, that is the way it is. You and I are individuations of a universality that has projected us into being. It has put within each one of us the seeds of perfection. That is why Walt Whitman said, "Enclosed and safe within its central heart, nestles the seed perfection." It is there; it contains everything we need. I sometimes think of it as a spiritual companion, a divine double, not with dualism, but it is there. No man does walk through this life alone. Emerson said that it seems as though when we entered this world something had given us a drink too strong for us, and that we act as though we are gods on a debauch. A sleepiness hangs around our eyes. But every once in a while, we look about us and open our eyes and see. And a new heaven and a new Earth is disclosed.

This is the mount of transfiguration; this is the pinnacle of faith; this is the secret place of the Most High; this is a light of the illuminati. This is a thing that Jesus and Moses saw, until a halo was visible around their heads and an aura of light around their bodies. I have experienced it many times, and I am sure you have. All at once, you look up, and there it is. You don't know where it came from; you cannot say whence it came. You hardly know what it is, but it is a light that is ineffable in its beauty and apparently flows in and around and through all things and encompasses all things in a softness that unlights the light of the sun. There is nothing harsh. It does not cloud the vision, and it seems as though you are a part of that light. I can well understand at least something of the meaning of Jesus when he said, "I am the light of the world. Let your light so shine before men, that they may see your good works and glorify your Father, which is in heaven."

Now we must know that back of every word we speak is power. That in such degree as this world has risen above the confusion and doubt, above the contention and strife, above the combativeness and argument of separation, above dualism, it will transcend all of them. This is what we practice. Very few people even in the metaphysical field actually know—and I don't pretend to very much—what the thing is that we are really teaching and treating that baffles known science, known medicine, known psychology, and most known theology. This is not a criticism of theology. We have our own theology. We know we are practicing a transcendence.

A couple of boys came to me and wanted to start a business and asked if they could treat for it. I said of course they could demonstrate the wherewithal if they thought they could, but to get above the denial, that you can't and don't try to know how you can. But know that it is, and the way and the how will come. Why is that? Because just as in the Divine, "in the beginning was the Word, and all things were made by the Word," and also was the creative energy and power and divine imagination and will, the image and the law to project it from an idea into a form by a logical and sequential evolution of that idea. This is what Jesus meant when he said, "The son can do nothing of himself but what he seeth the Father do, for what things soever He doeth, these also doeth the son likewise. For as the Father raiseth up the dead and quickeneth them, even so the son quickeneth whom he will."

How could it be otherwise? They call this the microcosm and the macrocosm. The Chinese called it the big world and the little world. We call it the universal and the individual, God in man. It doesn't matter what we call it, it is one indivisible, undivided, perfect eternal Presence, equally distributed through our time and eternity and space, and all of it is at the point of our thought. Now it really means this: When you give a treatment, there It will be, involuted in that treatment. That is clear, isn't it? Remember, involution wasn't something that started just a few days before Moses appeared. Everything the great bibles of the world have taught belongs to a timelessness, to an unborn moment in which the time shall be created for the time track of the revolution of the law and order that is to sustain the idea conceived when It gave birth to the time track.

I don't think that is very clear, so let's put it another way. Plant an acorn; it is an idea. In the acorn is everything that is going to make a tree. In it is the whole evolution and the creative soil. Now, it is the same way with your word. It operates in another kind of creativity and cosmos and soil, the soul of the universe. It has been called the womb of nature. Troward called it "the universal creativity," and Mrs. Eddy called it "the Divine principle," and it doesn't matter what you call it. It is the only possible explanation to the answer of any prayer because there is no God that likes a Jew better than a Gentile or a White man better than a Black man. There is only one race, and that is the human race.

When you think this thought, because of the creativity of this act, you didn't put the creativity in it; you took it out. You set the hen; you didn't lay the egg. We *use* a creativity. How wonderful to be the instrumentality of a Power and a Presence supreme—benign, magnificent, loving, containing the ineffable essence of beauty and givingness and forgivingness, implied in givingness, as they are two ends of the same act. How wonderful the concept that if these two boys can say, "We want to do this thing. Therefore, this is what we are going to do; here is the idea," they shall give birth to the time, to the place, already now involuted in a law beyond their comprehension and a Presence beyond their imagination, but personal and warm and colorful and responsive. This is the practice of Religious Science. It isn't an enigma hid within a riddle. It is simple, but we can't explain why because who can explain God? That is the way it works, and we know it.

I say then that in your thought is the law of that thought, which responds to it, now devoting its entire attention. How much gravitational force, how much of this entirety of gravitational force is holding the gloves to the desk? All of it. You can't say there is just a fragment of it. Is there more life in an elephant than a flea? Life has nothing to do with size. All of the law of God or good is invoked when you think. All of it, not some of it, not a fragment. All the creativity and mind and imagination and will and purpose of the entire universe is devoting all of Its time. Why? Because It can devote all of its time to infinite variations of itself without confusion. We can't do that, but we must imagine a creativity to which no limit is set. The means, the method, the end, all of the minute details that shall transpire from the thoughts of the thing are involuted in the law. And all the Presence is pushing it out. Therefore, we shall forget the process and think only of the culmination. How then shall we arrive at and satisfy ourselves that all law sustains all thought—and it must at every level—that the law that binds the ignorant is the same law that will free the wise, the thing that makes us sick is the only thing that can heal us, and that is ourselves. Jesus said, "Destroy this temple and in three days I will raise it up." The absolute immutability of the law that responds, whether we call it faith or prayer or treatment, the absolute creativity of a Creative Imagination that flows through us into self-expression in the cooperation of the only two realities that you will ever know, God and yourself. Shall you ever discover anything else?

Does not everyone live mostly alone? Even in the biggest crowd on Earth, you can feel lonely. God and I, in space, alone. There is nothing but me, there is nothing but you. And everything transpires in the divine arena of this eternal drama of self-existence.

Religious Science teaches you have a secret partnership with the Eternal, that it is not a limited one, it is on an equal basis. Jesus said, "All things that the Father hath are mine." And James Russell Lowell said, "Not what we give, but what we share/For the gift without the giver is bare/Who gives himself with his alms feeds three/Himself, his hungering neighbor, and Me." Only he who gives all gets all. Only he who loses all finds all. And it isn't easy for us to give up our little bloated nothingness. There is nothing in the universe that wishes to wipe us out. God has honored us by incarnating Himself in us.

"Know ye not that ye are the temple of the God and that the Spirit of God dwelleth in you?" That which the Almighty has created in us, that which existed before Abraham, is God, not to be belittled even in us, but to be exalted. Therefore, instead of attaching the possibility and hope of life and future in everything to that weakness that runs around tied to puppet strings of experience, to live and breathe and die. "What is man, that thou art mindful of him?"

Lifting up our vision from the valley of dry bones and the slain, we shall see that which neither slays nor is slain and hear the grand march of the further evolution of our soul to the conscious union of the finite and Infinite and start, for the first time, with the Divine companionship self-conceived, self-regulated. And for the first time in our evolution, we have arrived at that place where everything is put behind us that was compulsory. And we may choose to some degree, even now, what the pathway shall be.

Spiritual Maturity

FRIDAY, AUGUST 14, 1959

This Friday evening talk concludes Ernest Holmes's five-part series on the underpinnings of Religious Science. In this wrap up, he encourages us to develop what he calls "spiritual maturity" and offers his thoughts on what that means. Holmes provides a brief summary on what he hopes attendees learned this week and ends with a call for all to use our divine gifts in conscious cooperation with the Divine.

I trust we have learned this week certain definite techniques for the use of the principles and, above all, something that gives us a deeper and broader and higher and more comprehensive understanding and realization and knowledge of what we mean by the kingdom of God, what the Christian philosophy means by Christ, what the Hindu philosophy means by Atman, what the Buddhist philosophy means by the enlightened, because they all mean the same thing.

We have been studying the age of maturity, or dawn or hope of maturity. Remember this: No person is mature who thinks only one religion is the right religion. No person is spiritually mature or intellectually mature, and therefore he isn't emotionally mature, who thinks one race is the only race there is, or one philosophy, or any one human being represents and stands for the totality of humanity. That is not maturity.

Remember, every age has had its saviors, its avatars, its Christs—and they all have been good and necessary—and that taking from each and all of them, no one can be mature spiritually or in religion unless he knows what the great and the good and the wise have taught. No secularist, no "creed-ist," no dogmas leaning only on one belief or one system of thought or principle or person or group of people can possibly be religiously mature, because he has left out more than he has shut in. How much landscape do we leave out when we put a wall around our small estate?

But because we have a need of the security of authority, the world goes on hundreds and thousands of years believing what is not true because they feel unsafe to put their foot out in that seeming and apparent void, not knowing that they should do so, and if they did, they would find it placed on a solid rock. If we are mature, we shall have to know there is one God who is over all, in all, and through all. And if we have gained a little greater maturity, we shall have to know that God is all, and that nothing is left out, as Robert Browning said, "when God has made the pile complete."

If we are mature, intellectually and logically, we shall have to know that a universe that begins will end, that there is no such thing as an eternity snipped off at either end. If we are mature, we shall have to know that there are no cosmic purposes, as most theologist taught them, else God himself is incomplete and is trying through experience to find out something that He didn't know. If you had to energize energy, where would you go to get the energy to energize energy? If God had to find out something, where would God go or what would He do to find out what He did not know?

Therefore, if we are mature, we should expect to believe certain things. Whether we really understand them or not, they would have to be so, merely because other things are so. We are living. There is a universe; we are living in it. We have called the cause of all things "God." If we had called it a stick of wood, we would be worshiping whatever the thing is that we believe in, by calling it a stick of wood. If we are mature then, we must know that a universe that didn't start, will not finish. A universe that did start will finish. What gets born will die; what ends will end. We would have to know this. But, if we are mature, we shall be able to accept theoretically that which no human logic can necessarily explain, which no philosophy has completely fathomed, no religion absolutely revealed, and no science captured; the simple self-evident proposition that we are alive, awake, and aware, and there isn't anyone living who knows what that life is.

No biologist has ever seen life, yet his entire time is devoted to the study of life in the human body. No psychologist has ever seen the mind. No physicist has ever seen energy. No artist has ever seen beauty. No theologian has ever seen God. "Only the son has revealed the Father," and this means creation reveals a Creator. And if we were to study creation very carefully, we should come nearer to finding out what the nature of the Creator is than we would in reading all the books of theology that were ever written, including the ones I wrote, for they are theology. We are theologians, too, but I don't like to admit it.

If we are mature in a universe that cannot be born and cannot die, in which things are transpiring, and they don't always look alike, we shall have to accept the proposition that whether we understand it or not, there is an eternal action in the universe, an eternal manifestation, and an eternal expression, which did not start and will not finish. I do not even believe in the theosophical theory of *amandatara*—where God goes to sleep—because if God goes to sleep, who will wake Him up?

If we are mature, we shall not be afraid to think, no matter where that thought leads us. Should the conclusions we arrive at of a necessity contradict everything we ever knew, and should we go down the street someday and see someone walking on his left ear, we shall merely have to change some of our theories. And denying the fact will not produce the right theory to explain the fact.

If we are mature then, we shall see an infinite variety. Variation changes within a changeless, eternally. We shall see infinite beings in that which does not begin, and they will not contradict each other. We shall see limitless multiplicity in that fundamental unity, and that will not contradict each other. We shall see infinite variations of relativities from the fact that you scratch your ear, that Gabriel is blowing his horn, wherever that is. "That thou seest, man, become too thou must; God, if thou seest God, dust, if thou seest dust."

If we are mature, we shall have to know that in the beginning's endlessness, there is no contradiction. And we shall have to realize the whole thing is a sort of divine Maya or play of life upon itself, not for the glory of the Creator, because nothing can glorify God, but for the expression of that which you and I glorify and adore as the Infinite, the Absolute, God, the Father—no matter what we call it—that which we feel must be beyond us. But if we are mature, we shall again know that that which is beyond us cannot be perceived other than how that which is within us perceives it. This is why Immanuel Kant said we are able to recognize an apparently objective manifestation or some fact out here because it awakens an intuition within us. If we are mature, we shall have to know within us that there is one Mind common to all individual men. "Hear, O Israel, the Lord our God is one Lord," not two. "Cleave the wood, I am there; lift the stone, and thou shalt find me there!"

If we are mature, we shall have to know that this eternal play of life upon itself is a necessity of the Divine creative will and wisdom and is all going on and that we are a part of it. Only because there is that within us—and It is there—that is It. We can know It, for only life can understand, see, comprehend and only love can comprehend love, if we are mature. We shall have to accept the fact that, by observation and experience and human history and illumination, everything out here is in the process of evolution, and that its nature is to be more and never less, and that we are all hell-bent for heaven, no matter what it looks like.

If we are mature, we shall have to deliberately take 75 percent of the fundamentalist philosophy of all religions, not only the Christian but the Jew and the Greeks, and throw it in the trash can, because that is where it belongs, to garner such wisdom as the world has conceived, perceived. If we are mature in doing this, we shall not feel we have to deny any single fact. If we are mature, we do not expect to arrive at a basic unity by denying variety merely because we do not understand how variety is blended into the basic unity. Jesus was mature; he understood it, other people have. We are trying to comprehend it.

If we are mature, then we shall not try to deny one universe in order to affirm the other. We do not say people are not poor, sick, miserable, etc. We do say there is an Eternal Spirit that is birthless, deathless, and changeless and remains the Spirit forever. Death has not touched It at all. If we are mature, we shall no longer try to make something fit our theory where we have not found the fact to do it, and we shall try to find the theory to fit the fact and not search for facts to fit a theory that may or may not be right. We would be scientific and intelligent that way.

Then if we do not have to deny all this, we shall have to affirm it. But if we are mature spiritually, it will be a kind of an affirmation. In the first part of our experience, we shall see the cold hard fact of the world as it is and looks to be. Then we begin to study our abstractions, and our conclusion will be that there is nothing but God and mind. And the first thing we know, there isn't any mountain to overcome. Now we have lost the mountain we had, and yet the obstruction is still there. We haven't gotten anywhere, and we begin to deny everything we don't like and affirm everything we do.

But if we are mature, having had the mountain and lost it, we shall again find it. It is the same mountain, but it is the mountain we have not known before. It is no longer an obstruction. It, too, becomes a manifestation of the Divine Presence through the living principle of creativity, and it is logical. And so will every other fact become real to us, and that which should be more real than perhaps anything else would be the eternality and timeless time of a changing universe in a changeless principle of infinite variations in an unchanged and solid unity. And we shall have to reconcile all these facts to each other with such a simplicity that we shall not feel we are even profound when we are talking about them.

Every great thinker has always said the same thing. In a timeless universe where everything is changing, everything is eternally being made new, nothing can wear out. The essence and substance are eternal, changeless, and fluidic. The molding is a shifting thing upon the sands of time, where it belongs. Nothing shall be permanent and static.

Now, the human heart and the human mind long for and must have that which is near and dear to it as Presence, responsive to it as person, operating for it as law, acting in its experience as dynamics that are never static, where the world does forevermore become new, because that is the way we are born. Then we arrive at the conclusion that eternity itself is not broken up in fragments, that time is merely a sequence of events and not a duration—and there is a vast difference—that space and form are merely the very slightest outline of that which must express something, even in this fluidic state. It belongs to it but no form shall be permanent, no experience shall be permanent, no person as we now know him shall remain as we know him. Isn't it an interesting thing? Where is the person you fell in love with?

This means no sequence of time in and of itself has or can have or ever will have a history. It is absolutely impossible. Time has no existence separate from the movement of the timeless as sequence but never as duration. There is no god who can say yesterday, today, and tomorrow. God proclaims and doesn't explain. Plotinus said that if he were to personify nature, he would say, I do not argue, I contemplate, and as I contemplate, I let fall the seeds of my thought into the creative medium of a mind principle or force, not knowing, only doing, and giving birth to a nature that is more than nothing and less than something. It has an office to perform, which is to express the will of contemplation of the Spirit that creates it. That is Plotinus, whom Dean Inge called the king of the intellectual mystics of the ages.

He was saying what you and I believe. Yesterday, we sang and danced. There isn't any yesterday. The only way that song and dance can go on is on the time track of a psychic picture impressed upon the psychic wall of a subjective receptivity that holds everything in place for the duration of its experience. We call it a time track, but it doesn't matter what you call it. So, today we shall dance again. Now, the yesterday, today, and tomorrow are linked together in our memory as a sequence, which we call a duration, and actually in our imagination, shut yesterday off from today and today off from tomorrow. And by our morbid introspections of yesterday and our phobias and fears of tomorrow, we sandwich the possibility of happiness in the only day we shall ever live—today—between that which wasn't and that which isn't going to be, other than a time track, and all in a fluidic field. That is why one of the teachings of Zen Buddhism is to find where yesterday is no longer linked by a sequence of duration of cause and effect to tomorrow but where today, every day is a new beginning, every day is the world made new.

This is what you and I do every time we give a treatment, we rub out the duration of a fact, and write in by our mental explanation the expectancy of another one, and create it independently of the old one, if we do it consciously, which we should, or re-create the old one in a slightly modified form according to the principle which Troward discovered in human psychology: that a neurotic thought pattern will repeat itself with monotonous regularity throughout life.

These facts are well-established, so well-established that in his [Troward's] experiments with time, he sees the past imprinted on the walls of memory and the possibility and expectancy of the actuality of the future, which will probably logically carry itself out unless its sequence is changed. That, of itself, shows time is an eternal thing. Real time and what we call time exist in an eternal medium, but what we create in time can be uncreated. What God creates in time is forever shifting, never twice alike. The old swimming hole is never there. As we look in the hole, everything is changed, the flow of the water, etc. You can't dive in the same river twice. It is impossible. But it is brought down to us with a memory of yesterday and expectancy of tomorrow. Therefore, to find that time now, where yesterday is not only passed and gone and we have gathered what good we shall have from it and tomorrow is not yet here, we should most certainly look forward with pleasurable anticipation to whatever will happen when it comes, but where today shall remain the one sublime and divine and eternal fact in our experience.

"Beloved, now are we the sons of God." That is why every treatment has to be given without the concept of time. It is now. It is always now in a treatment because it is always now in life. There is no "was" and "is going to be," other than a sequence of events that we call a duration. And because we believe it is a duration, we tie one event to the other and repeat the monotonous pattern, and the world does it over and over and over again.

Now, we have learned a lot of things, theoretically, I hope this week, and one of them is—and perhaps most important of all—that we are individualized centers of God consciousness. Whether we like it or not has nothing to do with it and nothing to do with our opinion, not one thing. We are creative centers in the mind of God, and we can't help it. Until the time of our enlightenment, through the period of our ignorance, we didn't know it. But the law excuses no one from its consequences and it is no respecter of persons. And by the law that could free us, we have produced bondage and fear and everything else. And we have lived under a law of fear and been afraid of everything, from the meanest thing on Earth to the highest hope of heaven, and created a hell to bedevil ourselves with masochistic sadism. Isn't the perversity of the human mind a strange thing, that it has created so many illusions and worshiped them and, because in doing so, it projects on the screen of its temporary experience that which is logically the outcome of its movement of thought and mind. It says, "Here are the facts that prove it," and it isn't so at all.

The monotonous thought pattern repeating itself over and over and over again, not in a duration of time but in a sequence of events in an eternal time and a limitless time, plants and harvests and reaps and sows as automatically as gravitational force holds things in place. And we call it "fate" and "the will of God," and someday someone comes along and plants something else and sure enough, in a few years, in a few sequences, the old is blotted out. "Behold, I make all things new."

We know that 75 percent of all diseases, accidents, troubles, impoverishment are inevitably and irrevocably the result of what we call "yesterday," and all the yesterdays and bygone days back through history, into some dim obscurity of antiquity into which our vision does not penetrate, and all the expectancies of tomorrow to eternity itself in another end of another kind of obscurity, which we have been told is like this, that and the other, and we have either shuttered or fallen prostate in ecstasy. And we didn't know the only grace yesterday had, and the only possibility tomorrow will ever have, we gave it.

We shall have to learn to live today, no longer bound to yesterday, no longer living in the hope of tomorrow. Edward Rowland Sill, in his poem "Truth at Last," speaks something I never heard before, of the illusion of hope, where he says:

> 'Tis something, if at last,
> Though only for a flash, a man may see
> Clear-eyed the future as he sees the past,
> From doubt, or fear, or hope's illusion free.

We are not just a hopeful optimistic bunch of nitwits. We are people who are trying to awake from the long slumber of the endless generations of idolatry and division and separation and fear and pain and suffering because something stirs within our imagination, something which says: "Something lost behind the ranges. Lost and waiting for you. Go!" (Rudyard Kipling, "The Explorer").

Every man is on the adventure of a lifetime, with a known and unknown, but always in secret partnership with the Eternal, with an endless now and an everlasting here, fruitful from the world of nature and the divine impregnation of the thoughts and ideas of God and man, because the thoughts of man are the thoughts of God in man or else there is no man, or else there is no God, or else there is duality and not unity. And if that happened, there would be nothing and not something.

There is no such thing as adding nothing to something and increasing something by adding nothing to it. So we are trying to live right now, learning from the sequence of yesterday, of course, carrying over in today the beauty and the love and everything that has been hallowed, not because it is traditional. Remember this: For every death, there is a resurrection, and it is equally true that for every resurrection, there must be a death. I am not talking about the physical body. Hate has to be given up before love can resurrect itself in us. But you see the negative has no history other than that which we have given it. God has no history. No one will ever write a history about God. We can write a history of the doing of that Mind on this planet, that is all, because as Emerson said, "For it is only the finite that has wrought and suffered; the infinite lies stretched in smiling repose."

We have learned that these time tracks can be smashed, obliterated, rubbed out by affirmation and denial or by transcendent method of identifying the mind with that which is even beyond our previous or yet experience, until it accepts it and believes it and understands it and takes hold of it and lives by it and in it and of it and becomes one with it.

Now let us consider this: We have a partnership with the Infinite, every one of us. It is an adventure of life. It is glorious; it is now; it is here. We are the person. This is a drama, a stage, a setting, and we are going to speak parts that we ourselves have written. And no man shall give unto us and no man shall take from us, but only the good and gracious God shall find eternal fresh outlets through us for the glory and the power and the beauty. And we shall adore that God. We shall love that God. I don't care if you call him Christ or Buddha, it matters not. And we shall know that when the day is spent, we shall know the day or the darkness is over. There is a dawn.

We shall not fear what is gone or uncertain. It is terrible to be afraid of anything. I have never lived under caution or fear in my life, and I shall not start now. Emerson said that the soul is nimble and gives speed to hands and feet when it is identified with that which is life. But even the thought of that greater freedom frightens us. Isn't it strange? Now we have to create a new heaven and a new Earth, since we have freed ourselves from bondage of fear and doubt and uncertainty. "Behold, I make all things new." And don't ever think but the most humble among us might be Christ or Jesus or Moses, not by reincarnation, which may or may not be true. We are going to have to reverse a lot; we are going to have to expect it. Now nothing is too good to be true. You are emancipated from the thralldom and the slavery. We are not slaves, and we have no master other than the central sun of the eternal universe, which springs today and perennially every day, it springs full orbed from that which, to us, is invisible.

There is some divine gift if we are ready to receive it, some infinite possibility. And we have learned only through conscious cooperation with the law and the Presence that the new kingdom of God shall be ushered in, which comes not for the sight of the eye or the hearing of the ear but in the silence of the soul, in the long watches of the dark nights of human despair, alone with God. There is no other way.

The corpse was made of wax, and the sun came out and melted it. Where was the dream when we awoke? I have borrowed an expression from the ancient Jews: I will not let you go until you bless me, and then we don't have to. There is so much we have to move aside and get rid of. That is what practice is, that what is shall come always. There is a silent witness to this. That is what practice is, what the presence of God is, what the eternal now and the everlasting, until at long last we look out and yesterday is dead, and tomorrow is not born, but today stretches out around us, ever broadening its horizon until at last the world becomes one vast plane and boundless reach of sky.

But we shall create new times, new days, in conscious cooperation with that ineffable Presence, and you and I alone, here in the secret place of the Most High. The tomb is of yesterday, and the dawn is here. And the light of heaven now guides you wherever you go.

Sermon by the Sea

SATURDAY, AUGUST 15, 1959

We conclude with one of Ernest Holmes's most inspirational talks, his "Sermon by the Sea," given on Saturday before Asilomar attendees left for home. This would be Holmes's last talk at Asilomar before his transition in early 1960. In it, he expresses his desires for the future of the Religious Science movement.

Our religion is not something to be lived merely here at Asilomar, as much inspiration as we receive from it, but rather we are to take that consciousness we have arrived at here back with us into whatever activities we may be engaged in. I do not believe life is separated from its living, anywhere.

There is nothing in the world that can take the place of love, friendship, appreciation, and cooperation in our lives. I have thought so much about this all week, because these are the only things that have any meaning in the eternal values in which we are so interested. Emerson said that it is very easy for us to maintain a spiritual equilibrium in solitude, "but the great man is he who in the midst of the crowd keeps with perfect sweetness the independence of solitude."

I do not believe there is a single fact in human history or a single manifestation in the universe that is or could possibly be anything other than a manifestation of the One Divine Mind, the One Universal Presence, the One Infinite Spirit.

It seems to me that it is only as we view all life, everything from what we call great to what we call small, important or unimportant, it is only as we view the whole thing, as Alexander Pope said, "one stupendous whole, whose body nature is and God the soul," that we shall really enter into communion, into sympathetic oneness and rapport with the reality of all that is about us. Someone asked me, "What do you think God is?" I looked out the window and said, "I think God is that tree." And there was a squirrel running up the tree, and I said, "I think God is that squirrel."

It is going to be absolutely impossible for us, with our finite comprehension, to have the intelligence to divide the indivisible and to say this is real and that is unreal. The marketplace is as real as is the temple. That is why Jesus said that it is neither in the temple at Jerusalem nor in the mountain but in yourself that the secret of life is discovered, that the soul of the universe is consciously entered into, and the divine and benign Spirit, which indwells everything, is loosed in Its splendor and power through you, through your partnership with the Infinite, through your oneness with God, the living Spirit.

Everything that lives proclaims the glory of God. Every person who exists manifests the life of God. There is one Spirit in which we live, one mind by which we think, one body of which we are a part, and one light that lighteth every man's pathway.

We are a part of the evolution of human destiny. We are a part of the unfoldment of the divine intelligence in human affairs. It has reached the point of conscious and deliberate cooperation with that principle of evolution and out-push of the creative urge of the Spirit, on this planet at least, to bring about innumerable centers that It may enjoy. Also we may enjoy it through that divine interior awareness, which is the intercommunication of God with man, revealing our own divine nature.

Having had the privilege of starting Religious Science, I would wish, will, and desire above all things else that the simplicity and purity of our teaching could never be violated. There is a purpose of simplicity, a consciousness of unity, a straight-line thinking in our philosophy that has never appeared before in the world, outside of the teachings of men like Jesus and Emerson.

There was nothing obscure in the teaching of Jesus. He just said that it is "the Father's good pleasure to give you the kingdom." Why don't you take it? He said that there is nothing but God. Why don't you believe it? He was the last of the great Jewish prophets, the greatest line of emotional prophets the world has ever known.

The Greeks had the greatest intellectual perception of the ages. It appears in their literature and art, a perfect thing without a soul.

We also find a great intellectualism in Emerson, who never contradicted himself. He gave us the simplest statement of intellectual spiritual perception, probably that has ever been put into print. As that of Jesus, it was simplest, most direct, meaningful, and full of feeling. We inherit this.

It would be my desire that simplicity and purity and directness, that straight thinking should never depart from the teachings of our practitioners or instructions of our teachers or understanding of our laymen. It is the most direct impartation of divine wisdom that has ever come to the world because it incorporates the precepts of Jesus and Emerson and Buddha and all the rest of the wise. And I would desire that in our teaching, there would never be any arrogance, for it always indicates spiritual immaturity to me. Others will arise who will know more than we do. They won't be better or worse. They will be different and know more than we do. Evolution is forward.

I would desire that we should not build, out of the body of our simplicity and grandeur and beauty, other creeds loaded with superstition, a fear of the unknown, and a dread of the unseen. We have discovered a "pearl of great price." We have discovered the rarest gem that has ever been found, setting in the intellect of the human race complete simplicity, complete directness, a freedom from fear and superstition about the unknown and about God.

And we have rediscovered that which the great, the good, and the wise have sung about and thought about: the imprisoned splendor within ourselves and within each other. And we have direct contact with it. Whether we call it the Christ in us or the Buddha or Atman or just the Son of God the living Spirit, makes no difference. You and I are witness to the divine fact, and we have discovered an authority beyond our minds, even though our minds utilize it. Out of this, we have prepared ourselves, I think, I hope, I pray and believe.

One cannot but feel, from the human point in such meetings as these, that it is entirely possible one might not be here next year. This is of complete indifference to me because I believe in life, and I feel fine. Such an event is merely the climax of human events in anybody's life, and it is to be looked forward to, not with dread or fear or apprehension but as the next great adventure, and one that we should all be very happy and glad to experience.

But we must weigh and measure things somewhat from the human angle. No person or organization can make the provision for that which is paramount, for that which is of the most stupendous importance, that out of the ranks of all of us, innumerable people shall grow up who shall have caught a vision, who shall have seen a glory, who shall have experienced God.

The thing that interests me now is that every man shall find his savior within himself. If this is the only place he is going to discover God, you may be sure it is the only avenue through which any way-shower shall lead him to God. There is no other way. Jesus knew this, and when they sought to make Jesus, the man, the way, he said that it was expedient he go away that the spirit of truth should awaken within his followers the knowledge and understanding of what he had been talking about, that he had come to reveal them to themselves.

As we think, speak, talk, and commune with each other and with nature and God, there will never be an answer to us beyond the level of our approach. The level of our approach is the only avenue through which there could be an answer, else we would not be individuals. God cannot make a mechanical spontaneity, and that is why we are left alone to discover ourselves.

Those who bear witness in consciousness do not need to retire from life. The great man is he who, in the midst of the crowd, can keep with perfect simplicity the independence of his solitude. It is not in the mountain or the temple in Jerusalem. It is in our own heart, our own mind, our own consciousness, our own being, where we live twenty-four hours a day, awake or asleep, that the eternal share of the Infinite comes to us, because every man is some part of the essence of God, not as a fragment, as totality.

I think we have brought a blessing to the world, the possibility of something expressing through us that has never before been given to the world—a simplicity, a sincerity, and, I trust, a love and understanding. But we too little practice it because the human mind is prone, even when it has discovered a greater good than it had before, to compare the degree of good it thinks it possesses with a lesser degree of good it thinks someone else has. And this is brought about only through the psychological projection of some unredeemed past of a person's own psyche.

You will never discover a person who is full of emotional judgment and condemnation of others who is doing anything other than unconsciously releasing the tension of a burden, a burden so great to be borne that he does not even permit it to come to the light of day to be seen, for he could not face it. This has been scientifically proved. And that is why Jesus, with the profoundness of utmost simplicity, did not say, "Judge not lest God will judge you. He knew better. He said, "Judge not, that ye be not judged. For with what judgment ye judge, ye shall be judged." In other words, your judgment will judge you. "And with what measure ye mete, it will be measured to you again." God is not going to measure it back to you and say, "I will show you who is boss. You are the measure-outer. Troward said that we are dispensers of the divine gift, and we are in partnership with the Infinite.

It would be wonderful indeed if a group of persons should arrive on Earth who were for something and against nothing. This would be the *summum bonum* (Latin for the highest good) of human organization, wouldn't it? It is in the life of the individual.

Find me one person who is for something and against nothing, who is redeemed enough not to condemn others out of the burden of his soul, and I will find another savior, another Jesus, and an exalted human being.

Find me one person who no longer has any fear of the universe or of God or of man or of anything else, and you will have brought to me someone in whose presence we may sit, and fear shall vanish as clouds before the sunlight.

Find me someone who has redeemed his own soul, and he shall become my redeemer.

Find me someone who has given all that he has in love, without morbidity, and I will have found the lover of my soul. Is not this true? Why? Because he will have revealed to me the nature of God and proved to me the possibility of all human souls.

This is what Religious Science stands for. It is not a new dogmatism. It is not a new authority generated from a new alleged revelation of the God who never revealed anything to anybody, as such, else He could not have revealed all things to all people. There is no special dispensation of Providence, but there is a specialized dispensation that the great and good and wise and just have known, even though they knew it intuitively.

Find me one person who can get his own littleness out of the way, and he shall reveal to me the immeasurable magnitude of the universe in which I live.

Find me one person who knows how to talk to God, really, and I shall walk with him through the woods, and everything that seems inanimate will respond. The leaves of the trees will clap their hands; the grass will grow soft under him.

Find me one person who communes with cause and effect, and in the evening, the evening star will sing to him and the darkness will turn to light. Through him, as the woman who touched the hem of the garment of Christ was healed, shall I be healed of all loneliness forever.

Find me someone who is no longer sad, whose memory has been redeemed from morbidity, and I shall hear laughter.

Find me someone whose song is really celestial because it is the outburst of the cosmic urge to sing, and I shall hear the music of the spheres.

"All things are delivered unto me of my Father, and no man knoweth the son but the Father. Neither knoweth any man the Father, save the son and he to whomsoever the son will reveal Him." And each of us is that son. No use waiting for avatars. Jesus is not coming again; he is wiser than that. He has earned whatever he has. And to you and to me, no single kernel of grain shall come unless we have planted it. No meal shall be made unless we have ground it, no bread baked unless we have kneaded it and put it in the oven of our own consciousness, where the silent processes of an invisible and ineffable light precipitates itself into that which for us stands for the start of life.

But how we have put off that day! We say to each other that we don't know enough; we aren't good enough. The ignorance of our unknowing, the blindness of our unseeing, the condemnation of the ages weighing against our consciousness, known and unknown, conscious and unconscious, has created the greatest possibility of the larger progress of humanity, a burden so tremendous that even men's adoration of God has been saddened by fear. Like the man Ernest Renan said, prayed, "O God, if there be a God, save my soul if I have a soul." He did not know, so he was afraid to take a chance.

Find me one person who no longer doubts, no longer waivers, but not one who, with a proclamation of superiority, says, "Look at me. I have arrived!" I will not listen to that. Only that which reveals me to myself can be a message to me. Only that which gives me back myself can save me. Only that which leads me to the God within myself can reveal God. And only that person can do it to whom the vision has come through his own efforts, through the gift of God. Of course, the grace of God abounds by Divine givingness. God has forever hung Himself upon the cross of men's indifference. God has forever, but without suffering, given Himself, but we have not received the gift.

Find me one person who has so completely divorced from himself all arrogance, and you will have discovered for me an open pathway to the kingdom of God, here and now. Up until now, the search has been in far-off corners of the Earth. And we have knelt upon a prayer rug and been wafted away, in our morbid and fearful imagination, over ethers of nothingness, to places that have no existence—the temples of our unbelief—and we have come back empty. "What went ye out into the wilderness for to see?"

And now comes Religious Science. We are no more sincere than others. If we felt we were, that would be a projection of our insincerity. We are no better. If we thought we were, that would be a projection of an unconscious sense of guilt. Anyway, it would be stupid, and there is no greater sin on Earth than just plain stupidity.

What shall reveal the self to the self? The self shall raise the self by the self.

Find me somebody who has detached his emotional and psychological ego from the real self, without having to deny the place it plays in the scheme of things and without slaying any part of himself because the transcendence is there also, and I will have discovered the Ineffable in this individual and a direct pathway for the communion of my own soul.

Now, what does this all mean? I am talking about you and about myself. When I say, "Find a person," I don't mean to go over to Rome or London or back to your own church. The search is not external. All of these people I have been talking about have no existence as such, other than as figments of my own imagination, until they are finally centered in our own soul. Then this guest for whom we are looking will be the Self redeemed from the lesser self. This is a very interesting thing, for nature is foolproof, and when the fruit is ripe, it will fall. When the kingdom of God is perceived, it will be experienced simultaneously, instantaneously, and in its entirety.

But these people all exist in us. They are different attributes, qualities of our own soul. They are different visions, not that we have multiple or dual personalities, but that every one of us on that inner side of life is, has been, and shall remain in eternal communion with the Ineffable, where he may know that he is no longer with God, but one of God. If it were not for that which echoes eternally down the corridors of our own minds, some voice that ever sings in our own souls, some urge that continuously presses us forward, there would be no advance in our science or religion or in the humanities or anything else. But, "He left not Himself without witness."

These are simple things that call for discipline, not as one normally thinks of discipline, but a different kind of discipline that one discovers. I often sit for several hours at a time, sometimes all day, thinking one simple thought. No matter what it is, it isn't a waste of time to find out what this thought means to me or what it should mean in my life or what it would mean everywhere. This is something no one can do for us but ourselves. We are "the way, the truth and the life."

We have come to Asilomar, spent this wonderful week together on love for each other and adoration for the God we believe in. Many wonderful things have happened that would seem miracles if we didn't know about them. And now we meet for this fond farewell after the spiritual bath of peace, the baptism of the Spirit. Not through me but you to me and I to you, through each other, the revelation of the self to the self. We go back into the highways and byways of life with something so great that never again will anything be quite the same. A little more light shall come, a little greater glory added to the glory we already possess, a deeper consciousness, a higher aspiration, a broader certainty of the mind.

You are Religious Science. I am not. I am only the one who put something together. I do not even take myself seriously, but I take what I am doing seriously. You are Religious Science: our ministers, our teachers, our practitioners, our laymen. You find me one thousand people in the world who know what Religious Science is and use it and live it as it is, and I'll myself live to see a new world, a new heaven, and a new Earth here. There is a cosmic Power wrapped up in a cosmic consciousness and purposiveness that is equal to the vision which looses It.

What I am saying is this: There is a law that backs up the vision, and the law is immutable. "Heaven and Earth shall pass away, but my words shall not pass away." There is a power transcendent beyond our needs, our little wants. Demonstrating a dime is good if one needs it, or healing oneself of a pain is certainly good if one has it, but beyond that, at the real feast at the tabernacle of the Almighty, in the temple of the living God, in the banquet hall of heaven, there is something beyond anything that you and I have touched.

Find one thousand people who know that and use it, and the world will no longer be famished. How important it is that each one of us in his simple way shall live from God to God, with God, in God, and to each other. That is why we are here. And we are taking back with us, I trust, a vision and an inspiration, something beyond a hope and a longing, that the living Spirit shall through us walk anew into Its own creation and a new glory come with a new dawn.

"Now the Lord is in His holy temple, let all the Earth keep silent before Him," as we drink deeply from the perennial fountain of eternal life, as we partake of the bread of heaven, and as we open wide the gates of our consciousness that the King of Glory shall come in.

And may God bless and keep us. And for all the love you have given me, may I bless you.

Index A: People

A

Arnold, Edward — 50

Aurobindo — 32, 40, 76, 105, 163, 177, 187, 206, 218, 226, 229, 295, 308, 315

B

Barnhart, Ethel — 10, 329

Browning, Robert — xv, 8, 10, 21, 55, 60, 102, 127, 143, 168, 177, 183, 195, 263, 270, 293, 303, 322, 336, 346, 352, 356, 359, 367, 377

Bruyere, Jean de La — 53

Bucke, Richard Maurice — 48, 159, 172, 344

Buddha — 26, 81, 110, 112, 121, 164, 165, 186, 295-96, 305, 317, 336, 340, 346, 353, 368, 385, 389

Burnell, George Edwin — 185, 219

Burr, Aaron — 46, 344

Burton, Richard Eugene — 258

C

Cady, Emilie — 38, 263

Carpenter, Mark — 69, 79

Carruth, William Herbert — 24, 62, 309

Curtis, Donald — 157

E

Eckhart, Meister — 4, 15, 48, 59, 148, 174, 184-90, 204, 206-07, 216-18, 231-32, 280, 302, 319

Eddington, Arthur — 94

Eddy, Mary Baker — xvii, 7-8, 11, 32, 44, 49, 53, 98, 129, 165, 173, 189, 199, 214-15, 222, 225, 228, 301, 348, 359, 363, 373

Einstein, Albert — 9, 31-32, 45-46, 57, 94, **141, 177, 200, 262, 271, 300**

Emerson, Ralph Waldo — xvi, 5, 6, 9, 11, 13, 15, 23, 25-26, 30, 35-36, 45, 48-49, 51, 55-57, 59, 63, 69, 83, 93-94, 96-97, 109, 116-17, 122, 126-27, 129, 131, 134-35, 141, 146-47, 150, 166, 169, 173-76, 180, 183, 187, 191, 194, 197-99, 201-02, 204-06, 210-11, 214, 216, 219-20, 229-232, 261, 271-73, 275, 279-80, 282, 285, 289-91, 302, 305, 313, 316-17, 319, 335, 345-46, 350, 355, 357, 361, 363, 366, 368-69, 371, 384-85, 387-89

Eustace, Herbert W. — 201

F

Fillmore, Charles — 38, 263

Fink, David — 136, 144

Fleming, Rhonda — 134

Freud, Sigmund — 48-49, 287, 344

Froeber, Richard (Dick) — 77

G

Gandhi — 22, 23, 26, 53, 58-59, 61, 67, 70, 116, 118, 163, 217, 262

Garland, Hamlin — 260

Garrett, Eileen J. — 178

Gifford, Elmer — 69, 134, 330, 344, 347, 359

Glen, Rev Irma — 77

Goodspeed — 260

Graham, Billy — 131, 175, 221

Gray, Thomas — 148, 151

H

Harding, Dr. Esther — 163

Hemingway, Ernest — 280

Hermes — 189, 305, 366

Holmes, Anna Columbia — 45, 160

Holmes, Fenwicke — xxiii, 124-25, 128, 141, 284

Holmes, Oliver Wendell — 81, 130, 198, 310, 365

Hopkins, Emma Curtis — xvii, 104, 174, 184, 191-94, 220, 263, 275, 280

Hornaday, Dr. William (Bill) — xix, xxii-xxiv, 85, 160, 174, 213, 224, 242, 259, 285

Horney, Karen — 360

Hudson, Thomas Jay — 47, 227

Hutschnecker, Dr. Arnold — 50, 367

I

Inge, Dean — 273, 286, 345, 381

J

Jastrow, Joseph — 8, 44, 344

Jesus — 8, 11-14, 20-27, 30, 32-34, 36-37, 45, 47-49, 51-55, 59-63, 67-70, 72-76, 79-81, 83, 86-87, 95-96, 104, 110-13, 116, 118, 121-22, 126-27, 129, 132, 136-39, 142, 145, 147-49, 152, 155, 164-65, 173, 178, 186-87, 192, 194, 197, 205, 211, 213, 215, 220, 227, 261-63, 269, 271, 273-75, 278-82, 285, 288-90, 294-95, 300-01, 305, 307-09, 313, 317, 319, 333, 336, 339-42, 344-51, 356-59, 361-64, 366, 368-75, 379, 385, 388-92

Johnson, Barclay — 321, 337

Jones, Rufus M. — 108

Jung, Carl — 7, 47, 49, 174, 204, 214, 224, 338, 357

K

Kant, Immanuel — 179, 190, 379

Khayyam, Omar — 33, 147-48

Kimball, Edward — 8, 37

Kipling, Rudyard — 78, 81, 86-87, 154, 319, 384

Kunkel, Fritz — 36, 84

L

Lanier, Sidney — 164, 258

Lao Tzu — 188, 262

Larcom, Lucy — 154

Larkin, James — 174, 259

Larson, Christian D. — xvii

Lee, Peggy — 22, 135

Longfellow, Henry Wadsworth — 52, 78, 340

Lowell, James Russell — 21, 46, 60, 126, 138, 149, 208, 261, 302, 375

M

Mills, James Porter — 112

Morgan, Angela — xv-xvi, 119, 124, 281

Moses — 81, 100, 110-11, 121, 129, 165, 189, 285, 294-95, 305, 313, 317, 346-50, 366, 372-73, 385

O

O'Reilly, John Boyle — 108

P

Patanjali — 191

Plato — 37, 67, 103, 191, 220, 225, 317, 346

Plotinus — 3, 7, 14, 45, 47, 64, 82, 99, 188-89, 191, 224-25, 230, 279-80, 282, 287, 301, 348, 381

Pythagoras — 44, 366

Q

Quimby, Phineas Parkhurst — 8, 31-33, 36, 38, 132, 177-78, 199-202, 204, 212-15, 220, 222-24, 229, 261-63

R

Racine, Jean — 204

Reik, Theodore — 144

Rhine, Joseph Banks — 227

Riley, Frank L. — 185

Riley, James Whitcomb — 13, 307, 311

S

Seabury, David — 132, 229

Seneca, Lucius Annaeus — 46

Shakespeare — 4, 36, 57, 78, 86-87, 160, 169, 194, 321, 339, 350, 362

Sill, Edward Rowland — 188, 219, 383

Socrates — 67-69, 120-21, 211, 273, 279, 285, 317

Spinoza — 4, 31

St. Augustine — 13, 56, 189, 206, 273, 286, 352

St. John, Elaine — 160

Swedenborg, Emanuel — 177, 186, 222

T

Tagore, Rabindranath — 8, 43, 128, 163, 309

Tennyson, Alfred Lord — 52, 74, 76, 104, 141, 155, 283, 346

Trine, Ralph Waldo — xvii

Troward, Thomas — xvii, xxvi, 4-5, 7, 34-35, 37, 41, 47-48, 61, 64, 71-72, 74, 76, 113, 132, 134-36, 177-78, 199-202, 214, 219, 224-25, 232, 282, 286, 290-91, 295, 315, 334, 348, 357, 360, 373, 382, 391

Trowbridge, Dr. Carmelita — 125, 129

W

Watts, Alan — 175

Whitman, Walt — 26, 49, 94, 100, 122, 174, 185, 205, 208, 336, 356, 371

Whittier, John Greenleaf — 95, 138

Wilcox, Ella Wheeler — 26, 309, 323

Wood, Pearl — 132

Wordsworth, William — 11, 58, 97

Y

Young, Arthur — 273

Z

Zoroaster — 205, 315

Index B: Subjects

A

Absolute, The — 6-7, 136, 151, 220, 268, 294, 297, 299, 305-308, 335, 374, 379

Affirmations — 257, 263-265, 268, 358

Ain Soph — 148, 151, 220

Atman — 148-149, 151, 164, 336, 353, 376, 389

B

Bhagavad Gita, The — 7, 12, 49, 52, 126, 144, 149, 160, 193, 219, 259, 275, 337

Bible, The — xv, 4, 7-9, 12, 37, 46, 49, 53, 59, 94, 108, 112-13, 122, 134-35, 145-46, 159-60, 173, 178, 185, 188-89, 194, 225, 259, 285, 289, 292, 299, 305, 308-09, 315, 321, 331, 334, 348, 350, 359, 361, 365, 370, 373

Bondage — 51, 93, 103, 105, 118-19, 121, 129, 183, 194, 217, 261, 270, 275-76, 278, 281, 283, 286, 292, 306, 310, 335, 349, 382, 385

Buddhism — 110, 164, 381

C

Cause and Effect — 9, 13, 45, 62, 79, 111, 117, 129, 145, 147, 173, 195, 202, 208, 228, 266, 274, 295, 336, 347, 349-50, 353, 381, 392

Christ, The — xviii, 10, 19, 21, 23-24, 30, 36, 43, 45, 62, 68, 71, 75-77, 94, 112, 121, 127, 133, 148-149, 151, 153, 155, 157, 164-66, 169, 177-78, 190, 192, 201, 204, 211-12, 215-16, 220-21, 229, 285, 296, 306, 323, 347-48, 353, 371, 376, 385, 389, 392

Christian Science — xvii, 80, 177, 180, 199, 201, 212, 215, 222-223, 257, 262-63

Christianity — 32, 68, 111, 224, 301, 344, 351, 366

Consciousness — xix, xxviii, 6-7, 11, 15, 19-21, 23, 29, 32, 34-37, 40, 43, 48-49, 51, 53-55, 57-58, 60, 62-64, 75, 77, 86, 92-93, 95, 103, 105, 108, 114, 131, 136, 138, 159, 162, 164, 166, 172, 176, 187, 191, 203, 208, 269, 273, 277, 308, 315, 317, 330, 332-33, 337, 355, 361, 364-365, 370, 382, 387-88, 390, 395

Cosmic Consciousness — 6, 48, 60, 75, 159, 172

Creative Medium — 320, 381

D

Death — xxiii, 21, 24, 46, 49-50, 74, 99, 113, 118-119, 121, 161, 192, 195, 281, 295, 311, 343, 349, 351, 363, 379, 384

Denials — 257, 263-265, 268, 358

Divine Immanence — 98, 102, 154

Dualism — 73, 93, 95, 103-05, 114, 138, 195, 227, 266, 282, 334, 337, 355, 371-372

E

Ego — 13, 43, 48, 60, 76, 80, 97, 113, 128, 174, 181, 185, 278, 288, 333, 335, 340, 371, 393

Egypt — 110, 365

Enlightenment — 5, 70, 91, 105, 130, 143, 335, 346, 347, 349, 359, 382

Eternity — xxiv, 22, 123, 140, 146, 155, 165, 168, 175, 192, 196, 207, 221, 274, 282, 289, 303, 306, 308, 321, 335, 352, 356, 363, 370, 373, 377, 380, 383

Evil — 4, 5, 21, 34, 53, 55, 59, 72, 74, 99, 103, 120, 125, 160, 189, 192, 195, 266, 268, 276, 279, 331, 334, 343, 361

Evolution — xix, 19, 24, 39, 44, 57, 59, 61-66, 69, 70-71, 73, 76, 78, 81, 84-85, 92, 95, 102, 105, 129, 143, 146, 150-51, 158-59, 161, 178, 183, 190, 197-98, 205, 265-66, 269, 281, 287, 293, 297, 299, 303-04, 306, 308-10, 313-14, 318, 329, 332-34, 337, 339-41, 347, 349, 351, 356, 359, 365, 367, 369, 371, 373, 375, 379, 388-89

F

Faith — xxvi-xxvii, 29, 42, 46, 54, 82, 95-96, 98, 154-55, 174, 195, 215, 257, 259, 261, 263-65, 267, 269, 274, 292, 300, 311, 313, 339-40, 346, 356, 372, 374

Fate — 119, 281, 383

Fear — xvi, xxvii, 13, 24, 27, 74, 76, 83, 96, 98-99, 108, 112, 114, 118, 123, 127, 130, 138, 146, 160, 162, 166-67, 181, 188, 210, 219, 257, 259, 261, 263-65, 268, 272, 274, 276, 285-86, 293, 309-10, 313, 315, 339, 343-45, 349, 352-53, 360-61, 364, 382-85, 389-91, 393

Forgive — 12-13, 34-35, 155, 186, 352

Forgiveness — 86

Freedom — xxvii, 35, 51, 57, 72, 82-84, 93, 103, 105, 121, 128-129, 131, 157, 161, 182-83, 193-94, 203, 208, 261, 269-71, 273, 275-79, 281, 283, 292-93, 307-08, 310, 335, 350, 385, 389

G

Gnostic Man — 76, 296, 315

Grace — 22, 62, 70-72, 86, 124-29, 131, 133, 135, 137, 139, 337, 347-49, 352, 383, 393

Grief — 116, 121, 223

H

Hell — xvi, 9, 14, 19, 24, 49, 51, 55-56, 58-59, 73, 83, 94, 96, 99, 103, 105, 113-14, 125, 129, 134, 165, 168, 194, 218, 262, 276, 288, 300, 316, 323, 334, 346, 350, 379, 383

Hermetic — 189, 198, 257, 365-66

Hinduism — 25, 180, 209, 330, 346

Holmes Commonwealth — 330

I

Id — 60, 273, 286, 358

Ignorance — 4-5, 25, 61, 70-72, 81, 91, 96, 105, 125, 130, 140, 143, 151, 160, 162, 175-76, 193, 215-16, 228-29, 276, 285-86, 309-10, 313, 324, 335-36, 347, 349-50, 352, 359, 361, 364, 366, 382, 393

Illusion — 76, 98, 103, 111, 133, 146, 175, 179, 188, 191, 214, 219, 263, 268, 276-79, 282, 293, 301, 313, 324, 333, 343, 383

Individualization — 9, 44, 61, 64, 69, 120, 157, 190, 214

Infinite, The — xi, 13, 22, 27, 34, 39, 40-41, 44, 59-60, 62, 64, 79, 103, 117, 170, 187-89, 210, 265, 271, 273-74, 276, 279-80, 282, 284, 287, 292, 294, 299, 306-07, 309-10, 312-13, 315, 317-21, 323, 325, 334, 368-69, 379, 384, 388, 390-91

Influx — 99, 116-17, 119, 122, 202, 218, 279

Intuition — 20, 22, 40, 44, 46-48, 58, 117, 129, 133, 144, 161, 172, 175, 178-80, 183, 190, 206, 214, 230, 279, 288, 300, 308, 355, 379

Involution — 57, 61-62, 64, 71, 177-78, 265, 297, 303-04, 306, 329, 334-35, 337, 347, 356, 359, 373

J

Joaquin and Boaz — 195, 369

Judaism — 218, 330

K

Karma — 45, 62, 295, 320, 322, 349-50, 352

Koran, The — 160

L

Law of Correspondence — 222, 305

Law of Mind — 33, 36, 113, 117, 199, 264, 370

Law of Polarity — 195

Libido — 48, 60, 102, 273, 288, 335, 358, 360, 367

M

Meditation — xviii, 11, 36, 43, 97, 112, 115-16, 138, 142, 144, 155, 165, 167, 204, 315, 318-20, 370

Mental Equivalent — 41, 83, 100

Metaphysics — xiv, 35, 50, 187, 210, 224, 337, 368

Microcosm and the Macrocosm — 373

Mormonism — 80, 180

Multiplicity — 93-94, 210, 341, 355, 361, 365-66, 378

Mysticism — xxiii, xxvii, 31, 97, 104, 171-77, 179-85, 187-95, 197, 199, 201, 203, 205-09, 211, 213, 215, 217, 219, 221-23, 225, 227, 229, 231, 233, 280, 282, 319

N

New Thought — xiii, xiv, xvii, 177, 221-22, 225, 262, 294, 349

Nonresistance — 22-23, 43, 53, 262, 354-55, 357, 359, 360, 361, 363

O

Oneness — 258, 261, 268, 270, 284, 388

P

Panpsychism — 98

Practical Idealism — 161, 167

Praise — v, xxvii, 19-20, 27, 73, 80, 82, 86, 137, 154, 168, 353

Prayer — xviii, 9, 29, 36, 64, 97, 137-38, 148, 167, 203-04, 216, 280, 373-74, 393

Prodigal Son — 27, 281, 309, 334, 337, 349

Psalms — 73, 266

Psyche — 10, 30-31, 50, 71, 369, 391

Psychism — 69, 117, 172, 175

Psychology — 9, 14, 30, 44, 49-50, 65, 69, 107, 163, 181, 186, 204, 214, 220, 313, 335, 348, 357, 359, 367, 372, 382

R

Reincarnation — 25, 110, 157, 193, 218, 291, 352, 385

Relative, The — 151, 294, 297, 299, 301, 303, 305-11

Religious Science — xv-xviii, xix, xxv, xxviii, 10, 20, 44, 48, 66, 75, 77-85, 87, 134, 142, 157, 159, 161, 163, 165-67, 169, 171, 190, 194, 213, 218, 225, 257-59, 263, 276, 298-99, 312-13, 329-31, 337, 340-42, 344-46,

349, 351, 354-56, 365-66, 374-76, 387-88, 392-93, 395

Resistance — xxvii, 43-55, 116, 118-20, 296, 321, 336, 353, 359-62, 364

Revelation — 20, 22, 25, 27, 48, 52, 58, 70, 73, 81, 101, 158, 160, 163, 182-183, 206, 258, 287, 289, 333, 355, 392, 395

S

Science — xvii, 23, 29, 30-31, 34-36, 44-46, 50, 52, 59, 72, 75, 92-94, 107, 109, 129, 143, 153, 173, 178, 187, 194-95, 199, 201, 202, 216-17, 220, 227-29, 258, 262-63, 267, 287-88, 292, 298, 301, 308, 313-15, 318, 323, 336-38, 347

Science of Mind — viii-xv, xvii-xx, xxv-xxviii, 29-30, 58, 79, 84, 157, 213, 284

Self-Existent Cause — vi, 330, 342-43, 345-47, 349, 351, 353-54

Sin — 5, 12, 21, 51, 59, 79, 97, 105, 111, 130, 139, 143, 186, 194, 217-18, 228, 275, 335, 347, 350, 393

Spiritual Mind Treatment — xxvi, 29, 363

T

Theology — 5, 13, 31, 44, 50, 104, 142, 187, 190, 218-20, 224, 229, 262-263, 275-76, 296, 301, 330, 334, 337, 344-47, 352, 365-66, 372, 378

Transcendence — 21, 34, 53-55, 91-93, 95-102, 104-105, 116, 123, 126, 131-34, 136-38, 146, 148, 151, 153, 155-56, 162, 165-66, 169, 193, 232, 295, 355-57, 361-64, 368, 370-72, 394

Transcendent Realism — 167

Trinity — 68, 224

U

Unity — xvii, 24, 26, 43, 54, 68, 76, 82, 93-95, 149, 172, 181, 203, 210-11, 217, 231-32, 259, 261-263, 265, 273, 303, 309, 331, 341, 343, 348, 352, 355, 359, 362-363, 365-66, 368, 378-380, 384, 388

Upanishads — 58, 160, 371

V

Vedas — 160, 371

W

Will of God — 309, 383

Wonder — xxvii, 19-23, 25-27, 39-40, 64, 67-68, 91, 110, 125, 127, 157, 167, 203, 259, 265, 317-19, 366

Z

Zen — 22, 110, 112, 133, 179, 274, 381

ABOUT THE AUTHOR

Ernest Shurtleff Holmes

Ernest S. Holmes (1887-1960) founded the worldwide Religious Science spiritual movement, now known as Centers for Spiritual Living. A uniquely gifted scholar, Holmes had a vast command of the world's religions, as well as of psychology, philosophy, science, and the arts.

His seminal book, The Science of Mind, *is the clearest, most complete explanation of the spiritual psychology he founded. In it, he reveals universal principles that apply to all people, at all times, in all places. He presents powerful-life-changing ideas in straightforward language, and details this simple, practical philosophy.*

His discussions range from similarities and differences between Religious Science and other New Thought movements to the practical nature of healing those who are sick in body or spirit. He delves into the type of prayer called spiritual mind treatment, examining when and why it either works or doesn't. He leans on the wisdom of the ages, the words of prophets and poets as he examines the role of the human soul in relationship with the Divine.

To read Holmes is to experience the fascinating workings of one of the most respected and revered spiritual minds in the 20th century—and yet to marvel at the simplicity and power of his message.

In Ernest Holmes at Asilomar, *readers get to know Holmes through his lectures and classes presented in the 1950s. Readers will encounter ideas that challenge their thinking, spiritual concepts based in the philosophies and religions of the world and throughout time, and a speaker who is both brilliant and humble, witty and serious, as he engages his audience in principles that part the veil of philosophical mysteries in language all can understand.*

Made in United States
Troutdale, OR
10/01/2023